Acknowledgements

I would like to thank the numerous people who have helped bring this book into being. Luciana O'Flaherty at Oxford University Press commissioned it, and she and her colleague Matthew Cotton were extremely supportive throughout the writing and editorial process. Several other people at OUP also gave valuable assistance, notably Emma Barber. Edwin Pritchard made an excellent job of the copyediting, and Michael Parkin created the index. I am grateful too to the anonymous referee who made some valuable suggestions to help improve the manuscript, and to the other external readers who supported the project in the first place. Furthermore, as always, I am indebted to my wonderful agent, Natasha Fairweather, and her splendidly efficient assistant, Donald Winchester.

The University of Exeter remains a delightful place to work: no one could hope for better colleagues. Several of them discussed the issue of Second World War rhetoric with me, in particular: James Mark, Richard Overy, Matthew Rendle, Nicholas Terry, and Tim Rees. I benefited much from Andrew Thorpe's encyclopaedic knowledge of wartime British politics. A period of university research leave ensured that the book could be completed in a timely fashion.

Other friends provided valuable help and advice. Gary Love commented on the Introduction. Peter Clarke kindly allowed me to see the manuscript of his wonderful book *Mr. Churchill's Profession* in advance of publication. Warren Dockter similarly shared the text of his excellent forthcoming work *Churchill and the Islamic World*. Allen Packwood and his team at the Churchill Archives Centre provided their usual invaluable assistance. Jason Dinsdale persuaded me to go on Twitter (@RichardToye)—with what effect remains to be seen.

Churchill studies is now entering the electronic era, with the digitization of Churchill's own papers completed in 2012. Most of the research for this book was carried out in the conventional way, but the site's publishers kindly allowed me access to it shortly before the official launch, which assisted me in the final stages.

Mass–Observation material is reproduced with permission of Curtis Brown Group Ltd, London on behalf of The Trustees of the Mass Observation Archive Copyright © The Trustees of the Mass Observation Archive. Quotations from the speeches and writings of Sir Winston Churchill are reproduced with permission of Curtis Brown, London on behalf of the Estate of Sir Winston Churchill Copyright © Winston S. Churchill.

Throughout the writing of this book Kristine Vaaler and our sons Sven and Tristan were sources of pleasure and inspiration. My friends Gary Price and Mike Bush helped take my mind off work by, respectively, playing badminton and going running with me. I am also grateful to Katherine Waugh and Simon Stanhope for their friendship and it is to them that I dedicate this book.

Contents

List of Plates

Introduction

On 30 November 1954, Sir Winston Churchill turned eighty. That day, at a special ceremony in Westminster Hall, he was presented by both Houses of Parliament with gifts, including an overly candid portrait of himself by Graham Sutherland. Churchill hated it so much that his wife Clementine later ordered it to be destroyed. The public occasion, however, was all harmony. Labour Party leader Clement Attlee—who had defeated Churchill at the 1945 election and kept him out of Downing Street for six years—paid tribute to the Prime Minister, recalling his stirring wartime speeches. 'You offered us only blood and sweat and tears and we gladly took your offer,' he said. Then Churchill, a little unsteady on his feet, made his reply, which included a justly famous passage:

> I was very glad when Mr. Attlee described my speeches in the war as expressing the will not only of Parliament but of the whole nation. Their will was resolute and remorseless and, as it proved, unconquerable. It fell to me to express it, and if I found the right words you must remember that I have always earned my living by my pen and by my tongue. It was a nation and race dwelling all round the globe that had the lion heart. I had the luck to be called upon to give the roar.[1]

This was a superb piece of rhetoric, in which he neatly avoided appearing to take too much credit for the power of his oratory. As one of his acquaintances, the former Liberal MP Arthur C. Murray, had written: 'I have always held the opinion strongly that Churchill in the Second World War represented magnificently the will of the British nation to win the war, but it is nonsense to suggest—as has been done—that but for Churchill the British nation would not have continued the fight alone when France capitulated in the middle of June, 1940. The suggestion, indeed, is a libel on the British nation.'[2] Churchill skilfully negotiated this potential pitfall, on the one hand making proper concessions to modesty—he was a professional writer, and had got lucky—and on the other hand claiming to have acted as the mouthpiece of the entire British people. The speech was a master-class in the exercise of mock humility.

Although Churchill has received much criticism from historians over many aspects of his career, his Second World War speeches have been more or less immune. This, of course, is because most (but not all) of them were of a very high literary quality. Yet if, for this reason, they are justly renowned, most people's knowledge of them is nonetheless confined to a few famous phrases excerpted from a limited number of radio broadcasts made in the summer of 1940. And the iconic status of these has tended to deflect critical scrutiny from the speeches considered as an entire body, from the outbreak of war in 1939 through the election campaign of 1945. This book is—remarkably enough—the first to offer a comprehensive, archive-based analysis of Churchill's wartime rhetoric as a whole. It will analyse not just his (relatively rare) radio appearances but also his parliamentary performances, as well as speeches in the country and abroad. It considers his oratory not merely as a series of 'great speeches' but as calculated political interventions which had diplomatic repercussions far beyond the effect on the morale of listeners in Britain. Considering his failures as well as his successes, the book seeks to move beyond the essentially celebratory tone of much of the existing literature. It aims to offer insight not only into how the speeches were written and delivered but also into how Churchill's words were received at home, within the Empire, amongst allies and neutrals, and within enemy countries. It explores his speeches in the context of the global media war that was fought alongside the military campaigns.

In November 1941, Churchill observed in the House of Commons: 'It has been aptly remarked that Ministers, and indeed all other public men, when they make speeches at the present time have always to bear in mind three audiences: one our own fellow countrymen, secondly, our friends abroad, and thirdly, the enemy. This naturally makes the task of public speaking very difficult.' He also noted that 'no sensible person in war-time makes speeches because he wants to. He makes them because he has to and to no one does this apply more than to the Prime Minister.'[3] The multiple audiences ensured that the speeches became a tool of global diplomacy—not least as a means of appealing to public opinion in the United States—and as such were read carefully by neutral governments for clues about Britain's strength and strategy. The speeches were designed to communicate some types of facts and to conceal others; and, always subject to misrepresentation by enemy propagandists, they were a weapon used by both sides in the battle for psychological advantage.

Churchill's oratory, moreover, was itself shaped by political processes. Phrases such as 'this was their finest hour' now enjoy a timeless status, but they were produced in response to immediate political needs. The romantic image of Churchill as a lone genius conjuring masterly speeches out of the ether is misleading. It is true that he wrote them himself, but he did so as part of a collaborative process. Colleagues and officials supplied him with information and suggestions, and his drafts (which frequently reflected this advice) were often circulated within Whitehall for comment. It was not unusual for Churchill to accept recommendations that particular passages or sentences should be toned down or eliminated. This can be illustrated with evidence from the speech-writing files in the Churchill Papers, a neglected but valuable source.[4] The files include original drafts, often with handwritten amendments, as well as related information and correspondence. In combination with contemporary diaries and memoirs—as well as the resources of the National Archives at Kew—these files allow us to reconstruct the drafting process. This allows us new insights into the origins of famous passages and phrases. It also reveals the bureaucratic sensitivities and political pressures that combined to shape Churchill's statements. It also reminds us of his and his colleagues' ever-present awareness that a misplaced phrase or sentence—or indeed a tactless omission—could have serious diplomatic or even military repercussions, or adverse consequences for public opinion.

In addition to the many biographers who have commented on Churchill's oratory there is a considerable specialist literature. This body of work, which began to appear within Churchill's own lifetime, often couples his speech-making with his writing.[5] It has many strengths, not least in elucidating Churchill's rhetorical techniques, such as his use of metaphors and proverbs, and in showing how favourite phrases such as 'the English-speaking peoples' were used in different contexts throughout his career. But it also has important weaknesses, including an excessive focus on 1940, a failure to explore Churchill's speech-writing files rigorously, and a lack of examination of the speeches' global reception. Whereas it is acknowledged that Churchill was trying to appeal to world opinion as well as to the British public, there has been little exploration of how the rest of the world actually reacted. But perhaps the greatest failure—both of this literature and of historians more generally—is the near-total acceptance of the most powerful myth surrounding the speeches. This concerns the way in which they were received by the British people.

The picture that we all know—and which may even seem unchallengeable—was established during the war itself, early on. In September 1940, for example, a British propaganda leaflet dropped on the German-occupied Channel Islands asserted that Churchill's speeches had made 'brave men out of the weakest [...] Seldom in history have words taken such material effect'.[6] In August 1941 the popular magazine *Picture Post* ran a photo-spread entitled 'Listening to Churchill'. It was introduced with the following explanation: 'For weeks our photographers have had orders, whenever Mr Churchill speaks, to go out into pubs, clubs, streets and homes, and photograph the Prime Minister's audience. They tried again and again. At last they have obtained a set of pictures which sums up the spirit of the nation.' The result was an idealized set of photos, showing cross-class, urban-rural unanimity. City workers, factory hands, and housewives crowd the door of a wireless shop; a well-dressed family and penguin-suited waiter listen attentively in Piccadilly's Trocadero restaurant; a group of stolid agricultural types sit rapt in a country pub. 'He speaks to the nation,' explained one caption. 'He expresses the feelings of the whole nation.'[7]

After the war, this continued to be the accepted image, reinforced, of course, by Churchill himself, as in his eightieth birthday speech. One anonymous Londoner, interviewed for the TV series *The World at War* (1973–4) expressed the established view pithily when he spoke of Churchill's impact on his fellow East-Enders. 'Now he'd only have to open his mouth and say black was white and they would have believed him, such was their faith in him and such was the way in which he inspired confidence,' he recalled. 'You only had to listen to his broadcasts about fighting them in the fields and you could imagine people rolling up their sleeves.'[8] The politician Mo Mowlam made a similar case in the 2002 programme which led to Churchill being chosen as 'Greatest Briton' of all time in a public vote: 'He made war seem honourable and heroic, he made defeat seem impossible, he made every individual proud of the part they played in history.'[9] Central to this interpretation is the emphasis on unanimity; not only did every individual like the speeches, but they all liked them in exactly the same way. This, indeed, was crucial also to the whole popular image of the summer of 1940, supposedly the kind of moment when, as George Orwell put it, 'the whole nation suddenly swings together and does the same thing, like a herd of cattle facing a wolf.'[10]

Scores of historians have reproduced this story about the impact of the speeches, taking it more or less at face value. By no means all of them go so far as to claim that Churchill's words 'swayed the outcome of the invasion summer'.[11] Some suggest—as he did himself—that 'he expressed defiance, he did not create it'.[12] But it is generally agreed that the speeches served as 'an inspiration for the nation'.[13] They had 'an immediate, galvanizing effect'.[14] Churchill 'made the British people feel proud and strong'.[15] The populace was 'energized' by his rhetoric.[16] Even one Soviet scholar wrote that 'Churchill's speeches impressed the masses, who had, at long last, found a dynamic wartime leader who gave voice to their own feelings.'[17] Some historians have raised the occasional sceptical note, or have at least acknowledged that there was a degree of complexity in the reactions, but never in a sufficiently sustained way to disrupt the predominance of the normal account.[18]

This is in some ways surprising, for it has simultaneously been argued for many years that Churchill was not (at least at first) the leader of a united nation.[19] But although historians have identified many critics of Churchill's leadership, there has been a strong tendency to suggest that the doubters were those at the top of the social and political tree, notably within the Chamberlainite wing of the Conservative Party. There were 'many serious doubts in high places about Churchill as Prime Minister', but not, apparently, elsewhere.[20] Attacks on Churchill by elite figures merely showed how out of touch they were. In 1940, the new Prime Minister and the British people 'came together in what in retrospect was a sublime way, but which struck many in the British establishment at the time as dangerously romantic'.[21] This is convenient for traditionalists, because it allows criticisms of Churchill's speeches recorded at the time by MPs and civil servants to be explained away as snobbery. 'Whatever these influential and important people thought,' writes one historian, 'Churchill had captured the nation's heart.'[22] It is not always felt necessary to deploy evidence, as it is thought 'safe to assume' that 'the silent majority' were enthusiastic for Churchill's speeches.[23] Some historians do provide evidence, but in a highly selective way. Retrospective, nostalgic accounts are often given the same status as contemporary testimony, and although critical remarks by ordinary people are occasionally quoted, these are presented as aberrational.[24] However, Paul Addison, one of the most thoughtful scholars of the period, has acknowledged that there were 'pockets of society where pre-war distrust of Churchill still lingered' among the people. Nevertheless, he gives the impression that this was a very limited phenomenon.[25]

Therefore, although historians of Second World War society have long been aware of its many paradoxes and complexities, the question of how Churchill was viewed by the British people has received surprisingly little attention.[26] This is in part because the idea of his ubiquitous popularity seems at first glance impossible to question. His Gallup opinion poll ratings are widely cited as evidence for this. They were astonishingly high, and satisfaction with him did not fall below 78 per cent for the whole duration of the war.[27] Recently, however, the poll's methodology has been called into question, with one scholar suggesting that Henry Durant, who ran the poll in Britain, headed an operation that was far from perfect. The sample survey was not a precision tool for 'taking the pulse of democracy'. It contained irredeemable flaws that homogenized the private opinions of a skewed cross-section of British society, while commercial pressures forced Durant to make trade-offs between cost and quality, and clients' needs and best survey practice.[28] The sampling errors clearly cannot have been so large as to invalidate the poll's findings on Churchill completely.[29] Still, his ratings must be read in the light of the fact that he scored 83 per cent satisfaction in May 1945 and yet lost the general election heavily that July, after a campaign based very much around his own personality. The discrepancy is generally explained by saying that people tended to distinguish between Churchill the admired war leader and Churchill the potential peacetime leader.[30] They certainly did do so, and from a very early stage, but this did not mean—as reactions to his speeches show—that his war leadership was untouched by criticism. Dissatisfaction with his foreign policy was particularly pronounced from 1943 onwards; this fostered a sense that he was dictatorial and reactionary. It is clear, then, that 'satisfaction' with Churchill as expressed to Gallup did not always equate to unqualified admiration, even with respect to his conduct of the war.

In fact, as some observers noted at the time, what people said to pollsters and what they really thought were not necessarily the same thing.[31] Reduction of the issue of Churchill's popularity to a binary satisfied/dissatisfied question was problematic, and as one researcher argued:

> there may be forces at work which make the spoken opinion of a contact given to a strange interviewer no real indication of his true unspoken opinion. Such a situation could arise if it was felt that however bad Churchill may be, it was better not to stress this in public in order not to destroy internal unity in the country. Or there might be a fear that criticism of Churchill would call down the wrath of the powers that be, as would certainly happen if Hitler

were criticised in Germany. Or the contact may, perhaps wrongly, feel that he is exceptional in considering Churchill a bad Prime Minister, and weakly give the answer he feels is socially acceptable.[32]

There are, however, ways around these problems. We can obtain a richer perspective on opinions about Churchill than that revealed by the polls by examining contemporary reactions to his speeches. These reactions also cast light on important questions besides the issue of his popularity. But of course, his speeches and his popularity were bound up closely together, not least because his speaking gave people a regular cue to express their opinions about him.

It has been suggested that 'it is difficult to establish or measure' the impact of the speeches.[33] In fact, it is hard to imagine how the responses to them could have been better documented. Historians have tended to rely on the diaries of politicians and officials, notably Leo Amery, Henry 'Chips' Channon, John Colville, Hugh Dalton, James Chuter Ede, Cuthbert Headlam, and Harold Nicolson. These remain invaluable, but it is possible to go beyond them in order to gauge the opinion of the public. There are several important sources that are well known and are occasionally used and yet which have not been used systematically to explore reactions to Churchill's speeches throughout the war as a whole.

To begin with, there are the reports of the Ministry of Information (MoI)'s Home Intelligence Division. These were produced between May 1940 and December 1944 and surveyed the state of opinion 'with special reference to morale, rumours, and the reception of ministerial broadcasts and pronouncements'.[34] Then, there is the large volume of evidence collected at the time by the sociological research organization Mass-Observation (MO). This consisted partly of reports on morale collated from material supplied by observers and interviewers, similar to the Home Intelligence documents but both franker and less systematic. It also included a large number of diaries sent in by ordinary people. Over 200 of these—and probably more—make some mention of Churchill, and they may be supplemented by other diaries, published and otherwise. This evidence is extraordinarily rich and variegated, and reveals the complexity of responses to Churchill, including surprising levels of criticism and dissent.

There might have been even more open complaint if there had not been considerable social and even legal pressure to conform. There were a number of prosecutions under Defence Regulation 39BA of people accused of making statements 'likely to cause alarm or despondency'. In July 1940

Victor Muff was fined £10, later reduced to £2, for telling two women 'that old age pensioners would receive more under Hitler and that Churchill had caused miners to be shot' when Home Secretary before the First World War.[35] He was luckier than Elsie Orrin, who the following year was sentenced to five years' penal servitude 'for saying to two soldiers that Hitler was a good ruler, a better man than Mr Churchill'.[36] Of course, most critics held less extreme opinions than these, and faced only informal social sanctions. One anonymous woman diarist recorded being invited on board a naval vessel and listening to a Churchill speech whilst there: 'Only one other woman and myself had any criticisms and we were not well looked on for voicing them: in fact if we had been men I think that one of our hosts would have been rude.'[37]

Naturally, as one might expect, many contemporaries did record the 'classic' reactions to the speeches: the spirit of emboldenment and invigoration, the sense that Churchill was articulating feelings that listeners had but could not put into words.[38] Take, for example, Nellie Carver, a middle-aged single woman who lived in south-east London and worked as supervisor at the Central Telegraph Office. 'Winston's speeches send all sorts of thrills racing up and down my veins and I feel fit to tackle the largest Hun!' she wrote, three days after he became Prime Minister. 'I am certainly not the only Briton to be strengthened and inspired by our PM.'[39] But there was also a dissentient minority, which was much larger than we have been led to believe. Consider Mary Cooke, an art student living with her parents in Kent, who wrote: 'By the way we have got rid of our biggest bit of humbug namely Chamberlain, only to substitute something worse if possible, Churchill.'[40] In old age she recalled that 'the sound of Churchill's over dramatized speeches on the radio never inspired me, although Hitler's madly fanatical ones were much worse.'[41] Her views were not nearly as unusual as one might think.

The evidence that can be used to assess this claim is not without its problems. MO diarists were self-selecting, and were disproportionately drawn from the middle-classes and from those with 'progressive' views.[42] This would present a serious difficulty if the diarists had only reported their own thoughts, but in fact they also reported the opinions of others around them. For example, one diarist noted in 1942: 'Overheard in bus this a.m. "Well, he (obviously Churchill) is very good at speeches—lovely speeches 'e makes— but 'e don't *do* much." Grunts of approval roundabout.'[43] Of course, those who disliked Churchill may have been biased in terms of what they recorded. But, crucially, some people who did like Churchill's speeches recorded that others didn't, and expressed their surprise at this. Taken in combination with survey evidence—with which they often correlate—diaries can be a potent source. Although they cannot by themselves provide definitive evidence of *how many* people held a particular opinion about Churchill's speeches, they do give a good illustration of the *range* of views that were held.

It is the diversity and variety of responses that is the key. Yes, these were speeches that stimulated, energized, invigorated, and excited many people. But they were also speeches which caused depression and disappointment in many others—which was hardly surprising if Churchill brought bad news or no news—and which sometimes led to workplace or family arguments. Some members of the audience undoubtedly did listen in intense silence, but others cracked jokes, offered running commentary, or answered back to the radio. When the broadcasts were heard in public spaces, it is clear that not everyone listened carefully at all. Where there was hostility to Churchill, some of it was expressed in crudely abusive terms ('it's time the old b—— was dead') or was based on ridiculous prejudice ('Well I don't like Churchill's face. I hope Mr Eden is the next Prime Minister. He has a nice face').[44] Many people, however, were intelligent, reflective, and discriminating. They might like one speech but not another. A speech might strike someone as 'heartening' overall but have aspects that were 'disgusting'.[45] Someone else might have great faith in Churchill at one time but become 'bitterly disappointed' in him later.[46] A listener might get bored with his repetition: 'Does Churchill find himself incapable of making any speech without dragging in the Battle of Britain in 1940 & saying that we carried the burden of the War alone for 2 years?'[47] People could change their minds about a speech overnight, or after discussing it with others or reading newspaper commentaries. A speech causing 'extreme satisfaction' in Wales might get a lukewarm reception in Scotland.[48] (The reasons for such differences are not always clear.) Northern Irish Unionists, normally rock-solid behind Churchill, might read between the lines of a speech and get 'an uneasy feeling that he was hinting at some new effort to placate Eire on the border question at Ulster's expense'.[49] It is obvious, then, that failure to show complete enthusiasm for a Churchill speech was not necessarily a sign of outright political opposition to him. Some people were perfectly well disposed to him in general but happened not to care especially for his speeches. There were not many people who thought his delivery 'slow and boring' in general, but there were occasions when his delivery was the subject of considerable negative comment.[50]

One of the purposes of this book, then, is to draw out some of the wealth and heterogeneity of the domestic reactions to Churchill's rhetoric. Another is to show, in much more depth than has been attempted before, the ways in which the speeches were received abroad. They could not be ignored, even in enemy territory. The broadcaster Richard Dimbleby related a story told him by a man who had worked as a radio official in Hamburg during the war: 'He walked into the offices one night and found normal work at a standstill. [...] Asking what was up, the official was told to be quiet—"Churchill's broadcasting".'[51] The Nazis of course reported Churchill's words to their population in highly selective form. Some glimpses of ordinary Germans' reactions can be found in the reports—now published—of the *Sicherheitsdienst* (SD), the Nazi Party and SS intelligence service. Enemy propagandists did their best to turn Churchill's words to their own advantage, sometimes quoting his pre-war speeches against him. In occupied France in 1943, for example, 250,000 leaflets entitled 'Phrases de Churchill' were distributed by the Vichy regime's militia.[52] Britain's Political Warfare Executive (PWE) helped counter such efforts through their own leaflets, frequently quoting Churchill, which were dropped over occupied Europe by the RAF.

The impact of the speeches elsewhere in the world—most importantly in the USA—can be traced through newspapers, through diplomatic reports, and through the extensive records made of the contents of foreign broadcasts. Secret intelligence sources are occasionally useful too. Naturally, given the sheer volume of material, it is necessary to be selective when dealing both with the reactions and with the speeches themselves. It is impossible within a book of this length even to mention every wartime speech that Churchill gave, let alone analyse them all exhaustively. It is at the same time important, however, not to neglect the forgotten and even workaday elements of his rhetoric in favour of a gallop through 'Churchill's greatest hits'. The structure of the book is basically chronological, with most space given to the period before 'the turning of the tide' in 1942—the tensest years, when the potential implications of a Churchill speech were most serious. However, questions of post-war domestic politics (as opposed to domestic issues such as industrial production that were of importance to the war effort itself) are reserved for Chapter 8. This is because Churchill spoke on these issues only rarely prior to VE Day, and it is therefore convenient to consider these few occasions together with his 1945 election speeches. The book, moreover, does not claim to be definitive, but aims merely to stimulate debate, to widen the field of study, and to show how much still remains to be learnt about the origins and impact of Churchill's war rhetoric.

Before proceeding further, there is a false story to be disposed of. It has been rebutted authoritatively more than once, but it continues to enjoy wide currency among the public.[53] The tale is that Churchill did not make his famous radio broadcasts himself but was impersonated by an actor, Norman Shelley. It is true that Shelley did make a phonograph recording—not a broadcast—of a speech by Churchill, although what use was made of it (if any) is unclear. The speech related to events in North Africa in 1942. Shelley told the story, or a version of it, to the authors of a book published thirty years later: 'Of course, the old man insisted on listening to a trial run, for the European Service, and as he listened I'm told a slow slow smile spread over his face, as he said "He's even got my teeth!"'[54] The anecdote improved in the telling so that by 1979—at which point the story went global—it was the 4 June 1940 'fight them on the beaches' speech that Shelley had recorded. He did not however claim to have delivered it live on that day; indeed it was clear from his account that the recording had taken place at some point after the 1942 Battle of El Alamein.[55] In 1987—by which time Shelley was dead—the historian David Irving claimed that he had given the speech in 1940.[56] Irving is a Holocaust denier; variants of the story have appeared in the work of more reputable scholars, however, including that of the respected editor of the Roosevelt–Churchill correspondence.[57] It has often been pointed out that the 4 June speech was not broadcast at all—an announcer read out a summary. This, however, appears not to have dented the popularity of the myth very much. I have frequently been asked during the writing of this book, 'Isn't it true that…?' I make no claim to originality in saying, no, it is not.

The question remains, though, why people are so eager to believe the story. As a piece of psychological speculation one might hazard that they feel that the account of the almost mystical power of Churchill's oratory, as it is usually presented, is in some sense too good to be true. They appear to have reacted to this by latching on to a picturesque falsehood. Happily, the truth about Churchill's speeches is considerably more interesting than any myth or fiction.

I

'The Epitaph of Capitalism'

On the morning of 13 May 1940 Malcolm MacDonald MP obeyed a summons to see Winston Churchill, who had become Prime Minister three days earlier as German troops began their rampage across Western Europe. Churchill had not yet moved to Downing Street and was constructing his new government in crisis conditions from his room at the Admiralty, his previous ministerial posting. As he entered, MacDonald—son of Ramsay MacDonald, the first Labour Prime Minister—found Churchill 'striding up and down the chamber with his head thrust forward in deep thought on his massive shoulders and his hands gripping the lapels of his jacket, as if he were making a speech in the House of Commons'. Looking around without varying his footfall Churchill greeted MacDonald warmly. 'My dear Malcolm,' he said, 'I'm glad to see you. I've nothing to offer you except...' He hesitated. MacDonald—who had held Cabinet office under Churchill's predecessor Neville Chamberlain—felt a stab of disappointment. It seemed he was going to be given an unimportant role, such as Postmaster-General. Then Churchill went on: '...blood and toil, tears and sweat'. MacDonald was momentarily baffled, and wondered whether the Prime Minister 'had created a new war-time Ministry, and was asking me to become Secretary of State for Blood, Toil, Tears and Sweat'. Churchill inspected MacDonald's reaction, and then adopted an informal manner as he offered him the Ministry of Health. The visitor happily accepted and made his way out to the private secretary's office where he found Leo Amery, who had been appointed Secretary of State for India a few minutes earlier. 'Did he also offer you blood and sweat and toil and tears?' Amery asked, and when MacDonald said yes, revealed that Churchill had said the same thing to him. MacDonald recalled:

A few hours later we sat in a crowded House of Commons listening to Churchill making his first speech as Prime Minister. In the middle of it we suddenly heard him utter the well-rehearsed and now immortal phrase, 'I would say to the House, as I said to those who have joined this Government: "I have nothing to offer but blood, toil, tears and sweat." '[1]

Churchill, then, was not ashamed to practise; in fact, his rehearsals for this particular moment—or something like it that he had imagined—had begun decades before.

Churchill had been born into Britain's political aristocracy. He was a descendant of John Churchill, the first Duke of Marlborough, victor of the 1704 Battle of Blenheim, and was born at Blenheim Palace, the remarkable home built in honour of that triumph. Winston's grandfather, the seventh Duke, was a Conservative politician of some influence who briefly held Cabinet rank in the late 1860s. In 1874 Disraeli's Conservatives swept back to office at a general election, and Lord Randolph Churchill (the Duke's younger son, and Winston's father) was elected Tory MP for the 'family borough' of Woodstock. Lord Randolph was under paternal pressure to enter the Commons, and used the threat not to stand as a weapon in his fight with his parents over his hoped-for marriage to the beautiful young American heiress Jennie Jerome.[2] The battle won, Winston was born on 30 November the same year, just seven-and-a-half months after the wedding. Lord Randolph made a good start as an MP. According to Disraeli, 'Lord Randolph said many imprudent things, which is not very important in the maiden speech of a young member and a young man; but the House was surprised, and then captivated, by his energy, and natural flow, and his impressive manner.'[3] He soon ran into serious trouble outside the House, though. After he threatened to expose details of the Prince of Wales's private life (as part of a bid to cover up a scandal involving his own elder brother) Lord Randolph was ostracized from Society. This led the Duke to take up Disraeli's offer of the Lord Lieutenancy of Ireland; Lord Randolph went with him into social exile as his unpaid private secretary. So it was that Winston Churchill's first memory was of 'A great black crowd, scarlet soldiers on horseback, strings pulling away a brown shiny sheet, the old Duke, the formidable grandpapa, talking loudly to the crowd,' as he unveiled a statue of Lord Gough, a hero of the British Empire, in Dublin's Phoenix Park in 1880. This experience provided an early and vivid introduction to military rhetoric. As Churchill wrote in *My Early Life* (1930), 'I recall even a phrase he used: "and with a withering volley he shattered the enemy's line".'[4]

With the smashing Liberal victory of 1880, the family returned to Britain. Lord Randolph's social situation was now easing, and he resumed his brilliant but erratic political career. As a member of the so-called 'Fourth Party', a small group of rebellious Tory backbenchers, he both harassed Gladstone's government and assailed the staid and unimaginative leaders of his own party in the Commons. His tactics were controversial and, in the sense that he took little account of the consequences, irresponsible. He did not mind being offensive, and took delight in outraging his opponents. After one slashing attack on the prominent Liberal Lord Hartington, the *Leeds Mercury* accused him of taking a falsehood from the press 'as a street Arab picks a stone out of the gutter to throw at the head of any respectable person who happens to have excited his animosity'.[5] But in an age when the electorate was expanding it was increasingly important to appeal to the masses as well as to Parliament. Gladstone had pioneered the technique of the mass meeting, and Conservatives had to follow in his wake.[6] Lord Randolph became one of the party's most popular speakers; working-class audiences revelled in his verbal fireworks. Supposedly, the crowds used to cry out 'Give it 'em hot, Randy' by way of encouragement.[7] Winston Churchill's account gives a hint of the qualities he admired in his father's rhetoric:

> Wit, abuse, epigrams, imagery, argument—all were 'Randolphian.' No one could guess beforehand what he was going to say nor how he would say it. No one else said the same kind of things, or said them in the same kind of way [...] before the end of 1882 a speech from Lord Randolph Churchill had become an event to the newspaper reader. The worthy, pious and substantial citizen hurriedly turning over the pages of his *Times* or still more respectable *Morning Post* and folding it to his convenience, crouched himself up in his most comfortable chair and ate it up line by line with snorts of indignation or gurglings of mirth.[8]

Lord Randolph delivered his speeches from memory from full drafts prepared in advance, a technique his son did his best to imitate early in his career. Aided by his relaxed demeanour and use of gesture Lord Randolph was a great popular success. He complained that addressing big meetings caused him anxiety, and that 'the constant necessity of trying to say something new makes me a drivelling idiot'.[9] The effort paid off, however, and by the time the Tories returned to office in 1885, his position was such that it was impossible for the new Prime Minister, Lord Salisbury, to exclude him from the Cabinet. Gladstone—now in his eighties—came back to power briefly the following year, and made a failed attempt to enact his controversial policy of Home Rule for Ireland. In one of his most celebrated phrases, Lord Randolph claimed that the measure was only being put forward 'to gratify the ambition of an old man in a hurry'.[10] With the Liberals split, the Conservatives romped home at the 1886 general election, and Lord Randolph became Chancellor of the Exchequer. This was to be the pinnacle of his career—and a very brief one. At the end of the year he offered his resignation to Salisbury, in opposition to what he saw as excessive defence spending. This was simply a tactic, but he was outmanoeuvred. Lord Randolph might have been popular with the masses but he was difficult to work with and to the Tory establishment he was dispensable. Salisbury accepted his resignation and in so doing put an end to his ministerial career. Within a few years, his physical and mental health began to deteriorate, possibly as a consequence of syphilis. This became evident in his speech-making, which became increasingly painful to witness. Winston recalled that 'in spite of some brilliant successes [...] on the whole he seemed hardly to be holding his own'.[11] Lord Randolph's friend Lord Rosebery wrote that he 'died by inches in public'.[12] He eventually died physically in January 1895. He was forty-five. Winston had recently turned twenty.

Lord Randolph's influence on Winston was significant, but it was at a distance. Neither he nor Lady Randolph put much effort into parenting. The extent and the psychological impact of their neglect can perhaps be exaggerated—Winston did at least have the care of a loving nanny, Elizabeth Everest—but there was little communication between father and son. In spite of his pleas, his parents rarely visited him at boarding school. At the age of thirteen he started at the elite Harrow School where—although his general performance was indifferent—he soon met the challenge of committing to memory and reciting 1,200 lines of T. B. Macaulay's *The Lays of Ancient Rome*. It was Mrs Everest, not his mother or father, who came down to see him receive his prize. He followed his father's activities through the press: 'For years I had read every word he spoke and what the newspapers said about him.' In the early 1890s he had his first direct experiences of parliamentary rhetorical culture when he began to frequent the visitors' gallery of the House of Commons. There he saw Lord Randolph, Gladstone, and other titans in action. 'It seemed to me a very great world in which these men lived,' he remembered: ruthless political duelling went hand in hand with 'ceremonious personal courtesy and mutual respect'.[13]

Lord Randolph left Winston a substantial rhetorical legacy. It took him some years to get fully to grips with it: he gained his greatest familiarity with his father's career by researching his biography, published in 1906. But even before that he had taken the trouble of learning parts of his father's speeches verbatim. One man who knew him as a young soldier on the north-west frontier of India recalled him quoting them; a denunciation and ridicule of a proposal for a tunnel beneath the English Channel was apparently a special favourite, 'for before all things he was profoundly patriotic'.[14] Observers of the younger Churchill's maiden parliamentary efforts were divided over how his style compared with that of Lord Randolph. One journalist wrote: 'Mr Churchill does not inherit his father's voice—save for the slight lisp—or his father's manner. Address, accent, appearance do not help him.'[15] Another however thought that 'He has many of the gestures of his father, such as the sudden jerking forward of the head and clenching the fists and beating the air as though hammering home an argument.'[16] The question of technique aside, Churchill's claim to have taken his politics 'almost unquestioningly' from his father needs to be taken with a pinch of salt.[17] Lord Randolph's slogan of 'Tory Democracy' was an elastic, populist one, and Winston often interpreted his father's actions to suit his own ends.[18] Yet although early on in his career his father's memory almost threatened to overshadow him, he made good use of it as a valuable rhetorical resource on which he could draw.

Shortly after Lord Randolph died, Winston was commissioned into the Queen's Fourth Hussars, a cavalry regiment, having trained at the Royal Military College at Sandhurst. In November 1895 he and a friend took advantage of a period of leave to travel to Cuba, which was in revolt against Spanish rule, in search of adventure. This was his first sight of war, and also gave him a chance to make his name by writing about it for the *Daily Graphic*. Stopping off in New York on the way, he met Bourke Cockran, a Democrat politician (and friend of his mother) whom he claimed as a lasting influence on his speaking style. According to Churchill's later recollection Cockran—whom he quoted in his renowned 'iron curtain' speech—taught him 'how to use every note of the human voice like an organ'. Enthusing about him in the 1950s, he said: 'He was my model—I learned from him how to hold thousands in thrall.'[19] In 1896 Churchill shipped out with his regiment to India. There he launched himself into an ambitious programme of self-education. He felt dissatisfied with what he had learnt at Harrow, but there he had at least been taught to appreciate 'the ordinary British sentence—which is a noble thing'.[20] He read an eclectic range of authors including Macaulay and Edward Gibbon—the latter also having been an influence on Lord Randolph—the impact of whom can be seen on his grammatical style and use of irony.[21] Churchill's quest was driven both by a voracious intellectual curiosity and by a desire to put his learning into practice. Having already fixed on politics as his metier, he needed to acquire the rhetorical skills that would allow him to make a name for himself through speaking and writing.

There was also another motive. Churchill has been well described as 'the quintessential sensation-seeker', always searching, as in his military adventures, for some new thrill.[22] The public platform was another source of excitement and even, potentially, of physical risk. Churchill's first public speech—of sorts—was made as a Sandhurst cadet in 1894, during a rowdy episode at London's Empire Theatre, in defiance of morality campaigners who wanted to prevent alcohol being served in the auditorium. According to legend, he began: 'Ladies of the Empire! I stand for Liberty!'[23] He, however, counted as his real maiden effort the speech he made to a Conservative gathering in Bath when home on leave in 1897. He praised the government, sneered at the Liberals, and spoke of Britain's mission to carry 'peace, civilisation, and good government to the uttermost ends of the earth'.[24] Back in India, there was an uprising on the north-west frontier, and Churchill exploited his connections to ensure that he was part of the action. He wrote up his exploits as *The Story of the Malakand Field Force* (1898) and was later briefly attached to a further expedition in the Tirah. 'Even in those early days he possessed and was reinforcing his knack of coining felicitous phrases,' recalled a colleague.[25]

It was during this period that Churchill—trying to get himself taken seriously as a contributor to heavyweight periodicals—drafted an article called 'The Scaffolding of Rhetoric'. Never published in his lifetime, it displayed an essentially romantic view of the topic. The power of oratory made the man who wielded it into an 'independent force', who even if isolated from party and friends could bend crowds to his will. Crucially, the technique could be cultivated. It was important always to employ the 'best possible word' to express one's meaning; and all but the most sophisticated audiences preferred 'short, homely words of common usage'. Sentences, however, should be 'long, rolling and sonorous' and a speech should be brought to a climax through 'a rapid succession of waves of sound and vivid pictures'; apt analogies could achieve an electrifying effect. Finally, wild language should not necessarily be avoided. Used in a peroration, it could act as a safety valve, relieving the feelings of the crowd rather than inciting them to violence.[26] Although it would take a long time for Churchill to become a master rhetorician himself, it is clear that he had already established in his mind an ideal that would in many ways serve him throughout his career. This can also be seen in his only novel, *Savrola* (1899), in which the eponymous hero wins over a hostile crowd with an electrifying speech. Churchill described its preparation, in what is perhaps the closest thing we have to a detailed autobiographical description of his own methods:

> His ideas began to take the form of words, to group themselves into sentences; he murmured to himself; the rhythm of his own language swayed him; instinctively he alliterated. Ideas succeeded one another, as a stream flows swiftly by and the light changes on its waters. He seized a piece of paper and began hurriedly to pencil notes. That was a point; could not tautology accentuate it? [...]
>
> Presently he rose, and completely under the influence of his own thoughts and language, began to pace the room with short rapid strides, speaking to himself in a low voice and with great emphasis.[27]

This was the type of reverie in which Malcolm MacDonald found Churchill in May 1940.

With his Indian frontier experiences behind him, and with a small taste of fame from his writings, Churchill pulled further strings to ensure that he was present at the final stages of the British re-conquest of the Sudan. These exploits laid the foundations for another book, and he determined to leave the Army and earn his living through writing. In 1899, the same year that *The River War* was published, he fought an unsuccessful by-election campaign at Oldham. That summer saw the beginnings of a showdown between the British and the Boer Republics of South Africa that was soon to culminate in war. Churchill was rather blasé about the likely ease of defeating the Boers, whom he considered 'a miserably small people'.[28] When hostilities broke out in the autumn, he set off for South Africa with alacrity, as a highly paid correspondent for the *Morning Post*; the party on board his ship feared that all the excitement would be over by the time they arrived. But the British forces quickly faced major reverses. The war taught Churchill an important lesson: 'Never, never, never believe any war will be smooth and easy [...] Always remember, however sure you are that you can easily win, that there would not be a war if the other man did not think he also had a chance.'[29] It also brought him global celebrity. The circumstances of his capture by the Boers followed by his plucky and impulsive escape turned him into a hero. This status enhanced his authority when talking about war, and also made it easier for him to advance unpopular causes—such as his urgings of magnanimity, once they had been defeated, towards the Boer enemy he had now come to respect.

It also ensured his return as MP for Oldham at the general election of 1900. His first Commons speech, in defence of the conduct of the still-ongoing war, was a considerable success, although at least one observer detected nervousness.[30] Ideologically, however, he did not find the Conservative Party a comfortable home. All but immediately he launched an attack on the government's Army Reform scheme, and invoked the memory of Lord Randolph's resignation as he lifted 'again the tattered flag of retrenchment and economy'.[31] Accordingly, he was feted by Liberal commentators as a master debater and a 'born demagogue', the latter term being used as one of praise for someone capable of 'leading, inspiring, and inflaming masses of men'.[32] In their enthusiasm, they may have over-praised him. 'Mr Churchill and oratory are not neighbours yet,' stated one essentially friendly journalistic profile at this time, 'nor do I think it likely they ever will be.' The writer explained that 'His temperament is highly nervous, which may explain his tendency to overgesticulate. A favourite platform attitude, used whenever he has made a point, is to place both his hands on his hips, what time he beams the smile of satisfaction.'[33] Churchill later acknowledged that his early efforts had cost him some anxiety:

> When I first began to make speeches, I was in a fever lest some one should haul me over the coals for a verbal or trivial contradiction. Then I soon found that the greater part of a speech goes in at one ear and comes out at the other. [...] You can always silence a questioner, though it be only by a bad joke. Life would be too short if we had to set so rigid a watch upon our lips as all that. Besides which, if we were always calculating and hesitating over the precise effect, the painful consistency of every sentence, we should cease to be natural and spontaneous and therefore convincing.[34]

Churchill's political enemies would certainly have agreed that he was not excessively troubled by the need for consistency. In 1904 he incurred an enmity and suspicion that would dog him for decades when he left the Tories for the Liberals. This was over the issue of Free Trade, which the Conservatives now proposed to abandon and in which Churchill sincerely believed; but as he was abandoning a party in difficulties for one which looked likely to form the next government, the charge of opportunism was hard to shake off. In his view, trade was 'utterly different from war' and that therefore 'the ideas and the phraseology of the one should never be applied to the other', as was the habit of his protectionist opponents.[35] But he did not hesitate to describe politics itself as a 'battleground', and his Conservative foes were not inclined to give him quarter.[36]

Shortly before he joined the Liberals Churchill had a disconcerting experience when speaking. Up until this point he had done his best to commit as much to memory as he could; he had, for example, been able to reduce his notes for his maiden speech to 'a very few cryptic signs and jottings'. But now this method led him into trouble. When addressing the Commons on the issue of trade unions using only partial notes he found that he had written out only the first section of his closing sentence—and could not remember the end of it. After 'several prolonged pauses' he ended lamely and sat down. He recalled the reaction of his critics: 'some charitably suggested drink and other drugs, whereas the explanation was far less exciting.'[37] In fact, members may have thought of Lord Randolph's mental breakdown and wondered if it was repeating itself in his son. The effect of the episode was that Churchill from this point preferred when possible to speak from a full set of notes, as he was to do during the Second World War. But whether he worked from memory or from a text, it is clear that he was not at base a spontaneous speaker.

He was, however, extremely fertile in phrase, imagery, and humour. When the new Liberal government took office in 1905, Churchill was rewarded with the position of Under-Secretary at the Colonial Office. He seemed always to be in the public eye, much more so than was normal for a junior minister. This was in part because of his involvement in the high-profile question of post-war South Africa, but also because of his colourful character and gift for a phrase. Some of these—such as his use of 'terminological inexactitude' to describe misleading Liberal Party statements—came back to bite him. Some others made less of a splash at the time but were worked and reworked throughout his career, eventually to brilliant effect. Churchill can be seen as a 'phrase-forger' who—sometimes adapting the aphorisms of others—played with word combinations until he found a form that would stick.[38] For example, in 1906, talking about land settlement in South Africa, he commented that 'I do not think it is very encouraging that we should have spent so much money upon the settlement of so few.' In 1907, when talking of Kenya, he said that 'Never before in Colonial experience has a Council been granted where the number of settlers is so few.' Indeed, as far back as 1899, he had remarked that 'Never before were there so many people in England, and never before have they had so much to eat.'[39] Ronald Hyam has observed that this habit of Churchill's 'probably explains the ease and readiness with which the Second World War rhetoric flowed. Its most famous word patterns had been polished and perfected through thirty-five years of refurbishing.'[40] Sometimes, indeed, the quotations were not so much refurbished as recycled. The phrase 'let us go forward together', which he used in his first speech as Prime Minister and which became the slogan of a famous poster, had cropped up before in 1914 (in relation to Ireland) and 1928 (in connection with the Budget).[41]

When the ailing Henry Campbell-Bannerman was replaced as Liberal Prime Minister by H. H. Asquith in 1908, Churchill was promoted to the Cabinet. His (at times uneasy) political alliance with David Lloyd George, the new Chancellor, was highly productive, both men making important contributions to social reform legislation. Not coincidentally, Churchill came to be seen by many as a dangerous demagogue, whose populist rhetoric supposedly fanned the flames of class conflict. But the denunciation of dukes did not come naturally to him; of the two men, it was Lloyd George who spoke more credibly with a radical tongue. That was partly a matter of background and disposition; but Lloyd George also had the superior technique. Shortly before the government embarked on its celebrated battle with the House of Lords, the Liberal MP Edwin Montagu wrote to Asquith: 'Winston is not yet Prime Minister, and even if he were he carries no guns. He delights and he tickles, he even enthuses the audience he addresses—but when he has gone, so also has the memory of what he has said.'[42] This was catty but it was not fundamentally unfair. Robert Roberts, the chronicler of working-class life in Salford in this period, recalled how his father and a friend idolized Lloyd George but thought little of Churchill: 'Unlike their hero, the orator supreme, they considered him a shifty and mediocre speaker with a poor delivery.'[43] Lloyd George later said that Churchill 'was a rhetorician and not an orator. He thought only of how a phrase sounded and not how it might influence crowds'.[44]

This was perhaps because Churchill was so easily influenced by the words that he himself had produced. His alliance with Lloyd George initially involved opposition to excessive expenditure on the Royal Navy in the face of what they claimed was an exaggerated German threat. But after he was put in charge of the Navy, as First Lord of the Admiralty, he changed his tune. Early in 1914 he clashed with Lloyd George (and won) when the latter demanded he cut back his spending plans. Of course, given the outbreak of war later in the year, he could easily claim vindication over this episode. But one cannot help but be impressed by his capacity to argue essentially opposite cases with equal vigour. He had a great capacity for talking himself round. It was a common criticism that he allowed phrases to master him, rather than the reverse, and that he could persuade himself that something must be true simply because it sounded good.[45] Indeed he had once admitted the point in a letter to his mother: 'I do not care so much for the principles I advocate as for the impression which my words produce [...] I vy often yield to the temptation of adapting my facts to my phrases.'[46]

The coming of war with Germany might have seemed a great rhetorical opportunity for Churchill. As First Lord—the position to which he was reappointed in 1939—he was well placed to interpret the naval war to the public. That he loved warfare might have been an advantage, but he had difficulty concealing how much he was enjoying himself; this was not completely consistent with public dignity. In one of his first speeches he dismissively compared the German navy, corked up in its ports, to 'rats in a hole'.[47] Then the Germans sank three British ships in short order. It was Lloyd George—who had initially havered over British involvement in the war—who more authentically captured the national mood. At London's Queen's Hall in September he urged the spirit of sacrifice: 'They think we cannot beat them. It will not be easy. It will be a long job; it will be a terrible war; but in the end we shall march through terror to triumph'.[48] This was a great popular success which burnished Lloyd George's credentials as a war leader and helped set him on the path to the premiership. Churchill's career, on the other hand, now went into a downward spiral. In 1915, he fell out dramatically with Admiral John Fisher, the First Sea Lord, over the Dardanelles campaign—which was itself going badly wrong. The row forced Asquith to invite the Conservative Party into government as part of a coalition. Churchill was forced out of the Admiralty and was offered only a minor post in exchange. In the autumn, from a sense of frustration, he resigned from the government completely. During this period he made plenty of perfectly decent speeches but they were not in themselves enough to recover his shattered reputation.

After his fall from grace, Churchill joined the Army—whilst remaining an MP—and headed for the Western Front, but after a few months in the trenches the lure of politics proved too much, and he returned to Westminster. At the end of 1916, his old ally Lloyd George dramatically displaced Asquith as Prime Minister and formed a new coalition. Churchill was not included, but by mid-1917 Lloyd George was politically strong enough—and perhaps sufficiently nervous of Churchill—to bring him back to office as Minister of Munitions, a role in which Lloyd George himself had previously excelled. The Prime Minister went on to secure for himself the name of 'The Man Who Won the War'; his model of small War Cabinet with ministers freed from departmental responsibilities would often be used by Churchill's critics to reproach him when things went wrong during the Second World War. Effective rhetoric, both within and without the Commons, was an important part of the Lloyd George armoury. True, he did not leave anything that reads, on paper, as well as Churchill's 1940 speeches do today—although, if we had them, sound recordings might make his words live better. He must, however, be credited with an instinctive ability to read an audience and with a sound appreciation of the demands of media management. (He began speaking earlier in the day in order to better accommodate the newspapers.)[49] For his part, Churchill's position in the final years of the First World War did not give him many opportunities to provide broad, national leadership. A notable exception was his speech to a huge meeting in Westminster's Central Hall in July 1918. Speaking from a platform bedecked in flags, he declared that 'Germany must be beaten. (Loud cheers.) Germany must know that she is beaten, must feel that she is beaten. (Renewed cheers.).' In terms of parallels with his Second World War rhetoric, it is worth noting his description of the war as 'a conflict between Christian civilization and scientific barbarism'.[50]

The Lloyd George coalition won a resounding victory in the general election that followed the Armistice. Churchill held an important place in the government, although many of his colleagues thought him erratic. These years were notable for his crusade against Russian Bolshevism, his role in drawing up the new political settlement in the Middle East, and the part he played in the Anglo-Irish War and the peace treaty that followed. In 1922, however, the coalition collapsed, and Churchill lost his seat in Parliament. Two years later, with the Liberals in serious decline, he bounced back to become Chancellor of the Exchequer—in a Conservative government. Many of his new colleagues were understandably suspicious of this two-time switcher of parties. After the Tories lost to Labour at the 1929 election, Churchill's career foundered once more. He fell out with his leader, Stanley Baldwin, over the issue of India. Baldwin was determined to support the Labour government's moves in the direction of self-government; Churchill could not stomach this and resigned from the Shadow Cabinet in 1931. Later in the year, when economic crisis triggered the formation of a so-called National Government—a nominal coalition in which the Tories held the whip hand—he thus found himself left out. He spent the rest of the decade trying to talk his way back into power.

It is now widely accepted that the story of Churchill's wilderness years is much more complicated than the one that he presented in his memoirs. In his version, the 1930s were related as a straightforward tale of his heroic attempts to alert the British people to the need for rearmament in the face of the danger posed by the Nazis. The story of his equally vociferous campaign against reform in India was scarcely touched upon.[51] In addressing the question of why his warnings about Germany were for the most part ignored—that is to say, why his rhetoric proved unpersuasive—modern historians tend to point to the relationship between the two issues. The self-promoting Churchill was not only widely distrusted on grounds of character, and in some ways less consistent over Germany than legend would suggest; he discredited himself by prophesying doom over India, just as he had done over many other issues before. To MPs who had, as it were, heard it all before, his speaking style seemed not majestically impressive but overblown and hackneyed.[52] Moreover, his speeches revealed the weaknesses as well as the strengths of his mindset. Work in the field of political psychology suggests that he was extremely good at enumerating reasons why his opponents were wrong, but showed little ability to appreciate their point of view. This was wholly appropriate in relation to Nazism, but much less so when dealing with the leaders of the Indian National Congress. Negotiation with these men was undoubtedly difficult, but it was by no means as impossible as Churchill seemed to believe.[53] But if the India campaign was a political blind alley, he did gain something from it in terms of rhetorical technique. Because of the sheer number of interventions he had to make in the Commons on India, he briefly adopted a more spontaneous speaking style. He told his wife Clementine that he now spoke to the Commons 'with garrulous unpremeditated flow. They seem delighted. But what a mystery the art of public speaking is! It all consists in my (mature) judgement of selecting three or four absolutely sound arguments and putting these in the most conversational manner possible. There is apparently nothing in the literary effect I have sought for forty years!'[54] He soon reverted to his usual more formal and elaborate technique, but it seems that something had rubbed off. Harold Nicolson MP wrote in 1943 of how Churchill's mastery of the Commons was achieved by 'the combination of great flights of oratory with sudden swoops into the intimate and conversational. Of all his devices it is the one that never fails.'[55]

To anyone brought up exclusively on the popular myth, close examination of Churchill's 1930s speeches might be disconcerting. He was often willing to praise—or at least pay lip service to—those later demonized as the 'Guilty Men' of appeasement. In 1936, he acknowledged that Baldwin had in recent times made 'very serious statements about the need for rearmament' and 'fought, and largely won' the previous year's election on that issue.[56] In 1937 he spoke of the record of Neville Chamberlain, the new Prime Minister, in his previous post as Baldwin's Chancellor: 'no one was so active in pressing forward the policy of rearmament and in providing the immense supplies of money which had been rendered available, largely through his own foresight and prescience.'[57] Many such statements were purely tactical, made either because Churchill was making concessions to his opponents in order to establish wider points of argument, or because—to put it bluntly—he was sucking up to the party leadership in the hope of getting a job. He showed a blatant willingness to tone down his criticisms in exchange for office.[58] Sometimes, however, his remarks were awkward enough to him to require brushing under the carpet later. Thus the comments on Baldwin quoted above were quietly excluded from the speech in question when it was published in a 1938 collection—even though the reader was assured that none of Churchill's statements had been left out of the book on grounds of 'political inconvenience'.[59]

Yet what from one perspective looks like inconsistency or deviousness may from another look like subtlety—or at least attempted subtlety. It is worth reflecting on what Churchill was trying to achieve—or rather, what he thought was necessary to achieve it. From his point of view, if Britain was to be properly prepared for the possibility of war, he had to be in charge, if not as Prime Minister then at least in an important defence role. This might be through him being appointed to the existing government; hence his near-constant angling for a job. Alternatively, the government might fall to be replaced by a new one of which he was either the head or an important member. On the face of it, nothing in the 1930s looked less likely: the enormous Commons majority held by Baldwin and Chamberlain was by today's standards impregnable. However, to a generation brought up in the late nineteenth century it may have looked rather different. Then, the control of the party leaders over their MPs had been less secure, with the effect that governments with seemingly solid foundations could never exclude the possibility of overnight collapse. As Churchill put in his biography of his father, the Commons could be 'an organism of impulse. A sudden announcement; a brilliant and persuasive speech; powerful support coming from an unexpected quarter; panic, emotion, or excitement, and fine majorities may crumble into dust.'[60] In the era of appeasement, the increased muscle of the party Whips was evident, and Churchill sensed that the power of the Commons was in decline. But he still had in mind the possibility that the government might lose office as the product of some convulsion behind the scenes.[61] And if the government itself had not feared some such tectonic shift—as had occurred in a sense as recently as 1931—its bullying of the relatively few existing rebels would have been unnecessary. The Chamberlainites were afraid, not of the actual loss of their majority, but of a movement that might trigger some wider and more lethal forces. Indeed, that was exactly what happened when the government did fall in 1940. True, the circumstances then were extraordinary; but there was no shortage of 'panic, emotion, or excitement' in 1938–9 either. Although Churchill was terribly isolated at that time, it was by no means irrational for either him or his opponents to think that the situation might suddenly change. Pragmatically, then, it was less important that his speeches should be 'right' than that they should put him in the right place to benefit from events.[62]

Indeed, what was noteworthy about Churchill during the 1930s was not merely his capacity to deliver self-inflicted wounds—such as getting howled down by MPs for his support for Edward VIII during the abdication crisis—but his ability to recover from them afterwards. 'Of course Winston will come back,' noted one MP after a spectacular 'Churchill flop' over India; 'you knock him down and everybody says he won't get up again and then he is back in the ring as fit and as fierce as ever.'[63] And although he had few followers within the Commons his position with public opinion steadily improved, assisted by the rapidly deteriorating situation in Europe. He was perhaps more open to different viewpoints than the political psychologists suggest; at least, his rhetoric was calibrated to appeal to progressives and not just to traditionalist national security advocates. He emphasized that rearmament should go hand in hand with collective security, with Britain adhering firmly to the Covenant of the League of Nations and pursuing a 'Grand Alliance' that would include the USSR. The anti-socialist Churchill, by eschewing the more naked forms of power politics, thus began to win over the more realist elements of Labour and Liberal opinion. Early in 1938, for example, the *News Chronicle* editorial team 'agreed that since re-armament was now a necessity, it would be an immense advantage' to have Churchill in the government. The editor grumpily commented that things must be in a pretty state if the Liberal *Chronicle* was 'prepared to welcome to the Cabinet a man who had had the name of a war-monger'; but one of the journalists present replied that 'since then Churchill's attitude had changed, that he was now a supporter of collective security'.[64] By the summer of 1939 there was a growing popular agitation in his favour. Six hundred posters, funded by an anonymous donor, were plastered across London. They asked: 'What Price Churchill?'[65]

Therefore, at the point that war broke out in September 1939, Neville Chamberlain had little option but to include Churchill in his Cabinet, and also had good reason to fear him. The Prime Minister, it should be emphasized, remained popular. His opinion poll satisfaction ratings were in the mid-60s throughout the autumn and remained healthy almost until the end of his premiership.[66] He was, in fact, much loved, and if he was not an especially skilful speaker he was certainly a shrewd image-maker and manipulator of the media. In appointing Churchill to his old post of First Lord of the Admiralty—rather than letting him roam across all subjects as a minister without portfolio—he hoped to keep him busy with departmental tasks and prevent him making trouble. Churchill, however, quickly established a broader role for himself as one of Britain's most important propagandists, a task for which Chamberlain seemed ill-equipped. Some found the Prime Minister's radio and Commons speeches on the day Britain declared war to be 'simple and moving' and found Churchill's rhetoric, by contrast, to be indulgent.[67] (In Parliament, Churchill expressed 'thankfulness that [...] there is a generation of Britons here now ready to prove itself not unworthy of the days of yore' and denounced 'the pestilence of Nazi tyranny'.)[68] But others took a different view. Leo Amery, a former Tory minister and no uncritical admirer of Churchill, wrote that Chamberlain's address to MPs was 'good, but not the speech of a war leader [...] I think I see Winston emerging as PM out of it all by the end of the year'.[69]

Churchill's responsibility for the Navy helped establish him as the interpreter of the war to the British people and to global opinion. During the so-called Phoney War there was little action on land but British shipping faced a serious threat from U-boats. His first substantive Commons statement of the war was on the sinking of the civilian liner SS *Athenia*, with significant loss of life. In their efforts to cover up their responsibility, the Nazis resorted to claiming that the act had been 'planned by Mr Churchill'.[70] In the first two weeks of the war, the British merchant navy lost twenty-eight ships totalling 147,000 tons, a rate of loss (in terms of tonnage) about half that of the peak period of sinkings in 1917.[71] On 26 September, having pressed on Chamberlain the need for a morale-boosting statement, Churchill addressed the Commons on the anti-submarine war and the overall naval position.[72] After an uninspiring speech by Chamberlain—during which Churchill 'sat hunched beside him looking like the Chinese god of plenty suffering from acute indigestion'—the First Lord rose to loud cheers. He remarked with a grin on the 'curious change' in his fortunes, whereby he found himself back in the same job he had held in 1914; the House laughed but Chamberlain just looked sulky.[73] Churchill used his unique experience to argue that the position was now much stronger than it had been in the previous war. The security of shipping would improve as the convoys system came into operation, and attacks on U-boats were proceeding apace. He assured MPs, 'we have only to persevere to conquer.'[74] It should be noted that Churchill was quite prepared to be economical with the truth. Captain A. G. Talbot, who was in charge of anti-submarine warfare, once questioned his exaggerated figures for U-boat sinkings. 'There are two people who sink U-boats in this war Talbot,' Churchill told him. 'You sink them in the Atlantic and I sink them in the House of Commons. The trouble is that you are sinking them at exactly half the rate I am.'[75] In April 1940, still displeased with the figures he was getting, Churchill minuted that 'it might be a good thing if Captain Talbot went to sea as soon as possible'.[76] It was no thanks to Churchill that he did at least end up with the command of an aircraft carrier when he did so.[77]

Of Churchill's September statement, Harold Nicolson noted:

> The effect of Winston's speech was infinitely greater than could be derived from any reading of the text. His delivery was really amazing and he sounded every note from deep preoccupation to flippancy, from resolution to sheer boyishness. One could feel the spirits of the House rising with every word. [...] In those twenty minutes Churchill brought himself nearer the post of Minister than he has ever been before.[78]

These effects were not achieved without careful preparation. Pressure of work combined with Churchill's nocturnal habits meant that they were prepared late at night, after his normal 9–11 p.m. naval conference. Geoffrey Shakespeare, a junior minister at the Admiralty, described his technique, whereby he dictated directly to a typist as he padded up and down in his slippers, arms behind him, head bent forward, cigar in mouth.

> All those distinguished phrases which characterise his speeches came out fashioned spontaneously in the furnace of his imagination. The sequence of

thought and argument followed in due order, and as each page was finished he sat down at the table and altered a word or two, softening or accentuating their emphasis. For two or three hours he dictated thus without a break.[79]

When Churchill made a broadcast to mark a month of war, his speech was relayed via 275 wireless stations in the USA, where it was widely praised.[80] It is not clear exactly how many countries received the broadcast directly—his later radio speeches as First Lord reached least to Singapore—but press agency telegrams ensured full reports the next day as far away as New Zealand.[81] Churchill's ability to appeal to world opinion helped make him the special bugbear of Reich propaganda minister Joseph Goebbels: on this occasion some of his listeners heard interference from a German announcer who demanded answers to supposedly tricky questions such as 'What caused the sinking of the *Athenia*?'[82] But it seems likely that the *Irish Times* was right to suggest that Goebbels's 'vitriolic attacks on Mr Churchill have added enormously to the First Lord's popularity in his own country'.[83]

Churchill's 1 October broadcast was not merely a morale-boosting survey; he did not hesitate to warn that Britain might face 'great ordeals' from German bombers. Moreover, the speech was an important strategic statement, crafted to convey a range of messages to different international audiences. He began with a small but telling inaccuracy, claiming that Britain and France had been at war with Germany 'for a month tonight', when in fact, due to political manoeuvrings, they had not declared war until 3 September; he thus skated over the painful period in which the Poles had been forced to wait in desperation for pledges of international support as the Germans attacked. By the time of Churchill's speech, Poland had received no meaningful military help from her allies, and her resistance to the Nazis was almost at an end. Churchill therefore could only offer to the Poles the thought that their country would 'rise again like a rock, which may for a spell be submerged by a tidal wave'. He then provided a skilful treatment of the USSR which, following the pact it had made with Hitler in August, had moved in to seize eastern Poland for itself. Churchill held back from explicit criticism. Russia, he said, was 'a riddle wrapped in a mystery inside an enigma'; but the key, he suggested, was Russian national interest. In saying this he hinted that the Soviet action was in fact a positive development aimed at preventing further Nazi expansion. If Russia's behaviour was far from altruistic, it remained a source of comfort that Hitler had been 'warned off' further adventures in Eastern Europe and the Balkans.

Churchill also appeared to take a pre-emptive strike against Hitler's anticipated 'peace offensive' when—quoting Chamberlain—he emphasized that
Britain's war aim was to 'redeem Europe from the perpetual and recurring
fear of German aggression'. Britain was prepared for a three-year war, 'and
we are going to persevere to the end'.[84] Simultaneously, then, Churchill
offered (rather cold) comfort to the Poles; presented to non-belligerents
such as the USA the argument that Britain could win; tried to sow discord
between Russia and Germany; and gave an oblique hint to the Soviets that
Britain understood her territorial sensitivities. At the close of the war,
indeed, Churchill was to show his willingness to accept predominant Soviet
influence in Eastern Europe in exchange for recognition of British predominance elsewhere. As one Mass-Observation diarist noted after listening, 'the interesting point is he is not at all calling Russia names'.[85]

At the end of the broadcast, Churchill compared the current conflict with
the American Civil War. He said: 'All the heroism of the South could not
redeem their cause from the stain of slavery, just as all the courage and skill
which the Germans always show in war will not free them from the reproach
of Nazism.'[86] But afterwards he panicked, seemingly fearing that this would
be seen as an insult in the United States. Joseph P. Kennedy, the American
Ambassador to London, wrote to his wife, 'he called me up this morning in
a terrible state [because] of the slip up he made in his broadcast last night in
the closing paragraph he made reference to the South and Slavery in a comparison with the Nazis. Of course that isn't what he meant to say but that's
what happened. He asked me what he should say. I told him nothing until
I got a line on things with the US.' Kennedy was no true friend of Britain
and no admirer of Churchill, but in this case he helped out. He established
that President Roosevelt was 'very pleased' with the broadcast 'so I told
Churchill he was lucky and [that he should] say nothing'.[87] After the war,
Churchill bumped into Kennedy—who by that time had forgotten the
incident—at a racetrack in Florida and thanked him profusely for having
saved him from 'a great embarrassment' on that occasion.[88] Although
Churchill was in this case clearly oversensitive about the likely impact of his
words, the episode illustrates his awareness that giving a broadcast of this
type meant walking on eggshells.

In Britain, the speech boosted Churchill's stock even amongst some who
still dwelt on 'his record of untrustworthiness and instability'.[89] The radio
critic of the liberal *Manchester Guardian* praised his 'virile, athletic English'.[90]
Chamberlain thought the broadcast 'excellent', although he was irritated by

the pro-Churchill campaign in the left-wing press that followed it.[91] Although it is hard to be certain of the broadcast's popular reception, given the lack of systematic Mass-Observation or Home Intelligence analyses of reactions to Churchill at this time, individual diaries suggest that there was widespread enthusiasm. C. W. Smallbones, an electricity worker from Hampshire, thought it 'a good fruity speech'.[92] Eleanor Humphries, a London housewife, wrote that 'It certainly bucked us up no end & we loved the gusto with which he delivered it'.[93] At the same time, though, plenty of other diarists were sceptical or at least conflicted. Churchill had said that the Navy was hunting the U-boats night and day: 'I shall not say without mercy, because God forbid we should ever part company with that—but at any rate with zeal and not altogether without relish.'[94] Brenda Cobbett, a masseuse from Surrey, approved of this but could not quite dispense with her previous impressions of Churchill: 'He nearly got me, over the reluctance to say that we shall hunt the U-boats without mercy. I wish I didn't remember so clearly the intervention in Russia, and the General Strike in 1926.'[95] Miss E. Hill, a Northumberland teacher, also thought the speech impressive, but was shocked by the 'relish' in Churchill's remark: 'There are men in those U-boats and even though one realises the need to defend our shipping and destroy U-boats, it is still a dreadful thing that the crew and the submarine almost inevitably perish together.'[96] Elisabeth Crowfoot, an actress from Suffolk, wrote: 'I thought Churchill's speech very sensible, and calculated to make things easier whatever happened—Mummy wailed rather and said he was so dreadful because he enjoyed war; I said that if we'd got to have war the people who took an interest in it were more likely to get their jobs done well—I'm not sure that I agree with this in cold blood, but I was getting cross; all our tempers suffer a bit from the war.'[97] Some people treated Churchill with irreverent cynicism. One Oxford student noted how he listened to the speech with a journalist friend and his wife, who made 'occasional interpolations' such as 'for American consumption' and 'he's certainly the politician speaking'.[98] Towards the end of the speech, Churchill noted with approval the fact that (so far) Italy had remained neutral. The journalist Denis Argent recorded a conversation the next day with a pacifist vicar. 'Speaking of Winston's speech last night the Vicar picks out one rather hollow mockery. "We are fighting against totalitarianism", etc., says Winston in one breath; in the next he speaks of "the great & friendly nation of Italy."'[99]

Churchill and Chamberlain were now working together fairly well at the personal level and, even more crucially, they were in broad agreement on strategic matters.[100] This was illustrated by the way they both responded to Hitler's peace initiative made in speech to the Reichstag on 6 October. The Führer presented himself as a reasonable man who would pose no threat to the British Empire if his (lengthy but vague) terms were met. The conquest of Poland was complete; why, then, should the French and British continue in the war? He was now making his last offer, he said; but if the view of Churchill and his followers prevailed in England, 'we should then fight'.[101] There was a substantial minority in Britain that was potentially receptive to his message; Lloyd George had spoken out in favour of peace and as a result received thousands of letters of congratulations, in 'large batches by every post'.[102] It was several days before Chamberlain responded publicly to Hitler's offer, but when he did he rejected it emphatically. Churchill and other members of the War Cabinet helped refine his draft. The Prime Minister wrote to his sister: 'I must say Winston was most helpful not only in suggestions of phrases &c but also in his ready agreement with others particularly myself that I did not think he would like. In the end though he thought the speech might be criticised for not being sharp enough (which it was not) he was delighted with it.'[103] France and the Dominions were consulted on the statement; Canada's Prime Minister, W. L. Mackenzie King, hankering after a compromise peace, found it 'anything but satisfying' and concluded that Churchill rather than Chamberlain had written it.[104] In the British House of Commons, though, Chamberlain's words were warmly received. Echoing Churchill's broadcast, he emphasized that either Germany must demonstrate her sincerity by concrete action 'or we must persevere in our duty to the end'.[105] Some felt that Chamberlain's heart was not in it, but even if so this was an early and important (and rarely remembered) statement of British resolve.[106]

Nevertheless, the statement left a degree of wiggle room. Chamberlain had specified conditions that Hitler was highly unlikely to accept, but he had not said that Britain would never negotiate with the existing regime under any circumstances. In a further broadcast, on 12 November, Remembrance Sunday, Churchill did his best to shut off this option. (The Director-General of the BBC, a strict Sabbatarian, had tried to persuade Churchill not to broadcast on a Sunday at all.)[107] According to Chamberlain, 'he was so pleased with the success of his first effort that he insisted on following it up with a second, out of his [ministerial] turn and without having his speech "vetted" by the F.O. [Foreign Office] as other peoples are'.[108] The speech—filmed extracts of which were shown in cinema newsreels—was full of colourful language, including the description of Hitler as 'a cornered maniac'. With his characteristic and derisive mispronunciation 'Narzi', Churchill declared that 'either all that Britain and France stand for in the modern world will go down, or that Hitler, the Nazi regime and the recurring German or Prussian menace to Europe will be broken or destroyed'.[109] He also suggested, amongst other things, that neutral Italy was keeping Germany at arm's length, and that America was sympathetic to Britain's cause.

John Colville, assistant Private Secretary at 10 Downing Street, noted in his diary that the speech was 'very boastful, over-confident and indiscreet (especially about Italy and the USA), but certainly most amusing'. The next day he observed that 'Winston's speech has made a very bad effect at No. 10 but the FO and the City take a favourable view'. Italy and Holland made official protests, and R. A. Butler, the appeasement-minded Under-Secretary at the Foreign Office, thought the speech 'beyond words vulgar'.[110] Butler told the Italian Ambassador that Churchill's comments were 'in conflict with the Government's views' and that serious German peace proposals would be considered.[111] Hitler, somewhat later, told a Nazi rally that Churchill had 'publicly uttered what Chamberlain only secretly thinks. He admitted that it is his aim to annihilate and disintegrate the German nation as a whole.'[112]

Chamberlain, meanwhile, noted a division amongst members of the public who wrote to him. There were those who 'rejoiced' that Churchill 'should give it 'em good & proper'; those 'who felt that he had descended to the level of the gutter'; and lastly those 'who believed that time was on our side and who were therefore bewildered and alarmed by a challenge to the Germans to "come on, then"'. Chamberlain's overall impression, smugly recorded, was that Churchill had received a setback that would 'do him a lot of good'.[113] Examination of MO diaries suggests that the Prime Minister's assessment of the divisions in public opinion was about right. On the one hand were those who felt that 'Winnie expressed the pent-up feelings of many', and were amused, even if 'semi-shocked', by his 'strong language'.[114] On the other were those who thought the speech 'rather cheap' and even 'half-Nazi', and thought that Churchill sounded 'like a big public school bully'.[115] Jean Tayler, a teacher, wrote a couple of weeks after the speech: 'Frankly I enjoyed it, and I have been very much surprised to hear so many people say they thought it was bad form & that we do not want our statesmen speaking like German broadcasters.'[116] Whether or not the episode was really much of a setback for

Churchill is debatable, but there are signs that it helped establish, or at least reinforce, a view of him that would stick. This was encapsulated in the comment that 'Winston is a not a man I admire in peacetime but right now he seems like the right man for the job'.[117] This was obviously advantageous to him for the time being, but the idea that he was an unsuitable peacetime leader would in due course return to haunt him.

Churchill made a further broadcast just before Christmas, in which he described the bravery and achievements of the Royal Navy, notably its success in forcing the crew of the German pocket battleship *Graf Spee* to scuttle her at Montevideo.[118] He was praised for the dignified treatment of a 'lofty' theme, and for refraining from the abuse into which he sometimes descended.[119] The difficulty of pleasing everyone was shown by Prime Minister Mackenzie King's anger at Churchill's 'outrageous' announcement of the arrival of the first Canadian troops in Britain: Canada should have been allowed to declare the news, he thought. Mackenzie King suggested in his diary that Churchill 'was trying to monopolize the stage for the Admiralty' at the expense of Canada and that his voice sounded as if he had been 'taking stimulants', i.e. alcohol.[120] Churchill had apparently breached a previous understanding about the announcement, but Mackenzie King's sensitivity—to be displayed throughout the war—was absurd. Nevertheless, the question of what military information should be conveyed in broadcasts and when was a serious one. Earlier in December, for example, Churchill made the first official public mention of the Navy's use of the ASDIC system of sonar submarine detection.[121] Its existence was at any rate an open secret, and he calculated that, without revealing technical details, fear could be struck into the enemy's mind: 'We want to spread the idea of vague terror of remorseless process.'[122]

The fumings of Mackenzie King did not matter much; in fact, he was probably made additionally angry by the knowledge of how safely the British could ignore him. Much more significant for Britain's calculations at this time were the views of the neutrals. We are accustomed to thinking primarily of the United States in this category; indeed, Churchill was already courting President Roosevelt through an exchange of personal messages. But states from Scandinavia to the Balkans had to be considered too, as did some states beyond Europe such as Turkey; Mussolini's Italy was basically hostile but had not yet committed itself to the German side. In this situation, the British wanted not only to avoid gaining enemies, but to chivvy as many countries as possible into active cooperation, and of course if possible into belligerency on the Allied side. This context is important for understanding not only Churchill's speeches and activities in early 1940 but for the chain of events leading to the disaster in Norway that propelled him to power as Prime Minister.

Again, it must be emphasized that the strategic differences between Churchill and Chamberlain were not large. Chamberlain was himself one of those who believed that 'time was on our side'. He held that economic blockade of Germany, enforced by Churchill's Navy, would enforce such deprivation on the German people that, realizing that they were suffering to no purpose, their morale would collapse. Like Churchill, he believed that Hitler was likely blocked from further victories in the East. He did not believe that he would dare to attack in the West, and stuck to this view even when contrary evidence was staring him in the face. Churchill was less complacent than Chamberlain about the threat in the West, although (in the autumn of 1939) he did not believe it was imminent. He was, above all, more *activist* than the Prime Minister, always eager to take an opportunity to say or do something; and these things might be provocative. The cruder examples of Churchill's public language, Chamberlain thought, risked throwing away Britain's moral advantage in the face of world opinion. But although the men had their differences on issues ranging from rationing to talks with the German opposition, these were not of great import.[123] Churchill's view was that Hitler should be left 'to stew in his own juice during the winter while speeding forward our armaments and weaving-up our alliances'.[124] It was the public diplomacy aspect of this 'weaving-up' process to which Churchill turned—more than a little clumsily—as the new year began.

In January 1940, Churchill targeted a broadcast directly at the European neutrals. The speech was heard by 34.3 per cent of the potential UK audience.[125] He contrasted the courage of the Finns—who were putting up a strong resistance to the Soviet invasion launched the previous November—with other countries' cowardly inaction. 'They bow humbly and in fear to German threats of violence,' he said, adding: 'Each one hopes that if he feeds the crocodile enough, the crocodile will eat him last.'[126] This might seem like fair comment—it certainly did to the French, who warmly welcomed the speech—but to the neutrals themselves it looked like an attempt to browbeat them. The Belgian Ambassador complained that 'it was unjust to pillory the smaller neutrals, whose position was one of infinite difficulty, while there were larger neutrals notably the United States [...] who were in a position to give expression to their feelings and convictions without running into the immediate dangers by which the smaller powers were confronted.'[127] Press reaction in the other countries concerned was thoroughly negative. Although the reaction may look short-sighted today, the experience of the 1930s had left its scars and, to many, British attempts to seize the moral high ground smacked of hypocrisy. In Holland, *Het Handelsblad* commented that 'There is every reason for Mr Churchill to mention the fate of the unfortunate neutrals, but he goes too far in telling them that it is their duty to join the Allies according to League [of Nations] principles. The great Powers neglected their League principles whenever it suited them. It is too much to expect that the neutrals should lend their countries for "battlefields".'[128] At home, Churchill's comments on the League made him a target for satire: one music hall show included a song 'by Fairy Wish Fulfilment remarking that Mr Churchill has just discovered what the League of Nations is for'.[129] Meanwhile—doubtless because of his praise of Finland—the Russian press branded Churchill the 'greatest enemy of the USSR'.[130] Churchill's remarks had once more not received official clearance and he may have realized that they had been ill-judged. According to the understandably irritated Foreign Secretary, Lord Halifax, he demonstrated as much contrition 'as Winston ever shows' and began to ponder how he might undo the damage.[131] However, in a Commons speech a month later he appeared impenitent, claiming that 'the neutral Press makes more fuss when I make a speech telling them what is their duty' than they did about murderous Nazi attacks on neutral shipping.[132] Chamberlain began to ponder a speech of his own 'correcting (but not letting down too hard) WSC'.[133]

A week after his broadcast, at Manchester's Free Trade Hall, Churchill shied away from repeating his sentiments about the neutrals. In addition to his stirring message—'It is the time to dare and endure'—he defended rationing (about which he had been privately sceptical) and called for more than a million women to enter munitions and aircraft factories to boost production.[134] It was a splendid occasion, billed as part of the 'Ministerial public enlightenment campaign', and the demand for tickets had been extraordinary.[135] Although Churchill's speech was well received by the vast majority of those present, it was interrupted more than once by supporters of the Fascist leader Oswald Mosley, and three men were ejected from the hall.[136] One journalist noted: 'Those passages in Mr Churchill's speech that were interrupted by hecklers were recorded and broadcast by the Germans, while the cheering at the end of the speech was eliminated by the BBC. So that German listeners would have the impression of a stormy meeting and of a speech that was in the end rewarded by icy silence on the part of the audience.'[137] MO diarist M. M. Corfe recorded that, at the ambulance station where she worked, the disturbance brought listeners from other rooms to find out what it was all about. She also noted her fellow workers' 'ironical comments' which were 'mostly appreciative'. These included 'He's got a commanding voice but I don't like it', 'He's lovely, isn't he? Beautiful sarcasm', and 'He's well wound up today. He's had a damned good lunch.'[138]

In the speech, Churchill claimed vindication for his earlier view that, if Britain could reach the spring without her sea trade being interrupted, 'and without anything happening in the land or in the air', she should have gained the upper hand in the war's opening phases. He also stated that the policy of dropping leaflets on Germany, rather than bombs, had been the right one.[139] A cynic might say he was influenced in this last by the fact that some of these leaflets contained quotations from him![140] But in reality he was acceding, perhaps reluctantly, to the common opinion that it was unwise to incur the moral opprobrium of harming civilians or the risk of retaliatory bombing. Undoubtedly, though, he itched to take the war to the Germans.

But how was this to be done? Soon after his return to the Admiralty the previous September, Churchill had been alerted to Germany's heavy dependence on Swedish iron ore which, during the winter months, was transported via Norway. He therefore pressed for military action to halt the trade; as this would mean violating Norwegian neutrality his colleagues were reluctant, but by the turn of the year he seemed to be making headway. With the crisis-ridden French government pressuring the British to do something to help the struggling Finns, planning began for land operations across Norway and Sweden, with the ostensible aim of helping Finland, but with the seizure of the Swedish ore mines as a core objective. When a Soviet-Finnish peace deal was reached in March, the plan was abandoned, to Churchill's chagrin. In essence, the British were hoping that the Germans would commit some breach of neutrality that would justify a response in kind, without any sacrifice of moral authority. Churchill, more than most in the War Cabinet, was prepared to test the boundaries of international law, seemingly in the hope that Hitler would do something that would justify full-scale retaliation. He did not, however, realize how drastic the consequences of this might be. Thus the *Altmark* incident—when Churchill ordered the Royal Navy to rescue 299 British prisoners from a German ship in Norwegian territorial waters—sent Hitler into a rage and determined him to launch his plan to invade

Norway and Denmark.[141] Churchill was quite right to warn, in a broadcast at the end of March, that neutral countries might soon be exposed 'to an avalanche of steel and fire'.[142] MO diarist Nance Leacroft wrote: 'Churchill's speech last night—bringing in God—and boasting. It's awfully funny—but I find my idea is very widespread—i.e. directly we boast, the next day we lose a ship or something disastrous happens. It really is beyond me why he is so utterly popular—and with every class he most certainly is.'[143] Popular Churchill undoubtedly was, but, as other diary evidence shows, there were also continuing undercurrents of suspicion.[144]

The avalanche Churchill predicted soon came. On 8–9 April Hitler's invasion began—just after the British had finally got around to mining the port of Narvik. A few days earlier, Churchill had told the Cabinet he 'personally doubted whether the Germans would land a force in Scandinavia'.[145] In the Commons on 11 April, with MPs desperate for concrete information, he appeared tired and—according to Harold Nicolson—gave a stumbling speech that left the House deeply worried. 'He starts off by giving an imitation of himself making a speech, and he indulges in vague oratory coupled with tired gibes,' wrote Nicolson. Moreover, 'He hesitates, gets his notes in the wrong order, puts on the wrong pair of spectacles, fumbles for the right pair, keeps on saying Sweden when he means Denmark, and one way or another makes a lamentable performance.'[146] John Colville was much more positive, writing that Churchill was 'witty, but less polished than usual'.[147] After giving a detailed account of events, Churchill said that 'For myself, I consider that Hitler's action in invading Scandinavia is as great a strategic and political error as that which was committed by Napoleon in 1807, when he invaded Spain'.[148] This was less quotable than Chamberlain's comment, made just before the invasion, that Hitler had 'missed the bus', but it was scarcely more accurate.[149] Over the next weeks, the Cabinet muddled along while the Germans carried all before them. The British sent troops for operations against Trondheim (in the centre of Norway) and Narvik (in the north). The Trondheim operation failed, and on 2 and 3 May the troops were withdrawn from the central region. Narvik was eventually taken but then quickly abandoned. A first-class political crisis was in the offing. As both a service minister and as the (newly appointed) chairman of the Military Coordination Committee, Churchill was potentially extremely vulnerable to the criticism now being flung at the management of the war effort.

He knew this full well. In a draft passage of his memoirs he admitted that 'it was a marvel—I really do not know how—[that] I survived and maintained my position in public esteem while all the blame was thrown on poor Mr Chamberlain'.[150] The answer to the riddle is simple enough. The famous 'Norway debate' of 7 and 8 May—a pivotal moment in British political history—was only partly about investigating what had gone wrong in Norway. Rather, the defeat there appeared symbolic of broader failures, going beyond who had been responsible for particular military decisions. As the Labour Party leader Clement Attlee put it on the first day, Norway came as the culmination of discontents stretching back through the 1930s: 'People are saying that those mainly responsible for the conduct of affairs are men who have had an almost uninterrupted career of failure. Norway follows Czecho-Slovakia and Poland. Everywhere the story is "Too late".'[151] Labour, though itching to turn out Chamberlain, could of course do nothing without Tory help; and the hard core of rebels on the government side was too small to achieve anything unless a significant number of Conservative loyalists started to peel away. This now started to happen. Crucially, whereas the Chamberlainites would have been happy for Churchill to take the fall for Norway, Chamberlain's critics, now gaining strength, were keen to make sure that this did not happen. If the Prime Minister were to fall, Churchill—as one of the few plausible candidates—had to be preserved as a potential successor. He had to be dug out of the hole in which he found himself.

Accordingly, speaker after speaker, on both government and opposition sides, went out of their way to heap praise on Churchill, exculpate him from any special responsibility for the Norwegian fiasco, and distinguish between him and the Chamberlainites who before the war 'treated his warnings with contempt'.[152] The renowned example of this technique came from Lloyd George, in his last great Commons performance. Whilst describing the Trondheim expedition as 'half-baked', he also said 'I do not think that the First Lord was entirely responsible' for everything that had happened in Norway. This provoked an intervention from Churchill, who said that he took complete responsibility. Then came Lloyd George's celebrated rejoinder: 'The right hon. Gentleman must not allow himself to be converted into an air raid shelter to keep the splinters from hitting his colleagues.'[153] Already, the debate had gone badly for Chamberlain. Leo Amery, channelling Oliver Cromwell, had told him on the first day 'In the name of God, go'.[154] When Herbert Morrison announced, on the second day, that Labour would force a vote, Chamberlain responded 'in a carefully prepared impromptu' with an appeal to 'my friends in the House' for support.[155] This remark got him the 'great roar of cheers' that he wanted from

MPs on his own side, but to others it looked like partisanship at a time of national crisis.[156]

In these circumstances, Churchill's job of winding up the debate (that is, making the final speech, in the government's defence) was on the face of it a difficult one. Rising at 10.11 p.m., he had just over three-quarters of an hour to put his case, 'offering in his most persuasive manner a quite incomprehensible account' of some of the key decisions of the campaign.[157] His explanation of the decision to withdraw from Trondheim—the Narvik operation was still ongoing—was interrupted by MPs trying to get him to admit that the War Cabinet had overridden naval advice. (It had not; rather, practically everyone concerned, military officers as well as civilians, had changed their views multiple times.) He rejected this idea, and also scorned the claim that 'I, personally, proposed to the Prime Minister and the War Cabinet more violent action and that they shrank from it and restrained it'.[158] Eventually, the mood became bad-tempered. When Churchill, reiterating his argument that Hitler had made a strategic mistake, claimed that three-quarters of Allied shipping losses had already been made good through captures and building, the Labour MP Neil Maclean shouted 'Oh!'; Churchill turned on him, accusing him of 'skulking in the corner', and when Maclean persisted in asking the Speaker if it was in order to accuse another member of 'skulking', Churchill 'rose from his seat and stood shouting angrily at the Labour members, but so great was the noise that his words could not be heard'.[159]

Once order was restored, Churchill concluded by arguing against a precipitate decision to turn out the government and by urging unity in the face of the common foe. In spite of the stormy atmosphere, his 'slashing, vigorous speech' strengthened his position.[160] With every word he reinforced the impression created by Lloyd George and others that he was standing up for his colleagues because of his honourable personal steadfastness. As the Liberal Chief Whip Percy Harris wrote in his diary: 'A scene of great excitement [and] a lot of ill temper during Winston's speech defending the Govt. but very wise of him to take full responsibility'.[161] As Nicolson noted, Churchill had managed the 'almost impossible task' of both defending the armed services and refusing to undermine Chamberlain 'with absolute loyalty and apparent sincerity, while demonstrating by his brilliance that he really has nothing to do with this confused and timid gang'.[162] Amery observed how 'In the last two minutes he adroitly suggested that a Debate on Norway had only at the last minute been turned into a challenge of the Government's competence and that that there ought to be another debate before members on our side committed themselves to a vote of no confidence'.[163] Strikingly, when this speech was published in the 1941 collection *Into Battle*, the interruptions and the row with Maclean were excised, as was the final passage which included a defence of Chamberlain's remark about his 'friends': 'He thought he had some friends, and I hope he has some friends. He certainly had a good many when things were going well.'[164]

Immediately after Churchill's speech MPs filed through the division lobbies to vote. The government won by 281 votes to 200—but as Chamberlain's majority was nominally 213 it was clear that he could not continue without, at least, a major reconstruction of the Cabinet. When the result was announced, the Labour MP Josiah Wedgwood broke into 'Rule Britannia', the Tory Harold Macmillan joined in, and others shouted at Chamberlain to resign. On the Chief Whip's signal, the Prime Minister's supporters cheered him as he stalked out of the chamber.[165] The vote itself did not force the Prime Minister's resignation—that was ensured only by the manoeuvrings of the next two days, which culminated in the refusal of the Labour leaders to serve in a coalition under him.[166] On 10 May, when the news came of Germany's invasion of the Low Countries, it briefly looked as if he would attempt to stay on. He quickly bowed to the inevitable, however, and recommended Churchill to the King as his successor after Lord Halifax, the other chief contender, had ruled himself out. In the early evening of that day Churchill went to the Palace and was appointed Prime Minister. It was Chamberlain who announced the news to the nation, in a BBC broadcast at 9 p.m.; he also said that he had agreed to stay in the War Cabinet in view of Churchill's strong desire that he should do so.[167] For some of his critics, this was just Chamberlain's 'usual dreary stuff, drearily delivered'.[168] For others, his 'fierce denunciation of the Germans for invading Holland and Belgium' was 'a magnificent statement' which led to their previous hatred for him melting away.[169]

10 May was a Friday. Parliament reconvened on the Monday. In the meantime, Churchill had set about appointing his ministers and—as Malcolm MacDonald witnessed—running through his lines. At 2.54 p.m. he rose to address House of Commons. He introduced a motion of confidence in his new government and detailed the steps he had taken to form it, emphasizing its breadth and inclusiveness. After these preliminaries he hit his rhetorical stride, declaring, 'I would say to the House, as I said to those who have joined this Government, "I have nothing to offer but blood, toil, tears and sweat"'. After this echo of Garibaldi—who at a moment of crisis had offered his followers 'hunger, forced marches, battles, and death'—Churchill asked and then answered two rhetorical questions:

> You ask, what is our policy? I will say: It is to wage war, by sea, land, and air, with all our might and with all the strength that God can give us; to wage war against a monstrous tyranny never surpassed in the dark, lamentable catalogue of human crime. That is our policy. You ask, what is our aim? I can answer in one word: It is victory, victory at all costs, victory in spite of all terror, victory, however long and hard the road may be; for without victory, there is no survival.

The repetition of that single word 'victory' five times within one sentence created an impressive sense of Churchill's single-mindedness and determination; he did not promise victory but he did promise not to stop short of it, and this meant that his warnings of blood and terror were accompanied by a sense of optimism. He stressed indeed his own 'buoyancy and hope' as he took on his new task. Having spoken for not more than seven minutes, he finished with a plea for national unity: 'At this time I feel entitled to claim the aid of all, and I say, "Come then, let us go forward together with our united strength".'[170] The speeches that followed were not memorable, although things might have been different if William Gallacher, the sole communist MP, had been present. According to *The Daily Worker*, he had not been informed in time of the recall of Parliament. 'Speaking of Mr Churchill's statement to the House that he had nothing to offer but "blood, toil, tears and sweat," Mr Gallacher said if he had been there he would have described the phrase as the epitaph of capitalism.'[171]

Churchill might well claim the aid of all, and he won the motion of confidence with no votes against, but he would have been well aware that he did not, as yet, have the enthusiastic support even of all the MPs from his own Conservative Party. True, *The Times* reported the next day that when Churchill arrived in the Commons chamber he 'was received with loud cheers'.[172] But according to some witnesses Churchill's welcome was only lukewarm.[173] It is sometimes suggested that only Labour MPs cheered Churchill, but it seems unlikely that *all* Tory MPs remained silent.[174] Moreover, *The Times* report discreetly passed over the fact that Chamberlain—now Lord President of the Council—'received an even bigger cheer' when he came in shortly after Churchill.[175] According to the *Glasgow Herald*, 'Members rose from their seats cheering lustily'.[176] According to one loyal Chamberlainite, 'MPs lost their heads; they shouted; they cheered; they waved their Order Papers'.[177] In his first weeks and months as Prime Minister Churchill would face not only a military struggle in Europe but also a political battle at home to ensure that his old enemies within the Conservative Party did not wreak revenge on him for their sudden and unexpected defeat.

2

'Winston Will Explain Everything'

Less than a week passed between Churchill's 'blood, toil, tears and sweat' speech and his first broadcast to the nation as Prime Minister. Those six days, though, must have seemed like an eternity. On the evening of 14 May Churchill reported to the War Cabinet a phone message he had received from French Premier Paul Reynaud: 'The German Army has broken through our fortified line south of Sedan.'[1] The following morning Churchill was awoken by a despairing phone call from Reynaud who told him that the battle was lost. The same day, the bulk of the Dutch forces surrendered. On the 16th, Churchill flew to Paris in an attempt to put heart into the French government, returning the next day. He found that the evacuation of the capital was being readied, and was staggered to learn that the French Army had no strategic reserve to deploy.[2] As time went on, things continued to get worse. Above all, though, the situation was confusing. There was the very real problem of establishing what was actually going on in the midst of large-scale retreat. There was also the sheer psychological shock induced by massive defeat—an emotion shared by Churchill himself, even though he had been predicting disaster for years. The very fact that it was hard to believe that things could be as bad as they appeared at times itself appeared to give grounds for hope. In their bewilderment, the British people wanted to be told what was occurring; to have it explained to them; and to be told what to do. This is not to say that they did not also want to be 'inspired'. But for this to occur, they needed an understanding of what was going on.

Churchill was by no means the only person equipped to provide this. There were plenty of other voices that, if they are forgotten today, were well received at the time. We know this through the Home Intelligence Reports, production of which began on 18 May. The very first report argued the need

for chosen 'interpreters' of the news, such as the independent MP and journalist Vernon Bartlett, to be broadcasting constantly. It also suggested that
'Even at the eleventh hour people are seeking and needing a *positive purpose*,
something aggressive, dynamic, beyond themselves, worth dying for, not just
survival or "blood, sweat and tears".[3] (There is little concrete evidence of
any strong popular reaction to that speech.)[4] Churchill was probably unaware
of the reports at this stage, and later in the war cast doubt on their value; there
is no sign that he took them into account when drafting his speeches.[5] But
although they have their limitations, they are excellent sources for tracking
reactions to the rhetoric of Churchill and that of his colleagues.

During the second half of May there were several speakers who went
down well with the public. These included Anthony Eden (the Conservative
Secretary of State for War), Ernest Bevin (the union leader recruited to be
Minister of Labour), and the King. The most striking, success, however, was
the debonair womanizer Alfred Duff Cooper, the only member of the
Cabinet to have resigned over the Munich agreement. Churchill had offered
him the Ministry of Information—not a very high-status post—almost
apologetically.[6] His tenure there is generally ranked as a failure. However,
during the first crucial fortnight, far from being overshadowed by Churchill,
he helped plug a gap which the Prime Minister was too busy to fill on his
own. He used his broadcasts to warn against rumour-mongering, to boost
Churchill, and to praise 'the calm spirit of inflexible determination' that he
detected amongst the populace.[7] His early broadcasts drew forth comments
such as 'first rate', 'shows we're being taken notice of', and 'just what we
want'. His grave but confident manner meant that he was trusted to tell
the truth, helping to steady morale.[8] In early June, the US journalist Mollie
Panter-Downes, writing for the *New Yorker*, observed: 'As the danger grows,
Mr Duff Cooper seems to be in increasing demand to make the kind of
speeches that the public previously expected from Mr Churchill, and he
does the job excellently.'[9] Churchill is now mythologized as the sole individual with the oratorical capacity to rally the nation in its supreme crisis.
This is plainly wrong. That is not to say that the speeches of Duff Cooper,
Eden, Bevin, or the King, were just as good as his were. What it does mean
is that Churchill should be seen as the outstanding performer in a rhetorical
chorus—or rather a series of talented soloists—dedicated to delivering the
same central messages. Given that there were limits to how often the Prime
Minister could broadcast, and that he in fact did so rather infrequently, the
collective nature of the effort was essential to its success.

Although Churchill's first prime ministerial broadcast was undoubtedly good, it is not much celebrated today. Perhaps surprisingly, it was Neville Chamberlain who suggested making it. Chamberlain had been asked by Churchill to advise on the likely consequences of a French collapse. Reporting to the War Cabinet on 18 May, he advised that if Britain were forced to fight on alone, 'it would be imperative that we should abandon our present rather easy-going methods and resort to a form of government which would approach the totalitarian'. In order to prepare the country for the needed emergency measures, Churchill should make a radio speech. 'This statement should be in very general terms,' Chamberlain said, 'and should indicate that we were in a tight fix and that no personal considerations must be allowed to stand in the way of measures necessary for victory. The situation might deteriorate and, if so, further sacrifices would be called for.'[10] The next day, Churchill went down to Chartwell, his house in Kent, to write the speech, but was called back because of further bad military news. He at last wrote it in the few hours before he was due to broadcast, which he did before the 9 o'clock news bulletin. Chamberlain had provided some draft paragraphs and Churchill took a few lines, none of them especially striking, more or less directly from his suggestions.[11] John Colville wrote in his diary, 'It was good and it brought out the full seriousness of the hour, but it was not Winston at his best, nor quite the clarion-call I had expected.'[12]

In fact, Churchill did not bring out 'the full seriousness of the hour', solemn though his words were. He did not—indeed for diplomatic reasons could not—admit that the War Cabinet was already contemplating the fall of Paris and the forced withdrawal of the British Expeditionary Force (BEF) from France. It would be foolish, he said in his speech, to disguise the dangers of the situation. However, 'It would be still more foolish to lose heart and courage or to suppose that well-trained, well-equipped armies numbering three or four millions of men can be overcome in the space of a few weeks, or even months, by a scoop, or raid of mechanical vehicles, however formidable.' That, of course, was exactly what was about to occur, but Churchill predicted that 'We may look forward with confidence to the stabilization of the Front in France'. Even though the possibility of a worse scenario was already in his mind, this more optimistic expectation may also have struck him as credible. After all, something similar had happened in 1914, and in March 1918 the Germans had made a big push forward only to be defeated within months.

Churchill also predicted—prematurely as it turned out—that Britain itself would experience large-scale bombing 'in a few days'. (The British had now started bombing German industry and swift retaliation seemed likely.) This would be the 'supreme emergency' that would justify drastic interference with property and labour rights. Churchill emphasized that he had received 'the most sacred pledges' from the French 'that whatever happens they will fight to the end, be it bitter or be it glorious. Nay, if we fight to the end, it can only be glorious.' The Allies were living through 'one of the most awe-striking periods' in their joint history, which was 'also beyond doubt the most sublime', as they sought to rescue mankind from the incomparably foul tyranny of the Nazis. Churchill concluded with a quotation from the Book of Maccabees: 'Arm yourselves, and be ye men of valour, and be in readiness for the conflict; for it is better for us to perish in battle than to look upon the outrage of our nation and our altar.'[13] In his more famous speeches over the coming weeks and months he invoked the language of Christian civilization more explicitly, as he had done in 1918. He was not a conventional believer in Christianity, and he had not developed these themes much during his pre-war fight against appeasement. This, then, was a pragmatic choice of a discourse which seemed likely to appeal to the recent upsurge in public religious sentiment.[14] Indeed, Churchill did not come up with the quotation himself. It was suggested by Andrew Stewart, a Ministry of Information official, who thought it appropriate for Trinity Sunday: 'It occurs to me that if the PM broadcasts he might like to use it, or if he does not want it the BBC will try to include it somewhere.'[15]

To have referred even to the possibility that France might be forced to sign a separate peace would have undermined the French war effort terribly, at a time when the British were desperate to keep it going. Churchill's necessary silence, though, led to a tension in the speech. There was a disjuncture between his seeming confidence that the front would stabilize and his apocalyptic talk of fighting to the end. This helps explain why, even though the popular reception was favourable, the effects on opinion were not all that he might have hoped. He achieved 51 per cent of the audience (Chamberlain's resignation broadcast had got 54.2 per cent). According to Home Intelligence, 'All comments are favourable. "A good fighting speech", "makes you feel we're taken into his confidence", "he's not hiding things". There does not seem to be, however, any general realisation that the Prime Minister's speech had any extremely grave import.' It was taken most seriously in Scotland, where the 'Appeal to "faith in God" [was] considered to be ominous'. There was at this moment no widespread sense that Britain should give up the fight in the face of overwhelming odds. In a poll taken in May, only 3 per cent of people thought it possible that Britain would lose the war (although 11 per cent expected a stalemate and 10 per cent had no opinion).[16] In fact, Churchill's problem at this point was to persuade people of how bad things were. In this the broadcast was broadly successful but its impact on listeners was not uniform. 'Complacency was disturbed by it and although many people were worried by the serious implications of the speech, others were stirred by it and are now definitely "facing the facts". Of 150 house-to-house interviews in the London area, approximately half said they were frightened and worried by the speech; the rest were "heartened", "made more determined", "stiffened"'.[17]

Mass-Observation's morale report gave a more optimistic account of the speech's effect, but evidence from individual diaries seems to confirm the mixed picture.[18] Nella Last, a 50-year-old housewife from Barrow-in-Furness, approved of the speech wholeheartedly whilst recognizing the limits to its frankness. 'I thought Churchill's speech most impressive in its "restraint" and I felt that what he did not say I would learn some day and that I would just trust him and follow.'[19] Richard Brown, a middle-aged engineer from Ipswich, was heartened by the speech because he drew the conclusion that the Allies were dealing with the raging battle 'well and truly' and that 'we have the best staying power'.[20] M. M. Paton, a London house-wife, liked the broadcast but also noted alternative reactions: 'Why people should have been depressed by Mr Churchill's speech I do not know.'[21] Yet depression was a natural response if it was read as 'More or less a warning to expect war in England'.[22] C. Miller, a woman teacher in Sussex, found the speech 'invigorating' but reported a comment made by her headmaster: 'But why does he [Churchill] talk as if we might have invasion?' he asked. 'It's up to them to build the aeroplanes to stop it.'[23] Thus a substantial portion of the audience failed to respond to Churchillian rhetoric in the way that legend would lead us to expect; and given that many diarists failed to comment on the speech at all it seems safe to assume a fair measure of popular indifference too. Even the enthusiasts did not tend to suggest that they had been listening to extraordinary, epoch-making oratory.

It was a tall order to be sufficiently grave without inducing despondency. On 21 May Reynaud made a speech to the French Senate which many in Britain took as an admission that 'only a miracle could save France', although in fact he was trying to argue that the Allies could not be beaten. This induced shock and depression, successfully countered the same evening by one of Duff Cooper's broadcasts.[24] On the 23rd, Churchill made a 100-word statement to the Commons reporting that the Germans had 'penetrated into the rear of the Allied Armies in Belgium' and that Abbeville had fallen to the enemy.[25] Five days later he told MPs that Leopold, King of the Belgians, had used his authority as Commander-in-Chief to surrender his army, contrary to the wishes of the Belgian government. Churchill promised a further statement to MPs the following week and warned of the 'hard and heavy tidings' that were likely to come.[26] Backed by his Labour colleagues, he was now locked in a tense debate within the War Cabinet over whether or not to explore the possibility of securing peace terms from Germany, using Mussolini as an intermediary. The evacuation of the BEF was at the same time under way, although how well it would work was not yet known. On the afternoon of the 28th, Churchill addressed a meeting of ministers outside the War Cabinet, and made the case against negotiations. According to one witness account, perhaps rather too highly coloured, he said: 'If this long island story of ours is to end at last, let it end only when each of us lies choking in his own blood upon the ground.'[27] The precise phrasing is less important than the fact that he found unanimous support from those present. This strengthened his hand when the War Cabinet resumed its discussions that same evening. It now rejected the idea of an approach to Mussolini. The question of making a public appeal for help to the United States was also considered.[28] Although Churchill rejected the idea as premature, the need to win over American opinion was much in his mind as he devised his next crucial statement to the House of Commons.

Faced with strong isolationist opinion at home, and in an election year, President Roosevelt was sympathetic to the Allies but inclined to sit on the fence. Churchill's friend, the South African Prime Minister J. C. Smuts, had suggested the British send a message in the following terms:

> We are going to fight on even if we have to stand alone. We want nothing for ourselves. We are only concerned with the defence of world liberty against what will undoubtedly mean the domination of the world by Nazi power. Will the United States help or will they stand aside and take no action in defence of the rights of man?

Churchill's thought that an explicit appeal in these terms, before Britain had managed to make 'a bold stand' against Germany, would look like 'grovelling' and would only court rejection.[29] However, it was still perfectly possible to cast the same central message in oblique terms and to send it indirectly via a speech to the Commons that was bound to be reported globally. This was a key part of the thinking behind the 'Dunkirk' speech, as it was to become.

Churchill constructed this speech with the help of input from his colleagues. This help concerned rhetorical strategy as well as points of detail. On 2 June, Duff Cooper passed on to the Prime Minister a memo written by William Philip Simms, the pro-British foreign editor of the influential Scripps-Howard chain of American newspapers. Simms warned that US public opinion was increasingly concerned at British and French defeats and that the moment was ripe for an unambiguous declaration by Churchill that Britain intended to fight on. The Prime Minister should state '*that Britain intends to carry on this war until she has won—whatever the cost may be*'. The message should not be too nuanced but should be aimed at the American public, 'whose taste *in the mass* runs to bold, posterish effects'. In order to scotch the growing belief that the Allies could not take much more punishment, Churchill should say something on the following lines:

> We intend to fight this thing through to a finish and to victory however long it may take....Come what may, Britain will not flinch....We, over here know full well that difficult times are ahead....We have taken the measure of our foe [...] We know in short exactly what we are up against and that Hitler intends to throw everything he has in mechanical power or manpower into the struggle in the hope of a quick victory, no matter what the cost. Knowing all that, we are in it and, *in it to stay*.

Simms knew that Churchill would use his own phraseology. But in terms of structure the similarities between this passage and Churchill's peroration (with its repetition of 'We shall') are striking. Churchill was much more eloquent but the basic idea was the same. Simms's suggestions continued:

> The proposition is simple: It is whether the kind of world we know in Scandinavia, the Low Countries, Britain and the Americas is to survive, or whether most of the progress made by human kind since the Dark Ages is to be wiped out. For her part Britain intends to fight until Germany's power for evil has been broken. Give in—NEVER![30]

Simms proposed that Churchill should put this all in a written statement. Duff Cooper saw its potential as speech material. 'The line of the isolationist in [the] USA is "Too late",' he noted. 'The answer is not at all. We are still bound to win—but we need help to win *quickly*.'[31]

It seems plain that Churchill saw Simms's memorandum either before starting the drafting process or during it. The fact that there is a paper trail to follow makes clear that Churchillian speech-making was a matter of bureaucracy as well as of inspiration. In this respect he was much better supported as Prime Minister than he had been as First Lord, and mechanisms evolved around his way of doing things. We do not have eyewitness descriptions of how he wrote the Dunkirk speech, but the more general recollections of John Martin, one of his private secretaries, illustrate what became the usual Whitehall procedure. Martin emphasized that Churchill wrote the original draft himself, dictating to a shorthand writer 'very slowly', making a 'very careful selection of words and phrases', trying them out almost in a whisper before pronouncing his final choice out loud. After the draft was typed out, he would make alterations in his own hand. The new, 'semi-final' draft would then be typed out, checked by officials, and circulated to the requisite military experts and government departments. Churchill was supplied with the resulting comments by his private secretaries. This, Martin recalled, was one of their most difficult tasks, because the Prime Minister 'never liked criticism and often reacted very fiercely'. 'What fool suggested that?' was a typical comment. According to Martin, though, 'the interesting thing was that if there was any validity in the criticism one always saw that it had been taken into account' in the final version in some way. But as the time of delivery approached, Churchill would tense up, and it was difficult to make further suggestions to him at that point.[32]

Churchill's draft of the Dunkirk speech was circulated on 3 June, the day before it was delivered. Comments came back within hours. Eden suggested that Churchill had been 'a little rough on the French High Command'.[33] Archibald Sinclair, the Secretary of State for Air, was also sensitive to French feelings. At this stage, the French were still pressing to be sent more squadrons of fighters; the British resisted, fearing that to do so would risk harming their capacity for self-defence. In these circumstances, Sinclair noted, it 'might be unwise [...] to suggest that we did not employ our main Metropolitan Fighter Strength until the occasion came to evacuate our own forces' from Dunkirk. 'We, in fact, threw a considerable proportion of our strength into the battle, to assist our Allies as well as ourselves, in its earlier stages.'[34] Churchill took the point on board. He also received from the Admiralty the final numbers of evacuees from Dunkirk: 335,900 had got away, of whom 224,318 were British.[35] On one important point Churchill had second thoughts of his own, without prompting. He deleted from the draft text by hand the observation that 'the United States continues to watch with a strange detachment, the growth and advance of dangers which menace them ever more darkly'.[36] He wanted to wake Americans to the dangers that would be posed by a Nazi victory, but at the same time he was careful to avoid alienating them through excessive frankness. The result was that the speech contained no overt reference to the USA at all, even though it was aimed at winning over American opinion.

Churchill began making his speech in the Commons at 3.40 p.m. on 4 June. Significantly, eighteen foreign diplomats were watching from the gallery.[37] He spoke for just over half an hour. He started by reviewing the military developments that led up to Dunkirk, before dealing with the evacuation itself. He had a difficult course to steer between, on the one hand, presenting the facts in the most encouraging way possible and, on the other, not appearing to gloss over defeat. He achieved this by stressing that although the picture was negative it was better than could have been predicted. He noted that the previous week, when he had warned the House to expect bad news, he had thought that only 20,000–30,000 men might be re-embarked; and that that had been before the Belgian surrender had struck a further blow. Colville observed: 'He did not finally mention in his speech (although he had originally intended to do so) that King Leopold, whom he castigated soundly, had given Lord Gort [Commander of the BEF] a pledge of continued resistance.'[38] Since the surrender, there had been a 'miracle of deliverance', Churchill said. He warned that 'We must be very careful not to assign to this deliverance the attributes of a victory. Wars are not won by evacuations.' Nevertheless, 'there was a victory inside this deliverance', gained by the Air Force, which he said had vindicated itself in its struggle with the *Luftwaffe*. Overall, though, the recent events in France and Belgium had been 'a colossal military disaster'. He raised the possibility of a German invasion, whilst also mentioning 'the solid assurances' against it provided by Britain's sea and air power. He was confident, he said, that Britain could continue the war for years, 'if necessary alone'—a crucial phrase. What did the words mean, wondered the journalist Alexander Mackintosh: 'Were they a rhetorical flourish? Or was there the possibility of our being deserted by our Ally?'[39]

At last came the most famous passage:

> We shall not flag or fail. We shall go on to the end. We shall fight in France, we shall fight on the seas and oceans, we shall fight with growing confidence and growing strength in the air, we shall defend our Island, whatever the cost may

be. We shall fight on the beaches, we shall fight on the landing grounds, we shall fight in the fields and in the streets, we shall fight in the hills; we shall never surrender, and even if, which I do not for a moment believe, this Island or a large part of it were subjugated and starving, then our Empire beyond the seas, armed and guarded by the British Fleet, would carry on the struggle, until, in God's good time, the New World, with all its power and might, steps forth to the rescue and the liberation of the old.[40]

Here we see the influence of Simms ('whatever the cost may be', 'We intend to fight', 'Britain will not flinch', 'Give in—NEVER!'). Churchill may also have reached into his memory and summoned up the ghost of Lord Rosebery, who during the Boer War had declared that the British Empire would not 'falter or fail'.[41] It is worth noting too that the reference to the British Fleet was no mere afterthought. On 31 May Mackenzie King of Canada had sent a telegram to Churchill reporting his conversations with Roosevelt, who felt it impossible to give 'immediate belligerent aid', but thought that such aid might be possible in a few months if Britain and France could hold out. 'If further resistance by the Fleet in British waters became impossible before such aid could be given, the President believes […] it would be disastrous to surrender the Fleet on any terms, that it should be sent to South Africa, Singapore, Australia, the Caribbean and Canada.' If this were done, American intervention could be expected to follow quickly.[42] 'When I saw his concluding words,' wrote Mackenzie King when he read Churchill's speech, 'I recognized at once that the despatch that I sent him had been helpful.'[43] As a matter of fact, Lord Lothian, the British Ambassador to Washington, had earlier sent Churchill similar information, but precisely who deserved the credit is not important.[44] The point is that Churchill knew he was sending a message that reflected what the American administration wanted to hear.

According to 'Chips' Channon, 'several Labour members cried' when they heard the speech, although not, apparently, any Conservative ones.[45] That is not to say that everyone on the Labour side was won over. 'Far from coming away inspired, we sometimes went away depressed and dispirited after one of the Churchillian orations in the House,' recalled Emanuel Shinwell. He added:

> We were very much depressed as a result of the events that led to him making this [Dunkirk] speech, and all his oratory could not remove that depression.
>
> Members were beginning to murmur. Some suspected that this very fine speech, delightful to listen to, was just an elaborate cover-up for what we believed to have been a failure on the part of the military leaders.[46]

Doubts seem to have been more extensive on the Conservative side. According to Lloyd George, Churchill's reception was 'very half-hearted [...] in spite of his magnificent speech, he got far less applause than was usually accorded to Chamberlain'.[47] Churchill's wife Clementine was of the same opinion: 'a great section of the Tory Party were not behind Winston & had received his great speech [...] even in sullen silence'.[48] Anti-Chamberlainites were supportive if not completely uncritical. The arch-imperialist Leo Amery wrote that Churchill's 'note of defiance threatening to carry on the war even in the Empire outside if we were driven out of Britain was all that I could have wished, though unfortunately so worded as to give [Charles] Corbin [the French Ambassador] the impression that he was hinting that France might drop out of the war'.[49]

By this stage, Corbin's alarm did not count for much. It was more important to convey to the USA Britain's determination to carry on if the worst should happen than it was to avoid upsetting a crumbling ally. However, there were other aspects of the speech's conclusion that were potentially problematic. German propaganda aimed at the UK claimed that no sooner had Churchill raised the idea that he would die in the last ditch with his people than he dashed it to the ground with his suggestion that the fight would be continued from the Empire if Britain succumbed:

> We hardly know whether to compliment this miserable despot on being so frank as to express the possibility that Britain will be completely subjugated, or to exhaust the vocabulary of condemnation in stigmatising his implicit intention of deserting, in the hour of supreme need, the millions whom he has led to disaster. [...]
> [T]he war could, of course, never be conducted from another hemisphere unless Churchill and his confederates were there to conduct it.[50]

There is no sign that this notion ever caught hold in Britain, but another interpretation of the passage was potentially more worrying. Lord Lothian wrote to Churchill of his fear that it had encouraged those Americans 'who believed that, even though Great Britain went under, the Fleet would some-how cross the Atlantic to them'.[51] In his reply, Churchill claimed, rather disingenuously: 'My last words in my speech were of course addressed primarily to Germany and Italy, to whom the idea of a war of Continents and a long war are at present obnoxious; also to Dominions, for whom we are trustees.' As we have seen, it seems likely that his words had been intended to meet Roosevelt's wishes. But he now suggested that Lothian should point out to the President that a pro-Nazi British government might well surrender the Fleet, giving Germany and Japan mastery over the New World. 'You should talk to him in this sense and thus discourage any complacent assumption on United States' part that they will pick up the *débris* of the British Empire by their present policy.'[52]

Notwithstanding Lothian's worries, the speech was received with great enthusiasm in America. Listeners to the CBS network heard Ed Murrow's vivid account, which emphasized the contrast with Churchill's earlier parliamentary style: 'Today he was different. There was little oratory; he wasn't interested in being a showman. [...] there were no frills or tricks.'[53] The President liked the speech 'very much'.[54] The press went into raptures.[55] Even the staunchly isolationist *Chicago Daily Tribune*, which made clear to its readers that Churchill was calling on America to discard her neutrality, said that 'he is worth a quarter of a million or more soldiers to Great Britain'.[56] The New York correspondent of the London *Times* wrote that praise of the speech could be heard everywhere: 'People are even stopping each other in the street to talk about it.'[57] Indeed, the US reaction seems to have been distinctly warmer than that in Britain.

Amidst all his other concerns at this time, Churchill did not go to lengths to maximize the impact of his message on the British people. He did not act on a suggestion to schedule his speech earlier than customary to make sure that the evening papers were able to cover it the same day.[58] The Ministry of Information originally intended that a full report of Churchill's Commons speech on the radio evening news on 4 June would be followed by a broadcast by him the following day, as part of its campaign to prepare the public for the danger of invasion.[59] The report was broadcast—'even the BBC announcer got all het up about it'—but the further Churchill speech did not follow.[60] Presumably he was too busy to write a new one and it had not yet occurred to anybody that he could simply repeat what he had said in Parliament over the airwaves. The morning papers bathed the Dunkirk speech in superlatives. But as Home Intelligence noted, the coverage was not as prominent as might have been expected. Nor did the speech suddenly make the British people more determined:

> The final evacuation of the BEF has brought with it a certain feeling of depression. There is a deflation of tension without a corresponding increase in resolve.
>
> The grave tone of Churchill's speech made some impression and may have contributed in some measure to the rather pessimistic atmosphere of today. It should be remarked, however, that only the *Daily Mirror* and the [communist] *Daily Worker* gave Churchill's speech headline value ('We

Never Surrender', 'Not Blind to Colossal Military Disaster'). The contents of the speech were on the whole expected but some apprehension has been caused throughout the country on account of the PM's reference to 'fighting alone'. This has led to some slight increase in doubt about the intentions of our ally.

Only in Birmingham were 'excellent effects' positively noted, with workers showing greater eagerness to speed up war production.[61]

This overall picture is borne out by letter and diary evidence. Churchill's statement was undoubtedly recognized as 'A great speech—no gilding the lily'.[62] The novelist Vita Sackville-West was 'stirred' by it and praised it to her husband Harold Nicolson: 'Even repeated by the announcer it sent shivers (not of fear) down my spine.'[63] Yet other reactions were more muted. Nella Last wrote: 'We all listened to the news and the account of the Prime Minister's speech and all felt grave and rather sad about things unsaid rather than said.'[64] Evelyn Saunders, a housewife in her thirties, wrote: 'Churchill's speech yesterday hasn't raised my spirits yet, I still feel sick through me.'[65] It was not that the British people failed to spot that it was a good speech. It is just that, on the whole, it failed to cheer them up. This was only natural, given that it warned them that their country was under threat of invasion. It was equally only natural that the Americans, at a distance, should draw more optimistic lessons. As Key Pittman, Democratic Chairman of the Senate Foreign Relations Committee, observed: 'Churchill's assurance that Britain will never surrender even if the British Isles are subjugated and will continue the war against Hitler from Canada, substantially guarantees the Western hemisphere against successful attack for a long period of time.'[66] Hence the room for concern that Americans might conclude that they could rest easy for the time being rather than rushing to help Britain at once.

On 16 June Reynaud resigned as Prime Minister. Within hours, the new government of Marshal Philippe Pétain, a hero of the First World War, requested an armistice. 'The news from France is very bad,' Churchill announced in a seven-sentence broadcast—but it was not yet clear exactly how bad, as there were still some hopes that the French Fleet might not fall into German hands.[67] He was apparently pressured to speak to the nation by Duff Cooper: 'Churchill didn't seem to see the point' of doing so.[68] The public were depressed by the capitulation but appear to have assumed the war would continue. There was no popular movement in favour of peace, although the mood was one of resignation as much as of steely determination. One man in Bolton commented: 'You heard what Winston Churchill said—we would fight on even if it came to street fighting and if the country was swimming in blood. That will be nice won't it?'[69]

On the 18th, the Prime Minister addressed the Commons once more. Part of his speech was dedicated to calming demands that Chamberlain, Halifax, and other former appeasers be driven from the government. Insisting that the war effort would be undermined by efforts to lay the blame for recent disasters, he declared: 'if we open a quarrel between the past and the present we shall find that we have lost the future'. The political unity of the summer of 1940 was a fragile construct and needed continual reinforcement. Whilst Churchill again acknowledged the catastrophic nature of recent events, he also emphasized Britain's strength and capacity to deal with the new situation. David Edgerton has recently claimed that 'Britain was not "alone" between June 1940 and June 1941 [i.e. between the Fall of France and the entry of the Soviet Union into the war]; nor did it believe itself to be'.[70] In his analysis, the concept of 'alone' was largely invented later in the war at a time when the British, in need of American economic help, wanted to emphasize the burdens they had shouldered on behalf of civilization as a whole. There is something in this idea but it needs to be qualified. Churchill had already used the phrase 'if necessary, alone', and he now repeated it.[71] However it is right to emphasize that 'alone' in this sense referred not merely to Great Britain and Northern Ireland but to the whole British Empire, with a particular focus on Canada, Australia, New Zealand, and South Africa, the governments of which had deliberately chosen to throw in their lot against Germany. Churchill made no mention of the African colonies or of India, which had been committed to war without consultation and certainly, in the latter case, without wholehearted consent.[72]

This emphasis on the support of the Dominions was part of a broader argument about Britain's ultimate power to win the war. Churchill did not choose to revel in die-in-the last-ditch rhetoric, but underscored 'the solid, practical grounds upon which we base our inflexible resolve to continue the war' and emphasized 'that our professional advisers of the three Services unitedly advise that we should do so, and that there are good and reasonable hopes of final victory'. As well as speaking of the strength of the Air Force and Navy, he even presented the fact that Italy had joined the war as a source of strength to Britain, as extending the blockade to the Italians would help prevent resources getting through to the Germans. Although it was impossible to predict how victory would come, he said, he noted that during the First

World War no one had known that either, 'until at the end, quite suddenly, quite unexpectedly, our terrible foe collapsed before us, and we were so glutted with victory that in our folly we cast it away'.[73]

The peroration justly became the most famous part of the speech. Churchill made some minor amendments by hand to his final text; the words he added are shown in italics:

> What General Weygand calls[74] the 'Battle of France' is over. I expect that the battle of Britain is about to begin. Upon this battle depends the survival of Christian civilisation. Upon it depends our own British life and the long continuity of our institutions and our Empire. The whole fury and might of the enemy must very soon be turned on us. Hitler knows that if he will have to break us in this island or lose the war. If we can stand up to him all Europe may be ~~liberated~~ *freed*,[75] and the life of the world may move forward into broad, sunlit uplands; but if we fail then the whole world, including the United States, and all that we have known and cared for, will sink into the abyss of a new Dark Age made more sinister, *and perhaps more prolonged*, by the lights of perverted science. Let us therefore brace ourselves to our duty and so bear ourselves that if the British Commonwealth and Empire lasts for a thousand years men will still say, 'This was their finest hour'.[76]

There is no sign of any direct influence on this passage by anyone other than Churchill. Although Simms had referred to the 'Dark Ages' in his memorandum before the Dunkirk speech, Churchill himself had already used that phrase in his speech at Manchester in January. It was a term that had an especially powerful resonance at a time when the blackout was in force as a defence against bombing, although of course the restrictions were felt less heavily in the summer months.[77] Although both the 'Dark Age' idea and 'sunlit uplands' were established commonplaces, the contrast between the images was a powerful one which equated the British with light and virtue and the Nazis with the opposite.[78] Equally conspicuous is Churchill's willingness now to make explicit reference to the threat posed by Germany to the United States.

Again it was noticeable that Churchill was 'much more loudly cheered by the Labour Party than by the general body of Tory supporters'.[79] One suspects that some Labour MPs did this precisely because they wanted to drive a wedge into the Conservatives: it was a way of having a dig at Chamberlain, as he himself appears to have believed.[80] This time Churchill did repeat his speech on the radio, although he was not keen to do so. Initially Duff Cooper had proposed that it should be broadcast live from

Parliament, but this would have required the approval of the Commons and the idea lapsed.[81] Churchill's decision to reprise what he had said earlier rather than prepare a new speech seems to have been the result of resentment at being pressured to go on the radio when he did not want to. The press were annoyed at the bland Foreign Office response to the French collapse and urged 'very strongly that Churchill should say something to the nation'.[82] Harold Nicolson, now a junior minister at MoI, wrote in his diary:

> How I wish Winston would not talk on the wireless unless he is feeling in good form. He hates the microphone, and when we bullied him into speaking last night, he just sulked and read his House of Commons speech over again. Now, as delivered in the House of Commons, that speech was magnificent, especially the concluding sentences. But it sounded ghastly on the wireless. All the great vigour he put into it seemed to evaporate.[83]

This helps explain why, according to the Home Intelligence Report, public enthusiasm was less than complete:

> Churchill's speech was awaited anxiously and when heard was the subject of varied reactions. What he said was considered courageous and hopeful and the speech was welcomed for its frankness. 'He gives bad news frankly', 'Cool and businesslike', 'The sort of facts and figures we want'. On the other hand there was widespread comment on his delivery and his references to France have brought a recrudescence of anti-French feeling.[84]

According to Mass-Observation's initial report the speech 'was generally deemed satisfactory. People think that he did not say much, but that he said everything which could be said.'[85] The following day's report was more detailed:

> Churchill's broadcast at 9 o'clock last night was well received as regard[s] subject matter, and has certainly had some settling effect. But his delivery was frequently criticised. Some suggested that he was drunk, others that he did not himself feel the confidence he was proclaiming. A few thought he was tired. It would seem that the delivery to some extent counteracted the contents of the speech.[86]

Diaries show a range of reactions. Eleanor Humphries, a London housewife, viewed the broadcast in epic-heroic terms: 'Churchill made the speech of a lifetime. [...] I cannot remember when I was last so thrilled'.[87] Margery Davis, a cookery demonstrator from Margate, wrote that 'Everyone seems much more cheerful since Mr Churchill spoke'.[88] Mollie Panter-Downes, writing for publication, thought the speech 'less stirring than sensible—a carefully reasoned balance sheet of the chances for a British victory, well suited to the grimly sane public mood'.[89] By contrast Agnes Norman and her husband, of London, gained the impression that Churchill had 'dined a little too well to-night, and we do not doubt that Germans who turned on the wireless at 9 o'c will hold a similar view. Needless to say we do not take all this stuff designed for popular consumption too seriously.' The next day she wrote of her home-help's opinion: Churchill had 'tried to sound sure but wasn't sure'.[90] One member of the public was concerned enough about Churchill's seemingly halting speech to send a telegram to No. 10 suggesting that he had a heart complaint—although apparently the true problem was that he had a cigar in his mouth as he spoke.[91]

In the midst of adulatory newspaper press coverage the left-wing *Daily Mirror*—which had led the charge against Chamberlain's continuation in the government—showed a hint of ambivalence. Saying that it would respect Churchill's request to 'forget the past', it ran his speech as a front page story under the headline 'LEADERSHIP, GIVE US LEADERSHIP'.[92] This seemed to imply that there was some doubt that Churchill would. Cecil King, who directed the *Mirror*'s editorial policy, denounced the broadcast in his diary. He wrote that the Prime Minister's words added up to the claim that 'the situation was disastrous, but all right. Whether he was drunk or all-in from sheer fatigue, I don't know, but it was the poorest possible effort on an occasion when he should have produced the finest speech of his life.'[93] All this said, Churchill was undoubtedly moving towards a position where he was recognized as the pre-eminent ministerial broadcaster. By contrast, Duff Cooper's reputation as broadcaster was a little fragile. While his most recent speech was well received by the citizens of Wales and the Midlands, it was thought 'a little too literary' in Nottingham, and in London it was 'Considered "vague and too poetical" after Churchill's realistic talk'.[94] Churchill was appreciated as much for his straight-speaking and his delivery of facts as for his higher flights of rhetoric.

Two days after the 'finest hour' speech the Commons went into secret session, to allow MPs to debate sensitive issues confidentially. As no press or Hansard reporters were present, we only have a record of Churchill's speech in the form of his own typed notes. Although he did not say much that he could not have said in public, he spoke more candidly about the attitude of the USA than he likely would otherwise. It was not yet clear if Roosevelt would run in November for a third term. But Churchill, who was 'in really rollicking form', held out the too-great hope that if Britain could just last 'until Election issues are settled there' the Americans would enter the war: 'I cannot doubt the whole English-speaking world will be in line together.'[95] 'Winston wound up with his usual brilliance and out-of-place levity,' wrote 'Chips' Channon. 'His command of English is magnificent; but strangely enough, although he makes me laugh, he leaves me unmoved. There is always the quite inescapable suspicion that he loves war, war which broke Neville Chamberlain's better heart!'[96] Amery, for his part, judged that 'The extreme [anti-Chamberlain] agitation of a few days ago has gone and the one idea seems to be to stick out for the next few months and then prepare really effectively for the reconquest of Europe.'[97]

The continued coolness of some MPs towards Churchill cannot be put down solely to Chamberlainite sour grapes. Labour members may have made a point of cheering him but, as we have seen, their enthusiasm for the Prime Minister was not unanimous. Shinwell was to emerge as one of the government's chief critics; he and another sceptic, the Conservative MP Earl Winterton, were together labelled 'Arsenic and Old Lace'. It might be tempting to dismiss Shinwell as a malcontent but his retrospective comments on Churchill's rhetoric are worth taking seriously. Writing in the 1960s, Shinwell paid tribute to 'his capacity for crystallising in his oratory the sentiment of the nation'; and yet, 'my original doubts must remain as to their effectiveness at the time of their delivery and in the place they were delivered'. Shinwell felt that the perorations, 'splendid as they were', seemed to him detached from what he, Shinwell, suspected were the realities of the war situation. At the broadest level these suspicions were unfair, although Churchill did hold back some salient information, such as the sinking of the liner *Lancastria* with the loss of over 3,000 lives, for reasons of morale. Although it is not clear how widely they were shared, such doubts may help explain why Churchill's speeches did not impress the House as much as they might have done. Shinwell observed:

> No doubt many of these speeches were intended for consumption far away from Westminster—in the United States in particular. He sought to reassure the Americans, and, for that matter, the Russians too when they came into the war, that we were producing men and weapons to our utmost ability. [...]
>
> No doubt it was important that some of these speeches had to be made in this way—but it did not help Churchill to capture the House.

Shinwell was also right to point out that 'the effect of a speech on the House largely depends on timing: what may make a remarkable impact at one moment of time may, to the casual reader or listener twenty years later make no impact at all'.[98] It is a fallacy to assume that Churchill's 'best' speeches—judged in literary terms—must have been the ones that had the most effect at the time. By the same token, those that provoked the most powerful immediate reactions are not necessarily the ones that are most resonant today.

So it was with Churchill's speech on the French Fleet on 4 July. At the time Anglo-French relations were mired in acrimony and bitterness. In his 'Finest Hour' speech, Churchill had urged the French government to 'continue the war in accordance with their Treaty obligations, from which we have not felt able to release them'.[99] This pointed comment was rightly seen as an attempt to appeal to the French people, over the heads of their new leaders, to continue resistance.[100] With Churchill's backing, the as yet unknown Charles De Gaulle was allowed to give his famous 'flame of French resistance' broadcast from London that same day.[101] A few days later the French accepted the proposed armistice terms; their Fleet would come under German control. This caused even greater depression amongst the British public than the initial capitulation, because people had continued to hope that the surrender would not be complete and that the French navy would go on fighting. According to Mass-Observation: 'The terms came as a big shock, and on the day they were announced 14 people were afraid, for every one who expressed hope and determination. Nevertheless people took it for granted that the war would go on, and most said they were anxious it should do.'[102] We can therefore see both that Churchill's speeches were in themselves insufficient to keep people cheerful in the face of catastrophic news, and that there was no necessary connection between cheerfulness and willingness to carry on fighting.

Churchill issued a statement expressing 'grief and amazement' at the terms and calling on 'all Frenchmen outside the power of the enemy' to help the British carry on the fight.[103] In response, the French government denied any difference 'between itself and the rest of the country'; the British public would understand their action once it knew the full facts.[104] Pétain expressed his 'stupefaction and pain' at Churchill's words, while claiming to understand the anguish that inspired them. The French could not accept lectures from a foreigner, he said: 'Churchill may be a good judge of the interests of his country, not of ours. He is still less qualified to judge of French honour.'[105]

There was now beginning a rhetorical battle between Gaullists and Pétainists, as both groups fought to establish their respective claims to represent the true national spirit. De Gaulle's eventual recognition as the legitimate national leader was by no means seen as inevitable at the time. The Americans recognized Pétain's regime—which made skilful appeals to US opinion based on shared revolutionary history[106]—and Churchill for the time being kept De Gaulle at arm's length. And whatever his moral qualities, Pétain was no politically lightweight Quisling. With his war hero's prestige, he claimed almost literally to embody the nation and presented the path he had chosen as the one of honour, which would allow France to restore her greatness. The Armistice was generally welcomed or met with indifference by the population, who for the time being rallied behind him.[107] The circumstances made the British decision to seize or if necessary destroy the French Fleet a painful one. To act against a nation that had been so recently an ally and was now suffering under German rule was, Churchill recalled, 'a hateful decision, the most unnatural and painful in which I have ever been concerned'.[108] It was this heartfelt regret that gave his speech explaining and justifying the British démarche an unparalleled emotional power.

The speech, in common with many of Churchill's others, also gained in effectiveness from the sheer fact that it revealed new information. The language, by Churchillian standards, was fairly plain; there was nothing for the editors of dictionaries of quotations. The Prime Minister did not merely offer a vindication of what had been done; he delivered the news in the form of a compelling narrative. He began by outlining how the UK government had offered to release the French from their treaty commitments, if only their Fleet would head for British harbours before armistice talks were complete; and how, in breach of the promises of Admiral Darlan, the Pétain government had treacherously allowed its navy to fall into German power. He told how British forces had successfully taken over French craft at Plymouth and Portsmouth the previous morning. However, the Commander of the French force at the port of Mers-el-Kébir in Morocco had refused to respond to the British ultimatum (which Churchill read out to MPs at length). Accordingly, the British had attacked, and the French had resisted with severe loss of life; they had fought with characteristic courage albeit in an 'unnatural cause'. The end result was that a large part of the French Fleet had passed into British hands or 'been put out of action or otherwise withheld from Germany by yesterday's events'. Churchill concluded by saying that the action taken gave the lie to the idea, 'so industriously spread by German propaganda', that the government intended to enter peace negotiations. 'We shall, on the contrary, prosecute the war with the utmost vigour by all the means that are open to us until the righteous purposes for which we entered upon it have been fulfilled.'[109]

Lord Harmsworth, a former Liberal MP, was watching from the gallery. 'Only once before have I seen the House of Commons in a mood of such tense excitement as this afternoon,' he wrote in his diary, 'and that was when in 1914 Edward Grey put to the House the issue of war with Germany.'[110] General Raymond E. Lee, American military attaché in London, also observed the scene. He noted how at the start 'Churchill bounced to his feet, a most ordinary and undistinguished little rotund figure'. Then, 'with the most dramatic effect and yet with the most superb composure, he narrated as a historian this vivid passage of history'. When he finished, 'the decorum of Parliament vanished. All were on their feet, shouting, cheering and waving order papers and handkerchiefs like mad.'[111] According to the *Illustrated London News*—which provided a dramatic drawing of the scene—'While Parliament stood and demonstrated its approval, Mr Churchill sat with his elbows on his knees, his chin cupped in his hands, visibly moved.'[112] In fact, he wept.[113] In Churchill's account, 'Up till this moment the Conservative Party had treated me with some reserve, and it was from the Labour benches that I received the warmest welcome when I entered the House or rose upon serious occasions. But now all joined in solemn stentorian accord.'[114] It should not be concluded from this, though, that the Tories were now fully united behind Churchill; there were signs that the demonstration was deliberately brought about by David Margesson, the Conservative Chief Whip.[115]

The action against the French Fleet—rather than any of Churchill's earlier speeches—seems to have been the factor that led to a long-lasting boost to the public's levels of cheerfulness.[116] There was a sense that Britain was now 'getting to business'.[117] There is not much evidence that Churchill's speech itself—as distinguished from the events that it announced—had a dramatic impact, although apparently it had a 'rousing effect' in London.[118] 'Had to smile at the statement that Churchill had tears of emotion in his eyes,' wrote John Howard, an electrician, after reading the *Daily Telegraph*. 'The old —— casehardened —— never shed a tear since the day he was born.'[119] Churchill did not perform the speech again on the radio, but his awareness of the benefits of broadcasting direct to the people was growing. Within a few days he was planning a new broadcast speech, to be delivered on Bastille Day. He told the Cabinet that he would say that the government did not intend to take further action against the remaining units of the French Fleet. 'He proposed to strike a restrained and not unfriendly note, and might refer to the French as an oppressed people, who would be liberated by the defeat of Germany.'[120] When the draft was ready, he read the relevant passages to the Cabinet for their approval.[121]

The speech also had another dimension. According to Colville's diary, Churchill thought that 'the great invasion scare' provided 'a most useful purpose: it is well on the way to providing us with the finest offensive army we have ever possessed and it is keeping every man and woman tuned to a high pitch of readiness'. He therefore did not wish the scare to die down, 'and although personally he doubts whether invasion is a serious menace he intends to give that impression, and to talk about long and dangerous vigils, etc., when he broadcasts on Sunday'.[122] The speech thus summoned up a vision of invasion opposed at close quarters by soldiers and civilians in every village, town, and city: 'we would rather see London laid in ruins and ashes than that it should be tamely and abjectly enslaved.' Churchill also looked to the future: 'we must prepare not only for the summer, but for the winter; not only for 1941, but for 1942'. Then, he hinted, Britain would be ready to go on the offensive.[123] According to Mass–Observation, though, 'a great many people' remained convinced that the war would be over before the time 'mentioned by Mr Churchill as a likely date for offensive action'. There was a widespread belief that Hitler 'can't last another winter'.[124]

Asserting that this was 'a war of peoples and of causes' rather than of princes or dynasties, Churchill labelled it 'a War of the Unknown Warriors'.[125] This was perhaps the most memorable phrase in the speech, but it has not exactly rung down the years. Nevertheless, this broadcast was a landmark. For the first time we can find evidence of a Churchill speech evoking mass popular enthusiasm and boosting morale and optimism *throughout* society. This time, there was no depression and little if any carping. His previous efforts had been well received by many, but the unanimity of the response to the 'Unknown Warriors' speech was a new and remarkable phenomenon. The evidence for this comes, firstly, from the audience figures. According to the BBC's researchers at the time, the 9 o'clock news on 14 July, which was preceded by Churchill's statement, was heard by 64.4 per cent of the adult population—a not quite unprecedented statistic. (The King had secured 66.7 per cent of the audience for his May broadcast.) 'There is no doubt that the explanation of this high figure was the previous announcement that it would include a statement by Mr Churchill.'[126] Secondly, the Home Intelligence Reports were for the first time unambiguous about the effects of his oratory:

> Reports from all Regions agree that the Premier's speech last night won universal approval, and the assurance that there will be no peace discussion was welcome and heartening. A typical comment from Bristol is 'that's the sort of thing we want and he's the fellow we can follow'. Reference to 1942 elicits much comment. Reading RIO [Regional Information Officer] reports more spontaneous messages of commendation than after any important speech.[127]

By implication, then, it was approved of more strongly than Churchill's own previous speeches. It made people confident and cheerful and the references to defending London street by street led them to believe that 'we shall not be sold out as the French were by their Government'.[128] However, Sergeant L. D. Pexton, who was captured after Dunkirk, recorded a different atmosphere in his POW camp. He wrote: 'Heard today that Hitler had broadcast some peace terms and that Churchill had told him what to do with them. Don't know how true it is as the camp is always so full of rumours that you can't believe anything you hear. Hope they do patch up some sort of peace terms up as everyone here wants it, and to get home.'[129] As a matter of fact, Hitler had not make his peace offer until after Churchill's broadcast, and Churchill never deigned to make an explicit reply.

Churchill's technique catered to the public's taste for a 'virile' and 'martial' style of speaking. According to comments garnered by the BBC's researchers, people wanted announcers to show 'a less restrained manner' when referring to the Germans and Italians. 'They love to hear them called names. One of the reasons for Mr Churchill's popularity is that he talks and sounds as if he really hates the Germans and despises the Italians.'[130] Not all his rhetoric was belligerent, however. In mid-July he told the Commons that the government had agreed to the Japanese demand to halt the supply of arms via Burma to China, with which Japan was at war. (The agreement was for a three-month period.) It was not a heroic decision but appeasing the Japanese was understandable given Britain's perilous circumstances at the time. According to Channon, Churchill 'successfully quashed the Leftist Opposition's eagerness for war in the East as well as everywhere else'.[131] There was some popular resentment, but, with the public being fairly ignorant of Far Eastern affairs, people were generally willing to accept Churchill's lead.[132]

The Battle of Britain was now approaching its height. The RAF was reaching the limits of its capacity in its struggle to deny the *Luftwaffe*'s efforts to establish air superiority over southern England in preparation for invasion. Churchill's next major speech, on 20 August, is indelibly associated with the air battle, and with one phrase in particular. General Hastings Ismay, the Prime Minister's military secretary, recalled visiting No. 11 Group Fighter Command with him and following the progress of the afternoon's battle via a table-top map. At one point, every squadron was engaged and there was no reserve, even as new waves of German fighters crossed the channel. According to Ismay:

> I felt sick with fear. As the evening closed in the fighting died down, and we left by car for Chequers. Churchill's first words were: 'Don't speak to me. I have never been so moved.' After about five minutes he leaned forward and said, 'Never in the field of human conflict has so much been owed by so many to so few.'[133]

But the speech was not simply a well-deserved tribute to—and effective propaganda for—the RAF and its men. (It praised bomber crews as well as fighter pilots although the term 'the Few' quickly attached to the latter.)[134] It dealt with a range of complex and controversial issues at a time when Britain was angling for concrete US support. Churchill had not only to illustrate once again Britain's determination to continue the fight but also to tiptoe tactfully around domestic and US political sensitivities.

The speech as a whole presented the arguments for confidence in Britain's ability to win the war. These included not only the prowess and devotion of her airmen, but also the numerical strength of her army, her command of the sea, and her scientific superiority. They also included her ability to maintain a strict blockade of Germany and occupied Europe, but here Churchill had to tread carefully. Former US President Herbert Hoover had proposed a plan for relieving the populations of France, Belgium, and Holland by delivering food supplies, involving a partial lifting of the blockade.[135] Some, not only in America but in Britain, were concerned on humanitarian grounds about 'Winston's plan to starve Europe'.[136] European governments-in-exile worried that blockade might alienate their hungry populations from the British cause. Churchill—using material submitted by the Ministry of Economic Warfare and reworked by the Foreign Office—made the case for its military necessity and laid the blame for any suffering at the door of the Nazis.[137] The News Chronicle thought this 'Possibly the most important part of the Prime Minister's statement'.[138] Churchill also made the pledge that 'we can and will arrange in advance for the speedy entry of food into any part of the enslaved area, when this part has been wholly cleared of

German forces, and has genuinely regained its freedom'.[139] Thus even at a time when Britain faced major challenges to maintain its own food supply, she made a promise that helped lay the groundwork for the post-war programme of relief and rehabilitation.

Also significant for the audience at the time was his explanation for the British withdrawal from Somaliland—which he had announced the previous week—in the face of Italian attack. This was not an issue of great military significance but it concerned the public at the time, who felt that British prestige had been damaged. 'Fancy, the Wops, it's disgusting', was one comment picked up by Home Intelligence. 'Many people, however, are reported to be saying "Winston will explain everything".'[140] He did so by saying that the French decision to drop out of the war had made the British position there impossible to defend. Contemporary observers were also alive to Churchill's comment that Hitler was likely to continue his air onslaught 'as long as he has the strength to do so, and as long as any preoccupations he may have in respect of the Russian Air Force allow him to do so'.[141] This was read as a reference to a possible attack on Germany by the USSR.[142] The *Daily Mail* thought it a 'very pregnant sentence' in the light of the previous week's boast by the Soviet Union to have the strongest air force in the world.[143]

Of equal or greater interest to contemporaries was the vexed question of the so-called 'destroyers for bases' deal. Roosevelt was now willing to provide Britain with fifty out-of-date warships in exchange for long leases on military bases in British territories in the Caribbean and Newfoundland. In order to do this, he required Churchill to make a public statement about the future of the British Fleet 'similar to his statement to Parliament of the 4th June' (the Dunkirk speech). Part of the purpose of the 'Few' speech was to give the necessary assurance.[144] There were complications, however. For legal reasons and to help Congressional opinion Roosevelt needed to make the trade a formal one. From the American perspective this would appear an excellent swap, as the ships were of little military use. By the same token, though, Churchill wanted to avoid a formal arrangement as the exchange—judged in practical rather than symbolic terms—appeared a bad one. He later recalled, doubtless with right-wing Conservative imperialists in mind, that if the question 'were presented to the British as a naked trading away of British possessions for [the] sake of the fifty destroyers it would certainly encounter vehement opposition'.[145] Therefore, although the likely nature of the bargain was now public knowledge (in spite of Roosevelt's denials)

Churchill presented the decision to grant the leases as a spontaneous act made purely in the interests of mutual security.[146] There was no mention of the destroyers: he hoped that the Americans might make a gift of them as a 'separate spontaneous' act in reply.[147] But although the Cabinet hoped that his speech 'might increase confidence in the United States, and dispose the Administration to accept less rigorous terms' there was no avoiding a formal agreement, which followed in early September.[148]

In his peroration, Churchill presented the ceding of the bases as part of a process by which the British Empire and the United States would have to be 'somewhat mixed up together in some of their affairs for mutual and general advantage'. He did not, he said, have any misgivings about this tendency. 'I could not stop it if I wished; no one can stop it. Like the Mississippi, it just keeps rolling along. Let it roll. Let it roll on full flood, inexorable, irresistible, benignant, to broader lands and better days.'[149] In the car back to Downing Street afterwards he sang 'Ol' Man River' out of tune all the way.[150] But if the idea that eventual US involvement in the war was inevitable gave comfort to British listeners, it was anathema, of course, to American isolationists. Under the headline 'BRITONS URGE CLOSE TIE, EVEN UNION, WITH U.S.', the *Chicago Tribune*'s report dwelt on the fact that other MPs had followed Churchill's lead. One, the former War Minister Leslie Hore-Belisha, had even advocated common Anglo-American citizenship.[151] Overall, though, the speech appears to have had the desired effect of boosting American confidence in Britain's capacity to win.[152]

In the Commons, the speech was warmly received by MPs on all sides, even if it provided less drama than the story of the destruction of the French Fleet. Nicolson thought it 'a moderate and well-balanced' effort which 'did not try to arouse enthusiasm but only to give guidance'.[153] Colville, watching from the gallery, thought that there was 'less oratory than usual' and that MPs had been most interested in the bases issue. 'On the whole, except for bright patches—like that about "the Führer's reputation for veracity", which had a great success—the speech seemed to drag and the House, which is not used to sitting in August, was languid.'[154] This may have been a little harsh: Channon dismissed it as 'only another tour de force' but thought his colleagues had loved it.[155] Nevertheless, according to Reuters's parliamentary correspondent, 'there was nothing spectacular about the speech, only the plain facts, the usual touches of humour and the usual contempt for rhetorical devices.'[156]

The popular reception was much more effusive. Churchill had not wanted to repeat the speech over the airwaves in person. 'It would save me a lot of trouble if a record could be taken at the time, so that the speech could be repeated over the wireless in the evening, or such parts of it as are of general interest,' he wrote.[157] Neither Labour nor the Liberals favoured the plan, so it was allowed to drop, but Churchill later returned to the issue more than once.[158] He found broadcasting what he had already said 'a very heavy strain' and thought it 'unsatisfactory from the point of view of delivery'.[159] On this occasion, though, it is clear that the British people did not think so. 'The Prime Minister's speech was received extremely well, according to all reports,' noted the Home Intelligence branch. Furthermore, 'References to the Russian Air Force & closer relations with USA are particularly noted, and many consider this to be the most heartening speech the Premier has yet made.'[160] This suggests that the mass enthusiasm evoked by Churchill's 'War of the Unknown Warrior' speech had now intensified further. There was however 'some danger that people may mistake the Premier's optimism in ultimate victory for a feeling that it is already in sight, and more thoughtful people realise that hard times are ahead and that we may suffer reverses in different parts of the world'.[161] The references to the RAF were 'thought to be completely right—epitomises the feeling of the country'.[162] Nevertheless, the remark about 'The Few' was not as central to the speech's original reception as its later iconic status might lead one to expect.

Diary evidence confirms this, as well as showing that the speech did have some critics. These, however, were few in number and made positive remarks as well as negative ones. O. Smith, a housewife and voluntary worker from London, found it 'as usual splendid and most heartening, although to my mind, it was slightly flawed by the glossing over of the Somaliland debacle and the accustomed refusal to be drawn into any declaration of war aims'.[163] Churchill had resisted the left-wing demand to do so, refusing to offer 'elaborate speculations' about the post-war future.[164] A. N. Gerrard, a clerk from Manchester, commented beforehand that a pacifist friend thought Churchill's speeches 'excellent just lately'—but he didn't agree with her. 'He gives the impression, when he speaks, of knowing he's expected to "deliver the goods" & of endeavouring to make his speeches of such quality that they will be handed down to posterity as in Lincoln's Gettysburg address for instance. I think he fails miserably.' Once he had read (not listened) to the speech Gerrard wrote that 'apart from one or two phrases' he found 'nothing interesting or remotely inspiring in it'. Nobody wanted Churchill to make elaborate speculations, 'just a plain statement of what we hope to build up if and when we win this war'. However, even this stern judge liked 'the warning of trials ahead—perhaps 1942. This is surely the way to over-come apathy & false optimism.'[165]

A couple of weeks before 'The Few' speech, Cecil King recorded in his diary a conversation with Duff Cooper. Cooper 'mentioned that Churchill had said to him how odd it was that in the last war he could never say the right thing [...] while in this war everything he said was right, though he felt now just the same as he felt then'. Cooper also said he agreed with King's analysis 'that Churchill was quite unaware of his power in the coun-try and strangely afraid of the Tory majority in the House'.[166] In June 1940, a Mass-Observation survey suggested a 58 per cent approval rating.[167] In July, the Gallup poll gave him a rating of 88 per cent.[168] His speeches surely contributed to this rapid surge in popularity, although to exactly what degree is hard to establish; and, as we have seen, the figures themselves need to be taken with a pinch of salt. A more important and in fact more easily answered question is whether or not the speeches were the crucial factor that persuaded the British people to continue the war when otherwise they might not have done. Here it is important to separate out the evidence of contemporaries in the summer of 1940 from assertions based on memory.

Not all memories of speeches were positive, of course. After Churchill's death, the novelist Evelyn Waugh described him as 'simply a "Radio Personality" who outlived his prime. "Rallied the nation" indeed! I was a serving soldier in 1940. How we despised his orations.'[169] However, it is much harder to find retrospective negative comments than it is to uncover critical judgements made at the time. The broadcaster Ludovic Kennedy offered this recollection of the Dunkirk speech: 'when we heard it, we knew in an instant, that everything would be all right'.[170] Elisabeth Small, a school-girl in 1940, recalled: 'the atmosphere just *turned* and I can hear Churchill's voice now, "we shall fight on the beaches…we shall fight in the field and in the streets…We shall never surrender." Everybody was cheering, quite *extraordinary*.'[171] Nella Last remembered shortly after the war that when she heard 'that husky, rather stuttering voice acclaiming we would "fight on the beaches, on the streets"' she felt her 'head rise as if galvanised and a feeling that "I'll be there—count on me; I'll not fail you"'.[172] Kennedy, possibly, was recalling the newsreader's recitation of the speech. But as Churchill did not broadcast the speech himself, and as both Small and Last recalled hearing his *voice*, it is clear that their memories were at fault.[173] Furthermore, there are no contemporary accounts of radio listeners—as opposed to MPs in the

Commons—cheering the speeches as delivered. There was a natural tendency later for people to exaggerate their reactions. Hugh Dalton was one of those present at the ministerial meeting in May at which Churchill signalled his intention to fight on. His words were indeed received enthusiastically: Dalton's diary that day recorded 'a murmur of approval round the table'.[174] When he published the entry in his autobiography he altered the key words to 'loud cries of approval'.[175]

A common theme in memories of the speeches is their supposedly instantaneous effect. They are said to have wrought an immediate change in the atmosphere and to have given people new strength at once. Such claims need to be treated with considerable caution. Last did record such a reaction in her diary after hearing Churchill's first speech as Prime Minister. However, contrary to her later memory, the Dunkirk speech at the time made her feel 'grave and rather sad', as we have seen. This is not to imply that she was not a genuine admirer of Churchill in 1940. It is merely to note that she projected her most positive memories of his speeches on to what, retrospectively, seemed like his most emotive rhetoric. More generally, we may hazard that the near-universal enthusiasm for Churchillian oratory that emerged in July and August was played back in many people's memories to include May and June as well. The 'best' memories of the period were taken to represent the whole.

There is no question that the British people did respond with much feeling to Churchill's speeches at this crucial time. Many of them did report feeling heartened and inspirited as a result. Myth, however, suggests that the impact of the speeches was immediate, that they worked their results on almost everyone right from the beginning, and that their effect was always to generate optimism. In fact, Churchill did not have an extraordinarily large audience immediately; he took time to build it and to develop its enthusiasm. His speeches, from the beginning, did make many people more optimistic, but initially they made plenty of others feel more pessimistic too. The broadcasts did not send an instantaneous thrill through everyone, and they at first attracted a fair amount of criticism, of varying degrees of thoughtfulness. And, as the contemporary evidence shows, the speeches worked their effects in complex ways, in part because they dealt with issues that now appear obscure but which were of vital interest at the time. As the immediate context faded, the famous phrases were repeated time and again, and other elements of the speeches dropped more and more out of view. The focus on the great quotations helped lend the desperate months of 1940, in retrospect, a 'terrible beauty' built of nostalgia.[176]

In sum, there is no concrete evidence *from 1940* to prove that Churchill's speeches were the decisive factor influencing Britain's willingness to fight on. Their strongest impact was felt only in late summer, weeks after the crucial Cabinet decisions of late May had been taken and after the publication of the French armistice terms made it clear that there could be no hope of Hitler offering a reasonable peace settlement. The Home Intelligence and Mass–Observation reports show neither any signs of the growth of a popular peace movement nor any indication that Churchill's speeches were the magic ingredient that prevented one emerging. The speeches' contribution to morale was undoubtedly genuine, but they were only one part of a rich and sophisticated propaganda diet, most elements of which have now been forgotten.[177] Churchill's rhetoric represented to the outside world, and to many of the British people themselves, Britain's determination to carry on the war until victory. But we must not overstate the speeches' effect on public opinion, or allow the vagaries of collective memory to trump hard-headed factual analysis of reactions recorded at the time.

3

'The Duke of Marlborough All Over Again'

In September 1940, the *Luftwaffe* switched its tactics. Abandoning the attempt to achieve air superiority as the prelude to invasion, it intensified its bombing attacks instead. The heavy raids on London and other cities lasted until May 1941. This created new problems for the management of morale. This, however, was not the only rhetorical challenge that Churchill had to face; and in fact, of the four broadcasts he made that autumn, only one of them was aimed directly at the British people. He needed to project himself internationally, both to neutrals and to peoples under enemy occupation. At the same time he worked to secure his political position in Britain, and to fend off criticism from both Left and Right. As the better war news of the winter turned to fresh disaster in the spring, Churchill required all his persuasive skills to maintain his position, at a time when critics of his leadership were hovering ready to pounce.

On 5 September, two days before the worst of the bombing onslaught began, Churchill gave a review of the war situation in the Commons. He insisted that the figures for air raid casualties should not be published in advance: he would give them out himself.[1] The speech 'invoked little enthusiasm' among MPs.[2] Amongst the public, according to the Home Intelligence Report, 'it aroused less interest than his previous speeches, though it was well-liked'. Churchill's promise to review the confusing and problematic air raid warning system was especially welcome.[3] The candid observation that 'In many cases it is physically impossible to give the alarm before the attack' was deleted from the speech draft.[4] The City found the speech reassuring.[5] A few days later, once the Blitz had begun in earnest, Churchill made a broadcast, possibly in response to a suggestion by Attlee.[6] Beforehand, the Ministry of Information provided the Prime Minister with a list of questions which its researchers had found to be of concern to the public. These included 'why are German bombers apparently allowed to circle round and round dropping bombs?' and 'Is it true that the Jews in the East End are seeking only to save their own skins?'[7] In her diary, the novelist Naomi Royde Smith provided an insightful analysis of how Churchill's broadcast—which did not address these issues directly—worked to allay public fears:

> In the first place, though there was no announcement: no revelation: no *news* in it, an impression of being taken into the speaker's confidence was given from the outset, by the simple device of quoting figures in such a way as to give them the full status of inside, official information.
>
> *You will understand* (our flattered attention is at once roused) *that whenever the weather is favourable waves of German bombers, protected by fighters, often 300 or 400 at a time, surge over this island, especially the promontory of Kent.*

She explained:

> The statement of facts made, a transition to conjecture follows and, as the imagined but not imaginary danger is presented, long successions of monosyllables beat on the ear like the sound of an army marching to drums. *We cannot tell when they will try to come. We can not be sure in fact that they will try at all. But no one should blind himself to the fact that a heavy, full-scale invasion…*
>
> […] It sounds simple enough, but how few men can do it, and how few leaders speaking on such an occasion would have had the judgement and restraint to set the prayer 'Let God defend the right' in the heart and not the end of their oration?[8]

Indeed, Churchill had ignored a suggestion from John Dill, Chief of the Imperial General Staff (CIGS), that he move the line to the conclusion.[9] The public received the speech 'with approbation and quiet confidence'. As Churchill clearly hoped, people's expectation of invasion increased, but it was believed that Britain was well prepared to deal with one.[10] Although Operation Sea Lion (the German invasion plan) was put on hold a few days later, this was by no means the last time that Churchill would make such a warning.

Churchill not only enjoyed wide public backing; he was also cementing his hold on the levers of power in Westminster. At the beginning of October, Chamberlain at last stood down from office, on grounds of ill-health. He was suffering from terminal cancer and died within weeks. His resignation enabled Churchill to reshuffle his government, albeit perhaps not as radically as he would have liked. It also allowed him to replace Chamberlain as leader of the Conservatives, and thus secure his political future, although at some slight cost to his reputation as a truly 'national' leader wholly above squalid party concerns.[11] Rather than basking in his new position, though, he remained extremely sensitive to criticism. The failed Free French raid on Dakar (in Senegal), which had been backed by the British, had turned into an embarrassing failure. With no sign that America would enter the war, and with Britain being pounded by bombs, it was unsurprising that he should overreact to the cavils of the press. Still nervous of the Tory Party and eager to overcome its past hostility to him, he must have intensely disliked having the *Daily Mirror* and the *Sunday Pictorial* suggest that his reshuffle was a mere 'shunting of mediocrities' and that the 'paralysing influence' of Chamberlain lived on in his own government.[12] (Both papers were part of the same editorial stable.) Nor can he have relished the *Mirror*'s condemnation of the 'imbecility' of the Dakar episode, or its accusations that the government was sucking up to General Franco's dictatorial regime in neutral Spain.[13] '[A]n endeavour was being made to poison relations between members of the Government,' he fulminated. 'It was intolerable that those bearing the burden of supreme responsibility at this time should be subject to attacks of this kind.'[14]

In his Commons review of the war on 8 October, Churchill said that 'there is a tone in certain organs of the Press […] not only upon the Dakar episode but in other and more important issues, that is so vicious and malignant that it would be almost indecent if applied to the enemy'.[15] The Labour MP Aneurin Bevan, who was to be one of Churchill's most persistent critics, responded with an excoriating attack on the government's deficiencies, including its internment of enemy aliens (many of whom were anti-Nazi refugees) and its failure to provide deep bomb shelters. The lack of these was causing resentment in the East End of London, Bevan claimed: 'sometimes the right hon. Gentleman's ear is too sensitively attuned to the bugle notes of Blenheim for him to hear the whispering in the streets.'[16] The Prime Minister, however, suffered little damage from the debate, even if he did not put all doubts to rest. The Conservative MP Cuthbert Headlam thought the speech admirable—'full of vim, but not too much buck'. He noted that Churchill had blamed the local commander for the errors that had led to the failure at Dakar (thus acquitting De Gaulle himself of blame): 'he got away with this, but surely this is no excuse for our not having taken Dakar weeks ago—when we decided to go for the French Fleet?'[17] In spite of Churchill's anger, the government took no action against the mainstream press, beyond some rather cack-handed attempts to lean on the offending papers in private. (The communist *Daily Worker*, however, was banned in 1941.)[18] Cecil King, who was on the receiving end of these efforts, concluded that 'the Press reaction to Churchill's speech had not been quite what they [ministers] had hoped for'.[19] The public reaction was also muted. According to Mass-Observation, the speech 'seemed to have rather a confused effect on people, perhaps partly owing to the mixture of confidence and depressing warnings. It was not so apropos to the feeling of the moment as most of his previous speeches.'[20] Private comments were favourable, although Home Intelligence noted: 'For the first time sympathetic papers criticised a speech of the Prime Minister—the *Mirror*, for its too optimistic note, and the *Herald* "for its unjustified rebuke of the Press".'[21] Churchill would doubtless have poured scorn on the idea that the *Mirror* was sympathetic.

In his speech accepting the leadership of the Conservative Party the day after his Commons statement, Churchill justified the move partly on practical grounds. As he was in continuous contact with the other party leaders on domestic issues, he said, it would be convenient if he himself could speak for the Conservative Party with its authority. He also addressed the question of whether he could sincerely identify himself 'with the main historical conceptions of Toryism'. He alluded obliquely to his Liberal phase, saying he would not attempt to justify it. But he declared 'that at all times according to my lights and throughout the changing scenes throughout which we are all hurried I have always faithfully served two public causes which I think stand supreme—the maintenance of the enduring greatness of Britain and her Empire and the historical continuity of our Island life'.[22] This claim to have represented Tory values even when outside the Tory Party was a nice piece of footwork; at later general elections he would spend much effort arguing that the Conservative Party was the inheritor and defender of *Liberal* values![23]

Even more skilful was his tribute in the Commons to Chamberlain, after the latter's death in November. Here he faced the difficult task of giving the customary eulogy without his praise appearing either implausible or insincere in the light of the two men's past differences. He did this by putting Chamberlain's mistakes within the context of the ordinary condition of human frailty and the unpredictability of events:

> In one phase men seem to have been right, in another they seem to have been wrong. Then again, a few years later, when the perspective of time has lengthened, all stands in a different setting. There is a new proportion. There is

another scale of values. History with its flickering lamp stumbles along the trail of the past, trying to reconstruct its scenes, to revive its echoes, and kindle with pale gleams the passion of former days.

Chamberlain's errors needed to be seen in perspective: he had above all acted with *honour*. 'Whatever else history may or may not say about these terrible, tremendous years, we can be sure that Neville Chamberlain acted with perfect sincerity according to his lights and strove to the utmost of his capacity and authority, which were powerful, to save the world from the awful, devastating struggle in which we are now engaged,' Churchill said. 'This alone will stand him in good stead as far as what is called the verdict of history is concerned.'[24] (Note the phrase 'according to his lights', which Churchill had so recently used about himself.) The picture he painted, of course, was an imaginative reinvention of the historical Chamberlain, who had often been arrogant, egotistical, rigid, and petty, as Churchill himself well knew. But Churchill was aiming less at accurate description than at a prescription for a model form of manly political conduct. By claiming that his great rival had lived up to this ideal, in terms of character if not judgement, Churchill was not merely demonstrating his typical magnanimity but was also putting past controversies to bed in the interests of party unity.

The domestic dimension of Churchill's speeches during the autumn was equalled, and perhaps eclipsed, by the international one. They continued to receive praise in those parts of the American media that were sympathetic to Britain's cause; at the same time there was little in them for the isolationists to latch on to and criticize.[25] This was not accidental. As Churchill publicly acknowledged after Roosevelt won his third term in November, 'Everyone in this island—Parliament, Ministers, the press the public—discreetly abstained from the slightest expression of opinion about the domestic, political, and Party conflicts of the great democracy of the United States.'[26] Churchill also tactfully abstained from making grand predictions about the future of Anglo-American relations of the kind he had offered in 'The Few' speech in August. When the 'destroyers for bases' deal had been officially signed, he did not repeat his suggestions that the two countries would have to become 'somewhat mixed up together'. Rather he emphasized the formal nature of the agreement (which he had initially tried to keep informal) and said that 'Only very ignorant persons' would think that it affected even 'in the smallest degree the non-belligerency of the United States'.[27]

The USA was not the only significant non-belligerent country. Spain was sympathetic to the Axis and formed a potential threat to Britain's position at Gibraltar. The British were anxious to avoid Franco throwing in his lot with Hitler and Mussolini and to prevent him supplying them with raw materials. (Spain was an important source of tungsten ore, vital for munitions.) To blockade the Spanish risked pushing them into the arms of the Axis; not to do so meant permitting leakage. The path chosen was essentially one of pragmatic appeasement. In his October war review, Churchill dressed up a 'pedestrian' Foreign Office draft speech section in his own characteristic style.[28] 'Far be it from us to lap Spain and her own economic needs in the wide compass of our blockade,' he said. 'All we seek is that Spain will not become a channel of supply to our mortal foes. Subject to this essential condition, there is no problem of blockade that we will not study in the earnest desire to meet Spain's needs and aid her revival.'[29] The heavily controlled Spanish press covered the speech extensively—but omitted all the references to Spain.[30] For the rest of the war, Franco successfully played both sides against the middle, keeping out of the war whilst at the same time shoring up his own precarious position for the future.[31] In the same speech Churchill took a firmer line against Japan—which had just signed a pact with Germany and Italy—announcing the reopening of the Burma Road. Noting that the Three-Power Pact was aimed mainly against the United States, Churchill observed that 'Neither of the branches of the English-speaking race is accustomed to react to threats of violence by submission'.[32] This could be read as a way of threatening Japan 'with the combined forces of the British and American navies'.[33] It was a clever way too of turning the tables on the isolationists, by seeming to offer backing to America rather than begging for its help.

By contrast with these other countries, neutral Ireland was merely an irritant—although, as far as Churchill was concerned, it was an extremely irritating irritant. His own involvement with the Irish question was long-standing. He had played an important part in the negotiation of the Anglo-Irish Treaty of 1921, which had given Southern Ireland de facto independence, Northern Ireland remaining part of the UK. Churchill's special bugbear was Eamon De Valera, the Irish Prime Minister, who in 1938 had secured from Britain the return of some key ports originally reserved to the British under the Treaty. With Ireland remaining neutral, their use was denied to Britain at a time when it needed all possible help to secure her Atlantic lifeline. As Éire was still technically a British Dominion, Churchill did not acknowledge her right to stay out of the war; many Irish thought 'that Mr Churchill hates Ireland and would not be sorry to set the clock back with a strong hand'.[34] Nonetheless, others viewed him as a 'grand wicked chap', and his summer 1940 speeches had been received with 'detached but genuine admiration'.[35] But he undid this good work during his November Commons war review. He stated that Britain's inability to make use of 'the South and West Coasts of Ireland to refuel our flotillas and aircraft and thus protect the trade by which Ireland as well as Great Britain lives' was 'a most heavy and grievous burden and one which should never have been placed on our shoulders, broad though they be'.[36]

He must have known that this would create uproar in Ireland, so why say it? Or rather, granted that the remark was the product of genuine, deep feeling, why say it exactly now? Churchill made the comment on 5 November, the very day of the US presidential election, knowing that it would be reported too late to have an impact on the influential Irish vote. That is to say, he could at this point let off steam with comparative safety. The UK representative in Dublin explained to the Irish that the episode should be seen as a 'typically Churchillian' intervention: the Dominions Office had not been asked for its view in advance.[37] There may have been a deeper political motive too. MPs were restive over a range of issues, including Britain's food situation in the face of U-boat warfare. Some Tories wanted drastic remedies, perhaps even a British reoccupation of Éire to secure the ports. That was a course that Churchill had rejected earlier in the year—he saw the danger to Anglo-American relations—but a bit of fighting talk might help ease the pressure for this risky action.[38]

Not everyone in Britain was persuaded. The right-wing *National Review* portrayed Churchill's Irish troubles as a form of poetic justice—he was now being haunted by his earlier support for nationalist aspirations. But overall he found strong backing for his words in the House of Commons and from the British press. Even George Bernard Shaw threw in his weight behind the Prime Minister.[39] In Ireland, of course, it was a different matter. De Valera told his parliament that as long as the country remained neutral there could be no question of handing over the ports. 'Any attempt to bring pressure to bear on us by any side—by any of the belligerents—by Britain—could only lead to bloodshed.'[40] Even Irish people who were sympathetic to Britain thought that 'Churchill has certainly dropped a brick this time'.[41] The *Irish Times*, for its part, declared that he had committed 'no breach of propriety' but criticized the rather less restrained remarks made by some

Labour MPs.[42] The Churchill–De Valera spat led to rumours amongst the German population of a Nazi invasion of Ireland to forestall a British one.[43] What is interesting, though, is that after this controversy Churchill did not make another speech so overtly critical of Irish neutrality until the end of the European war.[44] He must have felt that do so was either unnecessary or likely to be counter-productive. Either way, he was capable of restraining his impetuosity if he wished.

Churchill's messages to neutrals were not addressed directly to them but were made in the form of passing comments during speeches to the House of Commons. By contrast he made explicit efforts to communicate with the peoples of occupied Europe. A short broadcast to the Czechoslovaks on the second anniversary of the Munich agreement promised that 'The hour of your deliverance will come'.[45] He followed this in October with an address to the French. Some in the world's press assumed that he did this because he knew that Pétain's Vichy-based government was about to enter into talks with the Germans, with a possible view to rejoining the war on their side.[46] In fact, the crucial information was received after the broadcast was made, but the Prime Minister was already angry and despairing at Vichy's attitude.[47] Churchill read the speech twice—once in English and once in French. He insisted that the translation should be into 'not too French French'.[48] According to John Colville, on the day of the broadcast, 'just before dinner he came into the room, where the French BBC expert and translator, M. Duchesne, was standing and exclaimed: "Where is my frog speech?" M. Duchesne looked pained.'[49]

The translator's real name was Michel Saint-Denis. He was a well-known actor and theatre director; 'Jacques Duchesne' was the pseudonym he adopted for his wartime BBC work. Years later, Saint-Denis recalled the hours he spent helping Churchill prepare and translate the speech:

> He was satisfied when I suggested 'la guigne' for 'bad luck' and was delighted when we thought of 'rire bien qui rira le dernier' for all will come right. And he was delighted when he suggested himself that his first call to the Resistance Movement should end with a sentence which he had read all over France during the war of 1914–18: 'Les oreilles ennemies vous écoutent'.[50]

Saint-Denis also remembered that throughout the rehearsal Churchill was 'as attentive and docile as a good child, he was indeed, angelic, but with sudden fits of temper'. He could not pronounce the rolling French 'r' and 'he could not manage some of the pure vowels such as the "o"s which in

English he likes to exaggerate in a throaty way. He relished the flavour of some words as though he was tasting fruit.' An air raid was in progress as Churchill and his party aides set off to make the broadcast: 'we crossed Downing Street running behind him; the anti-aircraft guns were firing from very close by and the shell bursts over head were followed by the whistling showers of falling splinters'. The group made its way to the underground Cabinet War Rooms and into a room in which BBC technicians were readying their equipment. Churchill sat down in front of the microphone 'perfectly comfortable in his sky-blue siren suit'. But Saint-Denis had to speak first in order to introduce him, and was forced to ask where he should sit:

> He looked about him and seeing that there was no other chair in the room, he replied: 'On my knees'. And leaning back in the armchair, he tapped his thigh. I inserted a leg between his and next moment had seated myself partly on the arm of the chair and partly on his knee.[51]

After Saint-Denis had made his introduction and—presumably—clambered off the prime ministerial lap, Churchill began by repeating the prayer 'Dieu protège La France'. He warned against the enemy's efforts to divide the French and the British, whilst emphasizing Britain's strength and heaping abuse and ridicule on the Führer and the Duce. 'Herr Hitler with his tanks and other mechanical weapons, and also by fifth column intrigue with traitors, has managed to subjugate for the time being most of the finest races in Europe,' Churchill said, 'and his little Italian accomplice is trotting along hopefully and hungrily, but rather wearily and very timidly at his side.' These 'two ugly customers' were planning to devour the French Empire; Alsace-Lorraine was to 'go once again under the German yoke'. Churchill referenced Napoleon and the nineteenth-century statesman Léon Gambetta, as well as urging those in the French Empire and the unoccupied zone of France to acts of resistance.[52] As the US journalist DeWitt MacKenzie noted, the broadcast was 'in essence an effort to mend the bonds of a comradeship which had been sealed in blood, and instil in the French the spirit of resistance—or revolt if you will—against their German masters'.[53]

On the face of it, there was nothing controversial about his interpretation of French history. However, his use of the term 'fifth column' (first coined during the Spanish Civil War) meant that he strayed inadvertently into contested territory. This would have been understood by many French leftists as referring to the capitalist conspiracy that supposedly drove appeasement at the behest of a sinister network, 'the two hundred families'.[54] Churchill was surely unaware that his words might be received in such a way, and it is notable that he avoided any explicit criticism of Pétain. This was in line with other British propaganda which tended to portray the revered Marshal as 'a venerable, though unfortunate statesman unable to resist Axis pressure'.[55]

It is also worth noting that the broadcast went out to the French colonial Empire as well as to metropolitan France. This was significant because imperial rivalries had long been a cause of friction in Anglo-French relations. Recognizing this, Churchill's personal assistant Desmond Morton had suggested to him an addition to the speech: 'Do not believe the lies you hear on your Boche-controlled wireless, and in your Boche-controlled Press. We English are not trying to dismember the French Empire, or to steal the French Colonies for ourselves.'[56] Churchill inserted a comment on these lines in his draft by hand, adding: 'We do not covet anything from any nation except their respect.'[57] According to Saint-Denis:

> After he had finished there was a prolonged silence. It was 9.15. Nobody moved. We were deeply stirred. Then Churchill stood up; his eyes were full of tears.
>   'We have made history tonight,' he said.[58]

According to a British analysis of French radio output:

> Paris took a day to decide what notice, if any, to take of Churchill's call to the French people. Even then, it first adopted the indirect method: the French Ambassador in Washington had remarked on the omission of any reference to the British blockade. But it soon received fuller treatment. It was even acknowledged to be 'good for an Englishman'. The reply is that England intends 'to save France against the will of the French' and there follows a series of references to the past, ranging from the deportation of Napoleon to the evacuation of Dunkirk and the bombing of Dakar, each undertaken 'to save France'.

The first meeting between Hitler and Pétain was then used to distract attention from Churchill's speech.[59] However, it would seem that the broadcast was received with great interest by the French population; the BBC was very widely listened to. Pierre Dupuy, Canada's chargé d'affaires in France, related the following story:

> The headmaster of a lycée at Versailles [...] said to his pupils on the day of the Prime Minister's broadcast, 'Today is not an ordinary day. We are going to hear the Leader of the Allied Forces. In spite of circumstances, we still remain the

Allies of Britain and so you must do everything you can to hear him. The broadcast will be badly jammed; will each of you take down every sentence which he can hear properly and we will piece it together tomorrow'. The next day each schoolboy came back with everything he had heard and the form spent the better part of the day piecing together Churchill's speech in the right order.[60]

Churchill continued to take an interest in what was being done with the speech; Duff Cooper informed him at the end of November that it had been broadcast nine times already and that it would be frequently rebroadcast. 'Moreover, in the news bulletins, various quotations from the record of your speech have frequently been used as appropriate comments upon the news of the day,' Cooper wrote. 'Sometimes these have been placed side by side with quotations from *Mein Kampf*, to point a contrast between your feelings for France and those of Hitler.'[61]

Churchill's speeches were important not only to the French but to resisters elsewhere in occupied Europe. Excerpts were printed on leaflets and dropped by air.[62] They were also dropped on Germany but it is hard to believe they had much effect there. The Polish underground fighter Jan Karski recalled how his network received news in code from the outside world and supplied it to the illegal press: 'Speeches by Churchill and Roosevelt, important interviews with the members of the Polish government-in-exile and news from the fighting fronts arrived in Poland and were circulated widely within a few hours,' he wrote. 'The services supplied not only the texts of speeches but comments and explanatory notes.'[63] And in 1943, for example, one German paper in Slovakia claimed that after Allied victories 'Jews crowded the streets and squares grinning shamelessly and telling the people about the enemy's broadcasts, manufacturing rumours and spreading every speech made by Roosevelt, Churchill, or Stalin'.[64] It seems very doubtful that this was literally true but the allegation does show both how the speeches' impact was feared by the Nazis, and how they were used as an opportunity to whip up anti-Semitism.

At the end of December 1940 Churchill decided to address the Italians—a somewhat different proposition to his French speech, as he would be talking to an enemy people rather than an occupied one. He had been asked to do this by Hugh Dalton, Minister of Economic Warfare, in collaboration with the Foreign Office. According to Dalton, Rex Leeper, director of the FO's political intelligence department, had provided a 'draft broadcast by the PM telling the Italians that we love them, that the Germans don't, and that they should get rid of Mussolini'. Dalton and Lord Halifax—still Foreign Secretary, but about to be shunted to the Washington Embassy and replaced by Eden—then spoke to Churchill who agreed to the plan. 'We propose that in his broadcast he should cite his letter to Mussolini when he became PM and Mussolini's stuffy reply,' Dalton wrote in his diary. ' "Only", says the PM, "I won't agree to their keeping Abyssinia." We agree that, at this stage, this need not be mentioned.'[65] Churchill—who had praised Mussolini in extravagant terms during a visit to Italy in the 1920s—had not seemed overly concerned about the 1935 invasion of Abyssinia at the time that it took place, but recent events had clearly hardened his attitude. At the same time, when holding out the hand of friendship to the Italians, it was necessary to tackle the issue delicately. By now, the British were scoring victories against the Italians in North Africa, and, in a Commons war review the day before his chat with Dalton and Halifax, Churchill had suggested that the enemy troops did not have their hearts in their work.[66] Count Ciano, Mussolini's Foreign Minister, noted that this parliamentary speech was, 'naturally, hard on us, for he says cruel things as to the value of our forces in Libya, where the situation continues to be serious. It is an able speech, in which many hints can be read between the lines.'[67]

On the day of the broadcast Churchill secured the Cabinet's approval for the disclosure of his previously secret correspondence with Mussolini.[68] He also summoned Alexander Cadogan, Permanent Secretary at the FO, to discuss the speech. Cadogan recorded: 'he wanted to protest against all our amendments to his broadcast. I persuaded him to take one, but had to let him discard the others.'[69] The introduction to the speech included a paean to the Risorgimento, the Italian unification movement of the nineteenth century, and stressed the fact that it had been strongly supported by Britain. The FO advised: 'Sentence beginning "All that great movement of Liberalism". It may be as well to omit any reference to Liberalism. Moreover, reference to British aid may perhaps be regarded in Italy as patronising.'[70] Churchill removed the phrase about Liberalism but retained his comment on British aid.[71] Overall, however, the substance of his speech was in tune with the Foreign Office draft, even though he expressed it in different language.[72]

After opening with warm words about past Anglo-Italian friendship, Churchill lamented the fact that the two countries were now at war and hinted at more powerful British offensives in the future: 'Presently we shall be forced to come to closer grips'. How had this sorry state of affairs come about? Churchill's answer was to place the blame exclusively on Mussolini. 'That he is a great man I do not deny,' he said, but after eighteen years in power he had led Italy 'to the horrid verge of ruin'. He went on, 'It is all one, one man, who, against the Crown and Royal Family of Italy, against the Pope and all the authority of the Vatican and of the Roman Catholic Church, against the wishes of the Italian people who had no lust for this war—one man has arrayed the trustees and inheritors of ancient Rome upon the side of the ferocious, pagan barbarians.'[73] (Note the effort to enlist Italian religious feeling against the godlessness of the Nazis.) The Foreign Office had worried that to suggest that the Pope and the Italian royal family were opposed to Mussolini might put them in an embarrassing position. Churchill plainly did not mind that or may even have intended it.[74] As for the Abyssinian dispute, he played down its importance: 'I declare—and my words will go far—that nothing that has happened in that Abyssinian quarrel can account for or justify the deadly strife which has now broken out between us.' As agreed with his colleagues, he avoided any promise that Italy might be able to retain the territory if Mussolini were jettisoned, but he did not openly suggest that she would have to lose it. He threatened that if the war between Britain and Italy continued, the Italian Empire in Africa would be torn 'to shreds and tatters', but this left open the possibility that parts of it could be kept if Italy dropped out of the war.[75]

Churchill criticized Italy's recent invasion of Greece, but again pinned the blame solely on Mussolini. 'One man, and one man alone, ordered Italian soldiers to ravage their neighbour's vineyard.' He read out his May correspondence with the Duce—written before Italy joined the war, of course—in full. In his letter Churchill had declared that he had 'never been the enemy of Italian greatness, nor ever at heart the foe of the Italian law-giver', i.e. Mussolini. Mussolini's reply had stated that Italy's future conduct would be guided by honour and by its respect for existing German–Italian agreements.[76] (Harold Nicolson thought the exchange of letters proved that Churchill had not been 'a war-monger but a heroic pacifist'.)[77] Churchill now stated that 'Any one can see who it was wanted peace, and who it was that meant to have war'. He ended by looking forward to the time 'when the Italian nation will once more take a hand in shaping its own fortunes'.[78] The implication was clear. The repeated emphasis on Mussolini's unique guilt suggested that other members of his regime need not fear that, if they overthrew him, they would be held to account for any crimes they had committed at his behest. The speech also left open the possibility that Britain might be willing to make peace with a post-Mussolini Italy: it was he alone who formed an obstacle to renewed Anglo-Italian amity. On the other hand, the option of making peace with Mussolini himself was now very publicly shut down.[79]

The broadcast was certainly understood as a peace move by many at the time, but this was not portrayed in the Anglo-American press as a sign of weakness. *The Times* supported Churchill's message, arguing that the Italian people should be given the chance to show that Mussolini did not speak in their name.[80] *The Glasgow Herald* said that if Churchill's 'striking example of "open diplomacy"' was met by the overthrow of Mussolini, the British people would be willing to help a new Italian government to an honourable position in the Europe of the future.[81] In the United States—where the broadcast received a wide audience—Sol Bloom, the chairman of the House of Representatives Foreign Affairs Committee, described it as 'a last appeal to reason by the Italians before the Nazis penetrate Italy'.[82] According to the *St Petersburg Times*, a Florida newspaper, 'Winston Churchill, Britain's shrewd, eloquent Prime Minister, believed that the deeply religious Italian people might listen to peace proposals during the Christmas season'.[83] The *New York Times* said that Churchill's appeal would 'stand as one of the great documents of the war. This is a diplomatic offensive on a grand scale.'[84] This probably exaggerated the amount of thought that Churchill had given to the problem. It seems that he acceded to the FO's initiative without any great expectation that it would bear fruit: there is no evidence that he really thought that Italian morale was about to collapse and that his speech could make a decisive difference. But there was a strong tendency to assume that he must have had 'definite reason for his utterance', and there was an attendant risk that his seeming confidence would come back to haunt him if the Italian regime did not crumble.[85]

Considerable lengths were taken to ensure that Italians could actually hear the speech. It was broadcast on both the normal wavelength used for Italy and two adjacent ones. These were announced right beforehand 'so that if the usual Italian wave is jammed, people in Italy can quickly switch over'. The Italian translation was read out first; then Churchill broadcast in English.[86] In addition, the speech was relayed in Italian to the USA and sent back via short-wave to Italy. The text was also telegraphed to Cairo, Athens, and Jerusalem and broadcast from those places throughout the following week.[87] It is impossible to say how many Italians actually heard the speech, but they were allowed to read it—or rather, most of it. Two important sections were missing from the Italian press reports: first, Churchill's letter to Mussolini, and second, the passage where he blamed Mussolini alone for Italy's entry into the war.[88] An official statement characterized the broadcast as 'a substantial appeal for a compromise peace' and as a confession of British weakness.[89] Italian external radio propaganda took the speech as 'proof of the right corner that Britain is in' and saw in it 'a vain hope that Italy will throw down her arms'.[90] Fascists scoffed at Churchill's interpretation of history, 'emphasizing particularly that Britain's support of the Risorgimento was fictitious'. The Princess of Piedmont applied for membership of the Fascist Party, a move seen as an indirect protest at Churchill's 'interference' in Italian affairs.[91] Although the true popular reaction is difficult to gauge, there is no sign that the speech was particularly effective either in splitting the regime or in dividing the people from it.

The broadcast was widely heard in Britain, achieving 62.2 per cent of the home audience. (Churchill's speech to the French had been heard by 49 per cent of British listeners; it was liked but did not attract much comment.)[92] It was well received, but the impact was not deep. Using this speech as an example, a Mass-Observation report at this time noted that it was rare for people to express opinions about politicians except 'when a notable speech has been made or because some political personality has been featured in the news. Even when this publicity might be expected to arouse comment from each diarist it does not do so to any great extent.'[93] Of the few diarists who made comments, J. Lippold, a buyer in his thirties, was fairly typical. He saw the speech as 'a very straight statement and warning [...] the truth will out and Mr Churchill gave it to the Italian people fair and square'.[94] 'So glad [the] Govt does understand that a revolt of oppressed peoples is needed,' wrote the teacher C. H. Miller.[95] Evelyn Oakley, who worked in a Glasgow shipping office, thought it the greatest speech she had ever heard. The next day she recorded a conversation with her colleagues:

> Mr Churchill's speech formed the chief topic of conversation this morning. Miss Smith praised it. Mr Mitchell said, 'It was expected. It will have some effect.' Miss Bousie was shocked and antagonistic. 'What venom, I dislike such speeches. He made me quake'. I, 'You quake. It is to be hoped he makes the Italians quake'. She, 'Yes, but what will they not do to us in revenge.'[96]

According to J. H. Millington, a young civil servant, 'Mr Churchill's speech to the Italian people was discussed in all quarters with considerable interest, although many confessed that they failed to understand just what he was "getting at", and were a little sceptical of its effect on the Italians."[97] Although it seems clear enough that he was 'getting at' the need for regime change, it was understandable if some people felt slightly bemused. Churchill was, at the close of 1940, still feeling his strategic way and his efforts at 'open diplomacy' reflected this. He was temporarily flushed with military victory, and basically confident of ultimate success, but it was unclear what contribution the successes in North Africa could make to the ultimate defeat of the Axis. With the USSR and the USA not yet in the war, the road ahead was unclear. If the enemy forces could be fragmented, they might yet suffer internal collapse. Hence it was reasonable to float initiatives which, on the face of it, were not very likely to bear fruit. Thus on the last day of the year Churchill sent a message to Pétain in which he offered British military assistance if the French government should choose to cross to Africa to resume the war. No reply was ever received.[98]

Meanwhile, Churchill's speeches were disseminated widely, representing an important part of Britain's propaganda struggle. Some of the schemes for doing this now appear of rather dubious value, notably the making of a special record of Churchill's Italian broadcast for smuggling into Italy.[99] (The prize for futility must go to a leaflet drop over Germany carrying the text of a Churchill speech—in French.)[100] More obviously useful was the publication early in 1941 of Churchill's war speeches in book form. If this seems rather late, given the urgency of winning over US opinion, there was a reason. Publication of such a collection was under consideration as early as May 1940.[101] In July, Churchill received an offer from Cassell & Co. for an advance of £600 on a 15 per cent royalty in exchange for the US rights.[102] Cassell's—who eventually published the book in Britain—seem to have reached an arrangement with the American publishers G. P. Putnam's. But nothing happened. In early September Churchill received a telegram from Putnam's: 'Fully understand manifold demands on your time and attention but believe American publication your book of speeches this autumn will serve important purpose in crystallizing American opinion therefore respectfully urge you release title and manuscript now awaiting we understand only your approval'.[103]

Part of the delay was explained by the fact that Desmond Flower of Cassell's, who had been going to act as the book's editor, was taken into the army when the work was half-finished.[104] But, as Churchill's Parliamentary Private Secretary Brendan Bracken had already noted, there was also 'a snag' about the selection of speeches to be published. The previous collection, *Arms and the*

Covenant, had been published in 1938, so to continue from that point meant including a number of speeches that were critical of Chamberlain.[105] And Chamberlain, at this point, was still a member of Churchill's government. With his resignation and death, the way was clear for publication, although the topic was still sensitive. Kathleen Hill, Churchill's secretary, noted tactfully, 'It may be thought advisable in Washington to omit the speech made in the House of Commons on 12th November 1940—the tribute to Mr Chamberlain, as I suggest it does not quite come into line with the rest of the book'.[106] In the end, there were two slightly different books, *Into Battle* for the UK (published in February 1941) and *Blood, Sweat, and Tears* for the USA (published in April). The British version was a comprehensive compilation of forty-seven speeches from 5 May 1938 to 9 November 1940. It thus stopped short before the tribute to Chamberlain, which was however the starting point for the next volume, published the following year.[107] The American version, by contrast, published fifty-two speeches, beginning in the same place and continuing to 9 February 1941, with the Chamberlain speech left out. Churchill's son Randolph, the book's new editor, claimed to have made no excisions in the interests of political expediency.[108] But, as we saw in Chapter 1, the peroration of Winston Churchill's Norway debate speech, urging MPs to support Chamberlain's government, was cut. There was now an obvious awkwardness about being seen to have praised or assisted him.

For the remaining years of the war, the publication of a book of Churchill speeches was an annual event.[109] The most popular of these was *The Unrelenting Struggle* (1942), with 55,000 sales in English.[110] The government acquired large numbers of copies of these books in order to send them abroad.[111] This helped generate good publicity in neutral countries, where the reviews were often rapturous.[112] However, publication in those countries was not always easy. A strange story surrounds the Swiss edition of *Into Battle*. Emil Oprecht of the Europa Verlag publishing house, based in Zürich, was keen to publish the book: he was a great supporter of exile writers and of the Allied cause. However, the Swiss authorities, clearly fearful of Nazi pressure, decided that to allow this would be a violation of their strict neutrality policy.[113] In the end, a compromise was reached. Oprecht succeeded in having the book printed in the unoccupied zone of France, using—with their permission—Putnam's imprint rather than Europa Verlag's. It was then imported into Switzerland and released there.[114] It was thus easier to print the volume in German-dominated France than in neutral Switzerland!

Meanwhile, Churchill's efforts to win over the Americans continued. He also had to fend off the arguments made by domestic critics, who said that his government was not doing enough to maximize war production. (These complaints grew in strength throughout 1941.) The two problems were, in fact, related. How could the Americans be persuaded to help the British if it seemed that they were not doing enough to help themselves?[115] Britain was now reaching the limits of its economic resources. After his re-election, Roosevelt had proposed a major scheme of aid to Britain. However, the so-called 'Lend-Lease' programme faced opposition in Congress and took some time to pass into law. The President also sent his friend Harry Hopkins as a personal emissary to Churchill. Hopkins arrived in January 1941, and at a dinner with Churchill 'paid graceful tribute to the PM's speeches which had, he said, produced the most stirring and revolutionary effect on all classes and districts in America. At an American Cabinet meeting the President had had a wireless set brought in so that all might listen to the Prime Minister'.[116] Churchill, for his part, made sure to lay on the star treatment for his guest and to show him Britain's war effort in action. 'We in this island stand four-square in the path of European dictators,' Churchill declared during a surprise visit to Glasgow, a key centre of shipbuilding. With Hopkins sitting shyly behind him on the platform, he added 'I hope that by the end of this year or the beginning of next year we may, in the air and on the land, be at no disadvantage so far as equipment is concerned with the German foe.'[117] A few days later, on top form in the Commons, he defended the government's system for managing production and emphasized that 'this great nation is getting into its war stride'.[118]

Churchill's next major broadcast, on 9 February, was—although cast as a speech to the British people—'addressed very largely to American ears'.[119] Churchill began with a long review of the war. He dwelt on how well Britain had withstood the bombing, on Mussolini's frustrated invasion of Greece, and on the British triumphs in North Africa. He also warned, yet again, of the threat of invasion. This was in spite of the fact that almost a month earlier he had received Enigma decrypts that confirmed an invasion was not probable. But Churchill's willingness to talk up the threat meant that Hopkins went home thinking an invasion was likely soon—which if true added obvious urgency to American efforts to help Britain.[120] Axis propaganda emphasized Churchill's supposed pessimism, even though Goebbels in his diary saw the speech as 'insolent and certain of victory'.[121] At the same time, Churchill made it clear that his demands on America were limited. It now seemed certain, he noted, that the USA would provide the supplies needed for victory. But:

> We do not need the gallant armies which are forming throughout the American Union. We do not need them this year, nor next year; nor any year that I can foresee. But we do need most urgently an immense and continuous supply of war materials and technical apparatus of all kinds.[122]

Of course, he would have liked nothing more dearly than the involvement of the US military, but could not say so openly. The idea that material aid would be sufficient was the basis of the speech's famous conclusion. In addition to Hopkins, Roosevelt had also sent another emissary, Wendell Willkie, the man he had beaten for the presidency the previous November. He had given him a letter of introduction to Churchill, in which he had written out by hand a verse from the poet Henry Wadsworth Longfellow. Churchill read it out:

> ...Sail on, O Ship of State!
> Sail on, O Union, strong and great!
> Humanity with all its fears,
> With all the hopes of future years,
> Is hanging breathless on thy fate!

Churchill then said that his answer to Roosevelt would be:

> Put your confidence in us. Give us your faith and your blessing, and, under Providence, all will be well.
> We shall not fail or falter; we shall not weaken or tire. Neither the sudden shock of battle, nor the long-drawn trials of vigilance and exertion will wear us down. Give us the tools, and we will finish the job.[123]

This was magnificent rhetoric, but as the US military attaché General Lee noted in his diary sometime later, it was essentially 'bravado'. The shortage of manpower meant that, however many weapons it might have, the British army couldn't grow large enough to finish the Nazis off by itself.[124] Indeed, some American critics of Britain came to see the speech as deeply disingenuous.[125] In the end Germany's defeat depended on the involvement of both the USSR and the USA and the deployment of their massive human resources as well as their economic ones. On the other hand, the idea of Britain winning the war single-handed did not look quite as unreal at this moment as it would do shortly, after new Axis successes saw the roll-back of recent British gains.

Churchill was not deluding himself, however. To one sympathetic American he denied 'the idea that we did not want America in the war on our side'. He did not share the view that 'it would be better to have America's industrial help rather than to see the main output going to America's own armed forces if she came into the conflict'.[126] Rather, Churchill's optimistic view was calculated to help Roosevelt's efforts to pass Lend-Lease. The Democratic Senator Bennett C. Clark suggested that his broadcast was aimed at the Senate Foreign Relations Committee and should be considered Churchill's testimony in favour of the President's bill—or 'Roosevelt's dictator bill', as its opponents liked to call it.[127] The speech generated helpful headlines such as 'TOOLS OF WAR ONLY REQUEST' and 'CHURCHILL SAYS AEF NOT NEEDED'.[128] ('AEF' stood for 'American Expeditionary Forces'.) Churchill's statement that he could not foresee the need for US soldiers in any year 'set at rest a doubt that had arisen from an earlier one of Mr Churchill's addresses, in which by saying that American troops would not be needed in 1941 he had made it possible to infer that he saw a need of them later'.[129]

However, those opposed to American military involvement saw things differently. The isolationist Democratic Senator Burton K. Wheeler, a leader of the fight against Lend-Lease, argued that the legislation was in fact intended to give authority to send US troops. Asserting that Churchill's speech had been 'arranged by London and Washington to disarm opposition', he claimed: 'The tools to "finish the job" can be provided without any new legislation. But if we are going to send our men, then we do need this legislation.'[130] The Chicago Tribune argued that Churchill's oratory was invaluable—to Britain. It was the Prime Minister's job to squeeze every last drop of help from the United States if he could. But his speech raised the question of why, if invasion of the home island was really likely, Britain's forces had been dispersed to fight the Axis elsewhere. The paper concluded that American 'war birds' were lying about the urgency of the threat to Britain in order to give Roosevelt 'a free hand to do what he pleases here and abroad'.[131] But such criticisms were not enough to halt the impetus behind Lend-Lease, and the legislation passed the following month.

In Britain, Churchill's broadcast was heard by 70 per cent of the potential audience—his highest figure yet. The speech seems to have been warmly received, although its effects were not uniform.[132] Margery Davis recorded her mother's reaction: 'We must be doing well if he's as cheerful as that.'[133] Vere Hodgson, a charity worker, liked the speech but took a different view of its meaning: 'Mr Churchill's speech has rather sobered me. I was beginning to think there might be no Invasion ... but he thinks there will, it seems. Also I had a feeling the end might be in sight; but he seems to be looking a few years ahead!'[134] There were also some criticisms. Pamela Slater, an architectural assistant, wrote: 'Churchill's speech, rather long and rambling; it emphasised that his mind is still in the 18th century—the Duke of Marlborough all over again. No mention of Peace Aims or the use of any other than military means to bring the war to a successful conclusion.'[135] M. J. Hill, a housewife from Yorkshire, wrote that she admired Churchill's style but wished that he would stop calling the Germans and Italians names: 'I admit it is amusing to hear but it is most undignified to stoop to silly vituperation.'[136] A report by Tom Harrisson of Mass-Observation found that Churchill's broadcast increased the expectation of invasion but noted also 'an appreciable decline in *enthusiasm*' as compared to the response to his previous efforts. The speech had been, 'for the first time, the subject of a small amount of bored or cynical comment (as opposed to the occasional abusive and antagonistic [comment] that has always come from two or three per cent. strongly disapproving of him)'.[137] Home Intelligence painted a much more positive picture. 'Though parts of the speech were said "to have made some people's flesh creep", listeners were also "relieved to feel that they were really hearing the truth".' Churchill's cheerful delivery 'increased the feeling of intimacy with his audience'.[138]

Robert Menzies, the Australian Prime Minister, was of the view that Churchill's vituperative style on this occasion was unseemly. 'No doubt Winston is right to appeal to the lowest common denominator among men—a hymn of hate—"the black hearted, treacherous Italians" &c, but I am quite sure we have a loftier cause than the one his speeches indicate.'[139] Menzies heard the broadcast in Cairo, en route to London, where he was to inject himself into ministers' debates on strategy, as the war took a turn for the worse. An anti-German coup in Yugoslavia in March was followed by a rapid Nazi invasion. The British sent troops from the Middle East to support Greece but when Hitler attacked that country in April they were forced into a humiliating withdrawal. At the same time, the diversion of manpower weakened Britain's position in North Africa, and newly arrived German armoured divisions under Erwin Rommel scored quick victories, undoing recent British gains. Meanwhile, German submarine warfare in the Atlantic was in full swing. On 9 April Churchill gave a war review in the Commons. As 'Chips' Channon noted, 'The moment was ill-chosen, indeed: he had tabled a resolution thanking the Armed Services for what they had done in

Africa—just as news of defeats is pouring in'.[140] Headlam observed that
Churchill had 'to change what he hoped would be a song of victory in to
the old, old story of catastrophe'.[141] However the Commons remained calm
and, according to Mass-Observation, the speech was well received by the
public 'and was as usual praised for its honesty' in not covering up the
facts.[142] In the United States the speech was seen in part as an appeal for US
convoys, as Churchill said that it would be disastrous if American supplies
were to end up at the bottom of the ocean on account of U-Boat sinkings:
'I cannot believe that it would be found acceptable to the proud and resolute people of the United States.'[143]

At the end of April, Churchill gave another broadcast. The Foreign Office
was keen for a speech 'which would have the effect of counteracting any
pessimism which recent events have created in the United States, as well as
in this country', and again the message was tailored towards the Americans.[144]
There is no evidence to support Roosevelt's opponents' allegations that
Washington and London had cooked up the 'give us the tools' speech
together. However this new address did receive American input. W. Averell
Harriman, another Roosevelt envoy then in London, provided Churchill
with an assessment of US public opinion, which he thought was in a state
of jitters. Like a young girl who had agreed to give her hand to a man she
did not know well, America needed reassurance of Britain's strength and
fidelity. 'I believe your friends in America want to hear from you something
along the following lines,' Harriman wrote:

> Confidence in the inevitability of the ultimate outcome.
> British Empire production is still on the increase and will be augmented by the
> flood of material from America increasing monthly for the duration.
> Express faith that America is going to help see that it is delivered.
> The spirit and morale of British people are high—ready to face what may
> come this year. Next year America's industrial output should be mobilised and
> turn the battle to the offensive.

Churchill should not be afraid to 'flatter America a little for aid already
given', Harriman added.[145] Churchill's broadcast broadly reflected this
advice, although doubtless many of Harriman's ideas would have occurred
to the Prime Minister anyway. Churchill's message of faith in America's
power to help Britain win the war was encapsulated in his closing quotation
from a poem by Hugh Clough Ellis: 'westward, look, the land is bright'.
What is significant about the episode is that, as the Americans became
increasingly wrapped up in British affairs, they gained a growing interest in

influencing the public messages that Britain was putting out. Churchill was able to say some things that Roosevelt could not. The President had just announced that the US Navy would extend its patrols in the Atlantic. But whereas he was careful to cast this move as a defensive one, Churchill referred to American 'naval support' for Britain.[146] On Capitol Hill, such words were interpreted by some 'as proof that the step was calculated—at least incidentally—to furnish the greatest help possible to the Royal Navy in maintaining Britain's North Atlantic lifeline'. Here was fresh material for the debate about whether America should help Britain further by supplying convoys for her shipping.[147]

In her *New Yorker* column Mollie Panter-Downes wrote that the speech had gone down well with the British, although Churchill had seemed to gloss over the Greek withdrawal: 'many listeners felt that there was a rather too summary dismissal by the Prime Minister of the public uneasiness over a situation which surely only a ninny could feel completely easy about.'[148] Edward Stebbing, a former shop assistant serving in the army, listened to the speech in hospital where he was recovering from an operation. 'His statement that morale was best in the worst-bombed areas took some swallowing,' he wrote. '"You ——— liar," one of the other patients said.'[149] Mass-Observation, though, found that the speech had a more positive effect than most of Churchill's recent efforts:

> Several people said it made them feel we would win in the end, others that it reassured them or made them feel more confident. There were also a number who said that it made them feel depressed, however, and especially some who seemed disappointed that it contained *no more fresh information* than it did (a very unusual Churchill reaction).[150]

But if Churchill's public popularity remained high, at Westminster he was sailing in troubled waters. His critics started to muster ready for a showdown. The most prominent of them was Lloyd George, Churchill's former colleague and long-time rival. On 6 May Guy Liddell of MI5 wrote in his diary Lloyd George was surrounded by a group of about ten MPs (including former War Secretary Leslie Hore-Belisha) who intended to make an onslaught on the government. 'No personal attack on Winston is contemplated and Lloyd George's ultimate object is to get into the Cabinet on his own terms,' he wrote.[151] The occasion was to be the debate on the progress of the war that took place almost exactly on the anniversary of the Norway debate that had brought down Chamberlain's government the year before.

Lloyd George's particular obsession was the need for a more efficient War Cabinet on the model that he had created as Prime Minister during the First World War, but he was not the only person to be concerned about Churchill's leadership. Robert Menzies agreed with him that Churchill was 'a bad organiser' but at the same time too dictatorial and lacking advisers who would stand up to him.[152] These accusations were by no means wholly fair, but as people cast around for explanations of why the war was going badly, they achieved some plausibility. Lloyd George's Commons speech was not the only one to advance criticisms, but his showdown with Churchill provided the debate's most dramatic moments. He drew attention to the gravity of the situation, called for a 'real War Council', and argued that the brilliant Churchill needed 'a few more ordinary persons', to point out to him where he was going wrong.[153] According to Channon, 'Lloyd George fulminated for a full hour: he was weak at times, at others sly and shrewd, and often vindicative [sic] as he attacked the Government.' Channon noted that Churchill 'was obviously shaken, for he shook, twitched, and his hands were never still'. When the Prime Minister stood up to reply, though, he was 'pungent, amusing, cruel, [and] hard-hitting'.[154]

In the summer of 1940, Churchill had made strenuous but unsuccessful efforts to recruit Lloyd George to his government. As recently as December, he had tried to persuade him to go to Washington as Ambassador. It is clear, though, that Churchill's patience was now exhausted: he put the boot in. Lloyd George's speech had been unhelpful, he declared. 'It was not the sort of speech which one would have expected from the great war leader of former days, who was accustomed to brush aside despondency and alarm, and push on irresistibly towards the final goal,' he went on. 'It was the sort of speech with which, I imagine, the illustrious and venerable Marshal Pétain might well have enlivened the closing days of M. Reynaud's Cabinet.'[155] Churchill was not the first person to make the insulting comparison, but he must have known that saying it himself in public would make it 'stick'.[156]

Earl Winterton, another critic who was the victim of a Churchill attack on this occasion, felt that the Prime Minister was 'very aggressive and unduly recriminatory about L.G.'s and Hore-Belisha's speeches'.[157] Headlam, who was also something of a sceptic, wrote: 'Winston winding up for the Government, made an effective speech from a debating point of view but said little to convince me that he knew much more about how to win the war than I did myself.'[158] However, in addition to the *ad hominem* remarks,

Churchill also offered an effective vindication of his methods of government in answer to Lloyd George's critique:

> My right hon. Friend spoke of the great importance of my being surrounded
> by people who would stand up to me and say, 'No, No, No.' Why, good gra-
> cious, has he no idea how strong the negative principle is in the constitution
> and working of the British war-making machine? The difficulty is not, I assure
> him, to have more brakes put on the wheels; the difficulty is to get more
> impetus and speed behind it. At one moment we are asked to emulate the
> Germans in their audacity and vigour, and the next moment the Prime
> Minister is to be assisted by being surrounded by a number of 'No-men' to
> resist me at every point and prevent me from making anything in the nature
> of a speedy, rapid and, above all, positive constructive decision.

He was also willing to mock himself: 'I have never promised anything or
offered anything but blood, tears, toil, and sweat, to which I will now add
our fair share of mistakes, shortcomings and disappointments.' He was, however, confident of final victory, he said. His final passages paid tribute to the
American assistance that had already been received and the future help that
had been promised.[159] This was the result of an intervention by J. G. Winant,
the sympathetic new US Ambassador to London. Winant had suggested
amendments to the speech, apparently having been shown a draft.[160] This
close cooperation was another sign of Anglo-American cooperation over
communications.[161]

The speech contained a notable hostage to fortune, in the form of a
pledge to defend Crete—which had not yet been attacked—'to the death
and without thought of retirement'.[162] But it was a tour de force, and was
followed by a vote of confidence which the government won by 477 votes
to 3. 'Churchill's speech to the House of Commons: excuses and very little
information', noted Goebbels in his diary. 'But no sign of weakness. [...]
England's will to resist is still intact'.[163] But in spite of the Prime Minister's
triumph, some British figures were still uneasy. P. J. Grigg, the Permanent
Secretary at the War Office, wrote privately: 'I agreed with nearly all L-G said
& in some ways it is a pity that Winston's immense dialectical skill should
have enabled him to get away with it so easily—for unless more drive at the
top is shown there is trouble coming'.[164] J. L. Hodson, a progressive journalist
who wrote a successful series of diaries published during the war, wrote:

> I could wish Churchill were less arrogant; and less apt to think that by making
> a fine speech he is disposing of problems or actually winning the war—though
> a fine speech helps. Most of his speech yesterday was akin to scoring

points in debate. The criticisms that had been made were sound; he did not really answer them. This House of Commons is somewhat hysterical, as it was when Chamberlain returned from Munich. To be silenced by a good speech is childish, and it was so silenced.[165]

Three days after Churchill's speech, the chamber of the House of Commons was hit by a bomb during a night raid. After a short spell meeting in Church House, Westminster, the Commons relocated to the House of Lords, where it continued to meet, save for a period of weeks during the V-weapons attack of 1944, until the rebuilt House opened in 1951.

On 20 May Churchill informed MPs that an assault on Crete by German paratroopers had begun that morning. After nearly two weeks of fighting, in which the enemy incurred heavy casualties, the British were forced to withdraw. Churchill spoke twice in Parliament about the battle while it was going on. On the second occasion, he was able to obtain some relief by announcing the sinking of the German warship *Bismarck*. This provoked 'great enthusiasm' and helped obscure other bad news.[166] On 10 June, with the battle lost, he spoke on the topic again. He looked 'worried and wary and there was a rather reluctant coolness in the cheer which greeted him'.[167] According to Winterton, this coolness was understandable, given the unfulfilled pledge to defend Crete to the death.[168] 'It is a difficult defence but the PM makes the best of it,' noted Dalton. 'Someone says that, as between him and his critics, it is more nearly than usual a drawn battle.'[169]

Churchill argued that the battle for Crete had been well worth fighting in view of the heavy casualties and aircraft losses that the Germans had incurred: there would be a benefit for the defence of the Nile valley. It would be unfair, wrong, and silly 'to select the loss of the Crete salient as an excuse and pretext for branding with failure or belittling with taunt the great campaign for the defence of the Middle East', which overall, he suggested, was prospering 'beyond expectation'.[170] MO diarist Edward Stebbing offered an astute commentary on the speech. He noted:

As has been the case before in his speeches to Parliament (but not in his broadcast speeches), I felt some dissatisfaction with his attitude. [...]

Again, Churchill concentrated on disposing of the argument that we should not have defended Crete, which was, I am sure, the opinion of a small minority, in order to distract attention from the argument as to why Crete was not *better* defended. He seemed very vague on this point. And although he often says that he wants to give the public as much information as possible, he seems to find numerous excuses for not doing so.[171]

It would seem that Churchill at this time was feeling angry and defensive. Here, the draft of his 10 June speech was rather telling. Initially, in a passage on German paratroopers, he intended to say: 'There is no obligation to give quarter in war, though as a matter of compassion and also of convenience it is usually accorded.'[172] However, a sharp-eyed official spotted this and explained, 'The Land War Regulations (4th Hague Convention) provide: (Article 23) "It is expressly forbidden to declare that no quarter will be given"', a point also affirmed in British military law.[173] The remark was wisely deleted—but the fact that Churchill wrote it in the first place may have been a sign of his sensitivity to stories of British atrocities put out by the enemy.[174]

Similarly, Churchill was tempted to link his domestic critics with the Nazis. His particular bug-bear was Hore-Belisha, who had been dismissed from the War Office by Chamberlain in controversial circumstances at the start of 1940. He had been popular as War Secretary, there was a perception that his sacking had been unfair, and he wrote a weekly column in the mass-circulation *News of the World*. He was not a likely candidate for Prime Minister—except in his own mind—but he seemed to be in touch with the public mood.[175] Churchill, doubtless overreacting, saw him as a threat.[176] The draft of his speech for the Crete debate made a comparison between Hore-Belisha and the Nazi propagandist William Joyce:

> One day last week Lord Haw-Haw reminded us tt we had bn four times flung into the sea, in Dunkirk, Norway, Greece and Crete.
> On the same day, the r.h.g. [Right Honourable Gentleman] for Devonport [Hore-Belisha] spoke of our sustaining defeat after defeat through our sloth-fulness, incompetence and lack or foresight, of which he is certainly a good judge.
> It was a kind of duet and they sang in tune wonderfully.[177]

Although this passage was deleted before delivery, Churchill was still quite brutal, referring to Hore-Belisha's 'dismal legacy' at the War Office.[178]

The attacks seem to have backfired. The week after the debate Mass-Observation detected 'new and disturbing signs of criticism against the Prime Minister'. Although he was 'still far and away the most esteemed character in Great Britain', the feeling was spreading that he was 'insufficiently sensitive to other ideas or new developments'. Many people were disturbed by his assaults on Hore-Belisha. 'The PM has made it his policy to stand for national unity and against recriminations. Many people have commented that his attack on Belisha was not in keeping with his personal integrity or declared policy.' Hore-Belisha had only been saying publicly what many ordinary people had been saying to each other privately. The report insisted that '*there is no doubt at all* that Churchill's attacks on Hore-Belisha have not enhanced his own prestige and have aroused considerable sympathy for Hore-Belisha'.[179] In spite of the basic strength of his position, then, Churchill was seemingly feeling rattled. His instinctive response was to lash out at his opponents, but this was counter-productive. However, the war was about to enter a new phase, both reinvigorating him and providing him with new rhetorical challenges.

4

'If Hitler Invaded Hell'

On 22 June 1941 Churchill awoke at Chequers to the news that Germany had invaded the USSR. It came as no surprise to him. He knew Hitler's intentions from Enigma decrypts and had warned Stalin, who had ignored the danger. Rumours of an attack were also circulating within Britain, fuelled partly by the recent arrival in Scotland of Deputy Führer Rudolf Hess on a bizarre one-man peace mission.[1] Thus Churchill had had time to think about his likely response to the invasion and public opinion was to some extent prepared for it. The day before it happened, Churchill remarked that 'a German attack on Russia is certain and Russia will assuredly be defeated' but that he would 'go all out to help Russia'. John Colville suggested to him that, as Churchill was 'the arch anti-Communist', this was for him the equivalent of sacrilege. According to Colville's diary for that day, the Prime Minister 'replied that he had only one single purpose—the destruction of Hitler—and his life was much simplified thereby. If Hitler invaded Hell he would at least make a favourable reference to the devil!'[2]

Having been told of the invasion, Churchill made the decision to broadcast that same evening. There was a need to act quickly in order to make Britain's position clear to domestic and international audiences. British support for the Soviet Union in the new circumstances was a foregone conclusion, but not everyone realized this. Clare Sheridan, Churchill's artist cousin, had aroused his ire by visiting the USSR after the revolution; she sculpted its leaders. After the broadcast she wrote to congratulate him on his 'splendid' speech: 'I was so afraid you wouldn't stand by Russia.'[3] Alison Selford, an ordinary member of the Communist Party of Great Britain (CPGB) recalled her own fear that Churchill 'wouldn't take this line or not take it so forcefully'.[4]

It was important to send out a rapid signal that he would, not merely to reassure the Russians themselves, but also to head off attempts by Germany to divide Britain from the Soviets. The Nazis presented their war with Russia as a crusade for 'civilization and the future of Europe', which could be read as an attempt to divide public opinion in the US and the UK, and to establish 'a Nazi–Tory united front against Russia as a world menace'.[5] Churchill had to make it plain as soon as possible—not least to the Americans—that Britain would continue the war regardless of these efforts. On the day of the invasion, the German Ambassador to Turkey put out a peace feeler via the Turkish Minister for Foreign Affairs. The next day, the British Ambassador to Ankara read out sections of Churchill's broadcast to the Turks as his way of making clear that the answer was 'No'.[6]

Churchill's speedy response also allowed him to sidestep consultation with his Cabinet colleagues. It was not that he feared that they would press him to take a different strategic decision, but he seems to have thought it likely that throwing in Britain's lot with Russia 'would arouse a measure of hostility, albeit unspoken, among sections of his own Party'.[7] He was especially concerned about Eden, refusing to allow him to see the text of the broadcast beforehand, 'in case he should seek to tone the speech down'.[8] He may have been worried lest his colourful language be bowdlerized in line with traditional Foreign Office caution; Alexander Cadogan, the Permanent Secretary, wrote after the speech that Churchill was 'overdoing the mud-slinging'.[9] However, it is also notable that Eden shared the right-wing Tory view that 'politically Russia was as bad as Germany and half the country would object to be associated with her too closely', whereas Churchill thought 'we should forget about Soviet systems or the Comintern and extend our hand to fellow human beings in distress'.[10] Churchill was to show that he had his own, highly effective way of dealing with the Conservative objections, and one can well understand him not wanting to be faced with pressure to insert caveats to his support for Russia. Sir Stafford Cripps, the British Ambassador to Moscow, was also present at Chequers that day, and provided several pages of notes for the broadcast, to which Churchill does not seem to have paid much mind. Cripps did emphasize that the attack on Russia was probably intended as a prelude to the invasion of Britain, a point that Churchill was to make in the conclusion of his speech.[11] Overall, the broadcast did not produce much of a paper trail, precisely because it was so rushed. It was not ready until twenty minutes before Churchill was due to speak.[12]

'I have taken occasion to speak to you tonight because we have reached one of the climacterics of the war,' Churchill began. ('Climacteric' was one of his favourite words.) He described Hitler's perfidious behaviour in launching a surprise attack on the Soviet Union in spite of her non-aggression pact with Germany, which was a repetition 'on a far larger scale' of previous Nazi breaches of faith. 'All this was no surprise to me,' Churchill said. 'In fact I gave clear and precise warnings to Stalin of what was coming.'[13] This revelation caused surprisingly little comment at the time; it seems to have been assumed that these warnings had been based on geopolitical insight rather than hard intelligence.[14] Churchill emphasized the relentless character of the Nazi war machine, which 'cannot stand idle lest it rust or fall to pieces'. He attributed the invasion to the quest for Soviet oil to keep the machine going. Hitler was a 'bloodthirsty guttersnipe' whose victory—'should he gain it—he has not gained it yet'—would merely be the stepping stone to further conquests. Thus Churchill allowed for the possibility that the Russians might be defeated. At the same time he dwelt on the human cost of German brutality.[15]

In this way he laid the groundwork for tackling the question of his previous attitude to the Soviet regime. His reputation as an implacable opponent of the Bolsheviks since 1917, and his support for the Whites during the Russian Civil War, presented him with an obvious rhetorical problem. However, it was also a strength, for if Churchill, 'the arch anti-Communist', was prepared to collaborate with Soviet Russia against Hitler, why should anyone else object? He had exactly the credentials he needed to counter Conservative suspicions, and he made play with them in his broadcast. 'The Nazi regime is indistinguishable from the worst features of Communism,' he said, almost equating the systems with one another whilst at the same time suggesting that communism was in fact the better of the two. 'No one has been a more consistent opponent of Communism than I have for the last twenty-five years,' he continued. 'I will unsay no word that I have spoken about it.' This set up his next move, which was to argue that although he stood by his views, they were unimportant in the new conditions: 'all this fades away before the spectacle which is now unfolding'.[16] Churchill was to be angered that the BBC report of his speech emphasized the 'fading away' without making clear that he withdrew none of his past criticisms.[17]

In the next passage Churchill talked lyrically about Russia, as distinct from the USSR, building a romantic—and somewhat overwrought—picture of patriotic struggle:

The past, with its crimes, its follies and its tragedies, flashes away. I see the
Russian soldiers standing on the threshold of their native land, guarding the
fields which their fathers have tilled from time immemorial. I see them guarding their homes where mothers and wives pray—ah yes, for there are times
when all pray—for the safety of their loved ones, for the return of the bread-
winner, of their champion, of their protector.

I see the ten thousand villages of Russia, where the means of existence was
wrung so hardly from the soil, but where there are still primordial human joys,
where maidens laugh and children play. I see advancing upon all this in hide-
ous onslaught the Nazi war machine, with its clanking, heel-clicking, dandi-
fied Prussian officers, its crafty expert agents, fresh from the cowing and tying
down of a dozen countries.[18]

It is clear that when Churchill said that the past 'flashed away', what he
really meant was the memory of the 1917–41 period. From behind this
screen another, pre-revolutionary past appeared—a land of religion, laugh-
ing maidens, and soldier-peasants defending their homes—in which communists were notable for their absence. Against the backdrop of the Nazi
onslaught, this mythic past merged with the present: the true soul of Russia
was revealed and Stalinist ideology was rendered irrelevant. Churchill also
referred explicitly to the memory of the First World War: 'my mind goes
back across the years to the days when the Russian armies were our Allies
against the same deadly foe when they fought with so much valour and constancy and helped to gain a victory, from all share in which, alas, they were,
through no fault of ours, utterly cut off.'[19] In other words, Britain and Russia
were natural allies, and it had only been the revolutionary events of 1917—which
led Russia to drop out of the war—that had prevented them basking in
triumph together.

In the final sections of the speech Churchill made clear that Britain would
never negotiate with Germany. Anyone who fought against Hitler would
have British aid: 'It follows, therefore, that we shall give whatever help we can
to Russia and to the Russian people.'[20] It was notable that he did not actually refer to the Russians as allies, although whether we should read this as a
sign of his 'determination to avoid a genuine association' is doubtful.[21] To
have said that the Soviets were allies would have been inaccurate and premature—the two countries did sign a formal alliance, but this took over another
two weeks to negotiate. It is however also true that Churchill at this stage
offered the Soviets only technical or economic help; in military terms all he
promised was to keep bombing Germany. Sending equipment to the Russians
was one thing; sending men to fight alongside them was quite another.[22]

Having warned that Hitler's final aim was 'the subjugation of the Western hemisphere', Churchill argued in his conclusion that 'The Russian danger is therefore our danger and the danger of the United States'.[23] As usual, then, the American audience was of crucial importance. Indeed, the elderly Fabian socialist Beatrice Webb—herself an uncritical admirer of the Soviet Union—wrote in her diary of 'Churchill's sensational oration to the world, especially designed for the USA with its anti-Communist prejudice'.[24] George Orwell, also on the left, but strongly hostile to Stalin, noted:

> Churchill's speech was in my opinion very good. It will not please the left, but they forget that he has to speak to the whole world, e.g. to middle-western Americans, airmen and naval officers, disgruntled shopkeepers and farmers, and also to the Russians themselves, as well as to the leftwing political parties. His hostile references to Communism were entirely right and simply emphasised that this offer of help was sincere. One can imagine the squeal that will be raised over these by correspondents in the *New Statesman*, etc. What sort of impression do they think it would make if Stalin stood up and announced 'I have always been a convinced supporter of capitalism'?[25]

Certainly, Churchill's refusal to take back his criticisms of communism went down well in the USA.[26] There was some suggestion that he was urging the US to clasp communism to its bosom but this was a rather marginal viewpoint.[27] The American government's approach to the USSR was as pragmatic as Churchill's; 'any defence against Hitlerism' was to be welcomed, no matter what the source.[28]

What is striking about the speech is how well it played out not just in America, but to multiple audiences, including Soviet officialdom. *Pravda*—the only Soviet paper published the day after the broadcast—printed a detailed summary of it in prominent position. There was no editorial comment, but the space devoted to it was a sign of approval.[29] A long summary was given on Moscow radio; Churchill's references to his opposition to communism were left out, but his pledge of British help to Russia was quoted verbatim.[30] It is notable that—once the awkward bits had been censored—Churchill's speech was in tune with what would become the Soviet narrative, in which the 'Great Patriotic War' came to be cast in nationalist rather than Marxist-Leninist terms.[31] However, his remarks about the peasants and 'the ten thousand villages of Russia' and so forth were amongst the material omitted from the Soviet press account of the speech. It may be that, with most Russians still ignorant of the progress of the Germans at this early stage, the Soviet regime wanted to avoid any hint of the Red Army's

defeats and the horrors that ordinary citizens were starting to experience. It
did not want to inform its people of what was going on, and certainly not
through the words of a foreign capitalist politician. The patriotic narrative
came into play only when the full scale of the assault could no longer be
concealed. Stalin gave the definitive seal of approval to the broadcast in a
rare speech early in July, which referred to 'the historic utterance of the
British Prime Minister, Mr Churchill, about aid to the Soviet Union'.[32]

The speech also found resonance elsewhere. Poland had been occupied
by the Soviets as well as the Germans in 1939. In the new conditions, its
government-in-exile came under pressure to sign an agreement with the
USSR: a bitter pill to swallow. Władysław Sikorski, the country's exiled
Prime Minister, favoured the restoration of relations, but had great difficulties with his supporters, who hated the Russians intensely. After much agony,
the agreement was finally signed at the end of July.[33] John Colville later
reported to Churchill: 'The Poles say that it was only your broadcast on June
22 which enabled General Sikorski to push his policy through and that you
are the only person whose voice carries weight with the Polish people, at
home and abroad, in a matter so instinctively repugnant to them as an alliance with Soviet Russia.' With an eye on the risk of Soviet post-war domination, they urged him to speak of the 'faith, constancy and courage shown
by the Poles' and to say that Britain was to ensure that they received fair
treatment. This would help 'reassure the doubtful elements' in Polish opinion.[34] Churchill duly responded with the public promise that Poland would
'live again and resume its rightful part in the new organization of Europe'.[35]
This shows once more the diplomatic function of Churchill's rhetoric,
which could have very different repercussions depending on local context.

The Turks, for example, were alarmed by the speech. Turkey was neutral
but a few days before the invasion it had signed a non-aggression pact with
Germany. The Turks were delighted at the attack on the Soviet Union: they
were pleased that the Germans had not invaded them instead.[36] But they
reacted with anxiety, if not panic, to Churchill's statement. He had not mentioned Turkey at all, but the Turks concluded that Britain was prepared to
reward Russia at their expense.[37] His remark that Russia had not benefited
from its efforts in the First World War was read by them as a veiled threat to
do this.[38] The British had no such intention, but at the beginning of July the
Ambassador to Ankara reported: 'Absence of anything to correct impression
created by Prime Minister's remark is doing increasing harm here and
causes me gravest anxiety which I can hardly over-emphasize.' The Foreign

Minister's Chef de Cabinet, he said, was 'convinced that after the war there was a scheme to partition Turkey. If the Prime Minister made another such speech, the whole of Turkey would turn round to Germany.'[39] This was merely one episode in a long story of troubled Anglo-Turkish wartime relations. The Turks continued to see the British as the handmaiden of Russian imperialism; and the British continued to see Turks as atavistically anti-Soviet and prey to German propaganda.[40]

For their part, the Nazis saw Churchill's broadcast as a gift. 'Churchill's speech provides excellent ammunition,' wrote Goebbels. 'Opinion in the USA very much divided. As a result of our assumption of the battle against Bolshevism.'[41] (Here he overrated the strength of isolationist opinion.) The speech provided meat for the Nazi version of satire. *Kladderadatsch*, a supposedly humorous magazine, published quotations from the speech about the Russians defending their homeland as the captions to drawings of starving peasants brutalized by commissars.[42] In 1942, there was published in Berlin a compilation of past anti-Bolshevik comments by Churchill under the title *Mein Bundesgenosse* ('My Confederate'). One of the most telling quotations was his praise of Finnish resistance to the Red Army in the winter of 1939–40: 'The service rendered by Finland to mankind is magnificent.'[43] Now Finland was at war with the Soviet Union again, and Churchill was doing everything he could to frustrate its efforts.[44] But the Nazis failed to recognize that Churchill's broadcast was in fact an effective blow against them. In Italy, Count Ciano was more realistic. 'Churchill has made a speech which, it must be objectively recognized, carries the mark of a great orator,' he wrote in his diary. He also recorded that he had talked about it to Dino Grandi, Italy's former Ambassador to the UK, 'who forgetting himself for a moment, expressed an extreme admiration for Churchill. "In England," he said, "I had few friends, but Churchill was really a friend."'[45]

In Britain, the speech seemed to bring the significance of the attack home to the population, making it appear 'more our own affair, part of our war'.[46] According to Home Intelligence, Churchill's pledge to give aid to Russia was 'generally accepted as both a practical and a logical move', and people felt that he 'discharged a difficult task well when he spoke of our support for Russia, after he had for many years voiced his contempt, and at times his abhorrence, for the Bolshevik regime'. The widespread admiration for the speech 'more than offset the recent fear that his touch was not quite as sure as it had been'.[47] His description of Hitler as a 'guttersnipe' appealed 'to almost all classes'.[48] Mass-Observation found, however, 'some adverse comment on alleged insincerity, the way he had always been against Russia and now turned round but without frankly saying so, mixing it up with "maidens still smiling", etc. One comment, representative of a minority feeling was that Churchill had said to himself: "I wonder if I can get away with this speech."[49] In her diary, the teacher M. A. Pratt provided a different take on Churchill's alleged hypocrisy, noting his suggestion that China might be the next victim if Russia was defeated: 'One would think that he had never closed the Burma road to help the Japanese to do their appalling worst, or dream that we had supplied her with the means of destruction.'[50]

It seems likely that Churchill's decision to emphasize the Russian national struggle helped account for the generally positive reaction. Later in the year, the American General Raymond Lee noted a conversation with an anonymous source in Churchill's entourage. Churchill's friend Lord Beaverbrook, appointed Minister of Supply in the government changes that followed the invasion, had made a speech referring to the Soviet Union. Lee's source commented: 'Churchill took the right position when he praised Russia's people and their brave fight to defend their homeland and urged aid for them. But Beaverbrook in his speech praised Stalin. That's a very different thing. It didn't go down with the trade unions.'[51] The leaders of the labour movement, indeed, were deeply hostile to domestic communism, in spite of their generalized admiration for the Soviet Union. Churchill urged the Labour members of his Cabinet to 'continue to draw a line of demarcation between the tenets of the Labour Party and those of Communism', but he hardly needed to do so.[52]

In the aftermath of the attack the CPGB surged in popularity— membership reached 56,000 by the end of 1942—but its own rapid switch from opposition to the war to support for it created certain presentational difficulties.[53] Willie Gallacher, the party's sole MP, cleverly explained away the change of heart. The CPGB was merely showing 'adaptability' in the light of changing conditions:

> As a primary example of this sort of adaptability, he cited Mr Churchill's speech last Sunday as 'agreeably surprising' but as one 'which did not go as far as I would have liked. It went farther than I expected,' Mr Gallacher said, 'but I remember Churchill once said: "If I had to choose between Communism and Fascism, I would not choose Communism." Well, Churchill has changed very considerably.'[54]

Initially, the CPGB welcomed Churchill's speech only because they wanted 'to focus attention upon these statements of policy by the Imperialists and so make it more difficult for them when they subsequently seek to betray the Soviet Union'. However, the party was forced almost at once to change its line again: 'When Comrade Stalin refers to Churchill's declaration as a "historic utterance" this leaves no room for doubt as to what our attitude towards this Government should be.' The CPGB now claimed to give the Churchill government its wholehearted and unreserved support.[55] Following Churchill's lead, the authorities tried to channel enthusiasm for Russia into apolitical forms, and although this was sometime hard to sustain, the rise of the CPGB was contained.[56]

One sign that Churchill's Russian broadcast commanded widespread agreement was that a debate on the issue in the Commons was deemed unnecessary.[57] On 25 June there was a Secret Session debate on the Battle of the Atlantic which passed off uneventfully. Churchill was cautiously optimistic, and he believed that he had reassured the House, but the decision to hold the debate in secret was taken by the public as 'a bad omen' at a time when its confidence in the war effort was still 'considerably shaken by our losses in Crete'.[58] On 14 July, Churchill gave two speeches on the question of air raids, one to civil defence workers in Hyde Park and the other at London's County Hall. The Home Office had urged him to emphasize that—although the *Luftwaffe* had now turned its attention to the Eastern front—the threat of heavy raids on Britain continued. In order to secure as much publicity as possible for his remarks, the Hyde Park speech was recorded for broadcast later the same day.[59] R.W. Fenn, a middle-aged teacher at a secondary school, recorded how it was decided to get all the children to listen to the speech, on the assumption that Churchill would make some new comment on the alliance with Russia. 'It turned out hardly to be worth the time spent listening to it,' he wrote, and regretted that the sections of the speech 'received with most applause referred to the policy of reprisals, and particularly to the rejection of any suggestion to limit bombing'.[60] Pacifist organizations deplored the speech as marking an acceptance of the increased bombing of civilians.[61] That may have been predictable, but there was growing concern within society more generally, including amongst some bishops of the Church of England, about the policy of strategic bombing. Nonetheless, as the reactions recorded by Fenn indicate, such pangs of conscience remained the preserve of a minority.[62]

Churchill's next major speech was in the Commons at the end of July, on the topic of war production. Here his task was to damp down the growing anxiety about failures of industrial efficiency. Earlier in the month, a

two-day debate led by other ministers had failed to allay concerns. His decision to present the government's case himself was a sign of how seriously he
took the presentational problem, even though he was unconvinced by the
merits of the criticisms. The *Manchester Guardian* warned: 'Mr Churchill
mistakes the temper of the House and the country if he makes this new
debate an occasion for trying to charm away all honest doubt by the magic
of his oratory.'[63] Arguably, the fears about production were, at the broadest
level, misplaced. On the one hand, Britain's military failures were not really
caused by shortages of equipment. On the other, the British were at this
time out-producing Germany in most kinds of weaponry.[64] Edward Bridges,
the Cabinet Secretary, may have been right to think that MPs did not properly understand the system they were attacking.[65] There was, however, plenty
of anecdotal evidence of slacking, poor management, and waste.[66] There were
many calls, widely echoed in the press, to improve drive and coordination
by creating a Ministry of Production.

Churchill's speech generated a huge file, reflecting the enormous amount
of departmental comment and advice he received on it. He spent the whole
weekend beforehand working on it, staying up till nearly 5 o'clock one
morning, which was late even for him.[67] It was a very long speech, which
was natural given the complexity of the issues. Churchill made his typical
argument that the critics were undermining Britain in the eyes of the world.
'The picture so luridly drawn of the chaotic and convulsive struggles of the
three Supply Departments, without guidance or design, is one which will
no doubt be pleasing to our enemies, but happily has no relation to the
facts,' he said.[68] The Production Executive, created at the start of the year to
resolve interdepartmental allocation problems, was working smoothly, he
pointed out. Production was gaining steadily in volume and momentum.
The creation of a Ministry of Production would cause administrative friction, not resolve it, he claimed. And who was the 'super-personality' who
would fill the office, he asked. With heavy irony, he poured scorn on his
critics' vision of a dynamic individual who, without holding the office of
Prime Minister, would impose his will on the whole governmental machine:
'When you have decided on the man, let me know his name, because
I should be very glad to serve under him, provided that I were satisfied that
he possessed all the Napoleonic and Christian qualities attributed to him.'
Churchill further noted that, in contrast to the situation during the First
World War, industrial relations were quite harmonious. 'I received, a few
minutes before I rose to speak, a report that at 11 o'clock to-day there was

no stoppage of work of any kind arising from a trade dispute in any part of Great Britain,' he announced.[69] The Ministry of Labour had advised him to use the word 'stoppage' rather than 'strike': as strikes were illegal in war-time, their possibility could not be admitted![70] He also offered a stout defence of Ernest Bevin, the Minister of Labour and trade unionist, who had antagonized Conservative MPs with his criticisms of industrial manag-ers. Bevin might cause offence in some quarters, Churchill said, but he had a 'frightful load to carry' and was producing 'a vast and steady volume of faithful effort, the like of which has not been seen before'.[71] This was a sin-cere tribute to a man for whom Churchill had genuine respect, in spite of their very different class origins.

According to Home Intelligence, the debate had, in spite of its lukewarm reception in the press, 'a somewhat reassuring effect on the public'. Churchill's speech was said to have restored a sense of proportion and to have given much encouragement to factory workers. However, people tended to see his 'masterly array of facts' as being meant mainly for consumption abroad, and there were still reports of idleness in munitions factories caused by unexplained shortages of materials.[72] Churchill's problems on this issue, in fact, derived less from the public than from the political classes. And this group remained sceptical. 'Chips' Channon wrote: 'He held the House which was interested certainly, but not enthusiastic, though there were few of his usual rhetorical tricks. Someone has told him that we are weary of his elo-quence.'[73] The Conservative MP Victor Cazalet thought the speech was 'very bad' and saw it as a sign of Churchill's intolerance of criticism.[74] As *Punch* noted, the debate had been expected to be 'The Day of the Great Chastisement' of the doubters, but things had not turned out quite as planned.[75] The result can be seen as a draw: Churchill had seen off the attackers, but not permanently. The following year, at a time of political weakness, he did concede the establishment of a Ministry of Production. This was initially under Beaverbrook, who resigned after only a few days, to be replaced by the less than Napoleonic (though not ineffective) figure of Oliver Lyttelton.

A few weeks before the production debate, a new shorthand-typist joined Churchill's team. She was Elizabeth Layton (later Nel), a young woman who got the job, remarkably straightforwardly, through the employment bureau with which she was registered. She left in her memoirs a vivid picture of how alarming it could be to work with Churchill, especially at the beginning, because he did not like unfamiliar staff. She recalled the advice the other secretaries gave her. They warned that it was hard, at first, to understand what he was saying when dictating:

> He has a very slight impediment in his speech connected with the letter S, and that, combined with the ticking of the typewriter, makes for difficulty. Until you get used to his voice it's impossible to catch everything. There's always that cigar, and usually he paces up and down the room as he dictates, so that sometimes he's behind your chair and sometimes far across the room. You must be prepared to go fast in short bursts, to finish one sentence before he starts another—and for Heaven's sake don't make any typing errors.

And that was just the beginning of the list of dos and don'ts. Layton experienced a baptism of fire that included being shouted at for typing single rather than double spaced. But she succeeded in typing out the 10,000 words of the production speech with only a single mistake, and after this she had Churchill's confidence. She recalled how he would often walk up and down in his dressing-gown, brow furrowed, as he dictated:

> Sometimes he would fling himself for a moment into a chair: sometimes he would pause to light his cigar, which with so much concentration was neglected and frequently went out. For minutes he might walk up and down trying out sentences to himself. Sometimes his voice would become thick with emotion, and occasionally a tear would run down his cheek. As inspiration came to him he would gesture with his hands, just as one knew he would be doing when he delivered his speech, and the sentences would roll out with so much feeling that one died with the soldiers, toiled with the workers, hated the enemy, strained for Victory.

Layton was not, though, invited to accompany him on his next foreign trip—his shipboard rendezvous with Roosevelt at Placentia Bay, Newfoundland, in August. Although she did later go with Churchill on his travels, his attitude at this stage was that women were not wanted on voyage.[76]

The fact of the Atlantic meeting was supposed to be a closely guarded secret, but the absence of both leaders from their respective capitals could not go unnoticed for long, and the press was soon rife with speculation. Churchill, for his part, of course wanted the President to declare war on Germany. In the production debate, the Prime Minister had said that America was giving Britain 'aid on a gigantic scale and advancing in rising wrath and conviction to the very verge of war'.[77] When asked by journalists what he thought of this statement, Roosevelt's bland response was to say that he hadn't read the speech.[78] His behaviour at Placentia Bay was almost as frustrating. There was to be no declaration of war, but the Americans wanted the British to subscribe to a joint statement of aims for the post-war world, which became known as the Atlantic Charter. After discussion, the principles arrived at included 'the right of all peoples to choose the form of government under which they will live' and 'improved labour standards, economic advancement, and social security'.[79] This was exactly the sort of statement of war aims—or 'peace aims'—for which British left-wingers had long pressed, and which Churchill had resisted, on the grounds that sensible people of goodwill all knew exactly what they were fighting for, and being too specific about it risked unwanted complications later.[80] Indeed, there was an obvious similarity between the Charter and the idealistic 'Fourteen Points' that President Woodrow Wilson promulgated during the First World War. Given the unsatisfactory nature of the peace settlement that had followed, this was not a happy precedent, but of course Churchill was not going to turn Roosevelt down. The Atlantic Charter provided Churchill with a symbol of US anti-isolationist commitment and with a rhetorical resource that he could draw upon, but it also created, as he had feared such a document might, some significant hostages to fortune.

The Atlantic meeting was carefully orchestrated as a global media event, to be publicized (for security reasons) only once it was over, but it was not possible to exert complete control over how it was received. On 14 August, while Churchill was still out of the country, it was announced that Attlee was to make an important broadcast at 3 p.m. Rumours of something dramatic immediately spread, including the suggestion that America was to enter the war. But when Attlee merely announced the fact of the Roosevelt–Churchill parley, and explained the Atlantic Charter, a lot of people felt cheated. Home Intelligence estimated that the Charter itself nonetheless met with 'warm approval'.[81] Mass-Observation, by contrast, found that much of the population was underwhelmed by it, although the report in question anticipated that reactions would improve 'when the Prime Minister himself has returned and spoken on the subject with the punch and clarity which Mr Attlee's broadcast lacked'.[82]

Churchill did indeed broadcast soon after arriving back on home soil. Home Intelligence reported that the speech 'greatly enhanced his reputation among thoughtful listeners, many of whom regard it as the most impressive since he took office'. Supposedly it was only the 'less thoughtful' who were disappointed 'at being told nothing new'.[83] That sense of disappointment, in fact, was quite a common reaction even among Mass-Observers, who may not all have been thoughtful but who were certainly engaged with events.

Andrew Schvil, a civil servant from Stockton, wrote that he was 'left in the air when it was all over, with a vague feeling of dissatisfaction'.[84] Another diarist, a young office worker whose MO file does not record her name, thought that people were right to admire the Prime Minister. However: 'It annoys me to have to listen to Churchill making these speeches. I was dragged out of the office to listen, but everyone got bored and quite a lot stopped listening. I hadn't expected it to be remotely interesting but I had hoped for some amusement from the good fellow's obvious rhetorical devices and odd pronunciation.'[85] The British press was mainly enthusiastic, although the *Daily Mirror* complained that Churchill had not said what Britain would do to assist the USSR.[86] This view was echoed by Eden's Private Secretary, Oliver Harvey: 'Great broadcast by the PM last night—"Words, words, words,—" very little about what we are going to *do* to help Russia which is what the people want to know'.[87] Cripps, now back in Russia, 'thought it was a good effort and was glad that it was less abusive than usual'.[88]

As with the production speech, some people regarded the broadcast as 'chiefly for overseas consumption'.[89] That, certainly, was a sound interpretation of its purpose. Of course there was plenty for the home audience too: Churchill dwelt on the 'symbolic' importance of his meeting with Roosevelt, reviewed the progress of the war, and explained the Atlantic Charter. But he also sent a message of global diplomatic significance, which was captured in headlines such as 'PREMIER'S "KEEP OUT" WARNING TO JAPAN'.[90] In a resonant voice, he condemned Japan's ongoing war in China and its expansionist moves elsewhere. With emphasis, he said 'It is certain that this has got to stop'. Whereas he hoped that American negotiations with Japan would succeed, 'if these hopes should fail we shall of course range ourselves unhesitatingly at the side of the United States'.[91] The whole Japanese press attacked the speech with the conservative paper *NichiNichi* accusing him of a 'big lie'. The Domei news agency rejected his argument that Japan had emulated Hitler and Mussolini, on the grounds that 'the Chinese war started first'![92] The spokesman for the Japanese forces in China said that Churchill's 'threat' to Japan was not a worry: 'What causes us greater concern is his ulterior motive—that is, to induce the United States into war'.[93] Whereas Roosevelt's supporters in Washington welcomed Churchill's stand, isolationists were predictably angry. 'We don't need any help from Great Britain or anyone else,' declared Senator Wheeler.[94] The *Chicago Tribune* caustically noted that 'The job of talking about the meeting at sea was taken over by Mr Churchill'; Roosevelt hadn't broadcast. 'Probably the idea was that inasmuch as Mr Churchill hasn't promised the American people they're not going to war it would be more appropriate for him to tell them as much as was politic of what their President had been doing at the warship rendezvous.'[95] It is clear that those in Britain who thought that Churchill hadn't said much were quite wrong.

One passage in the speech was of great significance, although, surprisingly and perhaps shockingly, it aroused little if any comment at the time. Having described the fierce Russian resistance to the Nazis, Churchill gave a vivid picture of the cruelties perpetrated by Hitler's forces:

> As his armies advance, whole districts are being exterminated. Scores of thousands—literally scores of thousands—of executions in cold blood are being perpetrated by the German police troops upon the Russian patriots who defend their native soil. Since the Mongol invasions of Europe in the sixteenth century there has never been methodical, merciless butchery on such a scale, or approaching such a scale. [...] We are in the presence of a crime without a name.[96]

In terms of public knowledge of the atrocities that we now refer to as the Holocaust, this was a landmark statement. It referred to mass shootings and not to extermination camps, which were only established after the Wannsee Conference of January 1942. It is striking, however, that Churchill did not mention the Jews explicitly as victims. Nor did he mention them elsewhere in the broadcast, as the prominent Zionist Chaim Weizmann complained in a telegram copied to Churchill:

> Impossible convey you shock reaction Jewry here [London] to Prime Minister's failure mention Jews among peoples awaiting restitution and liberation after destruction Nazi tyranny. [...] Disappointment the greater since Prime Minister had word of consolation every people including Luxemburg. It seemed which is surely not the case as deliberate omission.[97]

Weizmann was protesting about Churchill's general failure to refer to the Jewish people, not about the 'crime without a name' passage in particular; he naturally did not know precisely what was occurring on the Eastern front. Churchill knew a lot more, but not everything, which helps explain his omission. His information came from decoded radio traffic from the German Order Police operating in Russia. The Order Police did not use the Enigma machine but rather hand-ciphers; their messages were decrypted at Bletchley Park. However, because the new codes adopted for the Russian campaign took some time to break, British knowledge of German activities in the first weeks was far from perfect. Therefore, although the analysts knew that large numbers of Jews were being massacred, they did not know the full extent of this by the time Churchill made his speech. They and Churchill appear to have deduced that, although many of the murdered people were Jews, most were not. Had the broadcast been made just a couple of weeks later, when it was clear that the Germans were killing all Jews they captured, he might have presented things differently. As it was, in mid-September, the Order Police changed their codes, very possibly because Churchill's speech had alerted them to the fact that their activities were known.[98] A couple of months later, Churchill did refer publicly to 'all these victims of Nazi executioners in so many lands, who are labeled Communists and Jews'—the ambiguity of 'labeled' doubtless explained by continued uncertainty over the true identities of the victims.[99] Of course, the German media did not report Churchill's revelations of Nazi crimes. It gave only a selective account of his speech whilst claiming that it was his weakest yet. But the SD reported some signs of scepticism amongst the population: it was often asked 'what Churchill had really said'.[100]

The lack of reference to the Jews was not the only striking absence from the speech. 'India comes nowhere in Mr Churchill's picture,' noted the *Indian Express*.[101] 'I wonder how Indians must feel if any were listening on the subject of oppressed nations,' wrote M. A. Pratt.[102] It was a pertinent question. People from many parts of the Empire had reacted enthusiastically to the commitment in the Atlantic Charter to the rights of all peoples to choose for themselves the form of government under which they would live; but Churchill quickly secured his Cabinet's agreement that the Charter 'was not intended to deal with the internal affairs of the British Empire'.[103] He included a passage to this effect in a speech to the Commons reviewing the war. Ambassador Winant recorded how his own objections to it were overruled:

> On September 9, the day the Prime Minister spoke in the House, he sent me over a copy of his speech as there were definite references to the United States.
> I also found a paragraph which I asked him to eliminate. [...] I thought it ran counter to the general public interpretation of the [third] article [of the Atlantic Charter] and that I thought it would have little support here and elsewhere and would simply intensify charges of Imperialism and leave Great Britain in the position of 'a do nothing policy' so far as India and Burma are concerned. We talked up to a few minutes before he actually had to appear in

Parliament to make the address. [...] I was not able to change his determination to use this section of his statement.[104]

This episode again shows the closeness of Churchill's consultations with the
Americans over public utterances that might affect them, and also demon-
strates that he did not always cave in to their wishes. Having rejected Winant's
advice, he told MPs that the question of the restoration of self-government
was 'quite a separate problem from the progressive evolution of self-governing
institutions in the regions and peoples which owe allegiance to the British
Crown', which were covered by previous declarations on constitutional
development within the Empire that were 'complete in themselves, free
from ambiguity and related to the conditions and circumstances of the
territories and peoples affected'.[105] Yet when officials sought to answer
questions about what these commitments were they struggled to do so. 'I do
not think the PM can have realised the true nakedness of the land when he
made the statement,' observed Harold Macmillan, a junior minister. 'The
declarations are not complete in themselves, nor are they free from ambiguity. They are scrappy, obscure and jejune.'[106] Churchill's statement could not
help but raise the accusation of British double standards. 'This will really
make us stink as hypocrites in the eyes of the world,' wrote MO diarist
Pamela Slater.[107] It also increased tensions with the Americans. Roosevelt
continued to insist that the Atlantic Charter applied to 'the whole world',
and when journalists asked if he was talking about India, he pointedly
refused to comment.[108]

Churchill's 'long and optimistic' speech as a whole was a success overall,
however.[109] Roosevelt had just given the British a new boost by announcing that US patrols would if necessary shoot German vessels on sight to
protect merchant shipping in the Atlantic, although Churchill now hinted
he wanted more help still. He also promised 'serious sacrifices in the
munitions field in order to meet the needs of Russia'.[110] Harold Nicolson
wrote of how Churchill stood 'very stout and black, smoothing his palms
down across his frame'. Although the Prime Minister did not attempt 'any
flights of oratory' he did quote some lines by Rudyard Kipling on the
activities of minesweeping ships and became so moved by them that he
had to pause in his delivery. Nicolson noted: 'the speech has had a good
effect, and the slight anti-Churchill tide which had begun to be noticeable
was checked.'[111]

On 30 September Churchill gave a further war review, which Cuthbert
Headlam described as 'a really admirable speech which cleverly and effec-

tively knocked out his critics'.[112] One MO diarist quoted the view expressed in a letter from a communist friend from Bristol: 'Quite encouraging. Less shipping losses, German shortage of planes, goal in sight. It's the first time that Churchill has given us anything that can be called cheerful. Incidentally, did you notice how he referred to Premier Stalin? Quite democratic and respectable Joe is nowadays.'[113] An MO file report found that ten people liked the speech for every one person who disliked it, and that just over half the people questioned the following day had heard about the speech or read it in the newspapers. But a lot of them took with a pinch of salt his suggestion that the threat of invasion would be renewed 'in a very grave and sharp form' in the spring. 'Many people thought that Churchill had said what he did about invasion just to frighten people and keep them on the alert.'[114]

Churchill also taunted Hitler with the fact that he had not spoken in public for months. This drew the Führer into making a speech in reply, although at the same time he denied that it *was* a reply. He announced that new operations were under way that would help 'smash our enemy in the East'.[115] But the German forces in Russia were now in trouble. In November, Churchill replied in turn, during the course of another war review. 'It is a month ago that I remarked upon the long silence of Herr Hitler, a remark which apparently provoked him to make a speech in which he told the German people that Moscow would fall in a few days,' he said. (Hitler had not actually been that explicit.) 'That shows, as everyone, I am sure, will agree, how much wiser he would have been to go on keeping his mouth shut.'[116] It was a classic example of how Churchill used sudden descents into colloquial language to make people laugh. According to the Labour junior minister James Chuter Ede, 'This vernacular phrase [...] greatly pleased the House'. Churchill, Ede wrote in his diary, was 'at his roguish best'.[117] This was not a period, though, that yielded many timeless Churchillian oratorical gems: he was quite able to use rhetoric as an effective tool of political management without them. However, during a visit to Harrow School, his *alma mater*, he made a highly memorable statement, when defining what he said was the lesson of the last several months: 'never give in, never give in, *never, never, never, never*—in nothing, great or small, large or petty—never give in except to convictions of honour and good sense.'[118]

War was now looming between the USA and Japan. During his Mansion House speech in November—the traditional annual occasion when the Prime Minister delivered a speech on foreign affairs in the City of London— Churchill gave another warning to the Japanese. This seems to have been at the behest of the Foreign Office, following pressure from the Chinese, who feared a new attack on them.[119] It was against the advice of Roosevelt, who feared that 'in Japan's present mood' a new formal warning might be counter-productive.[120] Although the Americans were doing their utmost to preserve peace in the Far East, Churchill said, 'should the United States become involved in war with Japan, the British declaration will follow within the hour'. He seems to have believed that Emperor Hirohito was a less aggressive figure than the military establishment that surrounded him, although he decided not to make this explicit in public. One sentence in the draft of the speech read: 'I hope therefore that the peace of the Pacific will be preserved in accordance with the known wishes of the Emperor of Japan.' In the version Churchill delivered, the phrase 'the Emperor of Japan' was deleted and replaced by 'Japan's wisest statesmen'.[121] In the media reports of the speech, the warning to Japan tended to eclipse an almost equally 'sensational' aspect: Churchill's claim that Britain had now reached air parity with Germany.[122] This statement was nonetheless found to be very heartening by the British public, according to Home Intelligence. 'There was, however, some comment on the fact that Russia, our Ally, was not also named when he stated that if America were involved in war with Japan, the British declaration would follow within the hour—a promise which has otherwise been unanimously welcomed.'[123]

According to the *Singapore Free Press*, the speech 'electrified the whole of the Far East' and meant that 'the White Ensign will soon be filling the Singapore horizon'.[124] It was warmly welcomed in Australia, another likely target of Japanese aggression.[125] In Japan the *Yomiuri* newspaper said that Britain was 'dancing to the tune of the United States and digging her own grave', whereas *Asahi* commented that 'War with England would be expected in the case of war with the United States; therefore, it is silly to mention such a matter.'[126] This was the reality: that Britain's intentions had already been discounted in Japan's calculations. Diarist L. N. Adamson, a male ARP (Air Raid Precautions) worker, observed presciently: 'Churchill's clear warning to Japan will I think go unheeded, as the Japs I am sure are determined to pick a quarrel with America, and inter alia with us.'[127]

Churchill was dining at Chequers with Winant and Averell Harriman when he heard the news of the attack on Pearl Harbor. After a brief conversation with Roosevelt, he made some phone calls in order to recall Parliament and to implement his pledge to declare war on Japan. After sending some telegrams, he went to bed 'and slept the sleep of the saved and thankful'.[128]

By 12.30 the next day Churchill had drafted a speech to deliver in the Commons; he read it to the Cabinet for their approval.[129] At 2.30 Winant rang to say that, having read it, he had no comments to make. But fifteen minutes later he rang again. Roosevelt had sent a message asking for a delay: 'I think it best, on account of psychology here, that Britain's declaration of war be withheld until after my speech at 12.30 Washington time.' By this point it was really too late to halt the announcement and Churchill went ahead.[130] Just for once, though, Churchill's rhetoric was overshadowed by the President's. Asking Congress for a declaration of war, Roosevelt described 7 December 1941, the day of the Japanese attack, as 'a date which will live in infamy'. Churchill, for his part, observed that 'it only remains for the two great democracies to face their task with whatever strength God may give them'. He also lavished praise on 'the heroic people of China' and 'their great leader, General Chiang-Kai-Shek'. He was even mildly apologetic about the closure of the Burma Road in 1940. That evening he repeated the speech over the airwaves, adding an extra paragraph in which he appealed to war workers to 'make a further effort proportionate to the magnitude of our perils and the magnitude of our cause'.[131]

His delivery was not of the best. Andrew Schvil wrote: 'Missed the PM but wife said he sounded anything but strong and resolute'.[132] 'Thought he sounded tired, but his talk was as well worth listening to as ever', wrote Phyllis Lewis, a health visitor from Surrey.[133] According to C. R. Woodward, a male teacher from Middlesex, the Prime Minister's voice lacked 'that characteristic vibrant pugnacity that is forever Churchill. [...] A poor speech'.[134] Robert J. Nichols, a London park keeper, observed: 'There was a gravity in his voice, a slow delivery which suggested that he was weighing his words or finding difficulties in framing them. But the address was the same as he had given in the Commons earlier in the afternoon. The 6 o'clock news had reported this fully. I had the impression that he was reading a typescript which he already knew but that his mind was on something else.'[135] George Harvie-Watt, recently appointed as Churchill's Parliamentary Private Secretary, was now providing the Prime Minister with regular reports on the mood of the Commons. From one of these, Churchill learnt that MPs had thought his broadcast had been 'ill-advised' as he had sounded 'very tired'. Against these last words Churchill scribbled 'yes' and in the margin wrote: 'Well, who forces me? & why am I not allowed a gramophone record of a statement in the House?'[136] Having to broadcast live rather than make a recording clearly still rankled.

Churchill now made the impulsive decision to travel to Washington to visit Roosevelt. He arrived shortly before Christmas. The conference—codenamed 'Arcadia'—was a crucial one, because the British secured the USA's commitment to a 'Europe First' strategy. The defeat of Germany, not Japan, was to be the American priority. On 23 December, Churchill gave a joint press conference with the President. On Christmas Eve, he made a brief speech before an audience of 30,000 during the switching-on of the White House Christmas tree lights.[137] After dinner with Roosevelt on Christmas day, he excused himself part way through a film-show in order to 'do some homework'.[138] By this he meant his preparation for the speech to a joint session of Congress that he was to give the next day. On the morning of the 26th, his doctor, Sir Charles Wilson (later Lord Moran) went to see him on his daily visit but he was still busy drafting it. According to Wilson, 'He went on working at it until they told him he would be late for Congress.'[139] Churchill recalled in his memoirs that he had approached the occasion 'with heart-stirrings'. It was important, he wrote, 'for what I was sure was the all-conquering alliance of the English-speaking peoples. [...] I had the feeling, for mentioning which I may be pardoned, of being used, however unworthy, in some appointed plan'.[140]

His American ancestry, he felt, gave him 'a blood-right to speak to the representatives of the great Republic in our common cause'.[141] In the opening of his speech he made brilliant play of his Anglo-American parentage:

> The fact that my American forebears have for so many generations played their part in the life of the United States, and that here I am, an Englishman, welcomed in your midst, makes this experience one of the most moving and thrilling in my life, which is already long and has not been entirely uneventful. I wish indeed that my mother, whose memory I cherish across the vale of years, could have been here to see. By the way, I cannot help reflecting that if my father had been American and my mother British, instead of the other way round, I might have got here on my own.[142]

Wilson wrote: 'When the laughter was dying down, it would break out again, and this, coming right at the beginning, convinced him he had got a grip on things.'[143] Churchill went on to praise 'the breadth of view and sense of proportion' he had found in Washington. He also noted that the resources of the Allies greatly outweighed those of Japan, to the degree that it was 'difficult to reconcile Japanese action with prudence or even with sanity'. And then the most memorable lines of the speech: 'What kind of a people do they think we are? Is it possible they do not realise that we shall never cease to persevere against them until they have been taught a lesson which they and the world will never forget?'[144] In Wilson's words: 'At this, Congress rose as one man and stood cheering as if they would never stop.'[145]

Churchill made it all look so effortless that, as with his speech on Russia's entry to the war, it can be difficult to remember that his situation was potentially problematic. One astute observer was David E. Lilienthal, a progressive public official who headed Roosevelt's controversial Tennessee Valley Authority. Lilienthal was blown away by Churchill's use of imagery and alliteration, and by his ability to use his voice to evoke emotion: 'Why, at one point he made a growling sound that sounded like the British lion!' The contents were as impressive as the style: 'It was a position of considerable difficulty, for the nation has been at war so briefly that he could have made a grievous mistake, and many men of his vigor but with less skill would have.' Lilienthal continued:

> His audience, the members of the Senate and the House, were a far better sounding-board than I had feared. For example, they applauded vigorously and long to his tribute to Russia, and this was as pleasing as it was surprising. When he promised Japan that she would be roundly punished, the place broke out in yells—the first sound of blood-lust I have heard yet in this war. It was not surprising that the reception to his concluding words, which took courage, was rather weak. In the very centre of isolation, standing before the chair that held [Republican Senator] Henry Cabot Lodge and that slew an effective League of Nations, he spoke of the desperate need, when hostilities cease, of an end to the fallacy of 'isolation' from world problems and world responsibilities.[146]

As he left, Churchill turned and made his characteristic 'V' sign. 'The effect was instantaneous, electric', reported the *Washington Post*. 'The cheers swelled into a roar.'[147] The British Embassy assessed that Churchill's 'public appearances at the President's press conference and before the Senate were such an unqualified success and made so strong a favourable impression on the public at large that they alone would have afforded sufficient justification for his visit. The only exception to the paean of praise for Mr Churchill's address to Congress was to be found in the comment of Senator Wheeler who was careful to dub the speech as "clever".'[148] Roosevelt had not been present but listened on the radio. Churchill recalled that on his return to the White House 'the President, who had listened in, told me I had done quite well'.[149] This was a less than generous tribute: perhaps Roosevelt didn't care for being overshadowed in his own capital.

Churchill's speech was heard by listeners in Britain loud and clear—a seeming technical miracle. According to Home Intelligence, it was 'generally welcomed as a "great historic utterance", likely "to knit the British empire and the United States more closely together, not only for the duration of the war but for a long time to come"'. There was relief the previous signs of weariness had gone. People noted

> that 'he said things which the Americans needed to hear but which no American could have said', particularly the point that 'American collaboration after the war might have saved this one'. There is some feeling, however, that 'America should not be played up too much and told she is going to win the war'.[150]

'Grand old boy how well you must have managed all those difficult old Senators,' wrote Edith Dawson, a housewife from Gateshead, in her diary.[151] But although the enthusiasm was widespread, it was not unanimous. R. M. Dhonau, a housewife and Food Office clerk, wrote: 'Churchill's speech seems to have had a depressing effect implying as it did that the war wouldn't be over until 1943—at the earliest.'[152] This was an observation, not a criticism—Dhonau liked Churchill. But teacher M. A. Pratt took a distinctly negative view. She wrote: 'I wish he hadn't said that from the point of view of history it didn't matter much whether victory came in 1943 or 1944. I don't agree with him: every day of this destruction and semi-starvation on the Continent is likely to bring the eclipse of civilisation nearer, and may quite conceivably affect the survival of the Western Races.'[153]

During the night following his speech, Churchill suffered a mild heart attack. Summoned to examine him the following morning, Wilson—fearing the impact of the truth on the patient and the news on the world at large—decided to tell him merely that he was suffering from poor circulation. But over the next few days, Churchill continued to fret, repeatedly asking Wilson to take his pulse. The doctor began to wonder if Churchill would make it through his next big speech—to the Canadian parliament at Ottawa.[154] In fact, the occasion was another triumph, although Prime Minister Mackenzie King felt that it was not quite up to the standard of the speech to Congress, and noted that Churchill 'showed evidences of fatigue in its delivery'. However, 'it had been prepared with the greatest care so as to say nothing which would possibly offend any party. He had been meticulously careful in that.'[155] By this, Mackenzie King meant that Churchill showed sensitivity to local opinion, including that of the Québécois. To that end, the speech included a few lines in French, looking forward to France's 'national resurrection'.[156] Churchill was of course quite prepared to offend the enemy, although he did have second thoughts about one line. A reference to 'the monstrous combination which we may call the JAPHUNWOPS' was modified to 'the enemies ranged against us' in the final version.[157]

The speech is remembered today for Churchill's recollection of his dealings with the French government after the French collapse of 1940: 'When I warned them that Britain would fight on alone whatever they did, their generals told their Prime Minister and his divided Cabinet, "In three weeks England will have her neck wrung like a chicken". Some chicken! Some neck!'[158] Wilson observed how Churchill 'spat out his contempt' and how the gales of laughter turned into applause that lasted a long time.[159] It would be easy for modern readers to miss part of the point. In the parlance of the time, 'Some neck!' was the equivalent of 'Some cheek!' It would be equally possible to miss the political significance of his ridicule of 'the men of Vichy' that followed the joke. Part of the context for this was a political crisis surrounding two small French islands of the coast of Newfoundland, St Pierre and Miquelon. These had been under Vichy rule, but just before Christmas De Gaulle's forces had seized control, without warning Britain and the USA of what they were about to do. The State Department, which still wanted to maintain relations with Vichy, was very angry, and pressed for a return to the *status quo ante*.[160] Churchill's public praise of De Gaulle and those other Frenchmen 'who would not bow their knees' was therefore especially welcome to the General.[161] (The Vichy press ignored Churchill's references to France.)[162] 'What you said yesterday about France at the Canadian Parliament has touched the whole French nation,' he telegraphed to Churchill the next day.[163] But in private Churchill pressed him to reach a compromise with the Americans and became angered at De Gaulle's intransigence. In the end, the Free French remained in possession of the islands and the episode was forgotten. But, as well illustrating the complexities of the Churchill–De Gaulle love-hate relationship, the episode was significant as the first thoroughgoing official British denunciation of the Pétainists. This did not imply, though, an irrevocable commitment to De Gaulle himself. Churchill kidded Roosevelt that between them they had a division of labour. 'You're being nice to Vichy', he told the President, 'we're being nice to de Gaulle'.[164]

British public opinion on the St Pierre and Miquelon incident was divided between those who were angry at American 'attempts at appeasement towards Vichy' and those who expressed 'astonishment that General de

Gaulle should have countenanced such piracy without the sanction of the Allies'.[165] Although there was no detailed Home Intelligence or Mass-Observation appreciation of the impact of Churchill's speech itself, it is clear that some British listeners did see its political importance. 'The speech was remarkable for the fact that it was the first occasion on which Winnie has come out into the open on Vichy and their methods,' noted J. Frewin, a male office worker from Middlesex.[166] It was also appreciated at a simpler level. R. M. Dhonau wrote of how her small son Timothy was greatly tickled by the 'some chicken—some neck' crack. 'He was saying it to himself and roaring with laughter afterwards in bed. It is a strange thought to me that Churchill speaking in the Canadian Parliament should also amuse a child of 5 in bed thousands of miles away.'[167] 'Such-like dashes of humour make the PM a much loved man,' commented L. N. Adamson.[168] But, as ever, there were sceptics, of whom C. R. Woodward was one: 'I listen to Churchill at Ottawa—the cheering, the dramatic "speech-for-effect-on audience", the vituperation, the French-Canadian sop of 2 paragraphs in French, were all reminiscent of Hitler in 1936, 7 & 8. The mob psychology again.'[169]

In spite of such complaints, it is clear that the June to December 1941 period was one of enormous political strength for Churchill. His oratory cemented this and helped him negotiate successfully the potentially difficult transition to fighting alongside allies. But although, once America had come into the war, he could be confident of final victory, severe new challenges were at hand. A few days after Pearl Harbor the Japanese sank the *Repulse* and the *Prince of Wales* off Singapore. Meanwhile, their land forces advanced on British positions in the region. At Christmas, Hong Kong fell. In Britain, anxiety spread. In January 1942, Home Intelligence reported: 'General confidence in the Prime Minister has been, if possible, increased by his American and Canadian enterprises; but his choice of lieutenants is more and more criticised.'[170] Over the next few weeks, catastrophe in the Far East led to political crisis for Churchill; in his attempts to extricate himself, he was to find his rhetorical skills severely tested.

5

'He's No Speaker, Is He?'

Oxford student F. B. Chubb listened to Churchill's Washington broadcast and found his prediction of a long war depressing. Still, he had to admit that the Prime Minister's previous prophecies on these lines had been justified by events. 'I noticed too that he admitted we had no aircraft in Malaya, but to excuse this on the grounds of Libya is not much consolation.' Chubb wrote. Churchill had argued that it would have been wrong to disperse Britain's forces; he had also spoken of Japan's attack on the USA as an irrational act, a remark which in Chubb's view 'savoured much of Chamberlain's "Hitler has missed the bus"'.[1] In the longer run, of course, Japan's actions rebounded upon her, so Churchill was in a sense proved right; but it is also clear that he underestimated the scale of the immediate Japanese threat. Asked at a press conference in Canada if he thought Singapore could hold out, he replied 'I sure do'.[2] Churchill was not usually guilty of over-optimism in public but here he was dramatically wrong (although admittedly it would have been hard to saying anything else). Six weeks later Singapore surrendered, in what he would describe in his memoirs as 'the worst disaster and largest capitulation in British history'.[3]

The degree of Churchill's own responsibility for the catastrophe has received much attention from historians.[4] Although the military errors cannot all be laid at his feet, it is clear that he shared the mistaken impression—promoted in the press from the late 1930s—that Singapore and its naval base formed an impregnable 'fortress'.[5] As Churchill's old friend Sir Ian Hamilton pointed out before the war, 'A land army can lay siege to and capture Singapore, exactly as Port Arthur was captured' by Japan from Russia in 1905—a point echoed by a *Times* journalist in April 1941.[6] Yet the British people were fed complacent and often racist media messages until almost the last minute.[7] One January 1942 newsreel, for example, featured film of soldiers digging trenches, over which the announcer intoned: 'North of

Singapore in the Malay peninsula Australian troops help to make every inch of the way to the fortress island a death-trap for the yellow plague infecting the Straits settlement.'[8] Lacking an understanding of Singapore's true strategic position, and prone to the common habit of viewing the Japanese as inferior, Churchill was in a poor position to explain the defeat to his bewildered British populace. In fact he was as stunned as they were. According to Churchill's doctor, 'The fall of Singapore on 15 February stupefied the Prime Minister'. He was both incredulous to learn of the inadequate state of the island's defences and self-reproachful for having failed to find out the true position himself earlier:

> There was another more crucial question, to which the Prime Minister could find no answer. How came 100,000 men (half of them of our own race) to hold up their hands to an inferior number of Japanese? Though his mind had been gradually prepared for its fall, the surrender of the fortress stunned him. It left a scar on his mind. One evening, months later, when he was sitting in his bathroom enveloped in a towel, he stopped drying himself and gloomily surveyed the floor: 'I cannot get over Singapore,' he said sadly.[9]

The weeks before the surrender saw Churchill in growing political difficulty, but managing it with some success. At the end of January, he demanded a vote of confidence from the Commons. Normally his periodic war reviews concluded without a division. Now, however, he urged 'a clear, honest, blunt vote' which would force MPs to show where they stood.[10] The debate lasted three days, and Churchill spoke both to open and close it. Of his first speech, Harold Nicolson wrote: 'One can actually feel the wind of opposition dropping sentence by sentence, and by the time he finishes it is clear that there is really no opposition at all—only a certain uneasiness.'[11] As Cuthbert Headlam noted, Churchill's 'line was that although faults had admittedly been made here, there and everywhere—and very little had gone according to plan—considering our original unpreparedness, the fall of France, etc., etc., we might have fared a deal worse. His defence of the Far Eastern Mess was not very convincing: it only amounted to what Attlee said the other day—with our available military potential we could not be strong everywhere and that we had to run the risk of Japan coming into the war.'[12] On the final day, Churchill offered a concrete concession—the creation of a Ministry of Production. He justified his change of heart of the grounds that the Americans had established a body on such lines, and that the British now needed to do likewise if Allied resources were to be effectively pooled and coordinated. 'I offer no apologies, I offer no excuses, I make no promises', he concluded. 'Let every man act now in accordance with what he thinks is his duty in harmony with his heart and conscience.'[13]

In his memoirs, Churchill recalled that he found the tone of the debate 'unexpectedly friendly'; in fact he feared that there would be no division, leaving the boil of disquiet unlanced. 'I tried by taunts to urge our critics into the Lobby against us without at the same time offending the now thoroughly reconciled assembly,' he wrote. 'But nothing that I dared say could spur any of the disaffected figures in the Conservative, Labour and Liberal Parties into voting.'[14] Fortunately for him, the fringe Independent Labour Party (ILP) decided to challenge a division. As two of its MPs were required to act as tellers, Churchill won his vote by 464:1. Lord Harmsworth, who watched from the gallery, wrote in his diary: 'Winston not at his very best in summing up and seeming uneasy about the result, walking about the floor of the House while the 464 take 20 minutes to go through the narrow Lords Aye Lobby.'[15]

Churchill's crushing victory was in some ways rather empty. 'It is a great pity that Churchill's oratory is not as effective against the German Army and the Jap fleet as it is against his critics,' commented MO diarist D. Hurley sarcastically.[16] Some members of the public felt that Churchill was talking 'eyewash' or that he had made 'the wrong appeal', unfairly cloaking the failures of his subordinates by asking MPs to be loyal to him personally.[17] According to a Home Intelligence report prepared while the debate was still going on, 'Many people seem to think it "unfair for the Prime Minister to try and subdue criticism by throwing his personal popularity into the balance". The majority would prefer "a robust admission of failure" and it is feared that "further attempts at 'whitewashing' might damage the Prime Minister's own reputation".'[18] A week later, though, 'the great majority of the public' seemed satisfied that the debate was already 'bearing fruit'. Churchill's closing speech 'gave great satisfaction in that he promised to take heed of advice'.[19] But with the fall of Singapore increasingly expected, and with a general sense of unease still lurking, Churchill was by no means out of trouble.

He now faced a threatening new rival. Having recently returned from his post as Ambassador to Moscow, Sir Stafford Cripps—who had been expelled from the Labour Party in 1939 but remained in Parliament as an Independent—made a triumphant re-entry to British politics as the great white hope of those who wanted a more vigorous war effort. In a brilliant broadcast in the regular 'Postscript' series on 8 February, Cripps contrasted the relatively comfortable conditions on the British Home Front with the suffering experienced by millions of Russians. 'I have felt in this country since my return a lack of urgency,' he said. 'I may be wrong but I feel it in the atmosphere in contrast to what I felt in Russia.'[20] Cripps had cross-party appeal. MO diarist C. R. Woodward, a left-wing teacher from Twickenham, listened to his speech with friends who held different views: 'This family of Conservatives agree with it all, say nice voice, nice man, cultured, he knows what we want.'[21] Cripps's 'common sense, "one man to another"' style formed a marked an impressive contrast to 'Churchill's rhetorical fireworks', thought teacher R. W. Fenn.[22] Unsurprisingly, Churchill thought the broadcast was awful.[23] Cripps's words were 'a great contrast to the complacent utterances of the PM', wrote F. E. Smith, a London chemist.[24] A Mass-Observation survey in March—albeit using what was probably an unrepresentative sample—found 79 per cent unreserved approval and 8 per cent qualified approval for Cripps; for Churchill the equivalent figures were 32 per cent and 37 per cent.[25] It was not that Cripps's admirers all wanted him to overthrow Churchill; most of them wanted him to be brought into the government to help Churchill as a colleague, not as a substitute Prime Minister. But for the first time there appeared a plausible answer to the frequently asked question, 'If anything happened to Winnie, who would replace him?' American journalist Mollie Panter-Downes wrote of Churchill:

> You hear people say that they have trusted him in the past because they knew that he would let them have the truth, however unpalatable; now there's an uneasy suspicion that the fine oratory may sometimes carry away the orator as well as his audience. You also hear people say that anyway they've had enough of fine oratory; what they would like is action and a sign from Mr. Churchill that he understands the profoundly worried temper of the country.[26]

On 15 February, the BBC six o'clock news announced both that Churchill would speak that evening at nine and that the Japanese had announced the unconditional surrender of the garrison at Singapore.[27] Churchill presented his speech as a general review of the war. He stressed that, with the USA as a new ally, and with the USSR fighting more successfully than had seemed possible a few months earlier, Britain was in a better strategic position than it had been at the time of his August 1941 broadcast after the Atlantic Charter meetings. He appeared resentful of the criticisms of his administration, commenting that when the Germans had been at the gates of Moscow, 'the Russian people did not fall to bickering among themselves. [...] They did not lose trust in their leaders; they did not try to break up their Government'. His discussion of the fall of Singapore was brief, but he did acknowledge it to be a very serious 'British and imperial defeat'. He was silent on its causes; an omission perhaps prompted in part by security concerns, yet perhaps also by the difficulty of providing an explanation that was both reassuring and credible. He concluded by the presenting the crisis as an opportunity which, as in 1940, would allow 'the British race and nation' to demonstrate 'their quality and their genius'.[28] We may surmise that his use of the term 'imperial defeat' was not just a reference to the fact that Australian and Indian troops had been present in Singapore. Leo Amery noted the next day that in Cabinet Churchill was 'eloquent [...] on the general loss of the white man's prestige. That indeed is pretty serious.'[29]

Some, Amery included, found Churchill's speech impressive.[30] The overall response, however, was at best lukewarm. Harold Nicolson felt that his call for national unity and not criticism was reminiscent of Neville Chamberlain, and wrote in his diary that the broadcast 'was not liked. The country is too nervous and irritable to be fobbed off with fine phrases.'[31] With the exception of the *Daily Express*, those papers that offered comment tended to be critical.[32] 'We must endure anything, certainly,' observed the *Daily Mail*, 'but to go on offering us tears, sweat and blood in monotonous gloom of stoical resignation is now to confess ...that something is seriously wrong with the conduct of the war as a whole.'[33] Amongst the public, some diarists welcomed Churchill's presentation of 'the plain facts', but there was also much criticism.[34] The speech was found to be 'weak and illogical', 'pretty puerile', and was thought to sound like the work of 'a parliamentarian rather than a great Prime Minister'.[35] Comments of acquaintances were noted, mainly negative: 'An obstinate man badly rattled'; 'If he really wonders at the lack of criticism in Russia, he is either blind or exceptionally obtuse'; 'I did not listen: I am sick of words, words, words'; 'I wouldn't like Churchill's job'; 'Give Churchill's job to Cripps'.[36] Judy Roberts, a secretary in her twenties, wondered, 'How long will he get away with it?'[37]

One of the most vivid accounts was written by the journalist Denis Argent, now in the Army and billeted in Luton. He wrote down in shorthand the comments of his friend George—a twenty-four-year-old French polisher from South London—as he listened to the speech, which could be heard from the radio in the NCOs' room. Like many others, George noted Churchill's failure to comment on an embarrassing incident that had taken place shortly before Singapore fell. Two German warships, the *Scharnhorst* and the *Gneisenau*, which had been bottled up at the port of Brest, made a daring daylight escape through the English Channel. Many people seemed more upset about this than about the loss of Singapore.[38] Argent wrote:

> The 'historical' preamble (how like Hitler's speeches!) annoyed George, & he exclaimed 'Never mind that. Tell us about the Channel affair'.
> Soon after: 'What a bleedin' cover-up for that Channel game'.
>   When Churchill was talking about America's entry into the war: 'F——bullshit! Get on with it! What a f——g cover-up. Any normal person could see it's just pulling the wool over their eyes!'

Later, another friend, Harry, came in and started noisily rummaging in his kitbag, looking for an item to give to for his waiting girlfriend. 'Harry was far too eager to find something to give to the girl to listen to take any notice of George's "Listen to that old bastard. F——g cover-up he's making". When the speech became "eloquent" George's remark was "He's wrapping up that f——g defeat well".' Afterwards, Argent recorded 'Harry's verdict on the imperialism that's lost us Malaya—"We wanted to grab all and now we've got fuckall"'.[39]

But although Churchill had described the Singapore debacle as an 'imperial defeat', it appears that most people saw it more as a military and leadership issue. This can be seen, for example, in the diary comments of Pam Ashford, a secretary in Glasgow: 'Singapore! That is news indeed! There are recriminations galore! People say Mr Churchill has taken on too much, he is a dictator etc., but when asked if they want Mr Churchill to go, they hastily reply, "No, but they want to see about half the cabinet go".'[40] This view is confirmed by non-diary evidence. In the immediate aftermath of the speech Home Intelligence found that criticism of the government was 'intense and widespread'. Churchill's broadcast itself had 'a rather mixed reception [...] Particular note seems to have been taken of his "call for unity", to which the reaction is reported that "unity depends on having the right men in the right places".' Churchill's reference to Russia was thought to 'cut both ways' as it led people to contrast 'the organization and efficiency of the Russian war machine' with 'our own half-hearted methods'.[41] Further evidence of the population's reaction can be gained from a BBC Listener Survey Report on the speech—a unique document, given that equivalent surveys were not conducted for Churchill's other wartime speeches. Among the adult population, 65.4 per cent heard the broadast and it achieved a 'Popularity Index' of 62, which the report considered 'undeniably a low figure'. It was 30 points less than that achieved by Cripps for his broadcast

the previous week. Although some positive comments from listeners were
reported—'Told us how things really are, straight from the shoulder'—the
general feeling was that Churchill had failed to allay people's fears. The survey concluded:

> The reports reveal that a number of elements clearly played a part in deter-
> mining the public reaction to the Prime Minister's broadcast. First there was
> grave concern at recent bad news. Secondly, long standing trust in
> Mr. Churchill as leader. Thirdly, considerable misgivings about some of the
> PM's colleagues. Over against these came the broadcast which some felt was
> 'making the best of a bad job', while others felt it to be 'beating about the
> bush'. It is impossible not to detect a note of disappointment, both from
> those who hoped for better news in the broadcast, from those who hoped for
> new light on the recent perplexing set-backs, and from those who looked to
> the PM to provide new inspiration in dark times.[42]

Mass-Observation found an even worse picture, with 55 per cent of respondents making unfavourable remarks.[43]

The loss of Singapore, of course, was not just a military fact or a domestic
political problem; it was a global media event. Enemy propagandists, therefore, rushed to exploit it, heaping scorn on Churchill's speech in the process.[44] Some of the German propaganda aimed at Britain was cack-handed.
'Well workers, Churchill has been spouting again, and we're just about sick
and tired about it,' ran one broadcast. 'The trouble about Churchill is that
he's a skunk, and that nothing can de-skunk him.'[45] William Joyce ('Lord
Haw-Haw') was, by contrast, comparatively subtle, making play with
Churchill's implicit admission that Britain was now reliant on the power of
the USA:

> It was [...] natural to wonder what Churchill would say to assure his people
> that some barrier would be created to arrest, if only for the time, the flood of
> defeat which is now pouring over the British Empire. Read the speech twenty
> times and you will find no such assurance. [...] In the past the British used to
> say: 'We may lose every battle but the last. The last battle, however, we win'.
> But now that hope is gone, for apparently Churchill is expecting the United
> States to win the last battle for him.[46]

It is doubtful that these arguments had much effect in Britain, where anti-
Americanism, although never absent, was for the time being at a low ebb.[47]
In Germany, the reaction to the surrender and to Churchill's speech was
surprisingly ambivalent. This is clear from an SD report on public opinion.
Although there was pleasure at the triumph of Germany's Japanese ally,

there was also a sense that not only the British but white people in general had suffered a defeat. There was much talk of the 'yellow peril' (*gelben Gefahr*). The extracts from Churchill's speech and commentaries on it that the German media provided attracted much attention. Many people noted that Churchill did not hesitate to report bad news and to outline the severity of Britain's situation. They concluded from this that in spite of their heavy defeats the British people were holding their nerve and remained steadfast.[48] Ironically, then, Churchill's defiant speech was perhaps more successful in Germany than it was at home. The Nazis, meanwhile, were belatedly realizing that home propaganda that compared Churchill's public prophecies with actual events was more effective than simply calling him an 'old crook' and a drunkard.[49]

Axis broadcasts aimed at India and the Arab world were potentially more dangerous to the Allied cause than those received in Britain. The 'Voice of Free Arabs' station noted that Churchill's speech had made no effort to turn the surrender into a 'heroic defeat' on the lines of Dunkirk:

> We thought that Churchill, as usual, would speak of so-called glorious British victories, converting defeats into outstanding victories, but we were surprised when this criminal butcher told the truth. [...] The fall of Singapore means the defeat of the British Empire. [...] We, the Arabs, are well aware of the fact that the British Empire[,] which has been built up on tyranny and savagery, will not survive this war.[50]

Similar messages, adjusted for the different audiences, were broadcast in Afrikaans to South Africa and in Hindustani to India. According to the BBC monitoring report, one broadcaster 'addressed himself to Churchill personally, saying that "your treacherous bastard nation has kept India in slavery"'.[51] Incidentally, the image of Churchill with his cigar proved to be a poor tool for the British in their own Indian propaganda. As one intelligence report noted, 'the Indians' conception of a leader involves the spiritual and the symbolic, not the prosaic and ordinary'.[52]

Meanwhile, Canadian Prime Minister Mackenzie King praised Churchill's broadcast in his diary as 'a manly endeavour to brace the country against the most desperate situation with which it has been faced since the fall of France', but he also commented on Churchill's 'terrible omission which was no reference to Canada'![53] United States reactions were of greater significance. A report from the British Embassy in Washington noted on 19 February that 'The events of the past week have led to greatly increased criticism of Great Britain in this country'.[54] From Churchill's perspective the chief danger was that perceptions of British military-colonial incompetence would contribute to an upsurge in US anti-imperialism, with consequences for the shape of the post-war world. His recent visit to the US had seemingly had the effect of persuading influential Americans of the need to defend the British position in the Far East.[55] But this was not without consequences. The celebrated and widely syndicated columnist Walter Lippmann now wrote:

> as Mr. Churchill explained in his speech on Sunday, the main burden of the Eastern war rests upon the United States. With this responsibility must go authority in the political conduct of the war. Now it is evident that for the American people the objective of the Eastern war is not and cannot be the recapture and restoration of the white man's empire. [...] And now that Singapore and what it represents and symbolizes have fallen, we are bound to wage the war on the principle that the freedom and security of the peoples of Asia is the best guarantee of our own future in the Pacific.[56]

In other words, the abject defeat was a signal of the failure of the British colonial system as a whole, and America needed to exert its own enlightened influence in order to fill the gap left by its decline. Throughout the rest of the war, growing US power combined with American hostility to the British Empire left Churchill struggling with the new realities. There was also a residue of isolationist sentiment to take account of; its sponsors were always ready to make trouble for the British. From the Washington Embassy, Lord Halifax wrote to Anthony Eden: 'I have been rather strongly pressed by our publicity people here to let Winston know the use that certain evilly-disposed sections of the press are trying to make of the sentence in his broadcast of the 15th February about his having "dreamt of, aimed at *and worked for*" American entry into the war.' This phrase touched a nerve because it evoked the familiar trope of smart Europeans inveigling honest American folk into war step by step. As Halifax put it, it 'gave the idea that a simple innocent people have been caught asleep by others cleverer than themselves'.[57]

Nor were Churchill's domestic difficulties over. He had been wise not to try to turn the surrender into a 'heroic defeat' in the style of Dunkirk, but two days after his broadcast he spoke in the Commons and quickly ran into trouble when he tried to explain the Channel incident in exactly that manner. 'The PM came into the Chamber and I saw him scowl,' wrote 'Chips' Channon. 'No cheer greeted him as he arrived. Nor as he answered Questions. He seemed to have "Lost the House". Then at twelve o'clock he rose and in a curiously nonchalant, indeed uninterested manner, read a prepared statement about the passing through the Channel Straits of the German ships.'[58] Churchill argued that the 'abandonment by the Germans of their position at Brest has been decidedly beneficial to our war situation', because a threat to British convoy routes had been removed, and it was no longer necessary to divert bombers from attacking Germany to try to hit the ships in the French port.[59] According to Channon, 'he convinced nobody, and particularly his attempt to turn an inglorious defeat into a victory displeased the House [...] never have I known the House growl at a Prime Minister'.[60] According to Nicolson, the statement 'started all right' but Churchill 'became irritable and rather reckless' when MPs asked questions. 'He spoke about "anger and panic" which infuriated people and will, I fear, be broadcast throughout the world by our enemies', Nicolson wrote.[61]

The public was sceptical of Churchill's explanations, and although—according to Home Intelligence—speculation about him being forced out of office had ceased, there were still 'indications that he has yet to recover the complete command of public confidence which he enjoyed a year ago'.[62] Nevertheless, his promise of an inquiry into the Channel affair assuaged MPs and anger to some extent, as did his decision to move the Adjournment—a device that allowed members to make speeches both on the issue of the ships and on Singapore. 'It was quite clear from the whole tone and temper of the House that if he had adhered to his original policy and flatly refused a Debate the House would have brushed him aside', wrote Amery. 'As it is he was reasonable [sic] conciliatory and got away with it.'[63] It was notable in fact that the critics held off from a head-on assault on the Prime Minister personally. Observing that Parliament was 'given over to intrigue', Labour junior minister Chuter Ede noted, 'The PM's position is very difficult but he is still too strong for direct attack.'[64]

A few days after the statement, the public learned that Churchill was reconstructing his government. After the blow of Singapore's fall he had no choice but to appoint Cripps to the War Cabinet—the condition that his rival had set for accepting office at all. This move secured the public's 'unanimous approval'.[65] The changes eased the pressure on Churchill in practical terms as well as political ones, as he relinquished the position of Leader of the House of Commons to Cripps. This was a post, normally held by the Prime Minister, that involved responsibility for the conduct of parliamentary business. 'I must admit that this Parliamentary task has weighed upon me heavily,' Churchill told MPs. 'During the period for which I have been responsible I find to my horror that I have made more than 25 lengthy speeches to Parliament in Public or in Secret Session, to say nothing of answering a great number of Questions and dealing with many current emergencies.'[66] Giving up the job was an astute political move too, because it helped answer those critics who suggested that, through his insistence on being Minister of Defence as well as Prime Minister, he was carrying too great a burden. He retained the Defence portfolio whilst reducing his work-load in another way, showing a willingness to listen without appearing to retreat.

But he was still on the back foot. The British collapse in the Far East forced concessions to nationalist opinion within the Empire, in the hope of enlisting it against the Japanese. Greatly against his will, Churchill was obliged to consent to a mission to India, headed by Cripps, carrying a plan to offer the country self-government after the war. Amery, as Secretary of State for India, had been pushing in a reformist direction since 1940 and had often been infuriated by Churchill's intransigence. Now he had to help him announce his volte-face. Early on the morning of 11 March—the day Churchill was to announce the mission in the Commons—Amery received a redraft of the proposed statement which the Prime Minister had prepared late the previous night. 'Some of it was good, but some bits were full of incredible mistakes,' he recorded. The government's pledges to the Indian princes—a group that formed a key part of the structure of British rule—were 'sand-wiched in between other minorities and the depressed classes and referred to as obligations we could get clear of'. Amery and his Permanent Secretary drafted some alternative passages. He then took his corrections round to Churchill's bunker 'and discussed with Winston in bed in his gorgeous silk dressing gown. I got him to accept most of the important alterations and entirely change the first bit.'[67] Later that day, Churchill was received in the Commons 'with a more cordial cheer' than had been heard for some time.[68] He told MPs that the mission would take place, but did not lay out the terms of the British offer, which was to be conveyed by Cripps in person. This was so that the government could assure itself that its scheme 'would win a reasonable and practical measure of acceptance, and thus promote the concentration of all Indian thought and energies upon the defence of the native soil. We should ill serve the common cause if we made a declaration which would be rejected by essential elements in the Indian world, and which provoked fierce constitutional and communal disputes at a moment when the enemy is at the gates of India.'[69] Channon wrote: 'The House appreciated the solemnity of the moment, and that our great Empire of India was perhaps to be bartered away.'[70] Amery saw it rather differently: 'Winston [...] read out the statement to a House completely surprised and a bit mystified but altogether approving as the meaning of what he said dawned upon them. I thought it significant of quicker intelligence than I had anticipated that the strongest murmurs of approval of Cripps' appointment came from the Conservative benches, the Socialists silent as if they suspected that their Left Wing Champion was being used for Tory purposes.'[71] Within a few weeks the mission failed, partly because of Gandhi's intransigence, taking some of the shine off Cripps's reputation.

Churchill continued to deal with the aftermath of Singapore. In the 24 February speech in which he explained the changes to his government, he offered some comments on the disaster. The first draft of his speech included a harsh comment on the performance of the defenders: 'In spite of the absence of Air support, it might have been thought that this garrison which was nearly equal to all the Japanese forces in the Malay Peninsula and incomparably more numerous than those who effected landings on the island, would have been able to throw the enemy back into the sea on several occasions and to maintain a protracted defence.'[72] P. J. Grigg, Churchill's new War Secretary, sent him a letter pleading with him to 'modify materially' the passage in question:

> We do not know all the reasons for the collapse of the defence though we can assign a good many besides cowardice & bad leadership. [...] But even if you think privately that cowardice & bad leadership are the real explanations I believe that to hint publicly that this is so will do great harm. [...] If the troops are a bit soft & timid I suppose everybody is until he has had a good deal of fighting[,] the worst thing in the world is publicly to proclaim them cowards. They won't be a bit better for being called 'pi' dogs & I beg you not to do it. And further imagine how the Japs and Germans & even Italians will exploit an admission to the effect that the British troops are n.b.g.[73]

Churchill took the point. In the speech as delivered, he said 'I shall certainly not attempt at this stage to pass any judgment upon our troops or their commanders [...] We have more urgent work to do.'[74]

Public discontent meanwhile continued. According to an MO report in mid-April, 'Feelings about Churchill are beginning to show distinct similarities with the Chamberlain pattern, especially among past enthusiasts for his leadership. People are beginning to think of him as a poor old man who is carrying more than he can reasonably be expected to carry at his age.' An important contributory factor in this was

> the flatness which people are finding in his oratory. Gratitude for his speeches in the past seems to have keyed people up to expect great and moving speeches every time. The breaking of the oratorical spell is thus a shock as well as a disappointment. On the one hand people are beginning to blame themselves for being spellbound by his oratory, and react in the opposite direction with epithets such as 'old windbag'. On the other hand, in tone [sic] with the general feeling for more action and less talk, they are feeling that the present is no time for oratory.[75]

He had not, however, lost his command of the House of Commons. Speaking in Secret Session on 23 April he rejected calls for an official inquiry into what had gone wrong at Singapore, whilst admitting that the army had underperformed. 'Australian accounts reflect upon the Indian troops,' he noted. 'Other credible witnesses disparage the Australians.'[76] To probe too deeply, he implied, would open a wide field for intra-imperial recrimination and thus damage the prosecution of the war. When the speech was published in 1946 it created a furore in Australia.[77] After his lengthy disquisition on the Far East, he remarked: 'I now leave the lesser war—for such I must regard this fearful struggle against the Japanese—and come to the major war against Germany and Italy.'[78] This undoubtedly reflected Churchill's sense of strategic priorities.[79] But it should also be noted that Churchill was making an astute rhetorical manoeuvre. By suggesting that too much investigation would damage the Empire and the war effort, and that the Far Eastern theatre was at any rate a second order problem, he successfully deflected some of the heat from his own government, whilst simultaneously insisting that the decision not to hold an inquiry was purely in the interests of the state and not out of 'any ignoble desire to shield individuals or safeguard the administration'.[80]

All witnesses agreed that the speech was a triumph. Cuthbert Headlam wrote: 'Today's effort was, I thought, a very fine one—and none of his critics made any reply to it—not even complaining at his refusal to hold an enquiry on Singapore—they prefer to speak in public so that they can advertise themselves.'[81] 'Chips' Channon—never easily impressed by Churchill—described the speech as 'a tour de force. No humour or tact, little oratory, no mea culpa stuff, but straightforward, brilliant and colourful, a factual résumé of the situation. Only at 1.50 when MPs began to think of their stomachs, was there any restlessness.'[82] 'He tells us of our present dangers and prospects and dwells at length upon the heavy sinkings which we are sustaining in the Eastern Atlantic,' wrote Harold Nicolson. Paradoxically, as the catalogue of catastrophe continued, MPs began to cheer up, with the feeling that 'no man but he could tell us of such disaster and increase rather than diminish confidence'.[83]

Chuter Ede wrote of Churchill's performance: 'No words can adequately describe the tremendous impression he made by a graphic account of the happenings of the past few months.'[84] The crux of Churchill's argument was that, in spite of the current difficulties, the huge US output of ships and aircraft provided strong grounds for confidence. This would take time to make itself felt, 'but it is only a matter of six or nine months before a marked preponderance of air power should manifest itself upon our side'. Finally, he read out an extract of a message he had received from Roosevelt in the early hours of the morning, in which the President said that he felt 'better about the war than at any time in the past two years'.[85] 'This most dramatically ends the speech', Hugh Dalton wrote.[86] There were 'Loud & prolonged cheers'.[87] 'Who wants a public session after that?' asked one Tory MP.[88]

The grumbles subsided, for a while at least. 'This has been one of the quietest weeks in the House for some time,' George Harvie-Watt, Churchill's Parliamentary Private Secretary (PPS), told him a few days after the debate.[89] Successful landings on Vichy-controlled Madagascar further boosted Churchill's stock—albeit not with a furious Charles De Gaulle, who had not been told in advance.[90] On 10 May Churchill made a broadcast to mark the two years since he had become Prime Minister. 'Can anyone doubt that if we are worthy of it, as we shall be, we have in our hands our own future?' he asked. 'As in the last war, so in this, we are moving through many reverses and defeats to complete and final victory.'[91] Leonard Adamson, an ARP Worker and Food Packing Manager from Surrey, wrote in his diary: 'It was a new Churchill who spoke yesterday—a Churchill as usual full of confidence, but this time he did not dwell on the troublesome and worrying times ahead for *us*—the latter was for the enemy.'[92] 'Made one proud to be British!' wrote Gateshead housewife Edith Dawson.[93] Just a few days before, Cecil Miles, a commercial traveller, had observed: 'I find from conversations, reception of newsreels etc. that Churchill's power to inspire has rather slumped.'[94] But now it had undoubtedly bounced back. According to Home Intelligence, praise was 'practically unanimous' and the speech was said to be 'his best ever'. A typical comment was 'How grand it was not to hear about blood and tears and toil'.[95] O. Sutherst, a Hampshire housewife, felt that the broadcast was full of clichés and that Churchill's message might as well have been delivered by BBC announcer Freddie Grisewood. But she knew she was in the minority: 'I am shocked by the number of people who asked me this morning if I hadn't heard the PM's speech, didn't I think it was good & wasn't he more hopeful this time, and so ad nauseam.'[96]

Still, Sutherst was not entirely alone in her scepticism. Christopher Gould, serving on board HMS *Lightning*, wrote to his fiancée: 'I was on watch last night for Churchill's speech but he gives me the pip anyway so I didn't miss much. I don't need him to give me moral support and if a vote was cast in the services for him he would not be there anyway, the navy has special dislike for him as we do all his dirty work for him.'[97] Some others were merely indifferent. Denis Argent listened to the speech in the saloon bar of a Luton pub; no one in the crowded public bar heard it, as there was no radio there. Just as the speech was about to start, one of the civilians present said 'Wonder what he'll say?' A man who appeared to be her husband replied, 'Oh, I suppose he'll explain why we didn't win that sea battle & tell us all that we've got to work harder.' As the speech went on the civilians became talkative, and Argent and some officers who wanted to listen had to move close to the loudspeaker.[98] It was of course quite possible to react in different ways to different parts of the speech. Teacher M. A. Pratt commented: 'For the minute, I found the speech heartening, though I object to the reiteration of the untruth that "Britain was alone." What about the Empire? […] I object to this continual patting of ourselves on the back.' She added: 'The reference to German citizens fleeing from their cities to watch their home fires burning I thought disgusting'.[99] Edward Stebbing, who had been discharged from the Army on medical grounds and was now working at a hospital, recorded a similar reaction from his boss, a strongly anti-Nazi Czech Jewish refugee, Dr Konrad Rosenberg. 'We're fighting for better things', Rosenberg said, and talked of 'all this nonsense of hating your enemies'.[100]

Some of the most significant passages in the speech concerned the Soviet Union. There was now considerable popular pressure for a Second Front in Europe—an invasion of the continent—to relieve Russia. It was the product of a 'strange alliance' between left-wingers, communists, and Churchill's friend Lord Beaverbrook, who had now left the government.[101] Cleverly, Churchill did not attack the campaigners for straining after the impossible. Instead he remarked, 'Naturally, I shall not disclose what our intentions are, but there is one thing I will say: I welcome the militant, aggressive spirit of the British nation so strongly shared across the Atlantic Ocean.' (There were demands for a Second Front in the USA too.) Was it not better, he asked, 'that demonstrations of thousands of people should gather in Trafalgar Square demanding the most vehement and audacious attacks, than that there should be the weepings and wailings and peace agitations which in other lands and other wars have often hampered the action and vigour of governments?'[102] By praising the Second Fronters and appearing to hint that something was in the pipeline Churchill took some of the sting from the campaign. According to Home Intelligence, the speech helped reduce demands for a Second Front 'because it is thought to be on the way towards establishment'.[103]

Churchill also gave a warning. The Soviet government had advised the British that the Germans in their desperation might use poison gas against the Russians. It is unclear whether they had in fact already done so during their successful assault on the Red Army at the Battle of the Kerch Peninsula.[104] Churchill said:

> We are ourselves firmly resolved not to use this odious weapon unless it is used first by the Germans. Knowing our Hun, however, we have not neglected to make preparations on a formidable scale. I wish now to make it plain that we shall treat the unprovoked use of poison gas against our Russian ally exactly as if it were used against ourselves, and if we are satisfied that this new outrage has been committed by Hitler, we shall use our great and growing superiority in the West to carry gas warfare on the largest possible scale far and wide against military objectives in Germany.[105]

This statement, which the Soviets had pressed for strongly, had been the product of considerable Cabinet discussion. The Chiefs of Staff took the view that while Britain was able to use air power to deploy chemical weapons against Germany and in the Middle East, 'the Army was not yet adequately equipped with chemical weapons in any other theatre'. They believed that the start of gas warfare 'in certain Eastern theatres would involve us in the gravest difficulties, especially in India' and believed 'that it would be to our grave disadvantage if we became involved in chemical warfare in the immediate future'. However, the politicians felt that it was impossible to refuse the Russian demand at a time when negotiations for a new Anglo-Soviet Treaty were at a sensitive moment. 'It was pointed out that it would be important that the declaration made should be so worded as to safeguard us against Russia initiating gas warfare against Germany, and to provide for our being satisfied that gas warfare had been started by the Germans.' Hence Churchill's careful wording.[106] The possibility of a British gas attack on Germany raised the possibility of Nazi retaliation, so this section of the broadcast evoked enormous interest. 'Churchill's message about gas certainly went home for the ARP office was thronged with people to have gas mask repairs,' noted B. S. Inglis, a surveyor's pupil from Trowbridge. 'Five of us had to go up to assist—there was a terrific queue!'[107] But although the warning to Germany was widely approved, there appeared to be no increase in the carrying of gas masks, notwithstanding an upsurge in people having theirs tested.[108] In Germany itself, the SD reported that rumours about the use of 'new German weapons' (likely code for gas) had led 'to anxieties among the relatives of soldiers stationed in the East that the Bolshevists one day—as Churchill threatened in his last speech—may start gas warfare'.[109] The next month, following reports that Japan had used gas against the Chinese, Roosevelt made a similar threat of retaliation. In 1943, the President committed himself publicly against the first use of such weapons. In the summer of 1944, Churchill pressed his advisers to consider deploying gas against Germany, in response to the V-weapon attacks. He was reluctantly dissuaded by their arguments that it was unlikely to prove decisive, and that it would lead to chemical warfare in other theatres where the British were less well prepared for it.[110]

In June 1942, Churchill travelled again to Washington. He was concerned that the Americans, notably Army Chief of Staff George C. Marshall, wanted an early Allied assault on Europe; he preferred to focus on North Africa. In terms of strategy, he secured the results he wished. But while he was in the USA the British suffered another terrible defeat—the surrender of the Libyan fortress of Tobruk to inferior numbers of Germans. General Sir Alan Brooke, the Chief of the Imperial General Staff, recalled: 'Churchill and I were standing beside the President's desk talking to him when Marshall walked in with a pink piece of paper containing a message of the fall of Tobruk! Neither Winston nor I had contemplated such an eventuality and it was a staggering blow.'[111] The following day Churchill was lunching with the President when some New York newspapers were brought in, with headlines such as 'TOBRUK FALL MAY BRING CHANGE OF GOVERNMENT' and 'CHURCHILL TO BE CENSURED'.[112]

Nevertheless, upon his return to Britain, Churchill felt politically confident. Although he thought it would have been difficult to demand another vote of confidence so soon after the previous one, dissenting MPs solved his problem by putting down their own motion of censure. It stated 'That this house, while paying tribute to the heroism and endurance of the Armed Forces of the Crown in circumstances of exceptional difficulty, has no confidence in the central direction of the war.' It was in the name of Sir John Wardlaw-Milne, an MP described in Churchill's memoirs as 'an influential member of the Conservative Party' and in Harold Nicolson's diary as 'rather an ass'—two things which, after all, were not necessarily incompatible.[113] The situation in North Africa was now getting worse, and some believed Cairo and Alexandria would fall to Rommel's forces. Perhaps realizing that to press the motion in these conditions might appear unpatriotic, Wardlaw-Milne offered to withdraw it. Churchill did not mean to let his critics 'escape so easily', he recalled, and the government insisted that the issue be brought to a head.[114]

The debate opened on 1 July. Wardlaw-Milne began well enough, criticizing Churchill's combination of the posts of Prime Minister and Minister of Defence. But then he suggested that the Duke of Gloucester—younger brother of George VI—should be appointed Commander-in-Chief of the Army. The notion seemed ridiculous. Even the Duke's friends thought him at best suited to be second-in-command of a regiment, and the idea of putting an aristocrat in charge was hardly likely to appeal to the Labour Party.[115] 'The House roared with disrespectful laughter, and I at once saw Winston's face light up, as if a lamp had been lit within him and he smiled genially,' wrote 'Chips' Channon. 'He knew now that he was saved, and poor Wardlaw-Milne never quite gained the hearing of the House.'[116] In fact, Churchill did not depend on this mistake for his survival. The next speaker was the motion's seconder, Sir Roger Keyes, who had made a highly effective intervention against Chamberlain's government in the Norway debate of 1940. But he seemed to take the opposite line to Wardlaw-Milne, arguing that 'The story that the Prime Minister rides roughshod over his Service advisers and takes the whole direction of the war into his own hands [...] is simply not true'. Rather, the problem was that those very advisers were letting Churchill down.[117] The critics looked incoherent. On the second day there were powerful speeches from Aneurin Bevan—'The Prime Minister wins Debate after Debate and loses battle after battle'—and from Hore-Belisha, but the motley nature of the attackers weakened their efforts.[118] As one Labour MP put it, 'I could not help asking myself if these hon. Members who have no confidence in the Government have any confidence in one another.'[119]

Therefore, although Churchill's winding-up speech was a good one, he owed his victory on this occasion less to his oratorical brilliance than to the divisions and incompetence of his opponents. Cuthbert Headlam wrote afterwards, 'he had a pretty simple job today because the censure motion was so stupidly framed. To vote for it was out of the question because if it had been carried it meant the fall of the Government in the middle of a great battle—had it been framed so as to condemn the work of the Ministry of Supply and demand a thorough overhaul of its machinery I certainly could not have voted against it.'[120] Churchill's speech did not hold much comfort, as Londoner Vere Hodgson noted in her diary: 'He dominated us as he always does, and we surrender to his overpowering personality; but he knows no more than any of us why Tobruk fell—that he expected it to hold! This does not cheer us.'[121] He was, however, able to announce that General Claude Auchinleck was now in direct personal command of the battle, and he poured scorn on those who sought to weaken confidence in his government. 'Every vote counts,' he said. 'If those who have assailed us are reduced to contemptible proportions and their Vote of Censure on the National Government is converted to a vote of censure upon its authors, make no mistake, a cheer will go up from every friend of Britain and every faithful servant of our cause, and the knell of disappointment will ring in the ears of the tyrants we are striving to overthrow.'[122]

The government won the vote by 475 votes to 25. 'Good for you,' cabled Roosevelt.[123] Churchill was not completely out of the woods—another big defeat could have seriously undermined his position—but the weaknesses of the opposition to him had been exposed. 'What a wily old bird Churchill is,' wrote Birmingham office-worker Lionel Randle, adding: 'He appears to have the Commons just where he wants them.'[124] Leeds shopkeeper A. White, by contrast, confessed himself 'disappointed in Churchill,'[125] There was also a familiar refrain to be overheard: 'Words, words, words and more words. I wish they would do something.'[126] The British public as a whole seems to have regarded the result of the vote as a foregone conclusion. 'It appears, however, that the overwhelming vote for the Government is not considered to reflect the amount of criticism that exists,' reported Home Intelligence. Production and equipment problems generated disquiet and 'increased frustration and bewilderment'. On the other side of the coin, 'there are signs of developing intolerance at the washing of a lot of dirty linen in public which serves no useful purpose, but only depresses the spirits of the British public and encourages the enemy'.[127] In

Germany, in fact, not much notice was taken of newspaper accounts saying that the British had lost faith in Churchill's war leadership, given the outcome of the vote in Parliament. The press had already suggested that Churchill would manage to talk himself out of trouble, but people did not expect the extent by which the motion of censure was defeated. Still, many Germans regarded Churchill as stubborn and thought they could be glad if he stayed in charge and led England to its final downfall.[128]

In August, Churchill travelled to Moscow. There he broke the news to Stalin that there would be no Second Front in Europe in 1942, although there would be an Anglo-American invasion of North Africa. Stalin angrily accused him and the Americans of breaching their promises. By the time Churchill returned home, relations had been patched up, although Stalin remained suspicious that the British wanted to see the USSR defeated and to do a deal with Germany at her expense.[129] Reporting to the Commons on 8 September, Churchill did acknowledge the fact that 'the Russians do not think that we or the Americans have done enough so far to take the weight off them'. But—in spite of his private anger at some of the Soviet behaviour at the summit—the overall picture he presented was one of harmony. He claimed to have largely succeeded in establishing the same relationship of 'easy confidence and of perfect openness' with Stalin which he had built up with Roosevelt. It was, he said, 'very fortunate for Russia in her agony to have this great rugged war chief at her head'. Stalin had bravery, will-power, and a 'saving sense of humour', Churchill said. Moreover, 'Stalin also left upon me the impression of a deep, cool wisdom and a complete absence of illusions of any kind.'[130] Although it was rather over-the-top, this may have been intended simply as necessary diplomatic flattery. It is also possible, though, that Churchill now believed that he had truly established a warm personal bond with Stalin, and that the problems in Anglo-Soviet relations were caused by shadowy Kremlin forces to which the dictator was supposedly accountable.

On this occasion, Churchill was able to point out to MPs that the worst predictions of the critics in the censure debate had not been fulfilled. Cairo and Alexandria had not fallen, and the defence of Egypt was assured for some time ahead. He also touched on the recent raid on Dieppe. This action had been a sop to all those demanding a Second Front. Churchill described it as a 'most gallant affair' and said that 'This raid, apart from its reconnaissance value, brought about an extremely satisfactory air battle in the West which Fighter Command wish they could repeat every week.'[131] This disguised the fact that the raid had been a fiasco. Of the 5,000 Canadian troops who made up the bulk of the force, only 2,211 made it back; over 1,000 were killed and the rest were taken prisoner.[132] But although the raid was to become a long-standing source of bitterness in Canada it caused little controversy amongst MPs at the time, doubtless because Churchill had for the moment succeeded in glossing it over. In fact, the political temperature was now so much lower than it had been in July that the debate petered out. Cripps, as Leader of the House, chose to lecture MPs for their inattention, rather pompously reprimanding those who had wandered out of the Chamber while Churchill was speaking. His presumption in lecturing members on parliamentary etiquette got him 'into very bad odour with all parties in the House'.[133] He also displeased Churchill, who said in Cabinet that Cripps's statement 'might be construed as an encouragement to Members to make speeches critical of the Government's conduct of the war. In his view, it was satisfactory that Members should have found in his speech nothing on which they wished to comment.'[134] Churchill argued: 'MPs don't work by making speeches: watchdogs can be silent'.[135] But Cripps's rebuke struck a chord with a majority of the public. MPs were referred to as 'old men who needed their lunch' and their behaviour incurred 'condemnation, contempt and disgust'. People said that parliament was 'a wash out'.[136]

The failure of Cripps's mission to India in the spring had been followed in August by a new nationalist campaign under the slogan 'Quit India'. Gandhi, Nehru, and other Congress leaders were arrested by the British, and demonstrations were violently suppressed. Churchill was due to make a statement on the situation in the Commons on 10 September. Amery sent him a note to help him prepare, but when he asked if he had read it, the Prime Minister reacted furiously. Yes, he had read it, he said, but 'If we ever have to quit India we shall quit it in a blaze of glory, and the chapter that shall be ended then will be the most glorious chapter of that country, not merely in relation to the past but equally in relation to the future, however distant that may be. That will be my statement on India tomorrow.'[137] However, he did sit down with Amery who managed to get him to modify his original draft.[138]

Amery noted that Churchill's statement 'evoked ringing cheers from our people and greatly upset many of the Labour people, including a good many moderates'.[139] Churchill made clear, however, that the government stood by the Cripps offer, should the Indians choose to accept it in the future. This ensured that Cripps, who was now pondering resigning, could not do so on the issue of India, even though he thought the speech 'harmful and foolish'.[140] The statement was undoubtedly provocative. Churchill described the anti-British campaign as a 'revolutionary movement' and suggested that the Congress Party had been aided by Japanese fifth-columnists. He noted that large numbers of reinforcements had reached India and that 'the numbers of white soldiers now in that country, though very small compared with its size and population, are larger than at any time in the British connection'. Therefore, 'the situation in India at this moment gives no occasion for undue despondency or alarm'.[141] The response of the Indian nationalist press was one of outrage.[142] Muhammad Ali Jinnah of the Muslim League—which was opposed to Congress—was also critical.[143] The India League, a Congress-supporting group based in London, produced a point-by-point rebuttal of Churchill's statement. It noted: 'The decisive factor in the British Government's sense of strength and security of its own power in India is the presence of "white" soldiers. There is not even the pretence here that India's defence is a popular concern or that this is a people's war. Mr Churchill's description can only apply to an army of occupation.'[144] The impact in America was bad as well. 'Winston's statement on India will not have done us much good here,' Lord Halifax complained. 'Why must he talk about *white* troops, when the "British army in India" would have served his purpose just as well?'[145] There was also some criticism from the British public, who did not wish to slam the door on progress in India, even though they were 'fed up with Gandhi and Congress'.[146] One RAF corporal writing in his diary thought it 'A most tactless and stupid speech [...] nicely calculated to cause further bitterness in India & fresh doubts about British Imperialism in American minds.'[147] A. L. Baker, a Buckinghamshire chemist wrote: 'Churchill's statement on India makes me despair'.[148] But it seems that few people felt about the issue anything like that strongly.

Although the next two months were dramatic ones on the battlefront in North Africa, they were rather quiet ones on the rhetorical front in London. On 12 October Churchill was awarded the Freedom of the City of Edinburgh and used the occasion to give an optimistic review of the war situation. He noted that the Nazi leadership had become 'more talkative lately', with Ribbentrop, Goering, and Hitler making speeches in which could be heard, Churchill said, 'the dull, low, whining note of fear'.[149] On the whole the public received the speech well, Home Intelligence noted.

There were complaints that 'he didn't tell us anything new' and that 'he buttered up the Scotch too much', but people appreciated 'his correct interpretation of the mind of the enemy' and his 'argument that, in spite of successes, the Germans cherish little hope of ultimate victory'.[150] At the end of the month, Churchill and South African Prime Minister J. C. Smuts addressed a gathering of miners, mine managers, and colliery owners in London in a bid to boost production. Three thousand men were there. It was billed as a private meeting, helping to give the miners the sense that Churchill was confiding in them. He spoke of the ongoing battle in Egypt ('It is going to be a fight through to a finish') and warned against complacency ('Do not let us suppose that the dangers are past').[151] The event appears to have led to an 'improved spirit' amongst the miners, which was also attributable to good news from North Africa. Those present on the day realized that 'Mr Churchill did not tell them anything they did not already know: it was "his personal touch that convinced them".'[152]

Events in North Africa now drove everything else out of the news. Churchill had sacked General Auchinleck in August, believing him guilty of excessive caution. Auchinleck's successor, Bernard Montgomery, was cautious too but was better at handling the Prime Minister. Further weeks of preparation, combined with Montgomery's skill at boosting troop morale, led to a successful offensive that fructified in November with the famous victory at El Alamein. Anglo-American landings in French North Africa— Operation Torch—provided further good tidings. 'I have never promised anything but blood, tears, toil and sweat,' Churchill remarked when he spoke at the Lord Mayor's luncheon at the Mansion House on 10 November. 'Now, however, we have a new experience. We have victory—a remarkable and definite victory.' Rommel's army had been routed, he said, and 'very largely destroyed as a fighting force'. Having emphasized that the Germans were now 'receiving back again that measure of fire and steel which they have so often meted out to others', Churchill delivered one of his most superb lines: 'Now, this is not the end. It is not even the beginning of the end. But it is, perhaps, the end of the beginning.'[153]

The speech also contained another famous line—'I have not become the King's First Minister in order to preside over the liquidation of the British Empire.' It is worth noting that this comment came just after a passage in which Churchill emphasized that Britain had no 'acquisitive appetites or ambitions' and would not exploit its victories to gain territory at the expense of France.[154] Vichy propaganda at this time presented the

British as the thieves of French imperial territory; the prickly De Gaulle needed reassurance too.[155] But the remark was obviously bound to be read as an assertion of Churchill's 'diehard' credentials. Churchill had reached a position where he was politically unassailable, and took the opportunity to publicly dig in his heels against pressure for imperial reform. His decision to do this needs to be read in the context of the growing demand, coming in particular from the United States, that in future colonies should be subjected to some form of international control or 'trusteeship'.[156] Churchill's recent Indian statement had done nothing to damp down US hostility to British imperialism, although many Britons felt that it was hypocritical for Americans—who operated a 'colour bar' in their own military—to seek to lecture them on race relations. In October, Wendell Willkie, the Republican candidate defeated by Roosevelt in 1940, had called for the 'orderly but scheduled abolition of the colonial system'. Willkie stressed that he wanted to see the Empire gradually transform itself completely into a Commonwealth of self-governing nations—the very ideal espoused by Churchill's friend Smuts in a speech to both Houses of Parliament days earlier.[157] But Churchill did not like this type of criticism, however moderately expressed. A sign of his concern is that he had extracts of Willkie's broadcast circulated to the Cabinet.[158] As Mackenzie King commented to Roosevelt, the 'liquidation' remark 'was an answer to Willkie'.[159] Willkie hit back in turn against Churchill's defence of 'the old imperialistic order'.[160] Churchill now also used his position of strength to move Cripps—who had differed with him on military strategy—to a position outside the War Cabinet. The Washington Embassy reported: 'Willkie's speeches, Indian situation, transfer of Sir S. Cripps and interpretations of [the] Prime Minister's "Hold on to our own" speech have tended to revive picture of Britain as a stronghold of reactionary imperialism.'[161]

Churchill's audience at the Mansion House greeted the 'liquidation' line with loud cheers.[162] The public's reaction was seemingly divided. Home Intelligence received reports suggesting popular satisfaction with the passage in two regions and criticism or controversy in two others. Perhaps the fact that the Pathé and Movietone newsreels omitted this part of the speech from their coverage is explained by the editors' awareness that it was likely to be divisive. More generally, as one would expect, the speech was received extremely well. Churchill's prestige was said to have reached its highest level.[163] A. Schofield, a Bradford housewife, grumbled about the 'confirmed grousers' who would never give Churchill his due.[164] Mass-Observation did pick up some critical comments: 'Churchill is the root of the trouble. You can't call regaining something you've lost victory'; 'Churchill's speeches occupy 6 Vols, and Stalin's 4 pages. Churchill and his lot should all go out'.[165] But even some habitual sceptics acknowledged his achievements. The victory 'provided Churchill with a grand text for his lord mayor's banquet speech', admitted R. W. Fenn. 'He had a great deal to crow about, and no-one can begrudge him his share in the credit for a great operation.'[166] Still, even at this moment of maximum triumph, Churchill's rhetoric was not for everyone. According to M. A. Pratt's diary: 'My aunt, listening to the Prime Minister's speech, remarked of "our greatest orator", "He's no speaker, is he?"'[167]

Plate 1 Winston Churchill as an orator. Sketches made in the House of Commons by Samuel Begg showing Churchill's parliamentary mannerisms.

Plate 2 Cartoon, 'Siege Guns of Rhetoric', showing politicians of different persuasions combining together against the common enemy in the early part of the First World War. Depicted as cannons, they are: Lloyd George, Winston Churchill, Asquith, John Redmond, Bonar Law, and Will Crooks.

Plate 3 Winston Churchill, 1939. The First Lord of the Admiralty gives a speech about the enlargement of the British Territorial Army.

Plate 4 *Illustrated London News*, 13 July 1940: 'Mr. Churchill cheered by the House'.

Plate 5 Second World War propaganda poster. Churchill's praise of 'The Few' was made in his speech of 20 August 1940. This poster helped the phrase gain iconic status.

Plate 6 *Daily Worker*, 22 August 1940: 'We few, we happy few'. This cartoon satirizes the survival of pre-war appeasers within Churchill's government.

Plate 7 Listening to Churchill. People in a pub listen to a radio speech by the Prime Minister, summer 1941. Diary evidence shows that people did not always listen with such rapt attention.

verdict was 'He's slipping fast.'

But the latter part of the speech, about the fall of Singapore, we both listened to intently. As I listened I contrasted the 'blood toil & sweat' stuff with what I'd seen in Luton streets an hour or so earlier.

The most dangerous part of the speech was where he made the false suggestion that Russia does not remove its failures, & (by implication) therefore neither should we. I sincerely hope the public won't be fooled by that lie.

No, it wasn't a good speech. Not inspiring: the old rhetoric is wearing thin. It was the speech of a man on the defensive. I don't think it's done anything to improve Churchill's standing with the public.

Plate 8   Winston Churchill broadcasting in 1942.

Plate 9   Extract from Denis Argent's diary, recording his army comrades' reactions to Churchill's broadcast on the fall of Singapore.

Plate 10   Cartoon, *Daily Mail*, 21 May 1943: 'After listening to Churchill he just ate his way clean through the carpet and out of the room.'

Plate 11   Scene in the Galleria Umberto, Naples, 13 March 1944, when left-wing Italian parties demonstrated against Churchill's support of King Victor Emmanuel and General Badoglio; the former partisan Eugenio Gentili Tedeschi is speaking.

Plate 12   Churchill speaking from a balcony to crowds of people celebrating Victory in Europe Day in Whitehall at the end of the Second World War.

Plate 13   Churchill addresses the party conference of the National Union of Conservative and Unionist Associations, London, 31 March 1945.

Plate 14 Cartoon by David Low, *Evening Standard*, 7 June 1945: 'Dreamland'.

Plate 15 Removal men outside 10 Downing Street, 1 August 1945.

6

'What a Wartime Speech
Should Be, I Suppose'

The victory in North Africa was followed by a new political crisis. This was a product of the Vichy–Free French split and conflicting Anglo-American views of how to deal with its consequences on the ground. At the insistence of the USA, De Gaulle had not been told in advance of Operation Torch, the landings on Vichy colonial soil. To add injury to insult, the Americans made a bargain with the collaborationist Admiral François Darlan, who agreed to call a ceasefire, in exchange for being named 'High Commissioner for North Africa'. The Germans reacted by seizing the previously Unoccupied Zone in France. De Gaulle of course regarded Darlan as a traitor, and Churchill's own first reaction was that the Admiral was someone who ought to be shot.[1] British public opinion was uneasy about the recognition of Darlan, who was seen as an Anglophobe and a Quisling: 'a statement is impatiently awaited'.[2] A further complication was the presence in North Africa of General Henri Giraud, who had recently escaped from Vichy imprisonment. For the British and Americans, Giraud was a potentially more pliable leader than the troublesome De Gaulle, to whom he was an unwelcome if rather ineffective rival. Although initially sympathetic to De Gaulle, Churchill throughout the affair prioritized his relationship with Roosevelt, who, at least for the time being, had no qualms about dealing with Darlan. This led to further ructions in the De Gaulle–Churchill relationship, as the Prime Minister struggled to assuage popular and parliamentary concern without offending the US President. De Gaulle became incredulous at Churchill's willingness to sacrifice British dignity in the interests of harmony with the Americans; Churchill showed both ruthlessness and a capacity for self-deception as he changed his position in the interests of *realpolitik*.

Meeting with De Gaulle at 10 Downing Street on 16 November, Churchill did his best to soothe his feelings, reminding him that 'in his speech the other day at the Guildhall, he had praised the General and the patriots who in France followed him in legions, while he let it be understood that Giraud was famous only for his escapes'. De Gaulle expressed his gratitude for 'this subtle distinction' but pressed Churchill to stand up to the Americans over Darlan.[3] Churchill did indeed cable Roosevelt attacking Darlan's 'odious record' and warning that a permanent arrangement with him would be unacceptable to public opinion.[4] But although the President—facing growing criticism at home—stated publicly that the deal with Darlan was only a temporary expedient, it seemed that in practice that expedient might last a long time.[5] Churchill pandered to Roosevelt's dislike of De Gaulle by blocking him from making a broadcast, which Eden had approved, a fact that soon became public knowledge.[6] Within a few days, Churchill seemed 'very anti-de Gaulle' and 'more and more enthusiastic over Darlan'.[7] In public, though, he skirted around the question. At the end of the month he gave a broadcast, which was expected, according to the Associated Press, 'to shed considerable light on French developments' and to include a plea for French unity.[8] But although Churchill referred to 'that reunion of France without which French resurrection is impossible', none of the French actors was mentioned by name.[9] 'Listened to Churchill's speech', wrote Yorkshire housewife M. C. Towler. 'Didn't think much of it. He said nothing quite well [...] I did not think his remark to the effect that now that France was completely invaded she was at last united particularly helpful or tactful—though I see the point.'[10] 'Found the Prime Minister's speech easier to listen to than on other occasions: less hesitant,' noted another diarist, Margaret Congdon, who gave her occupation as nurse companion. 'Evidently we are not to be told anything about Darlan—the turncoat...'[11] J. Hinton, a woman teacher from Bedford, found the broadcast 'Cheering in some ways; but was terribly sorry that there was nothing about De Gaulle, & no statement about post-war planning'.[12]

This is not to say that the speech was vacuous or generally unpopular. From the domestic morale perspective, Churchill maintained his usual balancing act, on the one hand warning that 1943 would be 'a stern and terrible year' and on the other stressing that Britain would meet it 'with the assurance of ever-growing strength'.[13] According to Home Intelligence, his warnings that the war would last a long time yet 'are thought to have done some good already, and if this speech has been less popular than some of the others, it is believed that this is partly due to disappointment among the optimists at his references to "more bitter and bloody years"'.[14] It was indeed a hard message to hear. 'I listened to Churchill with a shadow on my heart,' wrote housewife Nella Last. 'It's bad enough to think "privately" all that he said, without hearing them [sic] on the wireless, to see the long, hard and bitter road, to feel the shadows deepen rather than lighten, to envy the ones who think that Germany will collapse in the spring.'[15] Churchill's comments on the war's likely course were targeted at opinion abroad as well as at home, of course. He predicted that the war in Europe might come to an end before that in Asia, in which case, he said, 'we should at once bring all our forces to the other side of the world' to aid Britain's allies there.[16] This was seen at the time as his way of disposing of 'American and Chinese fears that Britain may pull out of the war once Hitler is defeated'.[17] Such fears may not have been widespread or realistic, but they nonetheless had to be addressed.

Churchill also denounced Mussolini. He warned: 'our operations in French North Africa should enable us to bring the weight of the war home to the Italian Fascist State in a manner not hitherto dreamed of by its guilty leaders or, still less, by the unfortunate people Mussolini has led, exploited and disgraced.' Once the remaining Axis forces were driven from the tip of Tunisia, a 'prolonged scientific and shattering air attack' on Italy could be expected. Churchill hinted, though, that the Italian people could avert it by overthrowing the Duce, the 'one man' who was responsible for Italy's predicament.[18] As if to drive home the point, the RAF launched a raid on Turin using 8,000-pound bombs known as 'triple blockbusters'. Churchill's speech was transmitted in twenty-four languages in total, and was repeatedly re-broadcast in French, German, and Italian.[19] The broadcast stung the long-silent Mussolini into reply. 'Churchill's address honours me because it proves I am the real antagonist of Great Britain,' he claimed privately.[20] Addressing the Fascist Chamber of Corporations, he coughed and breathed heavily as he tried to rebut Churchill point by point. Quoting the accusation that he alone was responsible for Italy's entry into the war, Mussolini asked scornfully, 'when did the Prime Minister ever ask the British people if they wanted war?'[21] But the speech was an own goal. Foreign Minister Ciano judged: 'It will not be difficult for English propaganda to refute it effectively, even if it does not avail itself of Mussolini's glaring slip about the "dinner jackets worn by the English while drinking their five o'clock tea".'[22] According to British Home Intelligence, those who thought at first that

Churchill's appeal to Italians was not especially effective were 'persuaded it was worth while by Mussolini's reply', which was ridiculed as 'a very poor comic opera effort'. Furthermore, 'Mr Churchill's "pungent references to Musso" were particularly enjoyed by workers'.[23]

Yet in spite of the speech's good reception, it had done nothing to tackle the disquiet about Darlan. In his memoirs, Churchill recalled how on 10 December 'the mounting pressures in the circles of which I was conscious led me to seek refuge in Secret Session of the House of Commons. The speech which I then made was conceived with the sole purpose of changing the prevailing opinion, and I chose with greatest care the points to make.'[24] Harold Nicolson wrote:

> I have never heard him more forceful, informative or convincing. He refers to Pétain (whose name he pronounces 'Peatayne') as 'that antique defeatist'. He convinces us (a) that we [the British] were never consulted about the Darlan move; (b) that when it happened, he himself realised at once what trouble would be caused, and warned Roosevelt accordingly; (c) that it is purely temporary.[25]

This was an accurate account, as far as it went, but Nicolson discreetly failed to mention some crucial passages. Having explained that many French people regarded Vichy as a legally constituted regime, Churchill noted the power of Darlan's (actually false) claim to be acting with the authority of Pétain when making his switch to the Allies. This gave Darlan the ability to get the forces under his command to change sides, whereas to have involved De Gaulle, seen by many as a rebel against the French state, would have been a 'red rag to the bull'. His participation, Churchill argued, would have destroyed all hope that the landings would be unopposed. Churchill's original speech notes show him speaking even more dismissively of De Gaulle later in the speech. Although the General had been recognized as head of the Free French since 1940, and the British had financed him and helped him as much as possible, he could not be viewed as the representative of France as a whole:

> I cannot feel tt de Gaulle is France, still less tt Darlan and Vichy are France. France is something much greater, more complex, more formidable than any of these sectional manifestations. I hv tried to work as far as possible w Gen. de Gaulle, making allowances for his many difficulties, for his temperament and for the limitations of his outlook. [...] However now we are in Secret Session the House must not be led to believe tt Gen. de Gaulle is an unfaltering friend of Britain. On the contrary, I think he is one of those good

Frenchmen who hv a traditional antagonism ingrained in French hearts by centuries of war against the English.

Churchill then outlined a series of complaints about De Gaulle's past behaviour and habit of spreading Anglophobia. In a notorious press interview in 1941, for example, the General had alleged that Britain coveted France's African colonies. On a 1942 visit to Syria, 'his whole object seemed to be to foment ill-will between the Brit. Military and Free French civil administrations' and to undermine Syrian claims to post-war independence. Churchill then said—arguably with some exaggeration—that he maintained friendly relations with De Gaulle personally and continued to help him as much as he possibly could. This was owed him because he had stood up against the French surrender in 1940. 'All the same, I could not recommend the House to base all their hopes and confidence upon him, and still less to assume at this stage tt it is our duty to place, so far as we hv the power, the destiny of France in his hands.'[26]

The 'red rag' comment and the long, scathing section on De Gaulle were so toxic that they were silently omitted when Churchill's *Secret Session Speeches* were published in 1946.[27] At first it was planned to insert a note in the text stating that 'The Prime Minister [...] referred to General De Gaulle in terms which, though courteous and friendly, were critical. As General De Gaulle is now the head of a friendly State, the publication of this passage would be premature.'[28] But this would have given the game away. Churchill did not reveal the excisions in his memoirs either, and even the supposedly *Complete Speeches* of 1974 reproduced the bowdlerized version.[29] For the immediate audience of MPs, though, the comments certainly had their effect. 'Chips' Channon—a less discreet diarist than Nicolson—noted that Churchill 'told much which surprised the House but which was no news to me. How the French hated de Gaulle and how the Americans refused to have anything to do with the free French movement, etc. [...] He was in the highest fettle, and I have never admired him so much.'[30] Labour MPs were also impressed. One, W. H. Green, commented that 'it was the best speech he had heard from the PM'.[31] According to Churchill himself, 'I do not remember any speech out of hundreds which I made where I felt opinion change so palpably and decisively. [...] The Commons were convinced, and the fact that all further Parliamentary Opposition stopped after the Secret Session quenched the hostile Press and reassured the country.'[32] Nevertheless, seemingly reflecting his own continued doubts, Home Secretary Herbert Morrison warned: 'The Prime Minister's speech in the Secret Session set at rest for the time being the doubts which existed in Parliamentary circles as to the wisdom of doing business with Admiral Darlan. When the argument of military exigency is no longer so pressing, we may expect a recrudescence of anxiety.'[33] The problem was solved comprehensively by Darlan's assassination on Christmas Eve at the hands of a patriotic young Frenchman—and also by the hasty trial and execution of the killer, which put paid to awkward questions about British and Free French complicity in the murder.[34]

In January 1943, Roosevelt and Churchill met at Casablanca. With Darlan out of the way, the two leaders forced a reluctant rapprochement between Giraud and De Gaulle. At Churchill's urging, the Americans agreed to delay a cross-Channel invasion until the following year, and in the meantime strike at Italy via Sicily. Roosevelt, at a joint press conference with Churchill, urged the 'unconditional surrender' of Germany, Italy, and Japan, a statement that took the Prime Minister by surprise but which became official Allied policy.[35] A Mass-Observation report found that just over half of those interviewed said that they were pleased at the meeting's outcome, but there was also plenty of caution. Those who expressed hostility generally did so on the grounds that it was action that was wanted, not words:

> It is notable that this is the general reaction to speeches and reports. This attitude has grown up gradually, but was accentuated last spring when the demand for a Second Front became urgent, and has grown up in the measure of public disappointment when this failed to materialise. Several people—all men, by the way—made comments which showed a more or less overt resentment of Churchill's sense of drama and unexpectedness. These people seemed to consider his travels as a form of 'gadding about.'[36]

After a series of further travels, Churchill arrived in Tripoli, where he greeted thousands of troops and generated much exotic newsreel footage. Addressing the Eighth Army, he poured scorn on Rommel and told his listeners that 'your feats will gleam and glow and will be a source of song and story long after we who are gathered here have passed away'.[37] It was stirring stuff but it did not please everyone. One Mass-Observer recorded a conversation in a canteen with a 50-year-old housewife, who criticized both Churchill's Tripoli remarks and his most recent (December) broadcast. 'She could not see the point of mere castigation. "Anybody can run others down but it takes more than that to be great".'[38]

Churchill's 'Odyssey' boosted his popularity at home, and this can be seen in the warm reaction to the Commons war review he gave after his return. He was able to boast of progress in the war against the U-boats and to assert that the Allies now had 'a complete plan of action' which 'we are going to carry out according to ability during the next nine months'.[39] Although German news bulletins were peppered with brief references to Churchill's speech, the population were told that the British still faced a desperate shipping problem.[40] The British public welcomed his optimism and was strengthened in its belief that 'something big will happen soon'—speculation raged as to where the Second Front would open.[41] Addressing concerns about former Vichy personnel now involved in the administration of French north-west Africa, Churchill stated that he was more concerned about the security of the Allied forces than about 'the past records of various French functionaries whom the Americans have deemed it expedient to employ'.[42] His comments on this topic reduced suspicion and criticism, although it did not go away entirely.[43] A few days later Churchill fell ill with pneumonia, with the result that he did not give another speech for over a month.

When he did, in a broadcast of 21 March, he at once set out to reassure the public that he was still fit for his job. 'Although for a week I had a fairly stiff dose of fever, which but for modern science might have had awkward consequences, I wish to make it clear that I never for a moment had to relinquish the responsible direction of affairs,' he said. This broadcast—the so-called 'Four Years' Plan speech—provoked a fair amount of criticism from the public, mainly on account of Churchill's treatment of post-war domestic policy. (This is discussed in Chapter 8.) However, the speech also dealt with the future of the world as a whole and the question of what international machinery to help keep the peace should supersede the League of Nations. Planning should be headed by 'the three great victorious powers, the British Commonwealth of Nations, the United States and Soviet Russia', Churchill said. At this time, the term 'United Nations' referred to the military alliance of which Britain, the USA, and the USSR were a part. Churchill stated:

> One can imagine that under a world institution embodying or representing the United Nations, and some day all nations, there should come into being a Council of Europe and a Council of Asia. [...] We must try [...] to make the Council of Europe, or whatever it may be called, into a really effective League, with all the strongest forces concerned woven into its texture, with a High Court to adjust disputes, and with forces, armed forces, national or international or both, held ready to enforce these decisions and prevent renewed aggression and the preparation of future wars.[44]

This was an early sketch of Churchill's ideas for what would become the post-war United Nations Organization. His idea of regional councils can be seen as a way of trying to ensure that a future world body did not get too closely involved with the affairs of the British Empire: the European colonial powers would band together, at arm's length from countries that might criticize them. Ultimately, he did not get what he wanted but at the time his proposals were well received internationally. According to the BBC, thousands of copies of a clandestine newspaper including a summary of the speech were sold in Warsaw under the noses of the Germans.[45] Elsewhere, commentators noted Churchill's intention to maintain post-war cooperation with the USSR, and a long summary of the speech was published prominently in the Russian press.[46] Those offering praise included former US President Herbert Hoover, who noted that the existing Pan-American Union formed a potential foundation for the regional councils model, although another Republican, Senator Joseph H. Ball, claimed that the regional approach would create 'a new balance of power which would eventually lead to war'.[47]

In the USA there was much pro-China sentiment as well as a pragmatic desire to boost the status of Chiang Kai-shek's Nationalists in order to help keep them in the war against the Japanese. Thus as the British Embassy reported, the initial warm reaction in America was followed by a 'stream of sharp criticism [...] directed by a number of radio commentators and in press against lack of reference to China among the powers on whose co-operation future settlement must rest'. This was echoed by Sinophile politicians such as House Majority Leader John W. McCormack.[48] Moreover, Churchill had not only emphasized that victory over Germany (rather than Japan) was 'our first and most supreme task' but had also said that 'there will certainly be a partial demobilisation following on the defeat of Hitler'.[49] This brought criticism from those Americans who wanted a higher concentration of effort against Japan, and led to 'widespread talk in Washington of the deep concern alleged to be felt by interested parties', i.e. the Chinese.[50] This talk was well founded. The American chargé d'affaires in China reported to Washington the findings of Everett F. Drumright, an official based in Sichuan province:

> Mr. Drumright reports that he has detected among Chinese officials, educators and others with whom he has discussed Mr. Churchill's speech an ill-concealed feeling of disappointment, frustration and even anger. The Chinese people appear to have been led to think in recent months that Germany's

collapse would be a matter of a short time and that pressure against Japan would not be relaxed. They are consequently dismayed at the prospect of a further delay in the attempts of their allies to turn their strength against Japan. Mr. Drumright states that the Chinese people appear to be becoming tired of a seemingly endless conflict and that they feel that China is being ignored with respect to assistance which is her due. Mr. Churchill's speech increased that feeling of discontent and disillusionment. The omission of China in the portions of the speech having to do with post-war conferences was also a cause of deep resentment, for the Chinese regard themselves as one of the four major powers and thus entitled to a suitable place in the discussion of world problems. Mr. Drumright concludes that this speech may have destroyed whatever goodwill that may have been built up in China by British propaganda efforts during the past year.[51]

Madame Chiang herself publicly joined the critics in a Chicago speech in which she warned 'the men who fathered the Atlantic Charter' not to 'tantalize the sorely tried, staunch people fighting against violence'.[52] It turned out that part of the problem was that a crucial sentence, in which Churchill explained the physical reasons why not all of the troops which would become available after VE Day could be transferred to the Far East, had by an oversight been left out of the British press bulletin published in China.[53] British efforts at reassuring the Chinese were, to an extent, successful. Eden made a speech in Maryland which put China on the same level as Britain, America, and the USSR: 'Let China not misdoubt us,' he said.[54] In America, there were 'universal expressions of relief, simulated or real', but although Madame Chiang went to lengths to praise Eden's comments, Sino-British relations remained troubled, not least over the status of Tibet.[55]

Churchill's speech had a surprise punch-line, not included in his original text.[56] He revealed that Montgomery had sent him a message that the Eighth Army was 'on the move' as it entered the final phase of its battle with the remnants of the Afrika Korps.[57] 'This news left a thrill as he finished his talk,' wrote shopkeeper A. White.[58] Axis resistance continued until May—Churchill made some short statements to Parliament but gave no major speeches—with its final collapse paving the way for the forthcoming attack on Sicily. In America again that month, the Prime Minister agreed with Roosevelt a target date for the invasion of France across the English Channel: 1 May 1944.[59] From Washington, Churchill made a broadcast to Britain in tribute to the Home Guard, in which he rather implausibly talked up the continued threat of a German invasion.[60] When the speech was about to start, R. H. Allott, an insurance clerk from Newport, was just finishing an evening's gardening. A neighbour came past with a spade over his shoulder. Allott wrote in his diary: '"Fancy knocking off early just to listen to *him*", I jeered. "Being a H.G. [Home Guard] I'm only obeying orders to listen", he countered.' Allott did in fact listen to Churchill himself but wrote: 'It was worse than I thought. [...] He couldn't think of much to say, which was just as well.'[61] Although the Home Guard were delighted by the speech, 'most other people were disappointed' according to Home Intelligence. They had been hoping for 'a paean of victory about Africa': after all, 'People hope for something juicy when he broadcasts'. Nevertheless, the public was pleased to hear from him irrespective of the content, welcomed his American mission, and expected to get more substance from the speech he was due to give to Congress a few days later.[62]

Before giving that address, Churchill was nervous. He said he felt like Sydney Carton in *A Tale of Two Cities* before he was executed, but he gave the speech 'in a very natural way, [with] not too much in the way of gesticulation'.[63] He began with a review of the seventeen months that had passed since he had last addressed Congress. The Anglo–American alliance had worked well he said, but he also noted the 'very heavy misfortunes' that had occurred in the Far East and observed that many of the territories conquered by the Japanese had yet to be retrieved. And then he came to the crucial point: 'let no one suggest that we British have not at least as great an interest as the United States in the unflinching and relentless waging of war against Japan.'[64] This was no idle remark. Churchill knew very well that Britain's commitment to the Far Eastern war had been publicly called into question and that 'Pacific first' sentiment was growing, fuelled in part by his own recent comments on demobilization.[65] Two days earlier, Democratic Senator Albert B. Chandler made a speech strongly critical of British policy in the Pacific and urging a swift death-blow against the Japanese. The press suggested that this reflected disputes within the American military. General George C. Marshall, Army Chief of Staff, wanted an early cross-Channel invasion; Admiral Ernest King, Commander-in-Chief of the Navy, prioritized the Pacific at the expense of all other fronts. Chandler's speech won bipartisan support (as well as criticism). The charge against the British was that they were not doing enough to help China and that British forces in India were not making sufficient efforts against the Japanese in Burma.[66] Churchill had worked on the Japan and China section of his speech until almost the last minute.[67] He pledged: 'I am here to tell you that we will wage war, side by side with you, in accordance with the best strategic employment of our forces, while there is breath in our bodies and while blood flows in our veins.' One particular remark was interpreted as a direct reply to Chandler:'Lots of people can make good plans for winning the war if they have not got to carry them out.'[68]

Churchill made an effort to reach out to his audience, giving it information which he thought it either did not know or fully appreciate—such as the fact that the majority of US forces were already deployed in the Pacific.[69] The speech was described by one Japanese newspaper as 'the pathetic groan of battered Britain'; Churchill was said to have appealed for American help like a prisoner in the dock.[70] According to notes of a Cabinet meeting after his return to Britain, he said 'U.S. Executive treats Congress as an enemy—surprised at the sort of speech I made, tho' I explained it was common-form for H/Commons'.[71] The technique seems to have worked well. 'When the PM first entered the House, the crowd was a bit aloof,' wrote the syndicated columnist Drew Pearson. 'The spectators sat back in their chairs. But as he warmed to his speech, they leaned forward, until every member of Congress was heartily with him.'[72] Supreme Court Justice Felix Frankfurter noted that Churchill had been wise to speak 'exclusively in his capacity as Prime Minister for War'. If he had mentioned other issues than those relating to the conduct of the war, he might have raised distracting controversies.[73] Criticism was not completely extinguished, however. Chandler claimed that the speech left important questions unanswered.[74] Some other Senators indicated their intention to continue to press for a reversal of strategy.[75] However, Washington opinion was undoubtedly mollified, and Roosevelt—who again listened on the radio—'seemed very pleased'.[76]

It was natural that he should have been, given that Churchill had dwelt on 'The wisdom of the founders of the American Constitution' in making the President Commander-in-Chief of the armed forces.[77] Churchill claimed that the successful prosecution of total war required the combination of political and military authority in one person. This was significant in the context of speculation about a fourth term for FDR. Pearson suggested that Churchill's comments dovetailed with the strategy 'already devised by high-up advisers of the president, that in any 4th term campaign it should be hammered home that Roosevelt is Commander-in-Chief and the job of Commander-in-Chief must not be changed in wartime'. Pearson, a notorious muckraker, added: 'it looks as if the Prime Minister had already laid the groundwork for '44'.[78] Churchill told Vice-President Henry Wallace that Wendell Willkie—who was to run in the

1944 Republican primaries—'disapproved of his speech before Congress as interfering too much in the internal affairs of the United States'.[79] The Free French were also upset, for rather different reasons. Churchill had referred to 'the gallant General Giraud' but not to his rival—in the sure knowledge of how sensitive De Gaulle was to such things.[80] Furthermore, the question of combining the roles of head of government and commander-in-chief was a known point of dispute between the two French leaders: De Gaulle insisted that it was undemocratic to combine the two functions in one man and Giraud held that it was essential.[81] Churchill may not have consciously had this in mind, but it nonetheless seems clear that he had been affected by the anti-Gaullist Washington atmosphere.[82]

In Britain, by contrast, the speech did not seem very controversial. According to Home Intelligence it was seen by many as 'his greatest speech yet'; people were cheered and inspired by his cheerful, confident tone. It was believed that his promise to prosecute the war against Japan to the end would put paid to American doubts: 'some irritation is reported that "Americans should be so worried about attack from the Japanese when they are so many thousands of miles away" and when we are so close to the Germans'.[83] There were some undercurrents of indifference or dissent. The speech was heard by 53.9 per cent of the potential audience, a figure that was not especially high. According to Army clerk J. R. Reber, the speech was considered good by 'the few' who read it or heard it.[84] 'To my surprise I found I was the only female member of the office staff who listened all the way thru to Churchill from Washington last night,' wrote housewife and clerk N. E. Underwood. 'One, an ardent Tory, said "I listened a bit but I wasn't interested really!" All are NOT in agreement with Churchill's promise to continue the war to the end. All are agreed that because we began the war without [the] USA and once stood alone, they shd end up on their own to balance things.'[85] In what was now a familiar complaint, railway clerk M. R. J. Wilmett wrote that Churchill's speeches 'are generally rousing and agreeable but sometimes he seems to have a vindictiveness that I cannot approve of'.[86] Similarly, but more strongly, office worker Lionel Randle observed: 'I'm beginning to dislike Churchill. He seems such a bloodthirsty hound. I thought some of the passages in his speech to Congress were nauseating. He, at least, is one man whom I believe to be thoroughly enjoying this war.' Randle knew he was in a minority, although he may have exaggerated his own isolation: 'I wonder how far I should get any support for such a view—not an inch, I bet.'[87]

Although Churchill did a good job of smoothing over strategic conflicts in public, he could be highly disruptive behind closed doors. Alan Brooke, the CIGS, complained during the Washington trip of Churchill's temperamental inconsistencies that threatened to derail sensitive talks with the Americans:

> At times the war may be won by bombing and all must be sacrificed to it. At others it becomes essential for us to bleed ourselves dry on the Continent because Russia is doing the same. At others our main effort must be in the Mediterranean, directed against Italy or Balkans alternatively, with sporadic desires to invade Norway and 'roll up the map in the opposite direction to Hitler'! But more often than all he wants to carry out ALL operations simultaneously irrespective of shortages of shipping![88]

Churchill returned to Britain via Algiers, where De Gaulle met Giraud for what the Prime Minister openly referred to as 'tense discussions'.[89] These resulted in the creation of a French Committee of National Liberation which included both men; but De Gaulle quickly gained the upper hand. When he reported to the House of Commons on 8 June, Churchill spoke optimistically of the apparent new-found French unity—but within a few days, and under pressure from Roosevelt, he was feeling exasperated by De Gaulle. He even briefed the press secretly on the General's 'undoubtedly Fascist and dictatorial tendencies'.[90]

If Churchill's 'extremely cautious and moderate' Commons speech contained little about impending operations, the public appreciated that 'he could hardly have told us more than he did' and admired his reticence.[91] At the end of the month he received the Freedom of the City of London at the Guildhall. In his speech he repeated the 'unconditional surrender' demand and said that it was 'very probable that there will be heavy fighting in the Mediterranean and elsewhere before the leaves of autumn fall'.[92] This helped dampen public impatience, with most people now taking it for granted 'that our next offensive will be opened before Autumn', although a few complained that 'they have heard about the second front until they are sick of it'. Amidst the enthusiasm, there was much discussion of when exactly autumn leaves start falling: 'Never has there been so much interest in trees'.[93]

In fact, Operation Husky—the invasion of Sicily—began on 10 July. On the 19th, the first bombing raid on Rome took place. A few days after that, Mussolini was forced from power after his associates turned on him. King Victor Emmanuel III imprisoned him and appointed Marshal Pietro Badoglio Prime Minister in his place. For the time being, though, Italy remained formally part of the Axis. At the same time, the Allies had grounds to believe that Badoglio would be willing to do a deal. Confusion reigned. Churchill had long been willing to offer peace to the Italians if they would overthrow Mussolini. To strike a bargain now might help maintain stability in Italy and avoid further Allied bloodshed. Yet the Casablanca demand for 'unconditional surrender' made it hard to settle for anything less. Moreover, Badoglio had been responsible for atrocities during the Abyssinian war; the King too had been complicit in the Fascist regime. There was the risk of another Darlan problem, although this time it was mainly American opinion that was hostile. Foreign Office Permanent Secretary Alexander Cadogan wrote: 'PM is keeping his head, but Washington are going off the rails with excited abuse of Badoglio and the King'.[94]

On 27 July, Churchill made a speech to the House of Commons which was noted for its lack of gloating over Mussolini's downfall.[95] He emphasized the situation's uncertainty, whilst arguing for the potential need to work with the new government: 'We do not know what is going to happen in Italy, and now that Mussolini has gone, and once the Fascist power is certainly and irretrievably broken, we should be foolish to deprive ourselves of any means of coming to general conclusions with the Italian nation.' For the meantime, the Italians should be left to 'stew in their own juice for a bit' in the hope that the unconditional surrender of Italy could in due course 'be brought about wholesale and not piecemeal'. If Italy did not surrender, the Allies would pursue the war against her without compromise.[96] Harold Nicolson liked the speech but thought the 'stew in their own juice' phrase unfortunate: 'Apart from the vulgarity of this, it is untranslatable into Italian. I tell our BBC people to be careful not to use words which could be twisted to mean, "Italy must boil in her own oil".'[97] 'Chips' Channon thought the speech restrained and statesmanlike: 'The consensus of opinion was that Churchill had been masterly'.[98] Leo Amery described it as 'a very fine performance, both adroit and wise, and incidentally a strong lead to the Americans not to persist in the idea that every form of Government in Italy must be smashed up first'.[99] The speech was a skilful attempt to maintain the 'unconditional surrender' line while at the same time leaving the door open for talks. In Britain, criticism was muted, although the left-wing weekly *Tribune* brought up the embarrassing question of Churchill's pre-war views on Italy: 'We were glad to see how much Mr Churchill has revised his previously held views on Mussolini and Fascism. But, in view of what he said so often on previous occasions in support of the Fascist dictator's battle against Socialistic working-class opposition, it might become the Prime Minister to be sparing in his estimation of what now is good for Italy; and perhaps to leave this matter to the judgment of his Socialist colleagues and the Italian people.'[100] Some US journalists criticized the speech as confusing, but Roosevelt said that although he had read it only cursorily he liked what he saw. He also denounced a US Office of War Information attack on Victor Emmanuel and Badoglio.[101] Rome radio's comment on Churchill's speech was that 'In the circumstances, Italy has only one choice—to continue to fight'.[102] It took weeks before negotiations came to fruition.

In August, Churchill travelled to North America once again, for a strategy conference (codenamed 'Quadrant') with the Americans hosted by the Canadians in Quebec. There was considerable criticism of the fact that Churchill took his wife Clementine and his daughter Mary with him. Adapting the official wartime slogan, people asked, 'Was their journey *really* necessary?'[103] But when it was announced that Churchill would broadcast, which after postponement he did on 31 August, there were high expectations. Due to technical problems the speech could not be heard directly in Britain and had to be read out by an announcer. This was a disappointment to many: 'Couldn't say anything but platitudes and in absence of personality was flat,' noted housewife G. F. Glover.[104] Retired policeman H. B. Monck had the opposite reaction: 'I heard Churchill's speech and for some reason it seemed to me the best I had heard him give, I think to some extent it was because I heard it read by someone else. I rather dislike Churchill's mannerisms perhaps unreasonable but I do.'[105] Lionel Randle, whose distaste for Churchill seems to have been growing, wrote: 'The part where he said that if Almighty God spared our labours all his servants would be pleased, nearly made me vomit.'[106] G. South, a secretary, recorded, 'Last night Churchill's speech proved a great disappointment—at least, all the people I have spoken to today said they were expecting something really dramatic and were wearied and irritated by the "nothingy" quality of the speech. I think people were really hoping for an announcement that Italy had surrendered.'[107] Home Intelligence confirmed that disappointment was 'widely reported'. In Wales and Scotland there was some criticism of Churchill's praise of France: 'So unnecessary after their miserable record.'[108]

But although it struck some listeners as just 'another pep-up talk', others appreciated that Churchill's seemingly rather general review of the war situation did include one point of political importance.[109] The Soviet Union was conspicuous by its absence in Quebec. Seeking to quell speculation about the state of relations between Russia and its two main allies, Churchill explained that the conference was mainly dedicated to 'heating and inflaming' the war against the Japanese. As the USSR was not at war with Japan, and indeed had a non-aggression treaty with it, it would have been embarrassing to send the invitation, he claimed. 'But nothing is nearer to the wishes of President Roosevelt and myself than to have a threefold meeting with Marshal Stalin'—and if this had not happened yet it was simply because Stalin was too busy directing his armies. Churchill even went out of his way to say that he did not resent Soviet criticism of the failure to establish a second front in France, but at the same time emphasized that 'our soldiers' lives will be expended in accordance with sound military plans and not squandered for political considerations of any kind'.[110]

Thus if the British public were on the whole underwhelmed by the speech, there was 'great interest in, and satisfaction with, Mr Churchill's statement on Russia'.[111] It was also welcome in the USA. Churchill complained about the *Manchester Guardian*'s claim that it had been 'received rather listlessly' there, saying that he had read 'at least thirty leading articles' in American newspapers which disproved this.[112] According to the British Embassy, 'The troubled American public looked forward to [the] Prime Minister's Quebec speech with exceptional eagerness and received it with clear satisfaction. Tension about Anglo-American relations with Russia has been rising sharply, and the speech, regarded as a bold grasping of the nettle by Mr Churchill, did something to relieve it.'[113] The speech was portrayed in the press as a boost to relations with the Soviets and as the first clear-cut statement on the Second Front.[114] It seemed clear that Churchill would not have referred to a tripartite meeting with Stalin unless he had known that the Soviets were basically favourable.[115] German propaganda, of course, denounced the speech as 'amazing, servile flattery of the Soviets'.[116]

The Allied invasion of mainland Italy started on 3 September. Returning to Britain via the USA, Churchill received an honorary degree at Harvard on the 6th. He used the occasion to deliver a paean to Anglo-American unity, and to lecture his audience on their country's global role: 'The price of greatness is responsibility.' He preached the doctrine of 'fraternal association' between Britain and America—a theme he would develop after the war into the concept of the 'special relationship'. He also dwelt on the role of the English language as a potential factor in political unity: 'The gift of a common tongue is a priceless inheritance and it may well some day become the foundation of a common citizenship.'[117] The Embassy noted that the speech 'was greeted with expected variations in warmth, ranging from enthusiasm on the part of the Anglophile section of East Coast broadcasters and press, to [the] usual barrage of opposition by Patterson-McCormick-Hearst papers', i.e. the isolationist tendency.[118] A systematic official analysis of reactions was circulated to the British Cabinet. This noted that the speech came 'opportunely, during a growing nation-wide demand in the United States for the formulation and adoption of a specific foreign policy, after proposals for an Anglo-American military alliance had been made by such conservative Republicans as [Clarence Budington] Kelland [National Committeeman for Arizona] and [New York Governor Thomas E.] Dewey, and at a moment when there was a strong sense of Anglo-American solidarity (tacitly acknowledged even by those who most condemned it) in the face of a disturbingly aloof Russian attitude'. In spite of its timeliness, the reporting of the speech 'encountered several accidental handicaps': a White House announcement that the speech would not contain much of political significance, the Labor Day holiday which delayed some coverage, and a series of train wrecks which monopolized the press's interest. Still, the headlines were mainly fair and positive, there was much praise of Churchill personally, and there was 'an exceptional volume of homage to his eloquence'. Beyond this, the responses to Churchill's proposals fell into several categories:

(a) Complete agreement with the Prime Minister's thesis that it is essential to maintain after the war the smoothly running Anglo-American machinery so effective at present. Such comment sometimes alludes to the necessity of adding Russia and China at some stage, but its first love is an Anglo-American alliance.

(b) A more qualified approval of the thesis, which it favours, provided that it is to be the first step towards a world structure of some kind, and not to a system of power politics likely to lead to another war. This attitude varies from pious hope to stern warnings against an exclusively Anglo-American alliance.

(c) Direct criticism, usually by liberal internationalists, on the ground that such an alliance is simple power politics.

(d) The nationalist-isolationist opposition, which harps on the old theme that America must not entangle herself once again in an alliance with the British Empire and its imperialist and European complications. [...]

(e) Speculation of varying degrees of detachment on the precise political significance of the speech and its probable effect on American politics.

The report also quoted a wide range of newspapers in order to illustrate the spectrum of opinion. In the view of the *New York Times*, 'Mr Churchill has opened up a vast and hopeful field of discussion. Down the grim corridors of war light begins to show.' By contrast, the *St Louis Post-Dispatch* judged that 'If Stalin and Chiang and Governments-in-exile feel slighted, or wonder if the great fraternal Power combine will be used in "service to mankind," it is because they have been given cause to be concerned, in the past and through Churchill's words at Harvard'. For its part, the *Chicago Tribune* thought that Churchill had the right idea from his own point of view: 'Regardless of who actually gives the orders in the field, the British are to start the wars and we are to fight them. England gets the benefit of our victories.' The *Wheeling Intelligencer* (a West Virginia paper) pointed out: 'As for common citizenship with England, we fought in this country to free ourselves from that a long time ago.' The *Baltimore Sun* suggested that Churchill had 'injected himself almost directly into American political discussion', giving 'direct support' to Kelland and Dewey, Republican internationalists who faced hostility from their isolationist colleagues. 'Mr Churchill, astute assayer of public opinion as he is, has clearly been watching the development of American thought under the pressure of events. He knows, as well as we know, that the shadow of the 1944 Presidential campaign hangs with increasing ominousness over every suggestion which this Administration makes and over every suggestion that he makes in reply.'[119] Churchill did not yet know that Dewey was to be Roosevelt's opponent in the 1944 election, and he certainly did not want to boost him at the President's expense, but it made sense to give encouragement to the Republican internationalists in the hope of securing bipartisan support for Churchill's own post-war vision.

'When the PM has a speech on the stocks, it takes possession of him, and he usually banishes from his mind everything that is not connected with his script,' wrote Lord Moran in his diary. 'But when he spoke at Harvard, I found that his thoughts kept wandering to the coming landing at Salerno.'[120] The Badoglio government had at last agreed to Italy's surrender, on the basis that the country was to be allowed at once to rejoin the war on the Allied side—so it was not strictly unconditional. Unfortunately the Germans quickly moved to disarm Italian troops, meaning that much of the Allies' advantage was lost. Mussolini was rescued by SS commandos and was installed as the head of a Nazi puppet regime. The Salerno landing met strong opposition: it was clear that the conquest of Italy would be no walk-over. Nevertheless, Churchill was on a political high. Back in Britain, he reported to the Commons on 21 September. He began by expressing his 'acute personal grief' at the sudden death that morning of the Chancellor, Sir Kingsley Wood. (In the Cabinet reconstruction that followed, Wood was replaced by Sir John Anderson.) Cuthbert Headlam wrote: 'Winston spoke for the best part of 2 hours (with a luncheon interval) and, needless to say, had a big reception—the House was packed and he looked in the pink—truly amazing for a man of his age.'[121] Nicolson noted how Churchill started 'as always, in dull stuffy manner', reading out dry matter from his typescript. 'But as he progressed, he began to enliven his discourse with the familiar quips and gestures', including a characteristic movement in which he patted his trouser pockets and then moved 'his hands up and down from groin to tummy'. Nicolson continued:

> It was obvious that he was in some logical difficulty over the implicit anomaly that we had asked for 'unconditional surrender' whereas the Italians had asked in effect to be allowed in on our side. He dealt with this sturdily and stubbornly but in a somewhat laboured way. And when he got through the argument, he leant across to the Opposition and said in a conversational tone, 'That all right?' They grinned back affectionately. When he came to discussing the escape of Mussolini, he took off his glasses, stepped back from the box, and put on an expression of rather perplexed amusement. By his manner, rather than by what he said, he was able to convey to the House that this escape was no more than an irritating and (if one looked at it in the right way) an entertaining episode.[122]

Churchill also expressed sympathy for the Italians. They had already suffered terribly, and now 'their own beautiful homeland must become a battlefield for German rearguards'. But he promised that as the British and Americans marched forward, the Italian people would be 'rescued from their state of servitude and degradation, and will be enabled in due course to regain their rightful place among the free democracies of the modern world'. The German case was different, though, he said. There, Prussian militarism was 'the source of the recurring pestilence', and this, along with Nazi tyranny, needed to be rooted out of German life.[123]

In the debate that followed, Aneurin Bevan accused the government of having failed to realize the revolutionary potential of Italian workers rising against Mussolini. The decision to deal with Badoglio, he suggested, reflected a conservative tendency to assume that 'we must approach and occupy Europe with the least disturbance of its political and social structure'. Even he, however, conceded that when Churchill was able to present his story as one of uninterrupted success, the government's critics were going to have a hard time.[124] Some MO diarists did record a small degree of dissent. Chemist J. Greenwood thought that Churchill had 'touched on most topics that were troubling people. The staff at lunch were mainly approving, though one man thought we had made a mistake in not invading Italy as soon as Sicily was captured, and that Mr C was stressing the supply problem, merely as eyewash.'[125] A. White wrote: 'Mr Churchill has just praised Marshal Badoglio for one of history's finest acts of treachery. Can you wonder if the peoples of Europe become cynical of authority.'[126] N. E. Underwood commented philosophically: 'Well, Churchill had a lot to say, but as usual, we are little wiser after it all, which is what a wartime speech shd be, I suppose.'[127] Home Intelligence found that a minority thought that Churchill had 'appeared too friendly towards Italy' and were 'uneasy at his references to the Badoglio Government'; nor did the speech wholly dispel the feeling that the Allies had been 'slow off the mark' in Italy and had lost opportunities. Nevertheless, it was 'very well received by nearly everyone' and was praised for removing 'many doubts, criticisms and symptoms of uneasiness'. 58.5 per cent of the adult public heard announcer John Snagge's reading of the speech, although it was so long that 'many people became confused during the broadcast reading and remembered only isolated points'.[128]

Churchill's awareness of his own political strength was reflected in his unusual decision to intervene in a debate on the coal industry in mid-October. The industry was in a troubled state, short of workers and simmering with discontent.[129] It was widely expected that the Minister of Fuel and Power, Gwilym Lloyd George, would announce some new measures that would satisfy the miners' leaders, but when he made his Commons speech it became plain he had nothing to offer. The Conservative Viscount Cranborne had intervened with Churchill to head off the idea of the government taking over operational control of the mines. Cranborne was not influential with the Prime Minister, but his letter was probably representative of wider Tory discontent, of which Churchill may have felt obliged to take account.[130] With a Labour rebellion looking likely, the Cabinet backed Churchill's decision to speak, reaffirming the government's decision to maintain the status quo. Even though the miners were not overtly demanding full and immediate public ownership of the industry, it was this question that Churchill made the key focus of his speech. Whilst emphasizing that he was not opposed to nationalization as such, he ruled it out during wartime: 'I certainly could not take the responsibility of making far-reaching controversial changes which I am not convinced are directly needed for the war effort without a Parliament refreshed by contact with the electorate', i.e. without a general election.[131] An astute if partisan article by *Tribune's* parliamentary commentator Jack Wilkes noted that the speech was highly significant. Churchill had been 'conciliatory and sympathetic to the miners' and had skilfully dampened opposition to the government's coal policy. But his speech went beyond the coal industry alone:

> He laid it down as firm Government policy that there was to be no alteration in our economic structure during the war. Such alteration, he asserted, without stating any reasons, would involve a General Election, which he was not prepared to contemplate. The status quo is therefore to remain until peace comes. If the Labour Ministers are not prepared to co-operate on this understanding they can get out. And the implication throughout the speech was that although Churchill would regret this, he and his Conservative colleagues now felt confident enough to face this possibility without any serious qualms.[132]

In the face of Churchill's decision to wield his authority, the potential Labour rebels decided to retreat.[133] MO diarists were divided between those who thought that the refusal to nationalize the mines without an election was 'quite right and democratic', and those who sensed in the speech a 'lack of understanding' on Churchill's part: 'I doubt if he can fully see the point of view of the poorer classes.'[134] *The Economist* observed that 'by one of the deftest political performances of his career', the Prime Minister had got his way. 'But the coal problem remained unsolved when he sat down'.[135]

Churchill's intervention is striking, because its singularity highlights how rarely he had to take active steps to defend his government in the Commons during this stage of the war. Of course, he was still required to deal with parliamentary questions, and he made a point of doing so even when he could have delegated the task to others. His willingness to answer 'as humbly as if he had been the youngest of Under-Secretaries' endeared him to MPs: he carried out the task 'dutifully, carefully, subserviently'.[136] Unlike David Lloyd George during the First World War he did not isolate himself from the Commons but took pains to present himself as its servant. Thus he remained in touch with Members even though he made no further politically important speeches in Parliament before the end of 1943.[137] This is not to say that his government faced no challenges at this time—the release from prison of Fascist leader Sir Oswald Mosley provoked a storm of protest—but none was so serious that it required Churchill to descend from on high in order to deal with it.

The tyranny of the calendar imposed one other significant public obligation that year—the Prime Minister's annual speech to the Lord Mayor's Day
luncheon at the Mansion House. He used it to launch an attack on over-
confidence and to quash expectations that Germany was about to collapse.
In stressing the need for continued vigilance he offered an implicit rebuke
of Sir Walter Citrine, the TUC General Secretary, who had recently called
for a relaxation of fire-watching and Home Guard duties. 'We must go forward with unrelenting and unwearying efforts through every living minute
that is granted to us,' Churchill urged.[138] This was a tough message to get
across. 'The Prime Minister's warnings of difficulties ahead are not treated
too seriously, except by those with relatives in the Forces,' reported Home
Intelligence; 'people continue to anticipate an early end to the war.'
Moreover, the speech provoked less discussion than normal. 'While many
thought its serious tone provided a needed corrective to over-optimism,
others appear to have considered it was gloomier than the situation really
justified. Some go so far as to think it was unnecessarily upsetting, especially
on the question of casualties.'[139] 'I think Churchill has overdone it this time;
he has misjudged the mood of the people,' wrote Edward Stebbing. He
added: 'Churchill's reiterated warnings of the hardness of the fight are now
merely boring. We know it will be hard, but let's get it over with.'[140] As the
war moved towards its final phase, it was a sentiment that many would have
endorsed.

7

'Throwing a Temperament Like a Bloody Film Star'

In terms of his speech-making, 1943 had not posed very severe challenges for Churchill. With the war—at last—going pretty successfully for a sustained period, he could finally count on having security of tenure in Downing Street at least until the end of hostilities. But at the end of the year, the scale of his future problems came home to him. His hoped-for meeting with Stalin and Roosevelt convened at the end of November, but over the next few days the President cosied up to the Russians at the expense of the British. Britain could not command equal political weight with the two emergent superpowers, and Churchill found the experience humiliating. 'I realised at Teheran for the first time what a small nation we are,' he said later. 'There I sat with the great Russian bear on one side of me, with paws outstretched [...] and on the other side the great American buffalo, and between the two sat the poor little British donkey, who was the only one of the three who knew the right way home.'[1] During 1944–5, Churchill faced the necessity of making difficult geopolitical compromises, which in turn required him to rationalize them in public. At the same time as he made unpalatable concessions to Soviet and American power he showed sympathy for authoritarian regimes elsewhere, leading to awkward questions about his judgement. In combination with a new challenge to civilian morale at home, in the form of German V-weapon attacks, these factors presented him with some tough rhetorical dilemmas even as the Allies' final military triumph approached.

En route back to Britain from Tehran, Churchill again contracted pneumonia; for a time his life hung in the balance. Following his convalescence at Marrakesh, he returned home in mid-January 1944. When he arrived he 'went straight to the House, where he made a "dramatic" entry' and answered questions, although he was still feeling weak.[2] Equally dramatic was his intervention in a by-election at Brighton, normally a safe Tory seat. (Skipton, a Conservative seat, had fallen to the radical Common Wealth party a few weeks earlier.) An Independent candidate was running, claiming to be standing 'in full support of the Prime Minister and the Cabinet'. Churchill issued a letter denouncing this as 'an attempted swindle'.[3] The Conservatives held the seat only narrowly, suggesting that his tactic backfired. There was considerable resentment at the Prime Minister's attempt at 'dictation' to the voters.[4] 'Very entertaining, the present temper shown to Churchill's dictatorship', wrote Margaret Kornitzer, a journalist, in her diary. 'He of course is an autocratic old devil, ruling a turbulent people—no doubt he appreciates the historical continuity of the whole position as much as anyone does. But he continues to bring his best broadsides to bear on local issues—it is rather like trying to crush a nit with a steam-hammer.'[5] Housewife Edith Dawson wrote: 'He's not the favourite he thinks he is. [. . .] *He's a born dictator* if he can get away with it'.[6] The charge that 'Winston is a dictator; he cannot be overruled' had been around for years.[7] It was inaccurate—he was not all-powerful, nor did he attempt to be—but it may have been fair to say that there was 'a childish and dictatorial streak in Churchill's nature'.[8] The prevalence of the claim now was in part a simple reflection of growing anti-Churchill sentiment. Harold Nicolson recorded at this time: 'In the station lavatory at Blackheath [site of an RAF station] last week I found scrawled up, "Winston Churchill is a bastard." I pointed it out to the Wing Commander who was with me. "Yes", he said, "the tide has turned. We find it everywhere".'[9] Over the coming months the 'dictator' accusation was to feed into a powerful critique of Churchill that presented him as an admirer of despots and an opponent of true democracy. It was a view that gained some traction on the basis of Churchill's own references in his speeches to European issues.

Hugh Dalton noted of Churchill's next Commons speech, on 22 February, 'There was more interest, for those who know anything about such things, in his reference to foreign affairs than in his references to the war.'[10] That is to say, the Prime Minister was now dealing with the likely shape of post-war Europe. His greatest difficulty was over Polish-Soviet relations, and the question of where the two countries' future border would lie. In advance of the speech, the British had been pressing the Polish government-in-exile to accept Stalin's demand that the frontier should lie along the Curzon Line—a boundary proposed in the aftermath of the First World War, much further to the west than the Poles now wanted. From the British perspective, the

Poles were simply stubborn. Churchill told Prime Minister Stanisław Mikołajczyk (who had succeeded General Sikorski after the latter's death in 1943) that

> this was the one and only chance for the Poles to take Stalin's offer of a Poland between the Curzon Line and the Oder. The Russians alone could liberate Poland. Nobody else could do anything. If the Poles accepted, they had a decent prospect before them. He, the PM, did not intend to let Anglo-Russian relations to be wrecked by the Polish Government if they refused what he regarded as a reasonable offer and he would then conclude direct agreement with Stalin without them.

Eventually, the Poles succumbed to the pressure and came fairly close to agreement, and Churchill put a proposal to Stalin in such a way as to help save their faces.[11] In his Commons speech, Churchill spoke of his 'great pleasure' at hearing from Stalin at Tehran 'that he, too, was resolved upon the creation and maintenance of a strong integral independent Poland as one of the leading Powers in Europe'.[12] Chuter Ede noted that 'There were Tory cheers when he professed friendship for Poland but he soon corrected the balance'.[13] Churchill said: 'I have an intense sympathy with the Poles, that heroic race whose national spirit centuries of misfortune cannot quench, but I also have sympathy with the Russian standpoint. [...] I cannot feel that the Russian demand for a reassurance about her Western frontiers goes beyond the limits of what is reasonable or just.' He added that he had reached an agreement with Stalin on the need for Poland to be compensated with territory at the expense of Germany in the north and the west.[14] Churchill's failure to mention the Baltic States was correctly interpreted to mean that the British viewed their annexation by the Soviet Union as a fait accompli.[15] FO official Oliver Harvey wrote in his diary a few days later, 'Polish Government have put out a foolish semi-official statement refuting the PM's speech [...] and affirming that they refuse the Curzon Line'.[16] The Polish Foreign Minister complained to the British that the speech 'had accepted the whole Russian case'. Stalin, for his part, would not be pinned down to an agreement and refused to deal with the London Poles. But Churchill's speech was undoubtedly welcomed in Moscow, which presented it as showing Britain's willingness to abandon the exile government.[17] There was, however, astonishment at Churchill's statement that he could not guarantee that the war would end by the close of the year.[18] Propaganda by the 'Union of Polish Patriots in the USSR', broadcast in Polish to Poland, emphasized that:

English public opinion as well as public opinion in all democratic countries fully realized the importance of the Polish-Soviet problem, both from a point of view of a quick termination of this war, as well as for a future peaceful collaboration between all nations. All the more, the harmful and undemocratic policy of the so-called Polish Government in London created anxiety in England and caused a good deal of embarrassment to the British Government. Therefore, Churchill dealt with this matter at some length and quite explicitly...[19]

The Germans meanwhile developed the potentially fruitful propaganda line that Britain had transformed her 1939 guarantee of security for Poland 'into a guarantee for the security of the Soviet Union'. Moreover, it was claimed, 'Churchill's speech is characterized by final capitulation to Moscow and by a willingness to give up a say in political developments in Europe.'[20] The British public, for their part, took 'considerable interest' in the issue. Most people seemed to accept Churchill's position as 'just and reasonable', although some feared that 'Russia will use all her strength to get what she wants' and that the USA and Britain 'will be unable to ensure Poland getting her due'.[21] Poles in America were reported to be 'gloomy and depressed' as a result of the speech, although the US media (like the British papers) hailed it with 'immense enthusiasm'.[22]

Churchill's speech also emphasized that King Victor Emmanuel and Marshal Badoglio remained 'the legitimate Government of Italy'.[23] He had the Cabinet's backing, but it was a controversial point, not least within Italy itself.[24] A rival leader, the anti-Fascist former Foreign Minister, Count Carlo Sforza, was now on the scene. Hostile to the King, Sforza had the backing of the State Department and also seemingly of many Italian-American voters. Churchill, however, loathed him, and was determined to resist the demands of the anti-Badoglio forces in Italy—the so-called 'six parties'—which were urging the King's abdication.[25] Sforza reacted to the speech by attacking Churchill's 'sympathetic' references to Badoglio and restated his demand that 'King Victor Emmanuel must go'.[26] The Rector of Naples University claimed that Churchill had abandoned Italy's anti-Fascist forces, and the six parties called a nominal ten-minute strike.[27] The former Labour MP Lord Stansgate, now serving as Vice-President of the Allied Control Committee for Italy, was depressed by Churchill's attitude, which he thought would cause the Badoglio cabinet to dig in its heels. 'What's the use of telling us to eradicate fascism if he won't give us an Italian Govt with the will to do it,' he wondered to his diary.[28] In Britain, the left-wing *New Statesman* denounced Churchill's supposed neglect of democratic ideals: 'The idea that the Allies are supposed to be fighting for certain political principles and rights seems to be cynically discarded from his mind.'[29] Churchill was able to fend off American pressure for the time being, but when Rome fell in June he could do nothing to stave off the King's abdication and the creation of a new government, which included Sforza.

It might be tempting to see Churchill's support for Victor Emmanuel simply as a knee-jerk product of his well-known monarchical tendencies.[30] It is true that he viewed constitutional monarchy as an ideal, but as his 22 February speech made clear, he would not back kings irrespective of circumstance. As regards Yugoslavia, he announced his backing for Tito's communist partisans, at the expense of Draža Mihailović's rival nationalist Chetnik group, which Churchill believed had drifted into collaboration with the Germans. The young exiled King, who had proved himself a weak reed, got only a lukewarm endorsement (although Churchill did later unsuccessfully press Tito to work with him). Eden had warned him about the dangers of overpraising Tito—giving the impression of too great a satisfaction might make it hard to extract further cooperation with British wishes.[31] But as Dalton noted, Churchill 'went all out for Tito with exuberant eulogy, brushed aside Mihailović and made only faint praise of King Peter, adding that we should not seek to force Monarchy on any country that didn't want it'.[32] Churchill undoubtedly saw himself as a pragmatist—he would back whoever was fighting the Germans hardest, regardless of their politics, he said—but there was also a strong romantic element in his judgements. This meant that the stirring tales he heard of the battles of 'Marshal Tito and his gallant band' were able to trump the magic of monarchy—or in King Peter's case, the lack of it.[33] In this case, the British people were with him. His 'generous praise' of Tito 'caused great pleasure, although some people asked why it 'took so long to find out that Mihailovitch was a quisling'. Overall, the speech was received very favourably: 'Little criticism is reported, but some considered it less vivid and colourful than usual, and it is suggested that the Prime Minister's speeches were "more inspiring when he was unhampered by consideration for our Allies".'[34]

By this time, Churchill was starting to find making big speeches a burden.[35] Even minor occasions were a nuisance; when he agreed to go to a lunch with the Royal College of Physicians, he was 'very fed up at having let himself in for a speech'.[36] Even a seemingly trivial occasion such as this had to be handled carefully. Lord Moran provided some speech notes, which were then vetted by Henry Willink, the Minister of Health. From the No. 10 Private Office, John Martin drily advised Churchill: 'It appears that if you spoke from Lord Moran's notes, not only would your speech be in many respects inaccurate but you would be endorsing certain pretensions of the College which are disputed by other medical bodies, particularly the General Medical Council. If Mr. Willink's comments are taken into account, not much of Lord Moran's notes is left.'[37]

Churchill's next significant effort was a broadcast at the end of March. He was partly motivated by a desire to damp down talk about future demobilization when D-day was in the offing.[38] He explicitly said that Ernest Bevin, as Minister of Labour, had devised a 'fair and healthy scheme', but that the public were not yet to be told about it, because 'The hour of our greatest effort and action is approaching'.[39] The speech was a misfire. For some listeners, this was because of Churchill's handling of domestic policy after the war—'a sad tired old man drooling on about things in which he wasn't particularly interested,' according to MO diarist M. C. Towler.[40] (The post-war aspect of this broadcast is discussed in Chapter 8.) But it was also because, in place of his general review of the war, many people were expecting a more dramatic announcement. They had hoped for a rousing speech to brace people for the coming invasion of France—and some had thought that they would hear that Allied troops had already landed. 'Many were disappointed because they felt Mr. Churchill lacked "his usual fire"—there is much sympathy and concern that he "sounded tired"—and because he told them comparatively little about the second front.'[41] The fact that the broadcast was heard by 65.5 per cent of the potential audience was a testament to Churchill's continuing ability to draw in listeners, but the mixed reactions show that he was by no means infallible when it came to managing people's expectations.

He also faced international difficulties. In April, on the eve of a conference with the Dominion Prime Ministers, he made a Commons speech on imperial affairs. It was essentially bland, but he suggested—arguably rightly—that the agreements made with America earlier in the war did not commit Britain to abolishing its protectionist imperial preference trading system.[42] As a former Liberal free trader he did not care much for imperial preference himself, but the Tory Party he now led certainly did. Equally certainly, US Secretary of State Cordell Hull viewed it as an abomination. Hull protested that Churchill's words 'gave the impression that the Prime Minister favoured the maintenance intact of Empire preferences and a tightening up of the

Commonwealth' and would not be persuaded that he was actually keen to promote open markets.[43] This was only low-level diplomatic grumbling, but a much bigger row was brewing on another front.

This was over Spain. Now that the war was running against the Axis, and with the Spanish desperately short of supplies, the Americans wanted to turn the screw on Franco's regime. They did so in January 1944, cutting off petrol supplies in an effort to get Spain to halt all supplies of wolfram—a key war material. The British, who were concerned about their own supplies of raw materials from Spain and their other economic interests there, sought to present themselves as mediators. After several fraught telegrams between Churchill and Roosevelt, the British at last gained grudging American agreement to a deal. Britain would supply Spain with petrol, in exchange for a commitment to restrict—but not halt—the flow of wolfram. Franco was off the hook. The episode was seen in Washington as a case of the British indulging in appeasement in the naked pursuit of their own economic interests; the Americans, who faced a press that was hostile to Franco, felt they had been undermined.[44] State Department official Dean Acheson recalled: 'the role played by Mr. Churchill in deflecting our economic pressure was my first experience [...] of a relatively weak ally by determined, sometimes reckless, decisions changing and even preventing action by a much stronger one charged with ultimate responsibility'.[45] In fairness, Churchill may have been motivated both by gratitude to Spain for having kept out of the war and by the quest for post-war stability there in the absence of a clear alternative to Franco.

However, the fashion in which Churchill discussed the Spanish question in public was certainly reckless, although what is most surprising is the Foreign Office's failure to detect that his comments would be controversial. His remarks made during a debate on foreign affairs on May 24 have become notorious. As Dalton observed, it was not very clear why Churchill found it necessary to make a major speech at this time; it may have been an effort to establish clear lines of European policy in advance of D-Day.[46] Much of the work on the speech was done within the Foreign Office. Alexander Cadogan wrote in his diary of the frantic atmosphere there: 'A good madhouse in A. [Eden]'s room at 10.30. A., and 16 other people, fluttering pages of PM's draft speech (for this morning!) looking over each other's shoulders and all talking at once. Towards the end when asked my opinion, I said that if I could have a chance to read the damned thing I might express one.'[47] Having listened to the speech in the Commons, Leo Amery commented that Churchill had spoken 'largely I think from FO briefs with just a touch of his own diction here and there'.[48] It would seem both that the passages on Spain genuinely reflected Churchill's views and that officials saw them as unproblematic.[49]

In the crucial section, Churchill dwelt on the fact that Spain had resisted German blandishments in 1940, and had remained 'absolutely friendly and tranquil' in the face of the British reinforcement of Gibraltar before the 1942 North African landings. The Spanish had compensated for their friendly gestures towards Germany by ignoring the British build-up at that time: they had rendered a service to the Allied cause. 'I have, therefore, no sympathy with those who think it clever, and even funny, to insult and abuse the Government of Spain whenever occasion serves,' he said. Furthermore, 'As I am here to-day speaking kindly words about Spain, let me add that I hope she will be a strong influence for the peace of the Mediterranean after the war. Internal political problems in Spain are a matter for the Spaniards themselves.'[50] Harold Nicolson wrote of the speech, 'To our surprise he went miles out of his way to shower roses and lilies upon Franco. [...] His humour and charm were unabated. But his voice was not thunderous and three times Members called out to him, "Speak up!"'[51] Dalton noted that 'There was little fire in the speech, and he stumbled over his words; "Communism" or "Christendom", he wasn't quite sure which he meant to say at one point!' Afterwards, Bevin 'shook his head over the PM's speech and hinted that his health and stamina were again rather poor'.[52]

The speech was, of course, played up by the Spanish media. The newspaper *ABC* hailed it as 'truly masterful'.[53] Valladolid's Radio Falange described Churchill as 'Spain's best panegyrist', and said that his statement was a vindication of Franco's policy.[54] According to British intelligence sources, 'Mr. Churchill's speech caused intense satisfaction in Franco's immediate entourage'. However, precisely because it boosted the *Caudillo*, the speech had a mixed reception with the Falange, Spain's sole political party: 'The moderate group—that is the group which is trying to present the Falange as a "unitarian" and not a fascist party—was jubilant and claimed that thanks to its efforts, the British now had more confidence in the Falange.' However, the extremists and all those who had been mixed up with the Germans were 'disgusted' by the speech. 'They described it as being "diabolically clever" in that it placed on record Franco's services to the Allied cause, thereby deliberately showing how Spain had betrayed Germany.'[55] Meanwhile, those opposed to Franco, 'and particularly the

Monarchists, have concluded that the Anglo-Saxons are not going to help them, and their hopes have been dashed'.[56] In Berlin, the Japanese Ambassador discussed the speech with von Ribbentrop, who agreed that it might be 'the result of a desire to estrange' Germany and Spain.[57]

For their part, the Soviets appear to have been displeased by Churchill's statement: they omitted the references to Spain from press and broadcast reports of his speech.[58] In the United States, there was outrage, although the controversy took some time to develop. Many of the initial American headlines focused on other aspects of the speech, such as 'CHURCHILL CALLS FOR NEW POST-WAR ORGANIZATION' and 'CHURCHILL REAFFIRMS SURRENDER TERMS FOR JAPS AND NAZIS'.[59] But as the British Embassy observed, 'While earliest reactions welcomed Prime Minister's frankness and completely restored vigour with only usual complaints from liberals, later press and radio reactions are unusually critical.' The passages on Spain overshadowed the rest of the speech, with some leftist syndicated radio commentators professing 'to be deeply shocked by Prime Minister's kindly references to Spain'. The Embassy received many letters of protest on the issue.[60] Also problematic was Churchill's claim that the war had 'become less ideological in its character' as it progressed.[61] The Embassy reported that a prominent member of the Democratic National Committee had told a British official 'that his colleagues regarded reference to "less ideological" character of war as likely to damage President's position in elections since it was in direct contradiction to Democratic Party line in favour of a fourth term' for Roosevelt.[62]

On 30 May, Roosevelt gave a press conference in which he said he was dissatisfied with the Spanish government's recent actions, 'thereby indirectly taking issue with Prime Minister Churchill', as the *New York Times* noted, although American diplomats rushed to deny a split.[63] The President's wife Eleanor weighed in at a press conference of her own. Asked about Churchill's remarks, she said 'I think he has thought a certain way for sixty years and I don't think he wants to change. And that's the way he thinks on Spain.'[64] In a telegram to Roosevelt, Churchill sought to justify himself. The press criticism was 'very unfair', he complained, as he had only been reiterating the policy he had laid down publicly in 1940:

> I only mention[ed] Franco's name to show how silly it was to identify Spain with him or him with Spain by means of caricatures. I do not care about Franco but I do not wish to have the Iberian Peninsula hostile to the British after the war.

[...] I do not know whether there is more freedom in Stalin's Russia than in Franco's Spain. I have no intention to seek a quarrel with either.[65]

In Britain, the public generally approved of the speech, but the references to Spain were found problematic. According to Home Intelligence there was some minority agreement, on grounds of diplomatic necessity and in the belief that Churchill must have 'superior inside knowledge'. However,

> There is widespread criticism of the remarks about Spain and about General Franco, who is greatly distrusted and regarded as 'an out-and-out fascist'. Some are bewildered by Mr. Churchill's 'conciliatory' attitude, and cannot understand what good it can do; others speak of appeasement and fail to see why, if fascism is to be eliminated from Italy and the world generally, Spain should be excepted. Others again feel Mr. Churchill must have been speaking with his tongue in his cheek.[66]

Amongst diarists, J. Greenwood wondered 'what on earth has come over Churchill and the Spanish issue. Why this sudden adulation of Franco'.[67] Edith Dawson wrote: 'I've been wild about the Fascism in Spain ever since the Civil War—And to hear Churchill give in to Frankau [sic] makes me sick'.[68] According to Edward Stebbing, 'This is simply the appeasement, non-intervention policy of Chamberlain in a slightly different guise. If Churchill lives long enough, he may well find himself in the same position with regard to Spain as those who were friendly towards Hitler before the war are now.'[69]

Churchill gained some UK press support, but he was stung by criticism from, in particular, *The Economist*.[70] It said that the speech as a whole had articulated few principles beyond simple pragmatism, and found the references to Spain 'quite inexplicable'. Moreover, they were bad propaganda: 'on the eve of invasion, Britain's Captain General has sent his forces out to meet their allies with the wrong words ringing in their ears'.[71] A few months later Eden had to dissuade Churchill from praising Spain again.[72] His irritation about the episode is clear from an exchange with his friend Violet Bonham Carter. ('Now why do people say I praised up Franco?' 'Because you did.')[73] It also provided Churchill's political opponents with ammunition to use in the future. During the 1945 election, the *Daily Herald*, the Labour movement's official paper, ran the headline 'A VOTE FOR CHURCHILL IS A VOTE FOR FRANCO'.[74] It has to be pointed out, though, that the Labour members of the War Cabinet did not protest about the speeches at the time; nor did the Attlee government once in power make any attempt to dislodge Franco.

The row was eclipsed by the Normandy landings and the battle for France. On the morning of 6 June, the BBC news reported that the invasion had started in the early hours. Churchill was due to address the Commons, but as George Harvie-Watt, his PPS, recalled, 'The PM was very late in getting down to the House. He hadn't quite finished the preparation of his statement and Questions went quickly. Naturally the House expected a statement and were impatient to hear it, so the House had to remain in suspended animation until Winston arrived. I'd never seen that kind of situation in the House before or since.'[75] Churchill at last went into the Chamber just before twelve. Harold Nicolson noted: 'He looked white as a sheet. The House noticed this at once, and we feared he was about to announce some terrible disaster.' Called at once by the Speaker, Churchill put two separate sets of papers before him. Reading from the first set, he reported on the fall of Rome to US troops two days earlier—tactfully not mentioning that General Mark Clark had taken the city in breach of his orders, thus missing an opportunity to cut off retreating German forces elsewhere. Then, having milked things for maximum drama, he picked up his other notes and began: 'I have also to announce to the House that during the night and the early hours of this morning the first of the series of landings in force upon the European Continent has taken place.' As he continued with his account, MPs listened 'in hushed awe'.[76]

In spite of the good progress on the Continent, a new threat to British morale now emerged. On the night of 12–13 June, the first German flying bombs (known as V1s or 'doodlebugs') hit London and the Home Counties. Soon they were coming at the rate of a hundred a day. Churchill had warned the public of the threat as early as February, but although about half were shot down the rest got through.[77] Home Intelligence found that in general confidence remained high, encouraged by military success and by the 'unusual optimism' of a speech by Churchill at the Mexican Embassy. However, 'A good deal of criticism of the Government is reported—with particular reference to the Home Secretary and the Prime Minister'. One of the main complaints was at the failure to publish details of casualties, bomb damage, and the numbers of weapons destroyed before they hit their targets.[78] At first, Churchill was rather dismissive of concerns about morale. He said to Harvie-Watt: 'What is all this about the people getting windy with the doodle-bugs? I want you to keep your eyes and ears open as to what the reactions are and let me know. Personally I think it is all balls.'[79] But on 6 July, perhaps somewhat belatedly, he did make a statement to the

Commons. The figures he gave were fairly reassuring: 2,754 flying bombs launched had resulted in 2,752 fatal casualties, 'almost exactly one person per bomb'.[80] He judged the mood of the Commons rightly, Harold Nicolson noted: 'I had feared that he might dismiss the thing as a mere nuisance and thus offend the many people who are really frightened of it. But he took the opposite line and, if anything, exaggerated its danger. This was most effective and the House felt generally that there was nothing more to be said.'[81] According to Chuter Ede, though, 'there was some cynical amusement when the PM announced that [junior minister and MP] Duncan Sandys, who is his son-in-law, was in charge of the Committee in charge of offensive operations'.[82]

Amongst the public, reactions were more mixed. Civil servant A. B. Holness was 'very glad' about the statement: 'Although the casualties are so high it is better to know the figures than to keep on wondering.'[83] J. Greenwood wrote that 'Churchill's speech although it hardly made a favourable impression put people's minds into a proper perspective about the F. Bombs'.[84] But neither Holness nor Greenwood lived in London, which took the brunt of the attacks. Telegraph worker Nellie Carver—no critic of Churchill—wrote: 'It was one of his fighting speeches but we in London feel very depressed. We've had so much to put up with and W sees no end to the attack until the troops take the bases in the Pas de Calais and Northern France and Belgium. Well—we must be patient I suppose.'[85] Although Mass-Observation reported that the speech 'was found rather disappointing', Home Intelligence painted a more nuanced picture.[86] Disappointment was largely restricted to London, and the speech did much to discourage rumours: 'Consternation at the unknown has to a great extent given way to concern for the sufferers.'[87] A follow-up report found that although the public regretted that Churchill had not spoken sooner they were gratified by what he did say: 'People in London and the South East seem better pleased now that his "brutal frankness" has made the rest of the country more sympathetic.'[88] There were some other signs, though, that London opinion remained 'very irritated and a little bit defeatist'.[89] It was said that when Churchill visited Bermondsey he 'got a rough reception when he gave the V (for Victory) sign [...] & suggested they could take it. They asked if he could take it, going down his deep shelter. They were in a mood to pull him out of his car.'[90] There is no proof that this actually happened, but the circulation of the rumour was itself suggestive of popular anger. A delegation from the TUC visited Churchill at the end of

July to warn him that 'the attitude of "London Can Take It" was far too negative and was depressing to the people'. They asked whether he was in a position to make a reassuring statement in the Commons, 'but he said he was loath to do this in view of the dangers that lay ahead'.[91]

The problems quickly faded as public spirits soared when the Allies scored new successes in France and as the V1 launching sites were progressively overrun (although the V1s were superseded by V2 rocket attacks which continued into 1945). On 2 August Churchill made a war report to the Commons. 'On every battle front all over the world the armies of Germany and Japan are recoiling,' he said, and also stated his belief that the interval between the defeat of Hitler and that of Japan would be shorter ('perhaps much shorter') than he had previously supposed.[92] This message fell on willing ears, and gained credence from his 'consistent caution' in the past.[93] Office worker Lionel Randle conceded: 'Much as I dislike the bloke I must admit that he was never one to hold out any hopes of false or easy success, and for this reason I am all the more heartened when he says that victory may come soon.'[94]

Although Churchill's optimism was by no means unwarranted, there was to be no quick collapse of the Third Reich, and the war's messy endgame threw up new diplomatic problems. At a further conference in Quebec, codenamed 'Octagon', Churchill again liaised with Roosevelt and—as so frequently—caused much frustration to his own military advisers through his interference with their discussions. He scored two significant successes, though. First, he secured agreement that American Lend-Lease aid would continue during 'Stage II', that is, the period between the end of the war with Germany and the final defeat of Japan.[95] Second—realizing the importance to US opinion of Britain appearing to punch her full weight in the war against Japan—he offered to send a fleet to the Central Pacific to operate under US command. Roosevelt accepted the gesture unhesitatingly, over the objections of his own Chief of Naval Operations, Admiral King, who allegedly 'did not want anyone else to intervene in his own pet war'.[96] At a joint press conference with the President, Churchill addressed US press suggestions 'that the British wish to shirk their obligations in the Japanese war, and to throw the whole burden upon the United States'. The reverse was true, he said: if anything, the Americans had wanted 'to keep too much' of the war there to themselves, but agreement had been reached and Britain would be 'represented in the main struggle against Japan'.[97] General Sir Henry Pownall of the South-East Asia Command characterized this as 'a strong speech in protest at the mud-slinging against the British Pacific effort' in the US media, adding that America was 'a very raw, immature and uneducated nation with no code of manners'.[98] The British public approved of Churchill's statement although some thought that his rather light-hearted phraseology showed 'a disregard for the horrors our men have to face'.[99]

After returning to the UK, Churchill gave another war review in the Commons.[100] As Harold Nicolson noted, the Prime Minister faced a potential dilemma in dealing with the disaster of the landings at Arnhem a few days previously, in which Britain's 1st Airborne Division had been all but annihilated:

> On the one hand, it was necessary to represent it as an episode of relative unimportance in proportion to the wide sweep of war. On the other hand, it was necessary not to suggest to anxious parents that it had all been no more than an incident. Winston solved this difficulty with great mastery. He spoke of the men of the 1st Parachute Division with great emotion: '"Not in vain" is the boast of those who returned to us. "Not in vain" is the epitaph of those who fell.[101]

Although Churchill's suggestion that the war might continue into 1945 came as a shock to many in Britain, the speech was very well received there, whilst generating little comment or criticism.[102] Not so in China where it sparked considerable controversy, arising from what was only a passing remark. Churchill had observed 'with keen regret' that 'in spite of the lavish American help that has been poured into China, that great country, worn by more than seven years of war, has suffered from severe military reverses'.[103] It was Churchill's use of the term 'lavish' to describe American aid that the Chinese press found so offensive. According to the American Consul-General at Kunming,

> Mr. Churchill's statement has brought into the limelight both the anti-British feeling among many Chinese and the Chinese attitude toward what many Chinese consider the inadequate aid given to China by her Allies. Many otherwise reasonable Chinese apparently agree with the Chungking military spokesman in his description of American aid as a mere trickle and some usually unbiased Chinese at Kunming describe Mr. Churchill's statement as one to be expected from the British 'when they feel that victory is assured and there is less need of the assistance of other nations'. Mr. Churchill has succeeded chiefly in fanning the flames of the already existing anti-British feeling in China but he has also drawn widespread attention to the question of American aid to China.[104]

Churchill was likely oblivious of all this, but the episode shows how even his chance observations could have far-distant repercussions.

In speech-making terms, the last three months of the year were quite frenetic. Churchill made twenty-four speeches or statements, whereas he had made only eleven during the same period in 1943. The increase was mainly due to the pressure of events, at a time when Churchill was increasingly tired and struggling to stay on top of his work. On 5 October, for instance he paid tribute in the Commons to the heroic stand of the Poles during the Warsaw Uprising, which the Nazis had finally crushed after sixty-three days. Happy to see the Polish Home Army destroyed, the Soviets had failed to give the help that might have allowed the rebellion to succeed. John Colville, now back working at Downing Street after a spell in the RAF, noted that Churchill made his statement 'very insipidly': 'The words, produced by the FO, were good; the delivery, due to the PM being too long in his bath and having to rush, was poor.'[105] Another tragedy, this time with a more personal dimension, was the murder in November of his friend Lord Moyne, the British Minister-Resident in Cairo, by Zionist terrorists. Churchill's Commons eulogy was demonstrably marked by personal grief, and MPs listened 'mostly in grim silence', broken by applause when he said that the Egyptian government was investigating the origins and associations of the assassins.[106] Ten days later he made a further statement on the 'shameful crime', which had, he said, caused him to revise his views on Palestine. 'If our dreams for Zionism are to end in the smoke of assassins' pistols and our labours for its future to produce only a new set of gangsters worthy of Nazi Germany, many like myself will have to reconsider the position we have maintained so consistently and so long in the past.'[107] In truth, as Britain's global power declined, Churchill's views about the desirability of Zionism were of declining relevance to the Middle East's future.

There were also the usual ceremonial occasions, such as the annual Mansion House speech. Roosevelt had just been re-elected, and Churchill expressed his pleasure, but it was the delivery not the content that made the speech notable. It was broadcast, and although some listeners thought merely that Churchill was tired or ageing, others judged variously that he was 'a little tipsy', 'slightly fuddled', or 'completely sozzled'.[108] Opinions differed as to whether or not this mattered. One Women's Voluntary Service (WVS) leader said that she 'thought it disgusting when other countries were listening', although her husband 'thought it a joke and stoutly defended the "culprit" when she protested'.[109] M. J. Brierley reported the view of the timekeeper at the factory where she worked. '"The b—— was drunk", he said with great indignation', but her other colleagues did not take the matter too seriously.[110]

However, Churchill was about to walk into a much more serious row, over Greece. Part of the context for this was the so-called 'percentages' deal that he struck—or thought he had struck—with Stalin when he visited him in Moscow in October. Churchill drew up a proposal that the Balkans should be divided into British and Soviet spheres of influence. In Romania and Bulgaria, Russia would be predominant. In Yugoslavia and Hungary, the divide would be 50:50. In Greece, Britain (together with the USA) would have a 90 per cent share and the Russians 10 per cent.[111] Although Stalin seems merely to have taken note of the proposal rather than formally agreeing to it, it is notable that the Soviets did not seek to interfere in the Greek crisis that subsequently unfolded.

Whilst Greece was occupied by the British as German troops withdrew, the communist-dominated EAM/ELAS resistance movement retained both its arms and its hostility to the rival National Democratic Greek League.[112] The Greek government-in-exile returned to Athens but struggled to establish a hold on the situation, which soon erupted into violence. In early December, British troops in the city failed to intervene when Greek police shot at unarmed EAM demonstrators. At least ten people were killed. Churchill cabled the British commander and instructed him to 'act as if you were in a conquered city where a local rebellion is in progress'. It was essential to 'hold and dominate' Athens, Churchill said. 'It would be a great thing for you to succeed in this without bloodshed if possible, but also with bloodshed if necessary.'[113] The telegram quickly leaked to the American press. With ELAS in direct conflict with British forces—and with Edward R. Stettinius, the new US Secretary of State, making unhelpful statements—Churchill faced severe criticism from British newspapers and anger from within the Labour Party.[114] He now faced perhaps the biggest threat to his government since the dark days of 1942. 'The left wing see a heaven-sent opportunity for saying that we are supporting by our arms the forces of reaction in Italy and Greece,' noted Colville.[115] For many, the crisis summoned up ghosts of the past. Teacher M. A. Pratt wrote in her diary: 'One can't forget Mr. Churchill's anti-communist bias (he once declared that he preferred Fascism) and the horrible mess he made of things by supporting reaction in Russia after the last war.'[116] Churchill was also thought to wish to restore the Greek monarchy, with one MO diarist commenting on the aptness of a *Daily Mirror* cartoon 'which shows Mr. Churchill breaking into a prison and handing the inmates a crown instead of letting them out'.[117]

The Labour MP Seymour Cocks put down an amendment to the King's Speech. The amendment regretted that 'the Gracious Speech contains no assurance that His Majesty's Forces will not be used to disarm the friends of democracy in Greece and other parts of Europe, or to suppress those popular movements which have valorously assisted in the defeat of the enemy and upon whose success we must rely for future friendly co-operation in Europe'.[118] This parliamentary move, Churchill was keen to stress, was equivalent to moving a vote of censure. In a sign of how seriously he took the debate, and of how keen he was to ensure ministerial unity, he took the unusual step of outlining his proposed speech very fully in front of the Cabinet. 'The specific points likely to be raised on our conduct in various countries could be dealt with without difficulty,' he observed, 'but he was clear that the debate would turn not on the answers to such points, but on the fundamental principles governing the policy of His Majesty's Government.' Because of the US State Department's criticism, Britain was faced 'with the suggestion that the policy of His Majesty's Government in Greece and other liberated countries was at the moment anti-democratic', a claim he denied emphatically.

> He proposed in these circumstances to make an overwhelming case for democracy, and to bring out that the object of His Majesty's Government and of this country was to ensure that in these liberated countries the ordinary humble man should be at liberty to express himself in freedom through the ballot box, and that in exercising his franchise he should not be subject to intimidation or spying. [. . .] He would make it clear that in going into those countries, we had been concerned solely to liberate them from the enemy, thereafter to re-establish law and order and to hold the fort until the recognised constitutional government of the country could hold free elections. The result of which we would be bound and were ready to accept.

The Cabinet expressed 'complete agreement' with this line. It was also noted, probably by Labour ministers, that 'There was a feeling in certain quarters that we had a preference for the restoration of dynasties, independently or against the will of the people of the country and it would be well to dissipate this'. There was then a detailed discussion of whether Churchill should speak at the start or at the end of the debate. It was decided that he should intervene after the mover and seconder had spoken, not least because 'an early speech would ensure that our case got immediate and effective publicity in the United States and throughout the world'.[119]

On the day itself, Churchill did as he had said, rejecting the idea that EAM/ELAS were friends of democracy, presenting them instead as brigands. 'We are told that because we do not allow gangs of heavily armed guerillas to descend from the mountains and instal themselves, with all the bloody terror and vigour which they possess, in great capitals and in power, that we are traitors to democracy,' he said. He added: 'I shall call upon the House as a matter of confidence in His Majesty's Government and confidence in the spirit with which we have marched from one peril to another till victory is in sight, to reject such pretensions with the scorn that they deserve.'[120] It was a stormy session. According to the *Daily Mirror*, Churchill had not had to face so many interruptions during a major debate since he took office in 1940: 'He was on his feet for eighty minutes and there was a running fire of comment the whole time.'[121] This gave Churchill the opportunity to show 'his quickness in debate'.[122] 'In fact,' wrote Harold Nicolson, 'he seemed to be in rather higher spirits than the occasion warranted. I don't think he quite caught the mood of the House, which at its best was one of distressed perplexity, and at its worst one of sheer red fury.'[123] Chuter Ede considered that Churchill was 'in his most truculent vein. [...] Bevan, in the guise of a question, made three or four insinuations about facts. The PM said that it would be difficult to give the exact opposite of the facts with greater accuracy.'[124] Leo Amery thought that the speech contained 'two psychological mistakes' from the perspective of its effect on Labour MPs. 'One was an occasional note of flippancy in dealing with this subject on which there is very deep feeling. The other was that he began his speech by a longish passage laying stress on his general definition of democracy and the kind of ardent gangsterism which is not democracy, instead of working up to that as his conclusion.' The result, Amery thought, was the kind of speech 'which would have gone down admirably with a French audience'.[125] Eden helped save the day with a lucid factual speech, and the amendment was lost by 279 to 30. 'Judging by his looks,' observed Chuter Ede, 'the PM did not regard this as a very favourable vote.'[126]

The speech received a decidedly mixed reception in the British press, and public opinion was split.[127] Home Intelligence considered that those opposed to government were 'certainly the more vocal' and 'possibly the more numerous'. This group was predominantly left-wing and included most industrial workers: 'Only in Northern Ireland are the majority of workers said to be solidly behind Mr. Churchill.' Those in favour of the government's policy 'are mainly described as right wing people, "better informed people", and those convinced by Mr. Churchill's speech'.[128] A Mass-Observation report found that at first people tended to blame the government as a whole for the Greek situation, but increasingly blamed Churchill himself after he emphasized that he was treating the matter as a question of confidence. Many negative comments were heard. 'I think it's disgusting,' said one 40-year-old man. 'We say we're the ones who are going to give freedom to all the poor devils we're fighting to liberate, and then when we've done the first bit we try to put a government of our choice— not yours and mine, mark you, but Churchill's—just like Hitler did afore we fought to liberate them.' 'HE doesn't want to cause bloodshed!' said a 50-year-old woman. 'Why, 'e's a bloody wholesale butcher—'im and 'is like!' A 20-year-old man complained that Churchill was 'turning into a proper dictator in his old age. Thinking he can always get his own way by threatening to resign—throwing a temperament like a bloody film star.' There was also a vocal 'Trust Churchill' minority, though. One 45-year-old man said: 'Well, from Churchill's speech, I think he was justified in the step he took. I think it puts a very different face on it, if that ELAS movement is run by communists and Germans leading them. I think if there's German intrigue behind it, well, it's a different matter to what I thought it.'[129]

Postal censorship revealed that Churchill's line was highly popular with British troops serving in Greece. From an NCO: 'Don't you go drawing any conclusions, darling, because on what you read in the papers you have no chance of grasping the true position. Mr. Churchill is nearer the mark than anyone.' From a warrant officer: 'Mr. Churchill and his speech bucked us no end, we know now what we are fighting for, and against, it is obviously a Hun element behind all this trouble.' From an officer: 'I have not met anyone here who does not think that Churchill is taking the only step possible—and they are a long way from being 100 per cent. government supporters generally.' And from another officer: 'What Churchill said is partially correct, but there is quite a lot left out. The press are doing much to hinder us by encouraging the rebels to think that we are not backed up by the people at home or America.'[130] Not surprisingly, Churchill circulated this evidence to his ministerial colleagues.

Although Harry Hopkins was pleased by the speech, there was not much comfort to be taken in American reactions more generally.[131] The British Embassy in Washington noted: 'The atmosphere resembles nothing so much as the outburst which greeted the Prime Minister's so-called "friendly words to Spain" in May.' The influential New York Times was supportive, and the

Hearst press group acclaimed Churchill as a 'long-wanted champion of humanity against the advance of the Red menace', but British foreign policy came under severe attack from other quarters.[132] The response was partly wrapped up with the Polish question, on which Churchill made a further speech in mid-December, urging the London Poles to reach agreement with the Russians on the basis of the Curzon line.[133] According to Colville, 'He couldn't think of anything new to say on the subject and so inserted long quotations from his own earlier speeches and a certain amount of padding'.[134] The speech was warmly received in Moscow, and the Soviet-backed Polish Committee of National Liberation said that Churchill now backed its policy.[135] By the same token, many exiled Poles felt it spelt their country's doom.[136] 'Churchill doesn't keep his word,' said one Polish cleric in Milwaukee. 'He's against the Communists in Greece but he's pro-communist in Poland. This will react not only on Britain, but it is putting the United States, as England's ally, on the spot.'[137] And such support as the British got over Greece was rather lukewarm, the embassy noted: 'Too often defence of us takes form merely of questions as to why USSR, which has been guilty of harsher intervention in affairs of other nations while Britain is treated to so full a measure of rebuke.'[138] Interestingly, a German propaganda directive insisted that press commentaries should *not* make use of US criticisms of Churchill's speech in order to illustrate Anglo-American divisions on Poland: 'You should rather assert that the United States as well as England shows obsequiousness as far as Moscow's claims on Poland are concerned, and that, seen from the outside, the American procedure is merely one of considerable diplomacy and care.'[139] As far as Roosevelt's position went, this was probably actually fair comment. He had long since endorsed the Soviet position on the border, but unlike Churchill had not made his position plain in public.[140]

On 19 December, Churchill had a tough Question Time in the Commons, particularly over Greece. 'The Chief Whip says it is the first time he has seen the House really irritated and impatient with him,' recorded Colville.[141] But things soon started to look up. Already, Ernest Bevin had made a strong speech of support at the Labour Party conference, although this did not wash with many of the critics. ('I got a big shock when I read Bevin saying he was a party to it,' ran one typical comment. 'Now I never thought that. I thought it was all our dictator Mr. Churchill.')[142] Then—not allowing himself to be distracted by the new German offensive in the Ardennes— Churchill made a lightning Christmas visit to Athens. His conversations there led to a policy shift: the King would not return to Athens at once, but Archbishop Damaskinos would act as Regent until a referendum on the monarchy could be held.[143] This concession to popular sovereignty reduced suspicions in Britain of 'wretched Churchill and his precious Kings'.[144]

As the crisis in Greece went off the boil, so did the criticism at home. Churchill returned to the Commons on 15 January; the news of his arrival back in Britain had been kept under cover. 'He came in just before 11.30 and smiled,' wrote 'Chips' Channon. 'The house cheered and rose, a courteous spontaneous welcome which under the circumstances was legitimate, but curiously cold. Churchill is not loved in the House.'[145] On 18 January, Churchill gave a war review and devoted much of it to Greece. He deployed eye-witness testimony of ELAS atrocities to great effect, and described the group as 'Trotskyists', a word, he said, which had the advantage of being 'equally hated in Russia'.[146] He made a scathing attack on newspaper criticism, deploring the 'melancholy exhibition [...] provided by some of our most time-honoured and responsible journals'.[147] This oblique assault on *The Times*—which had been in the forefront of the attacks—brought forth a prolonged cheer from resentful Tories.[148] Colville wrote that in rhetorical terms it was the best speech he had heard Churchill make 'since 1941 or even 1940'.[149] The Labour critics had not wholly given up. Seymour Cocks maintained that 'if it is necessary to fight the Prime Minister, we shall fight him on the beaches, on the hill-sides, on the Floor of the House, in the Division Lobbies, on the hustings and at the ballot box, and in the name of liberty we shall defeat even the man who, four years ago, did so much to defend the liberties of this Island'.[150] This time, however, only six other MPs joined him in voting against the government. According to a Gallup poll in February, public opinion was now 46 to 28 per cent in favour of Churchill's handling of Greece.[151] In America, the Washington Embassy reported, his speech was acclaimed by centrist opinion 'both as masterpiece of exposition and as a powerful argument for recent British action'. Nevertheless, 'both on the right and left, there has been increasing criticism of this or that portion of his speech, and in direct proportion as Americans appear to become more ready to accept their own responsibility for participation in political solutions abroad, there is a tendency to scrutinize even the Prime Minister's golden eloquence with a sharp eye to the merits or demerits of specific concrete proposals, and an almost discernible effort to resist being swept away by the sheer power of his hypnotic style'. The mood, therefore, remained 'puzzled or critical rather than acquiescent'.[152]

Much expectation, though, surrounded the forthcoming 'Big Three' conference at Yalta in the Crimea. This was held in early February and took important decisions regarding the proposed United Nations Organization, the post-war treatment of Germany, and, most controversially, the future of Poland. Churchill, Stalin, and Roosevelt—the latter now exhausted and close to death—agreed that the eastern frontier of Poland should follow the Curzon Line, albeit with some minor digressions from it in favour of Poland, which would also receive new territory in the north and west at the expense of Germany. The Soviet-sponsored provisional government based in Lublin was to be broadened to include members of the London government-in-exile, whereupon it would be recognized as the Polish Provisional Government of National Unity. On the way home, Churchill passed again through Athens, where he addressed a huge audience in the centre of the city, speaking of his pride in the British Army's role 'in protecting this great and immortal city against violence and anarchy'.[153] 'I have had great moments in my life,' he said later, 'but never such a moment as when faced with that half-million crowd in Constitution Square.'[154]

In contrast to the trouble over the Greek question, Churchill could rely on the Labour Party to be supportive of his line on Poland.[155] The Yalta decisions made some Conservatives angry, however. Although the outcome has often been seen as a betrayal of the Poles, it is hard to see what Churchill could have done to bring about a different result, given the overwhelming power of the Red Army in Eastern Europe. Still, his attempts to rationalize the deal to himself and others were less than wholly convincing. After his return he told ministers, 'Poor Neville Chamberlain believed he could trust with Hitler. He was wrong. But I don't think I'm wrong about Stalin.'[156] The draft of his speech defending Yalta in the Commons contained the statement 'Soviet Russia seeks not only peace, but peace with honour'. Next to this, Colville wrote '? Omit. Echo of Munich'.[157] It was duly left out of the final text, although Churchill nonetheless included some significant hostages to fortune.

When he rose to speak in the Commons on 27 February he appeared vigorous although he afterwards admitted that he felt 'tired all through'.[158] He was 'restrained and sober' in his manner but for the most part less fluent than usual.[159] The Polish question comprised only a part of his statement but it was, he acknowledged, 'the most difficult and agitating part'. He insisted: 'In supporting the Russian claim to the Curzon Line, I repudiate and repulse any suggestion that we are making a questionable compromise or yielding to force or fear, and I assert with the utmost conviction the broad justice of the policy upon which, for the first time, all the three great Allies have now taken their stand.' He further stated his impression 'that Marshal Stalin and the Soviet leaders wish to live in honourable friendship and equality with the Western democracies. I feel also that their word is their bond.'[160] Justifying this latter claim in his memoirs, Churchill wrote: 'I felt bound to proclaim my confidence in Soviet faith in order to procure it. In this I was encouraged by Stalin's behaviour about Greece.'[161] At the time, however, he claimed privately to be 'Profoundly impressed with the friendly attitude of Stalin and Molotov'.[162] Colville wrote: 'He is trying to persuade himself that all is well, but in his heart I think he is worried about Poland and not convinced of the strength of our moral position.'[163] Harold Nicolson observed: 'He makes a good case for arguing that Poland in her new frontiers will enjoy an independent and prosperous existence.' However, 'he rather destroys all this by saying that we will offer British citizenship to those Polish soldiers who are too frightened to return'.[164]

The following day, twenty-five MPs voted for an amendment regretting 'the failure to ensure to those nations which have been liberated from German oppression the full right to choose their own government free from the influence of any other power'.[165] Although the number of rebels was similar, this was not a potentially destabilizing governmental crisis like the Greek one.[166] As Cuthbert Headlam put it, 'no one seemed pleased with what Winston said, but I heard no one suggest what else he could have said in the circumstances'.[167] Once the amendment had been defeated, the House approved the Yalta settlement as a whole by 413 votes to 0. Nor was the Conservative rebellion backed by significant popular anger in Britain. With morale no longer considered an issue, Home Intelligence reports had been discontinued. We know, however, that reactions to Churchill's December statement on the Polish question had revealed sympathy for the Poles and some appreciation of the British government's difficulties as well as accusations of 'knuckling under'. But strong feeling was not widespread, and there is no evidence it developed in response to Yalta.[168] In his diary Home Guard Colonel Rodney Foster denounced Churchill's 'speech defending the Yalta betrayal, full of lies and verbal gymnastics', but the more common attitude was likely one of acceptance.[169] In the United States, criticism was not absent, but now that Roosevelt's agreement to the Polish settlement was known, Churchill was no longer such an exposed target. The President made a bland report to Congress, containing little new information: 'The familiar complaint is consequently again being heard that Americans are dependent on [the] Prime Minister's speeches for knowledge of what goes on at Allied conferences.'[170]

By mid-March, Churchill could proclaim (in a speech to the Conservative Party conference) that 'victory lies before us, certain and perhaps near'.[171] In the period before the German surrender, he made a number of speeches and statements, the two most notable of which were eulogies. At the end of the month, returning from a trip to the Western Front, Churchill was told of the death of his old colleague, the former Prime Minister David Lloyd George. He paid tribute to him in the Commons the next day, noting the contribution he had made to social reform and describing him as 'the greatest Welshman which that unconquerable race has produced since the age of the Tudors'.[172] Lifelong Liberal Clementine Churchill wrote to her husband that she 'loved' the speech: 'It recalled forgotten blessings which he showered upon the meek & lowly'.[173] John Colville, by contrast, considered the tribute 'eloquent in parts and well delivered but not, I thought, as good as that he paid to Neville Chamberlain in 1940'.[174]

On 12 April, Roosevelt died. 'I expect Churchill will go next,' commented one 40-year-old woman, perhaps not without relish. 'They say he drinks a lot. I liked Roosevelt better, he was a man of the people.' Another woman, aged 35, said: 'I'm afraid it will have serious repercussions for the peace. I had far sooner it was Churchill who died.'[175] Churchill's secretary Elizabeth Layton recalled that when the news came through she rushed into the Prime Minister's study to take dictation: 'Mr. Churchill was sitting crumpled up in his chair, his face white. When he dictated he was gentle as a lamb, but his voice sounded quite dead.'[176] The resulting speech described the late President as 'the greatest American friend we have ever known', but in truth the Churchill–Roosevelt relationship had been much more difficult than could be publicly acknowledged.[177]

On 8 May, Churchill was at last able to make the long-awaited victory announcement, via broadcast. It was heard by 71.5 per cent of the potential audience. The previous day, at 2.41 a.m., the Germans had surrendered unconditionally, Churchill said. Having promised 'a brief period of rejoicing' he noted that the war with Japan was not yet over, and concluded: 'Advance, Britannia! Long live the cause of freedom! God save the King!'[178] Lord Moran heard the speech in the House of Lords library: 'It was a short, factual statement, arranged by a man of letters, though the ending had a tinny sound.' The peer next to him thought it odd that there was no reference to God in the speech. Moran noted drily: 'There was, however, no doubt in Winston's mind to whom the credit was due'.[179] A. Riley, a retired woman teacher from Brighton, wrote in her diary: 'I thought C's speech well pointed but again he brought in the year Britain stood alone (I have not heard him make a single speech without that reference and had just before said so), and my friend & I exchanged a smile. C's last three sentences struck me as ludicrous coming after his solemn announcement & I laughed outright.'[180] Charity worker Vere Hodgson was less cynical. She described how she heard the speech over loudspeakers in central London: 'How wonderful to be standing in Whitehall, in the shadow of the House of Commons, listening to That Voice which had steered us from our darkest hours to the daylight of deliverance.'[181] The revels began, and continued through 9 May. Mary E. Lelean, a clerk in the Auxiliary Territorial Service, recorded:

> I left my parents at Victoria, and made for Westminster alone. Victoria St. and Parliament Sq. were practically empty, but Westminster Bridge was packed with people admiring the lights on the river. As I stood here, a roar went up behind me. I turned around, and started back towards Whitehall; I was soon swept along by the hurrying crowd, and cast up at the corner of Whitehall and Bridge St. As I expected, Churchill was on the floodlit balcony of the Ministry of Health, puffing at a huge cigar, and saluting the cheers through a cloud of smoke. After a few moments, he indicated that he was going to speak, and the crowd tried to hush itself. After a few attempts, he made himself heard over a microphone; it was a short, disconnected, but impressive speech, about London and the Londoners, and even I felt moved. Personally, I have no great admiration for the *man* Churchill, but as a war leader he has been unsurpassed, and his command of the language is wonderful. He recited the verse of 'Rule Britannia', then lifted his hand, and with a tuneless voice, roared out the first notes of the chorus: 'R . . . Rule'. . . .' And the crowd took up the refrain. It was impossible not to be moved.[182]

It would be nice to leave the story on that triumphant note. However, there was a less than happy sequel. In a further victory broadcast, on 13 May, Churchill urged the British people to maintain their efforts 'till the whole task is done and the whole world is safe and clean'. Since his comments in November 1940 he had been restrained in his public comments on neutral Éire, save for one or two oblique digs. But in his moment of triumph he could not resist dwelling on how Britain, instead of seizing the treaty ports, had 'left the De Valera government to frolic' with German and Japanese representatives in Dublin.[183] De Valera had indeed gone to the German legation to pay his condolences on the death of Hitler. Irish opinion was outraged, however: Churchill was seen as having offered an insult to the whole country. Even the *Irish Times*, a paper critical of Irish neutrality, thought that he had gone too far.[184]

Three days later, De Valera broadcast a much-anticipated reply, deliberately using a quiet and considered rather than an angry tone. 'Mr. Churchill makes it clear that, in certain circumstances, he would have violated our neutrality and that he would justify his action by Britain's necessity,' he said. 'It seems strange to me that Mr. Churchill does not see that this, if accepted, would mean Britain's necessity would become a moral code and that when this necessity became sufficiently great, other people's rights were not to count.' The speech allowed De Valera to stand on his dignity and recover from the mis-step of his visit to the legation by appealing to Irish national sentiment. 'Mr. Churchill is justly proud of his nation's perseverance against heavy odds. But we in this island are still prouder of our people's perseverance for freedom through all the centuries.'[185] After hearing the broadcast, Churchill was unusually quiet for a long time. He later admitted to his son that his own speech was one that 'perhaps I should not have made in the heat of the moment. We had just come through the War and I had been looking around at our victories. The idea of Eire sitting at our feet without giving us a hand annoyed me.' In his war memoirs he was not so candid and instead glossed over the episode.[186]

After VE Day, the Labour Party and most of the Liberal Party withdrew from the coalition. At the end of May, Churchill formed a new caretaker government. Sir John Maffey, the UK representative in Ireland, had written in frustration at Churchill's outburst at De Valera, 'Phrases make history here'.[187] They did so in Britain too, a point that the Prime Minister was to illustrate once again as the general election campaign opened.

8

'Hush, Hush, Hush, Here Comes the Bogy Man'

'No Socialist Government conducting the entire life and industry of the country could afford to allow free, sharp, or violently-worded expressions of public discontent,' said Churchill on 4 June 1945, in the first radio broadcast of the general election campaign. 'They would have to fall back on some form of *Gestapo*, no doubt very humanely directed in the first instance.'[1] That August, nursing his wounds after his defeat at the hands of Clement Attlee's Labour Party, Churchill claimed privately to have no regrets: 'He said the time would come when that particular speech would be recognised as one of the greatest he had ever delivered.'[2] In fact, the speech has retained all of the notoriety that it gained at the time of its delivery, a negative view quickly cemented by the brilliant reply made by Attlee the following day. The broadcast and the response to it are often seen together as a foundational moment for the post-war British political settlement, the point when calm, mild-mannered, un-rhetorical Mr Attlee skewered Churchill's bombast and demonstrated his own superior qualifications as a leader in time of peace.[3]

The central flaw of the speech appears obvious. Between May 1940 and May 1945, Churchill himself had worked with the leaders of the Labour Party who had taken ministerial roles in his coalition government. Yet, with only a slight qualification ('no doubt very humanely directed in the first instance') he now seemed to suggest that electing them would lead to horrors equivalent to those perpetrated by the Nazis. There was an appalling credibility gap, merely accentuated by the recent revelations of the nature of concentration camps such as Belsen. However, if the standard view of the speech cannot be rejected, it is also incomplete. Although leading Labour politician Herbert Morrison immediately labelled it 'Churchill's Crazy

Broadcast', it cannot be dismissed as a mere mental lapse.[4] To understand it fully, we need to appreciate how it fitted into Churchill's broader domestic political strategy during the war years, which this chapter investigates. Two conclusions emerge. First: rather than taking the speech as evidence that Churchill was becoming 'increasingly irrational', we should see it as part of a considered (albeit in execution misguided) effort to appeal to wavering Liberal opinion.[5] Second: from the moment he entered Downing Street in 1940, Churchill faced a losing battle to convince the electorate that he was a desirable peacetime Prime Minister. Although there seems little reason to doubt the consensus view that the 'Gestapo' speech harmed his chances of returning to office, he already faced an almost insurmountable challenge to be re-elected. He was leader of a Conservative Party that was widely perceived to have failed domestically and internationally in the 1930s, and his reputation as a war leader was in fact a rather dubious asset in the new conditions of 1945. With few political options to choose from to help him tackle opponents fighting skilfully on their home ground, there was little Churchill could do to reverse his fortunes. Seen in this light, the 'Gestapo' broadcast and the failed election campaign of which it was a symbol appear less as the cause of Churchill's problems than as their consequence.

From the point that Churchill returned to the Admiralty in the autumn of 1939, there was an idea in circulation that his natural aggression qualified him to be a war leader but made him unsuitable in peacetime. 'Think Winston is the man for the job in wartime—a first class Admiralty man', wrote J. R. Aldam, a London office manager, after his January 1940 Manchester speech. 'But distrust him greatly as a politician in time of peace, a view which seems to be shared by people of all shades of opinion whom I meet.'[6] The day that Churchill became Prime Minister, bank clerk W. C. Eyre Hartley wrote in his diary: 'A change for the better as he has go & drive but he is rather inflexible & we must not let him make peace but only war'.[7] Journalist Margaret Kornitzer wrote a few days later: 'Typical comments on Churchill: "Oh he's a ruffian. But he'll see us through this...he won't hesitate to be as ruthless as the Nazis." No man for the peace.'[8]

Such views were expressed throughout the war. In 1943, Mass-Observation asked its panel of observers to record their opinions of Churchill. As MO acknowledged, the panel did not represent a cross-section of society and was weighted towards the middle class. On the other hand, the panellists may have been more willing than people approached by interviewers in the street to give their frank opinion. It is important to stress that Churchill did have widespread popular support and that very few people disliked him as an individual. 'Individuals may be ardent socialists, or confirmed Tories; both speak of Winston Churchill as "the national leader".' However, 'a third of the whole sample mentioned quite spontaneously that, good as Churchill was as war Prime Minister, they did not want him as Prime Minister after the war, or were doubtful whether he would make an equally good peacetime Prime Minister.' The critics variously thought that he would be too reactionary, that he had old-fashioned ideas about economics, that he had 'too much of the old bulldog in him', or that he was too aristocratic. 'Let's hope he is the man to win the war and leave the peace alone,' observed a 42-year-old housewife. One 20-year-old man in the forces thought that Churchill's 'type of leadership is just what is needed in war-time, provided it can be done away with afterwards'. MO's report concluded 'that though Churchill is highly popular with a large mass of the people of this country, and while his prestige is perhaps higher at present than ever before, the feeling that his premiership should come to an end soon after the finish of the war is strong and certainly growing'.[9] It was a theme and a sentiment that the Labour Party came to exploit very effectively.

The question of post-war politics was first raised by Churchill in the Commons in January 1941. Post-war reconstruction would be easier, if the task could be done 'with something of the same kind of national unity as has been achieved under the pressure of this present struggle for life'.[10] This was understood at the time as a suggestion that some form of coalition should continue for a while once the war was over—and that indeed was to be Churchill's preference in 1945.[11] Until that point, however, he engaged little with domestic politics, and failed to give much of a lead to the Conservative Party, which itself was struggling to deal with the aftermath of Neville Chamberlain's fall. This was because he was busy with more pressing matters, not because he was indifferent to its fate, but Conservative officials were often frustrated by his lack of attention to their problems.[12] He was not always unresponsive. One thing that concerned Conservatives was their belief the other parties were not respecting the terms of the party truce agreed at the outbreak of war. As far as Labour and the Liberals were concerned, it was an electoral truce, not a political one—that is to say that, although the main parties would not fight each other at by-elections, there was no rule against making party political statements. The Tories saw things differently. On the eve of Churchill's first speech as leader to the Conservative Central Council in March 1941, the Party Chairman, Sir Douglas Hacking, sent him a series of allegedly partisan quotations from recent statements by leading Labour figures. Hacking wanted him to reassure Conservative activists that they were right to suspend their propaganda activities, and at the same time praise them for maintaining the party organization.[13] Churchill did this, but the result was a very bland deprecation of partisanship and an invocation of national unity. His position as 'national leader', very useful for the time being as far as the war was concerned, made it hard for him to offer his party anything more than platitudes. His future opponents had much freer rein.

Churchill's 1942 speech to the Central Council, which evoked only moderate public interest, was similarly free of political red meat, although he made sure to butter up the audience.[14] MO diarist R.W. Fenn wrote: 'In spite of his protests that party allegiances are suspended in the interests of unity, his real views peeped out this week when he told the annual conference of the Conservative Party that they were after all the people who really mattered,—"the main part of the rock on which the salvation of Britain was founded".'[15] Churchill dealt with the problem of reconstruction briefly and seemingly reluctantly, saying that he was 'perpetually asked to devote more time and attention to the rebuilding of the post-war world' but emphasizing that it was important not to lose focus on the war effort.[16] This was an attitude that became much harder to sustain after the Battle of El Alamein. From this point on, the prospect of ultimate victory seemed much more concrete, and the battle was quickly followed by the seemingly timely official report by Sir William Beveridge into the future of the social services. Beveridge's ambitious proposals were highly popular, but for Churchill they were a headache.

In February 1943, the government met a major Commons rebellion by Labour backbenchers who wanted ministers to commit themselves definitely to the report. Churchill for his part viewed Beveridge as 'an awful windbag and a dreamer', but he was not opposed to the extension of welfare provision per se.[17] As a Liberal minister before the First World War Churchill had been closely associated with significant social reforms, such as the introduction of National Insurance, and his reputation was closely bound up with that of his radical colleague, David Lloyd George.[18] As Conservative Chancellor of the Exchequer in the 1920s, Martin Daunton has noted, Churchill 'consciously seized' Lloyd George's mantle and aimed 'to appropriate the ideology of "new Liberalism" which had, to a large extent, migrated into the Labour party'.[19] As the 1945 election approached Churchill increasingly rediscovered himself as a social reformer and as an heir to the

Liberal tradition.[20] This was in line with the thinking of some Conservative social reformers and with the party's efforts to appeal to Liberal opinion and to ally itself with elements of the collapsing Liberal Party as they sheared off.[21] But until the war's end was immediately in view, Churchill continued to see debate about reconstruction as a distraction from his main task. Another reason for silence was that the Conservatives were themselves divided. The Tory Reform Group's sympathy towards collectivist policies was not shared by those sceptical of the growth of taxation and state control, and there were plenty of right-wing Tories willing to make trouble if the government made too many concessions towards Labour opinion within the coalition.[22]

Churchill did however make one major wartime speech on post-war planning—his so-called 'Four Years' Plan' broadcast of 21 March 1943. This was a clear attempt to seize the initiative in the wake of the Beveridge Report revolt the previous month and also perhaps a response to by-election setbacks.[23] Churchill dictated the first draft to his secretary Elizabeth Layton during a car journey; unsurprisingly, her notes were illegible. She appealed for help to, amongst others, Churchill's private secretary John Martin, his friend and adviser Lord Cherwell, and his detective Commander Thompson. She recalled: 'What I had missed or could not read they made up for me: they told me what he had probably said and what they thought he ought to have said, and what they would have said had they been Prime Minister; and Mr Churchill had later to admit that, while I had not recorded his dictation exactly, at least the words made sense.'[24] The drafting process as a whole took about three weeks. Those who gave advice included the eminent economist and Treasury official Lord Keynes.[25] Some intemperate passages about 'the Battle of Gandhi'—who had been fasting in protest at British rule in India—and the 'Battle of Beveridge' were dropped from the script.[26]

The War Cabinet reviewed the finished version and made suggestions. Labour ministers were part of this process, the most significant comment coming from Herbert Morrison, who prompted Churchill to agree to make clear that legislative preparations for reconstruction must start before the war's end.[27] Morrison told Hugh Dalton that 'he succeeded in improving some passages in the PM's speech, and in particular in getting him to say that there was an increasing field for State ownership, particularly as regards monopolies'.[28] The Labour contributions are striking, because Churchill was to fight the 1945 election using the pledges made in the broadcast as a key part of his platform. At the time, indeed, one Labour MP described the speech as 'the Tory election manifesto'.[29] To some, Churchill's hints that he would be himself prepared to act as post-war Prime Minister came as something of a surprise.[30]

Churchill's conception of a Four Years' Plan was that it would cover the period of the transition to peace and 'would cover five or six large measures of a practical character [...] which fit together into a general scheme'. He left open the question of what these measures should be, but he stressed his desire for the extension of National Insurance—a key component of the Beveridge scheme. Rather hypocritically—in view of what he really thought of Beveridge—he observed that he had been 'prominently connected with all these schemes of national compulsory organised thrift from the time when I brought my friend Sir William Beveridge into the public service 35 years ago, when I was creating the labour exchanges'. He also recalled his association with Lloyd George, the 'prime parent of all national insurance schemes'. He said that 'the best way to insure against unemployment is to have no unemployment', although he was unspecific about how this was to be achieved. He touched on agriculture, and on the importance of public health, on which he quoted Disraeli, perhaps as a counterweight to his praise of Lloyd George. His most memorable observation was that 'there is no finer investment for any community than putting milk into babies'. He spoke too on education, doing so 'with great earnestness and fervour'.[31] The speech committed Churchill to little that was concrete.[32] Nor could he fully disguise his resentment at being forced to speak about post-war planning.[33] But if the speech was vague it was not obviously reactionary. Churchill expressed his faith that 'if we can make State enterprise and free enterprise both serve national interests and pull the national wagon side by side, then there is no need for us to run into that horrible, devastating slump or into that squalid epoch of bickering and confusion which mocked and squandered the hard-won victory we gained a quarter of a century ago'.[34]

Churchill was, however, cautious enough to ensure that Tory traditionalists were not too dismayed. Cuthbert Headlam wrote wearily: 'while he was careful to tell us all that nothing could really be done until the war was over, he assured us that he was all for keeping us from the cradle to the grave—so I suppose that he will satisfy all the progressives. [...] It is certain to be greeted by a round of applause and undoubtedly was a fine performance of its kind.'[35] Leo Amery, more instinctively sympathetic to social reform, thought Churchill 'struck a fair balance between wholeheartedly endorsing the Beveridge scheme and yet warning us that we had to consider finance'.[36]

On the Labour side, some MPs genuinely welcomed the broadcast as a sign that reform would take place, whereas others feared that Churchill was planning a 'khaki' election 'dominated by a centre party loyal to him'.[37] But although the party's National Executive shared that concern, it decided not to make any public comment.[38] Its members probably realized they were walking on eggshells. There was talk at the time that a new centre party led by Churchill would attract some Labour ministers, triggering a Labour split of the kind that had so damaged the party in 1931.[39] 'For a man of his years so recently ill, it was a superb performance,' observed the journalist J. L. Hodson. 'But there is as much argument as to what he precisely meant, as there is over what Shakespeare sometimes meant. Did Churchill forecast a Centre Party? Did he mean there's nothing doing on Beveridge till Hitler is laid low? Is he going to lead in peace as in war? (Most folk read this into his words.)'[40]

Churchill had managed to seize some political ground, but to describe the broadcast as a proclamation of a new political consensus is perhaps to go too far.[41] Although Churchill did share some ideological territory with Labour moderates such as Morrison, his real aim was to relieve pressure for immediate reform by paying lip service to its importance in the future. Privately he remained emphatic that no big legislation could be expected before the war's end: 'he found himself being constantly told that he must talk about the post-war plans when we had nothing like won the war. People were always getting ahead of events.'[42] The public reaction was rather confused.[43] N. E. Underwood of Sheffield recorded: 'I went round the office today asking what each thought of the Churchill speech and found that 50 per cent didn't bother to listen. Those who did were disappointed as they expected something sensational whereas what he said wasn't a bit interesting! Can you believe that?'[44] 'Mother and Dad weren't a bit interested because it dealt with the future,' noted factory clerk M. J. Brierley sadly.[45] By contrast, ARP worker L. N. Adamson—likely projecting his own views—stated that 'the ordinary man and woman liked it. I was much struck by the fact that it was almost pure socialism, which is a considerable advance for a Conservative Prime Minister.'[46] Hospital lab assistant Edward Stebbing at first found the speech 'very encouraging', but changed his mind after reading the comments of the Liberal News Chronicle. 'His remarks on private enterprise were typically Tory,' believed Stebbing, adding: 'Churchill can never hide his Conservative background and party politics no matter how much he pretends that party politics has been put on one side.'[47] 'Listened to Churchill's speech', noted J. Hinton, a teacher from Bedford in her forties. 'Thought it excellent that he should consider planning necessary & that some of his points were very good. But our first exclamation was "We shan't want *you* any more when the time comes to put it into practice".'[48]

These and other diary comments bear out the findings of Home Intelligence, which suggested that reactions were more varied than for any of Churchill's previous war speeches:

> The Prime Minister's broadcast aroused much diverse comment—ranging from praise at 'his greatest ever', to disappointment because 'he barely touched on the war,' and did not refer to the second front—a subject uppermost in many people's minds. [. . .] Many less intelligent people, who never normally listen to the Prime Minister, were 'overwhelmed' and 'confused'. They turned on their sets expecting to hear a war review on a familiar pattern. At first, they were disappointed at the unfamiliar theme, then at times 'the speech got quite beyond them', and they are 'still assimilating its ideas piecemeal'. Among the more intelligent, it appears to have pleased and satisfied 'the majority who like the middle of the road', while giving those on the extreme right or left 'plenty to shoot at'.[49]

According to Mass-Observation:

> It was felt that to some extent talk about post-war problems at present was superfluous, although this reaction may have come from a strong feeling minority rather than the majority. There was some suspicion too that it was only words, and would not be put into practice. Apart from this, the speech was well received, and there was a numerous majority in favour of each of the somewhat vague statements made. There was practically no criticism of particular points of policy, although there was some doubt as to what Churchill's own attitude to the Beveridge report really was. The speech probably satisfied those who wanted to hear about post war plans, without doing any great harm with those who thought the time not yet ripe for such discussions.[50]

73.8 per cent of the potential audience listened—the second highest figure of the war. The BBC's Listener Research Department reported 80 per cent satisfaction, which was thought low for a Churchill broadcast, but good compared with other recent programmes in the same slot.[51]

Some weeks after the speech, the Gallup organization began to conduct polls on voting intentions. The first survey, in June, gave Labour an eight-point lead, and the party stayed ahead of the Tories until the general election.[52] Clearly, the broadcast had not done much for Conservative political fortunes. The results were more concrete in the City, which responded well to Churchill's talk of currency stability. According to the *Financial Times*, 'Radio Manufacturing shares were stimulated by the Prime Minister's forecast of great peace-time activity through the war-time development of radiolocation. Aircraft shares responded to his reference to the possibilities of civil aviation.'[53]

Of course, a single speech could not be expected to revolutionize Churchill's election chances by itself. It might be tempting to argue, then, that he might have done better in 1945 had he talked more often about reconstruction questions. There may be some truth in that idea, but the reactions to the 'Four Years' Plan' speech make clear that the results might not have been wholly positive for him. When it came to the point of choosing a post-war government, the voters in practice clearly wanted a party that had well-developed plans; but there was clearly a body of people who did not want their war leader to talk about such things while the war was going on and were disconcerted when he did so. These may well have been natural Tory voters; had Churchill made too much of a habit of talking about reconstruction he might have alienated some of his core support. In other words, his very position as 'national leader' in wartime placed some obstacles in the way of electoral preparation. This was evident again in the reactions to a broadcast he made a year later, in which he harked back to the Four Years' Plan idea and noted progress made, including the passage of the government's Education Act.[54] (But a few days later, Churchill insisted that the Commons reverse a vote in favour of equal pay for women teachers, which contributed to his reputation for being 'dictatorial'.) Although the domestic policy references in this broadcast were generally warmly praised, 'some objection is reported on the ground that it sounded like an election speech'.[55] One listener noted drily: 'There was no postscript to the News, but Mr Churchill gave what was almost a Postscript to the National Government.'[56] Another (albeit minority) complaint was that 'there was too much about post-war domestic planning, "in a world-wide broadcast with friend and enemy listening, and on the eve of the second front"', i.e. the invasion of France.[57]

As the end of the war approached, Churchill began to refine his political strategy. By March 1945, it was already clear that Labour and the Liberals would probably leave the coalition once victory in Europe was won. That month, Churchill addressed the Conservative Party conference in London. It was the first full party conference that he had addressed as leader. It was good, knock-about stuff, with digs at 'the stay-at-home Left Wing *intelligentsia*' and

the 'windy platitudes and glittering advertisements' that the Tories' opponents supposedly offered.[58] 'Churchill as Tory head had shown himself in his
true colours,' wrote housewife Edith Dawson, who defined her own views
as 'Anything but Tory'.[59] Churchill said: 'Should it fall to me, as it may do, to
form a Government before the election, I shall seek the aid not only of
Conservatives but of men of good will of any party and no party who are
willing to serve and thus invest our Administration with a national character.'[60] After Lord Croft (formerly Henry Page Croft MP) wrote to congratulate him on his speech, Churchill replied explaining his thinking:

> I do not intend a National Government founded on the official agreement of
> Labour and Liberals, unless of course we are denied an effective working
> majority. But both before and after the Election, I hope to have the help of
> eminent and capable men who can do their various heavy jobs to the highest
> public advantage. As an old political campaigner, you will realise the advantage
> of having 'socialists v. the rest' rather than 'Tories v. the rest'. I imagine this is
> even more true in an election where there must be an enormous vote unat-
> tached to any particular Party.[61]

Churchill's efforts to present himself as a 'national', non-partisan politician
was in line with the strategy adopted by previous Conservative leaders'
strategies. There was an irony in this. When the National Government was
formed in 1931, Churchill—denied ministerial office—was privately dispar-
aging although supportive of it in public. Churchill's own government of
1940 had a much more plausible claim to be genuinely non-partisan—but
only for as long as the other parties stayed on board. After VE Day the
Labour Party and the majority of Liberal ministers withdrew from the coalition, yet Churchill was determined to hang on to the 'National' label
nonetheless. The irony lay in the fact that Churchill was linking himself to
a brand that had paid great dividends for Baldwin and Chamberlain. But
because of the perceived failures of the original National Government, it
was a brand that was heavily devalued. Churchill would struggle to over-
come this even though his credentials as a national leader were apparently
exceptional.

When the coalition broke up in May, Churchill created a new caretaker
government. The election was to take place in July. Inevitably, the new government was dominated by Conservatives. However, Churchill also went to
considerable lengths to recruit non-Tories. One of these was the sixth Earl
of Rosebery, son of Lord Rosebery, the former Liberal Prime Minister, who
became Secretary of State for Scotland. Another was Lloyd George's son

Gwilym who had declared that he meant to fight the next election 'as a Liberal candidate supporting the National Government'.[62] Leslie Hore-Belisha, Churchill's sometime critic, was appointed Minister of National Insurance. Originally elected as a Liberal National, and later an Independent, he was to fight the coming election (and lose) as a National candidate. There were further similar examples, but there were no Labour representatives in this government; the vestigial National Labour Party was dissolved in June 1945. However, in the 'Gestapo' broadcast and in the election campaign generally Churchill would make much play of the government's supposed 'national' status. Strikingly, Churchill's election manifesto made no mention of the Conservatives, or of any other political party.[63] It is no surprise, then, that The Times was to headline its report of Churchill's first election broadcast—the 'Gestapo' speech—'"VOTE NATIONAL, NOT PARTY"'.[64] There was, however, a powerful disjuncture between Churchill's claim that he and his colleagues transcended party, and the 'Gestapo' comment itself, which sounded like a party political insult. Churchill had a long history of engaging in such gibes. It was easy for Labour, therefore, to portray him as reverting to type.

However, Churchill was by no means the only person to use 'Gestapo' as an insult. The term had long since entered the English language. The Gestapo—a contraction of Geheime Staatspolizei—was founded in April 1933, and received its first mention in the London Times on 13 October that year. In 1940, there was a media storm about the survey activities of the Home Intelligence Division. 'This house-to-house questioning will throw the shadow of the Gestapo over honest and loyal creatures,' warned the Daily Sketch.[65] In 1944, Labour's Arthur Greenwood (who had by that point left the government) suggested that British forces in Greece acting against the left-wing EAM/ELAS resistance movement were being 'driven into the position of a sort of Gestapo'.[66] More significant was the long-standing Labour critique of conservatism as a kind of crypto-Fascism. In this analysis, the pretension to 'national' values was particularly suspicious, and the critique extended to the Tory Party's allies.[67] During the war period some left-wing pamphlets claimed that there was a symbiosis between conservatism and Fascism. Aneurin Bevan MP wrote in 1944 that 'the Tory is a potential Fascist element in the community'.[68] Even Attlee, as party leader, was in on the act. In May 1945, he publicly rejected the suggestion that the coalition might be prolonged. Churchill had coupled that idea with a proposal to hold a referendum on whether or not the life of the current parliament should be extended. 'I could not consent to the introduction into our national life of a device so alien to all our traditions as the referendum, which has only too often been the instrument of Nazism and Fascism,' Attlee wrote. 'Hitler's practices in the field of referenda and plebiscites can hardly have endeared these expedients to the British heart.'[69] Sir Alan Lascelles, the King's private secretary, wrote in his diary that 'Attlee was guilty of a great breach of taste (and of tactics) in suggesting [...] that Winston's suggestion of a referendum savoured of Hitlerite methods'.[70] It may have been a breach of taste, but there is no reason to think that the tactic backfired.

Indeed, Labour candidates had official encouragement to link Conservatives with Nazism. The 1945 Labour Party *Speaker's Handbook* explained that 'The Tories' real policy all through was to let Fascist aggressors get away with their crimes because they wanted to keep Fascism and its oriental ally Japanese militarism strong enough to hold down the working class in Europe and to bolster up Imperialism in Asia and Africa.' Conservatives had been fully aware of Fascist methods, including the concentration camps, which had 'flourished all through the years the Tories were coddling and appeasing their friends Hitler and Mussolini'.[71] The concentration camps had been liberated between 11 April and 8 May. It was the liberation of Belsen on 15 April that made the strongest impression on the British public mind. Left-wingers tended to view the camps not in the light of the Jewish Holocaust, which was not yet fully understood, but rather in the light of what had been known about them in the 1930s. That is to say, there was a strong awareness that the camps had been used to repress Social Democrats and other political opponents of the Nazis, even as the Conservative policy of appeasement continued. Coming at the point that it did, Churchill's 'Gestapo' comment was obviously tasteless. Perhaps even more crucially, it was inopportune. At this moment, socialists could be far more persuasively portrayed as the likely victims of Nazi-style political terror than as its likely perpetrators. As one scholar has suggested, the news from the camps played into Labour's hands.[72] Conservatives, of course, did not take all this lying down, and often liked to point out that the Nazis called themselves National Socialists, hinting that British socialists cherished totalitarian ideals within their bosoms.

Thus, Churchill made his 'Gestapo' charge at a time when other figures in both main parties had been flinging similar insults and allegations around for some while. In no case did any of these other instances become notorious or create a media storm. This immediate context is important; in accounting for the 'Gestapo' speech it is possible to overemphasize intellectual influences on Churchill at the expense of other, cruder elements of contemporary discourse. Nevertheless, those intellectual influences may have been important. In 1944, F. A. Hayek, an Austrian émigré economist based at the London School of Economics (LSE), published *The Road to Serfdom*. This work argued that political and personal freedom was contingent on freedom in economic affairs; there was no third course between an economic system based on free enterprise, and totalitarianism; and that attempts by the state to plan economic life would tend to the destruction of liberty. Hayek later wrote ruefully that 'I am afraid there can be little doubt that Winston Churchill's somewhat unfortunately phrased Gestapo speech was written under the influence of *The Road to Serfdom*'.[73]

During 1944, Hayek made two efforts to get the book into Churchill's hands. In March he sent him a copy.[74] In October, he lunched with the Conservative MP Waldron Smithers and asked him 'most earnestly' to send Churchill a (further) copy. Smithers did so, suggesting that the Prime Minister could get the book's gist from the introduction and noting the 'tremendous interest' it had aroused in the country.[75] Again, however, it is unclear if Churchill actually read Hayek himself. It has been suggested by Richard Cockett that Churchill may have been influenced by the book at second-hand, via the Conservative Party Chairman Ralph Assheton. Assheton was so impressed by *The Road to Serfdom* that he bought fifty copies and sent them to colleagues and also to Attlee and Herbert Morrison. In April 1945, Assheton made a speech which not only had a clear Hayekian tinge but also associated Labour's policies with Nazi dictatorship, via a xenophobic take on Marx. 'We in this country have been fighting against totalitarianism in Germany and we do not wish to adopt as our creed the German-made doctrines of Karl Marx,' he said. 'I do not think that most of those who toy with Socialist theories and doctrines in this country sufficiently realise that Socialism [...] inevitably leads to a totalitarian State.' He sent his text in advance to Churchill, who thought it 'very good'.[76]

It is certainly possible that Assheton's speech had an impact on Churchill. It is worth noting though that Churchill had previously attacked socialism as leading to authoritarian rule.[77] It is also worth noting that Hayek (who saw himself as a liberal rather than a conservative) objected to full-scale centrally planned socialism, not to all forms of welfare legislation.[78] If this is understood, it is easier to see how Churchill could make use of Hayekian ideas in the 'Gestapo' speech whilst simultaneously championing social reform. The speech was to include appeals to two competing strains of liberalism that, to him, did not necessarily appear incompatible. He was not, in fact, the most extreme person on the National side. Rowland Hunt, General Secretary of the National Liberals, argued not long before Churchill's broadcast that the proposals of Beveridge were contrary to Liberalism and, 'if adopted would be Hitler's last triumph, for Britain would then become a completely totalitarian state'.[79]

Churchill wrote the speech at Chequers over the weekend of 2–3 June. Although many people, when they heard it, suspected the involvement of his cronies Lord Beaverbrook and Brendan Bracken MP, it was his own work.[80] There is no surviving account of how Churchill came to light upon the 'Gestapo' phrase. According to his youngest daughter, Mary Soames, his wife warned him not to use it: 'Clementine, to whom he had shown the script of his broadcast, spotted this unfortunate sentence at once, and she had begged Winston to delete the odious and invidious reference to the Gestapo. But he would not heed her.'[81] After the war he expressed a note of private regret—whilst defending the speech as a whole—that he had had to refer to the Gestapo rather than to the Soviet NKVD, forerunner of the KGB.[82] At the time that he made the broadcast, he was already highly concerned about Soviet geopolitical ambitions.[83] He was, of course, constrained from offering public criticism by the fact that Britain and the USSR were still allies. In the domestic context, moreover, it must have seemed doubtful that traditional 'red scare' tactics could be as effective against Labour as they had been at the elections of 1924 and 1931, given the Soviet Union's recently found popularity with much of the British public, which reflected admiration for the efforts of the Red Army. Nonetheless, his actual choice of words implicitly linked Stalinism with Nazism, because he was arguing that *all* socialist systems would require a Gestapo. Therefore, his speech can be seen as part of the process by which British reactions to pre-war and wartime Fascism and post-war communism became fused, with the USSR replacing Germany as the threat to 'civilization' in the early stages of the Cold War.[84]

On Monday 4 June Churchill delivered the broadcast in the study at Chequers. It lasted 21¼ minutes.[85] His private secretary John Colville observed that 'he was speaking against the clock which made him hurry unduly'.[86] Churchill devoted his first few paragraphs to his regret at the break-up of the coalition. 'I know that many of my Labour colleagues would have been glad to carry on,' he said. He did concede that political parties had always played a great role in British affairs: 'Party ties have been considered honourable bonds, and no one could doubt that when the German war was over and the immediate danger to this country, which had led to the Coalition, had ceased, conflicting loyalties would arise.' But he immediately went on to suggest that being bound by such ties was, in the current circumstances, dishonourable: 'Our Socialist and Liberal friends felt themselves forced, therefore, to put party before country. They have departed and we have been left to carry the nation's burden.' Churchill could certainly have relied on most of his listeners accepting his unstated axiom that it was wrong to put party before country. In his reference to 'the nation's burden' there was an echo of the charge levelled against the Labour Party in 1931 that it had run away from its responsibilities during the financial crisis that triggered the creation of the National Government. It is of course common for politicians to describe office as a burden even when they themselves are not in the least inclined to give it up.

Churchill then expounded his claim that his caretaker administration was a National Government. He himself, he said, would stand as a 'Conservative and National' candidate: he presented himself and his colleagues as men who, by selflessly shouldering the burden of office, were already putting the national interest first. 'Particularly do I regret the conduct of the Liberal Party', he said. 'Between us and the orthodox Socialists there is a great doctrinal gulf, which yawns and gapes.' There was, however, 'no such gulf between the Conservative and National Government I have formed and the Liberals. There is scarcely a Liberal sentiment which animated the great Liberal leaders of the past which we do not inherit and defend.' In order to justify this claim, he referred both to his government's 'championship of freedom' and to the Four Years' Plan. However, Churchill did not go into details about the Plan, appearing to assume that his audience was already familiar with it. He asserted that the programme of social reform it contained was 'so massive, so warm, so adventurous' that Gladstone would have felt it was going too far. 'But we still have a Rosebery and a Lloyd-George to carry forward the flags of their fathers'. Rather surprisingly, although he mentioned these family connections of members of his government, he failed to comment on his own concrete record of reform or his past association with Lloyd George.

Having explained how much in common Liberals had with his government, Churchill faced the tricky task of explaining why the Liberal Party had 'spurned' him and his colleagues by withdrawing from the coalition. His explanation verged on the comic: 'I am sorry to tell you that they have yielded to the tactical temptation, natural to politicians, to acquire more seats in the House of Commons, if they can, at all costs.' The Liberals, it seemed, had left office out sheer self-interest in spite of agreeing with the Conservatives on every significant ideological point! After attacking the Liberal leaders, Churchill attempted to win over their supporters. He appeared to assume that Liberals were in fact likely to vote Labour. He appealed to them to ask themselves whether his government 'has not more claim on their ancestral loyalties than has a Socialist administration, whose principles are the absolute denial of traditional Liberalism'. It was here that he segued into his philosophical denunciation of socialism, which he combined with an assault on Labour's liberal credentials:

> My friends, I must tell you that a Socialist policy is abhorrent to the British ideas of freedom. Although it is now put forward in the main by people who have a good grounding in the Liberalism and Radicalism of the early part of this century, there can be no doubt that Socialism is inseparably interwoven with Totalitarianism and the abject worship of the State.

A complete socialist state, he argued, would be unable to tolerate opposition. Socialism, moreover, was an attack 'upon the right of the ordinary man or woman to breathe freely without having a harsh, clumsy, tyrannical hand clapped across their mouths and nostrils'. Citing proposals made by both Herbert Morrison and Stafford Cripps to increase the efficiency of Parliament by curtailing debate on the details of policy, he claimed that 'a Free Parliament is odious to the Socialist doctrinaire'. He then went further and said that 'no Socialist system can be established without a political police'. He acknowledged that many advocates of socialism would be 'horrified' at this suggestion. 'That is because they are short-sighted, that is because they do not see where their theories are leading them.'

Then came the crucial passage:

> No Socialist Government conducting the entire life and industry of the country could afford to allow free, sharp, or violently worded expressions of public discontent. They would have to fall back on some form of *Gestapo*, no doubt very humanely directed in the first instance. And this would nip opinion in the bud; it would stop criticism as it reared its head, and it would gather all the power to the supreme party and the party leaders, rising like stately pinnacles above their vast bureaucracies of civil servants, no longer servants and no longer civil.

The power of the 'Gestapo' phrase came in part from the fact that it brought the alleged threat to freedom alive in a way that an abstract word such as 'Fascism' was unlikely to achieve. But the comment's infelicity was obvious, and this was actually increased by Churchill's use of the qualifying phrase 'no doubt very humanely directed in the first instance'. This was clearly an attempt to further convey that socialists did not intend to introduce a horrific state of affairs but would be forced to do so over time by the logic of their own doctrines. However, the idea of a 'humanely directed' Gestapo was self-contradictory. If a socialist government's methods of control were initially humane—no matter what they might later descend into—they could not at that point be considered equivalent to the Gestapo. And if they *were* equivalent to the Gestapo then they could not be considered humane. After all, the Gestapo's history was not that of a well-intentioned organization gone wrong.

Churchill's assault on Labour was not yet complete. He turned to the party's plans to nationalize the Bank of England. Once a socialist government began 'monkeying with the credit of Britain' no-one's nest egg would be safe, he argued.[87] This was an echo of the charge levelled in 1931 that the return of Labour would endanger savings held in the Post Office Bank. His own government stood for maintaining the value of the pound, he said, 'and we would rather place upon all classes, rich and poor alike, the heaviest burden of taxation they can bear than slide into the delirium of inflation'. Here was another echo of 1931 and the talk then of 'equality of sacrifice' across classes. Warning that electing him offered 'no guarantee of lush and easy times ahead', Churchill also gave a minor reprise of his 'blood, toil, tears and sweat' speech of 13 May 1940: 'our resolve will be that what has been earned by sweat, toil and skill or saved by self-denial shall command the power to buy the products of peace at an equal value in sweat, toil and skill.' He then justified having engaged in a long disquisition on socialism versus individualism, on the grounds that he had been forced into it. 'That is because for the first time the challenge has been made, in all formality, "Socialism versus the rest"'. This of course was the theme that he had earlier identified in his letter to Croft.

The concluding section of the broadcast contrasted the 'vast revolutionary change' supposedly represented by Labour's plans with his own proposals for 'practical and immediate action'. His peroration further emphasized the importance of practicality, combining the military themes of marching and returning warriors with a cosy vision of domesticity:

On with the forward march! Leave these Socialist dreamers to their Utopias or their nightmares. Let us be content to do the heavy job that is right on top of us. And let us make sure that the cottage home to which the warrior will return is blessed with modest but solid prosperity, well fenced and guarded against misfortune, and that Britons remain free to plan their lives for themselves and for those they love.

The reference to 'the cottage home' might have seemed misplaced in a country so heavily urbanized as Britain. Admittedly, Baldwin, whose career had ended only a few years beforehand, had made highly successful use of rural imagery; this was part of his appeal, that of a plain man of the people, who could be trusted because he was not 'clever'.[88] But if the high-living and mentally frenetic Churchill was aiming to emulate this home-spun technique, he did not do so successfully. In spite of the quasi-Baldwinian 'National' elements of the 'Gestapo' speech, it was also blatantly aggressive. Arguably, Churchill was returning to the platform techniques he had learnt in his youth, having assimilated only partially the lessons that Baldwin's example could teach.

Indeed, it is tempting to draw parallels between the 'Gestapo' speech and the popular Toryism of the late nineteenth century. The working man's right to live his life free from interference by busybodies (especially in regard to alcohol) had then been a classic theme. However, we may also note some important differences. For as long as the Liberal Party remained strong, Conservatives assaulted its principles head on, arguing that its commitment to laissez-faire meant that only Tories could be trusted to deliver legislation in the interests of the workers.[89] But in 1945, with the Liberal Party on its last legs, Churchill chose (as he had done in the 1920s) to reach out to its supporters by claiming to embrace its values. He presented conservatism and liberalism as allies, not antagonists, in the face of the greater socialist threat. Paradoxically, this putative alliance in defence of 'freedom' was made easier by the fact that liberalism itself had moved some way from laissez-faire. At the same time, ironically, the 'Gestapo' comment was actually a revival, in adapted form, of a charge that Churchill had levelled against the Conservative Party when he was a Liberal MP in 1905. He had argued then that Conservative policies, including the anti-immigration Aliens Bill, implied the use of Tsarist methods: 'At the coming election the country will have to decide whether it will follow in the regular, settled lines of English democratic development, or whether, by borrowing a tariff from the United States, a military system from Germany, and—when he thought of the Aliens Bill—a system of police from Russia, we will change the free British Empire, which we have known and cherished, into a greedy, sordid, Jingo, profit-sharing domination. That is the issue, and it is intimately inter-woven with the question of free trade.'[90] This again shows how Churchill might have expected his broadcast to appeal to Liberal opinion.

The day after the broadcast, Churchill was greeted in the House of Commons by ironical cries of 'Where's the Gestapo?'[91] Some Conservative MPs were buoyed up by the speech. 'Chips' Channon thought that 'the Labour boys seem very depressed and dejected by Winston's trouncing' and noted that his own colleagues were 'cock-a-hoop'. Nevertheless he thought their optimism was excessive.[92] Cuthbert Headlam's opinion was that the speech 'rather overdid the business I thought, so far as sensible people are concerned—but then there are few sensible people and the rank and file of the party may welcome a fighting speech from the leader'.[93] Journalists quickly began to report that some Tories were unhappy, although the Manchester Guardian's parliamentary correspondent suggested that Churchill's own good mood at Question Time indicated that he felt the broadcast had gone well.[94] Press comment tended to divide on predictable lines, but the contrast in coverage provided by two left-wing papers is interesting. In an astute move, The Daily Herald reported Churchill's speech quite fully, inter-spersed with rebuttals offered by Herbert Morrison. The paper took Morrison's 'crazy broadcast' remark for its main headline.[95] The Daily Mirror, for its part, ran 'JAP SPY PIGEONS TO FACE FALCON TERROR' as its chief story with 'CHURCHILL CLAIMS HE IS LEADING NATIONAL GOVT.' relegated further down the page. Although it reported accurately the gist of his attack on socialism, the 'Gestapo' comment itself was omitted.[96] By any standards, this was shoddy journalism: either the writer had failed to spot the most news-worthy quotation, or he/she deliberately held it back in the (as it turned out, false) belief that it was damaging to Labour.

Attlee's reply to Churchill was broadcast on the evening of 5 June. Several parts of it were in the form of direct rejoinders to the Prime Minister, nota-bly the masterful opening passage:

When I listened to the Prime Minister's speech last night, in which he gave such a travesty of the policy of the Labour Party, I realized at once what was his object. He wanted the electors to understand how great was the difference between Winston Churchill, the great leader in war of a united nation, and Mr. Churchill, the party leader of the Conservatives. He feared lest those who had accepted his leadership in war might be tempted out of gratitude to follow him further. I thank him for having disillusioned them so thoroughly. The voice we heard last night was that of Mr. Churchill, but the mind was that of Lord Beaverbrook.[97]

Here, Attlee skilfully combined the sarcastic suggestion that Churchill was deliberately undermining his own electoral chances with the powerful idea that there were two Winston Churchills. This was a trope that was to be taken up by other Labour speakers and, in the aftermath of the election, was represented visually in a famous cartoon by David Low.[98] As Mary Soames has put it, praiseworthy war-leader Churchill was contrasted with reprehensible party-leader Churchill, the latter portrayed as 'irresponsible, out of touch with ordinary people, subject to the malign influence of Lord Beaverbrook, and not to be trusted in peacetime'.[99] Beaverbrook was not only a powerful press magnate, but he had a reputation as an evil genius. Attlee's suggestion that he had inspired Churchill's broadcast resonated strongly. *The Daily Herald*, reporting Attlee's speech, gave a visual representation of it at the top of its front page: 'The Voice Was the Voice Of [arrow pointing to photo of Churchill] But the Mind Was the Mind Of [arrow pointing to photo of Beaverbrook]'.[100] Attlee had managed to undermine Churchill's apparently impregnable character-based claims, not via a direct assault, but by exploiting the perceived negative character of somebody else, i.e. Beaverbrook.

Attlee was similarly adroit when he dealt directly with the Gestapo passage. He pointed out that Scandinavian countries as well as Australia and New Zealand had elected left-wing governments without dreadful consequences.[101] He added: 'I shall not waste time on this theoretical stuff, which seems to me to be a secondhand version of the academic views of an Austrian professor—Friedrich August von Hayek—who is very popular just now with the Conservative Party.'[102] This suggests that he may well have read the copy of *The Road to Serfdom* that Assheton had sent him. (Morrison had definitely read it, as had key Labour intellectuals.)[103] Cockett has observed that Attlee 'subtly' emphasized 'Hayek's foreign origins to persuade his listeners that Hayek was nothing more than a mad foreign professor who did not understand the English way of doing things'.[104] That is true enough. Attlee, though, was himself contending with claims, such as those made by Assheton, that socialism's allegedly Germanic origins rendered it suspicious. Churchill's own reference to 'this continental conception of human society called Socialism' had been very much in that vein.[105] 'I wrote the book essentially to persuade the Socialists to act wisely, but I do not seem to have succeeded in that,' Hayek told *The Daily Telegraph*. 'I have no connection with the Conservative Party.'[106] He told Beaverbrook's *Daily Express*, however, that he was delighted 'if any party has the wisdom to profit' from *The Road to Serfdom*, which implies that he did not disapprove of Churchill's broadcast at the time.[107]

Many politicians left records of their reactions to the exchange between Churchill and Attlee. For example, Churchill's good friend, the Liberal politician Violet Bonham Carter, wrote in her diary on 4 June, 'have just heard W's broadcast which really does lay it on a bit thick!' Two days later she wrote, 'Attlee gave a good & dignified & reasoned & constructive reply to Winston'.[108] The reaction of Leo Amery, was a common one: 'Winston jumped straight off his pedestal as world statesman to deliver a fantastical exaggerated onslaught on socialism.' He described Attlee's broadcast as 'a very adroit quiet reply to Winston's rodomontade'.[109] After listening to Attlee, Leo Amery's son Julian, himself a Conservative candidate, 'had considerable searchings of heart' regarding his political allegiance.[110] Margaret Thatcher recalled in her memoirs: 'I vividly remember sitting in the student common room in Somerville [College, Oxford] listening to Churchill's famous (or notorious) election broadcast [...] and thinking, "he's gone too far." However logically unassailable the connection between socialism and coercion was, in our present circumstances the line would not be credible.'[111] David Renton, who successfully fought Huntingdonshire as a National Liberal, recalled that the speech 'didn't go down well. I made a joke of it in Huntingdonshire and found that other people made a joke of it too. Rather giving the impression that he'd intended it as a bit of a joke.'[112]

However, some government candidates took up the 'Gestapo' idea and ran with it. Howard Leicester, standing under the National label in Bethnal Green, prepared a circular which said: 'A Socialist State needs a Gestapo and Concentration Camps. Think this over and remember Belsen.'[113] The so-called 'Laski scare'—the allegation that the Labour Party National Executive Committee under its chairman Harold Laski would dictate policy to an Attlee government—was an attempt to extend the Gestapo theme. Some Tory candidates referred to 'Gauleiter Laski'.[114] For their part, interestingly, Churchill's left-wing critics painted the speech as absurd rather than—as might have been expected in the immediate aftermath of Belsen—obscene. They did not describe the broadcast as a disgusting insult to the victims of Fascism. Rather, they depicted it as 'crazy', cheap, and semi-comic, and as sad and undignified, but at the same time as predictable given the Con-servatives' previous record of election 'scares'. Some adopted a sorrow-not-in-anger approach, in which Churchill was pitied rather than excoriated.[115] As Attlee's broadcast showed, ridicule was a highly effective tool.

Yet it was certainly not Labour's only weapon. Historians tend to suggest that 'Hostility to blatant partisanship explains the response to Churchill's infamous first radio speech of the campaign'.[116] The implication is that Labour did not engage in similar tactics, but it is a myth that, during the elec-tion, Churchill and the Conservatives engaged in a form of 'blatant partisan-ship' that the Opposition responsibly eschewed.[117] It is true that Attlee refrained from repeating the comparison he had made when the coalition broke up. Others were far less restrained, taking Churchill's broadcast as a license to reply in kind. Emrys Hughes, editor of the left-wing weekly *Forward*, declared that if Churchill 'had been born in Germany he would have been a Nazi'. Admittedly, the British plutocracy had not yet needed a Hitler to maintain its interests, 'but if ever the time did come when Big Business and Vested Interests found it necessary to dispense with their pre-tended devotion to democracy, we have no illusions as to who would be running the Gestapo'.[118] Michael Foot, journalist and candidate for Plymouth Devonport, referred to Churchill, perhaps half in jest, as the Tory 'Fuehrer'.[119] Some such examples were fairly trivial.[120] But many of the attacks were serious, and cannot be dismissed as simply the work of the lunatic fringe or of obscure candidates. Senior Labour figures were happy to associate the Conservatives with Fascism. Cripps, speaking in Glasgow, found it sinister that there was no mention of the word 'Conservative' in Churchill's mani-festo: 'In Cumberland I saw someone was running as a "Churchill candi-date". We seem to be getting nearer and nearer the Fuhrer idea.'[121] A. V. Alexander, former First Lord of the Admiralty, declared that before the war 'Under Tory rule there were millions of wives whose housekeeping money consisted of a bare unemployment allowance under the Gestapo of the means test'.[122] In one of Labour's official election broadcasts Philip Noel-Baker MP argued, on the basis of the 1935 Anglo-German Naval Treaty, that 'the Tories helped the Axis'.[123] The Liberals also joined in. 'The Conservative Party claim the definite right to govern apparently in perpetuity,' claimed Lord Samuel, echoing remarks made previously by Herbert Morrison. 'That is the principle of Nazism and Fascism.'[124] To draw attention to these remarks is not to claim that they were precisely equivalent to Churchill's language. Opposition politicians did not tend to make the explicit claim

that the return of a Conservative government would lead literally to totalitarianism. The crucial point is that Tories and their press supporters would
have found it much easier to attack the claims they did make as extreme had
not Churchill spiked his own side's guns with his reference to the Gestapo.

The reactions of ordinary voters to the speech were broadly negative.
The speech was listened to by 48.1 per cent the potential total audience.
According to Mass-Observation's report on the election, 'It would be difficult to exaggerate the disappointment and genuine distress aroused by this
speech'. The report reproduced a large number of observations from citizens, many along the lines of this: 'The whole speech seems to have been in
bad taste. No one but the veriest baby in politics would believe his assumption that the Labour Leaders are potential Gestapo officials.' Attlee's contribution was often viewed positively, for example this comment: 'It was a fair
speech and very truthful. He didn't use any election stunting.'[125] Similar
comments can be found in MO diaries. A. White, a Leeds shopkeeper, complained of Churchill: 'Listening to him, I felt as if time had taken me back
forty years or so, and I was standing in some market square listening to some
soapbox oratory. [...] He, a former Liberal himself, seemed peeved that
some Liberals still had faith in Liberalism.'[126] According to chemist
J. Greenwood, 'The gist was "Hush, hush, hush, here comes the bogy man",
in this case the bogy being the socialists of course. [...] He went to length[s]
to criticize, nay castigate, the Liberals, and then raised the "National" flag'.[127]
M. Clayton, who worked in the film industry, wrote: 'Could hardly sleep last
night thinking of PM's speech, which I think will do infinite harm, both to
his own reputation and hope of reasonably friendly "get together" on
important issues.' To her, the speech appeared as 'trumped up insincerity.
I don't suppose it will appear in that light to hide-bound Conservatives, but
I think that many will feel that Mr Churchill has stepped down from the
position he occupied.'[128]

But the existence of these negative reactions should not be allowed to
obscure that of more positive ones. 'Although I wasn't really moved by what
he said I love to hear him make a fighting speech and I believe he enjoyed
it,' wrote civil servant A. B. Holness.[129] Shipping clerk Edith Oakley wrote,
'I *was* influenced by Mr Churchill, in part because there are strong Liberal
traditions on my father's side, and it was always the Liberal angle that was
praised up in my youth.' Her mother read the speech the next day and commented: 'Until I read Mr Churchill I had not realised what a peril the nation
stands in threatened by this Labour gestapo.' Both decided to support the

government candidate.[130] J. Lippold enjoyed Churchill's speech and found it 'full of fight', but soon wearied of Attlee's reply: 'we found him very expressionless to say nothing of being unconvincing and the whole speech was so obviously just being read from the script'.[131] It should also be noted that Labour's Gallup poll lead declined from 16 per cent on 28 May to 9 per cent on 18 June, although we should hesitate to attribute this to the impact of Churchill's speech, given that 69 per cent of those interviewed by Gallup thought it 'bad'.[132]

In contrast with the 'Gestapo' speech, Churchill's subsequent election broadcasts were rather anti-climactic. Harold Macmillan wrote to him tactfully:

> Your first broadcast has given a splendid start-off to the Party, by which I mean the old *Conservative* workers throughout the country. They liked its virility and forcefulness. But it must be made clear that your warnings were against the extreme Socialist tail wagging the moderate Labour and Trade Union dog.
>
> In your following broadcast you will no doubt direct yourself particularly to the *floating (and non-party) vote*.[133]

Perhaps in response to such advice, Churchill did tone down his second broadcast. A draft of it included the following remark: 'I am glad the word "Gestapo" stung, because it will show a lot of harmless and worthy people the way they are going, and where they will finish up if they are not stopped in good time while the nation remains free.'[134] When it came to the point, he did not say this, but he did renew the charge that under socialism 'all effective and healthy opposition and the natural change of parties in office from time to time would necessarily come to an end, and a political police would be required to enforce an absolute and permanent system upon the nation'. Macmillan had also advised setting out the Four Years' Plan anew because people had forgotten the details, and this Churchill did, albeit only at paragraph length. This time he remembered to mention that he was 'the oldest living champion' of National Insurance in the House of Commons and to name-check 'my friend Mr Lloyd-George', who had died earlier in the year.[135] 'I am a Liberal as much as a Tory,' he claimed a couple of weeks later. 'I do not understand why Liberals pretend they are different from us.'[136] His third broadcast was notable only for his endorsement of the 'Laski scare'.[137] His fourth and final broadcast—similarly lacking in inspiration—opened with a remark that hinted at how Churchill was really feeling. 'This strange, unnatural election, tearing asunder so many ties of mutual comprehension and comradeship which had grown up in our political life, is now, to everybody's relief, drawing to its close.'[138]

This is not to say that the broadcasts were a total disaster. MO's report noted that the question 'Which speeches on the wireless or in the papers did you like best?' found more people preferring Churchill to any other single speaker. However, unlike those who preferred other speakers, these respondents tended not to give concrete reasons for their preference. They offered reasons such as 'I've always listened to all his speeches' and 'He is a great man, and we should listen to him'. The report argued that 'This type of reply indicates a simple loyalty that transcends criticism; and it was the conflict between this feeling and the rational disapproval and disagreement that his actual statements aroused which formed one of the keynotes of the election.'[139] This remark may well be thought to reveal the report's pro-Labour bias. Still, the broadcasts did try the patience of some loyalists. Vita Sackville-West, instinctively conservative but not much interested in politics, wrote to her husband Harold Nicolson: 'You know I have an admiration for Winston amounting to idolatry, so I am dreadfully distressed by the badness of his broadcast Election speeches. What has gone wrong with him? They are confused, woolly, unconstructive and so wordy that it is impossible to pick out any concrete impression from them. If I were a wobbler, they would tip me over to the other side.'[140]

Churchill's national speaking tour was more successful, at least insofar as he attracted huge audiences, but he encountered hostility as well as much enthusiasm. One Mass-Observation report contains a vivid account of when Churchill spoke at Walham Green, the junction between the constituencies of East and West Fulham on 2 July, a few days before polling. Placards announced that Churchill was due at 5 p.m. From 4.15 small groups began to form; by 5.00 people were standing five deep. MO's investigators overheard various comments: 'I thought I must see him and give him a cheer'; 'He's no good for the working class—never was...'; 'Whether his politics are yours or not, you've got to hand it to him'; 'It's him what started the mud-slinging...'. Churchill finally arrived about 5.35. 'The crowd surged forward amidst a confusion of boos and cheers, with cheers predominating, to hear Churchill speak. But there was so much noise that none of the investigators were able to hear what he said. From a distance of 20 yards he was quite inaudible.' The investigators did overhear more comments, all of which agreed that he looked old and tired, although later press reports said he looked fit and healthy. 'I'm sorry for Churchill,' said one man. 'They're killing the old chap. He's the Tory dog that's got to be on show—they're killing him between themselves.' A woman replied: 'Shame on you. He's a tired old man, because he's old you want to cast him aside, and after what he's done too.'[141]

He still had some fight left in him, and he had not given up on the Gestapo idea. The final day of the campaign again found him in London. According to the *Manchester Guardian*:

> 'As you see, I am a very old and broken man, almost dead,' said Mr. Churchill when he stopped at Blackheath road, but he quickly dispelled this idea when dealing with a heckler. He maintained that if Socialism were established in a totalitarian form in this country it could only be defended by some sort of Gestapo. A man near him strongly objected, and Mr. Churchill exclaimed, 'I see an ugly look on your face. It looks just like what a Gestapo would resemble.'[142]

But privately he was not confident, even though he was unaware of the published opinion polls which suggested he would lose. 'I am worried about this damned election,' he had remarked to Lord Moran mid-campaign. 'I have no message for them now.'[143]

There was an interval between polling day and the announcement of the results, in order to allow time for the Service vote to be counted. In the meantime, Churchill travelled to Potsdam for a 'Big Three' meeting with Stalin and President Truman. Attlee was invited too as a courtesy. During the conference, Churchill introduced Stalin to Lord Cherwell ('the Prof'), his scientific and statistical adviser, for the first time. According to Roy Harrod's memoir of Cherwell, the Prime Minister

> had no ready formula for describing the Prof. He explained that he was a man who had been advising him about a balanced use of our resources for the war effort, drawing his attention to shortfalls, and generally keeping his eye on the whole scene of government, to inform him if anything was amiss; in fact he had acted as a kind of Gestapo for him. 'Oh!' said Stalin immediately, 'I thought it was only Mr. Attlee who had a Gestapo.'[144]

Attlee and Churchill returned to Britain for the election results which were announced on 26 July. Labour had a majority of 146 over all other parties. Attlee returned to Potsdam as Prime Minister. Churchill was back in the wilderness. What had gone wrong? Why had he been unable to capitalize on his position as 'national leader'?

Innumerable commentators have suggested that, having held that position, he threw it away at a stroke with the 'Gestapo' speech. ('Mr Churchill last night put off national leadership and became a party chieftain of the old-fashioned type,' claimed the *News Chronicle*.)[145] They all appeared to assume that this 'national leader' status was a tremendous advantage for him, and that only a character defect, mental spasm, or the sinister influence of Beaverbrook and Bracken could have led him to jeopardize it. Churchill himself clearly valued that status, but at the same time must have appreciated its fragility; the slightest mis-step could open him to the charge that he was failing to live up to it. This explains the lengths that he went to shore up his 'National' credentials, a strategy which, on the surface, made sense given the pool of former Liberal support which stood to be captured.[146] Yet his attempt to distance himself from Conservatives by identifying himself as 'National' backfired. This was because the Conservatives were themselves associated with the 'National' label, always portrayed by Labour as a fraud, a claim much more easily pressed after the events of 1940. Attlee's achievement in his reply was to manipulate the various senses of 'national' to Churchill's disadvantage. In his account, Churchill *had* been the great leader of the united nation—and had, with his broadcast, stopped being so. The addition of a few independents and domesticated Liberals did not make his caretaker government National, a point the demise of National Labour reinforced. In contrast to the sectionalism of the Conservatives, Attlee claimed, Labour was the true national party, capable of transcending class interests in a way that Churchill could not. And Churchill's wartime popularity was, for many people, contingent on the idea that he was a good leader *for the duration*. For many of them, the very qualities that made him a good wartime leader made him unsuitable during peacetime. Churchill's apparently winning card turned out to be a dud.

Churchill, in fact, was cornered. He tried to distance himself from the unpopular Conservative Party, but could only do so by playing on the 'National' label which offered no distance at all. It is true that he did not play his hand well. Although the reactions to the 'Four Years' Plan' speech suggest that he may have been right not to talk more about reconstruction in 1943–4, it was open to him to be both more positive and more detailed as the election approached in 1945. His appeal to individualism was intelligible in the context of an appeal to Liberals, especially given the Liberal Party's own wartime swing to the left, but the 'Gestapo' remark was an unforced error. He may have intended it as a broader, politico-philosophical point, but it is scarcely surprising that it was seen as a personal attack on the Labour politicians with whom he had recently worked closely. The standard explanations for the mistake are not without merit. He was indeed physically and mentally exhausted after five years as Prime Minister at war. Arguably, though, his rhetorical collapse was the product of his political predicament rather than the primary cause of it. The role of 'national leader' in which he found himself imprisoned was widely perceived to preclude various kinds of conduct in which, as a party leader at election time, it was hard to avoid indulging.[147] When protesting at his wife's suggestion that he should retire at the end of the war to avoid having to lead one section of the nation against the other, he liked to say that he was not yet ready 'to be put on a pedestal'.[148] His tragedy in 1945 was that he was already on the pedestal and that, if he wanted to continue in politics, he would inevitably come under attack for stepping down from it.

Conclusion

The intellectual problem posed by Churchill's speeches has normally been seen as that of how to explain their success. That success, and the nature of it, has largely been taken for granted. Churchill's achievement was either, on the one hand, to make the British people (or almost all of them) feel the same way or, on the other, to put into words what they were all feeling but could not express themselves. This book has challenged that assumption, by showing the multiplicity of ways that people reacted. It has argued that dissent—and differing reactions short of open criticism—was more widespread than previously thought and was not restricted to a small coterie of extremists and troublemakers.

Can one quantify this? To attempt to do so is hazardous, because most of the statistics we have are not directed to the reception of speeches per se but to approval/disapproval of Churchill as Prime Minister, voting intentions, and attitudes to specific policies. There were, of course, connections between his popularity and views of his speeches, and also between these things and the patterns of British military success and failure. A Mass-Observation report of December 1942 concluded: 'Ever since Churchill became Prime Minister, it has been noticeable that his personal popularity has risen and fallen in a way showing very close association with the general feelings of cheerfulness or depression about the war situation. [...] Churchill's popularity has a normal value of rather over 80 per cent, from which it falls off suddenly whenever there is a military reverse, and takes some few weeks to recover.' Criticisms of him such as 'Supreme careerist', 'He talks too much', 'Too much of a showman', were always present as a background minority opinion, and were present 'only in any considerable numbers at times of military reverses'. The adverse comments were 'nearly always the same ones, and they recur whenever the war news deteriorates, and particularly after a Churchill Speech during bad times. During times of military success, however, and during lulls, these critical opinions—while still being found—do not extend over more than 10 to 15 per cent of the population.'[1] There may, of course, have been more potential critics who were cowed into silence by social pressure. It may be noted MO's satisfaction figures for Churchill were sometimes quite dramatically lower than Gallup's—notably 66 per cent as against 81 per cent favourable in March 1942—but we perhaps should not worry too much about precise numbers, given that the methodologies of both organizations can be called into question and, either way, he clearly had a very strong bedrock of support.

It is worth, however, recapping the relatively small quantity of statistical evidence relating specifically to the reception of speeches. The Home Intelligence spot survey on Churchill's speech of 19 May 1940 found that about half of respondents were frightened and worried by it. The BBC listener survey on his February 1942 Singapore broadcast found that 38 per cent were not satisfied by it (and Mass-Observation found 55 per cent of respondents making negative comments on that same speech). The BBC also found that 20 per cent failed to express satisfaction with his March 1943 'Four Years' Plan' broadcast. It is undoubtedly the case that there were also a significant number of speeches where the volume of criticism was tiny. And perhaps more importantly, it was clearly possible for Churchill supporters to be depressed, concerned, or confused by the contents of a speech without this shaking their faith in him as a leader. If we acknowledge that expressing disappointment with a speech did not necessarily imply fundamental dissatisfaction with Churchill as Prime Minister, then we can get a better insight into the complexity of people's reactions. There seem to have plenty of people who at one time or another experienced some unease or disappointment at a Churchill speech without this implying political opposition. At the same time it is clear that many voters regarded Churchill as a good leader for the duration of the war and no longer; some who 'approved' of him in this way expressed this in terms such as 'He's the best of a bad bunch'.[2] These, we must imagine, were not generally people who were reduced to a condition of helpless ecstasy every time he opened his mouth.

The conventional story—that Churchill's oratory produced unanimous or near-unanimous rapture—is therefore unsatisfactory. A good speech by him might provide a few days' spike in morale, but it could not in itself effect a long-run shift in people's beliefs about how the war was going. It is hardly surprising that his speeches were best received when things were going well;

we should not exaggerate his capacity—even in the case of Dunkirk—to persuade people that things were better than they were. This does not mean that we need to reject the idea that Churchill's speeches were successful, but we do need to rethink the nature of their success. If they sometimes caused people to feel depressed, this was usually because of his accurate predictions that the war would last much longer than many expected. This enhanced his credibility in the long run, in spite of the negative emotions created in the short term. Ironically, moreover, the near-relentless focus on the speeches with 'the quotable bits' has distracted attention from some equally successful but seemingly less rhetorical ones, such as his speech on the destruction of the French Fleet and his broadcast on the invasion of the Soviet Union. Paul Addison has rightly suggested that part of Churchill's success lay in his capacity to inform people and put things in perspective.[3] This point deserves to be emphasized more. The corollary was that, however great the phrases, uplift without content didn't work. When Churchill had no new information to give—and of course he could not provide it infallibly—disappointment was often the result. The lesson for those who might seek to emulate his rhetoric is that excellent style, even from a master of the English language, is no substitute for meaningful content.

Looking at Churchill's speeches in a global perspective, and considering their diplomatic consequences, leads to a further conclusion. He did of course make some serious errors, perhaps most spectacularly over Spain in 1944, but given how often he spoke and how many subjects he ranged over, it is remarkable how few gaffes there were. (The 'Gestapo' speech falls into a different category: there were no serious effects abroad, although it was well liked in the USA and caused anger in Australasia.) This was a tribute to his judgement, not in terms of unfailing instincts, but with regard to his willingness to subject his speeches to a collective vetting process designed to minimize risk. Churchill is often portrayed as a man who 'charged ahead' stubbornly, paying little attention to the views of others.[4] But although he made a great deal of fuss when presented with criticism, he did not in the end usually resent it and frequently acted upon it to good effect. 'Collegial' may not be exactly the word; but nor should 'Churchillian' be taken as a synonym for riding roughshod over other people's opinions. Unfortunately, some modern politicians have not understood this and have drawn the wrong lesson from the history from which they claim to learn.

Equally, if we also reject the idea of the British as a nation that acted and reacted as one, we should not conclude that diversity meant division.

Heterogeneity and heterodoxy were not signs of societal weakness.[5] Those who criticized Churchill were generally just as keen as he was that the Nazis should be defeated, though they might disagree with him about how this should be achieved and what should be done next. Even if they were wrongheaded—and they certainly sometimes were—they still had a role to play. The existence of criticism—including the parliamentary and press criticism that Churchill hated so much—forced him to justify himself in public and provide a rationale for what he was doing. Hitler and Mussolini, when things started to go wrong for them, retreated into silence. For them, this was a luxury; it was also a chronic weakness of the political systems they operated. Their judgement went unchecked, with catastrophic consequences. It is a strange feature of British national mythology that we celebrate the idea that at a time of national crisis the entire population thought and acted the same way. The fact that it didn't is not in the slightest bit shameful; it was one of the strengths that helped democracy survive. The widespread accusation that Churchill was some sort of dictator was on the one hand grossly unfair and on the other an extremely healthy reflex against the fear of arbitrary power. And it is greatly to Churchill's credit that—even if he was sometimes overly defensive and angry at his critics—he was assiduous in presenting himself to Parliament in order that he might be held to account.[6]

In his diary, Lord Moran recorded a conversation with Churchill just after the war. 'People say my speeches after Dunkirk were the thing. That was only a part, not the chief part,' he grumbled. 'They forget I made all the main military decisions.'[7] This sensitivity was still in evidence on his eightieth birthday, when he was keen to emphasize that, if he provided the British lion with its roar, then that was not all he did: 'I also hope that I sometimes suggested to the lion the right places to use his claws.'[8] One can understand why he felt the need to stress his military credentials, but if he feared that his oratory was overshadowing his other, supposedly more important, achievements, perhaps he did himself an injustice. The American journalist Ed Murrow said that Churchill 'mobilized the English language and sent it into battle'.[9] Clement Attlee put it a different way: 'If somebody asked me what exactly Winston did to win the war, I would say, "Talk about it".'[10] If that was true, then perhaps 'talking about it' was a more significant contribution than even Churchill himself fully understood.

Appendix: Listening Figures for Churchill's Speeches

This table gives as complete a picture as is possible of the listening figures obtained by Churchill's broadcast wartime speeches. The data are derived from the BBC Listener Research Department (LRD)'s contemporaneous reports; the titles of the speeches are derived from those used in these documents. The LRD claimed at the time that 'Subject to the limitations of sampling, the figures [. . .] show the estimated percentage of the whole adult civilian population of Great Britain who listened to each item. 1 per cent equals approximately 300,000 persons'. Notably, then, those serving in the forces were excluded. Two other points are worth noting. Churchill did not broadcast his 'Dunkirk' speech of 4 June 1940, but extracts were read out on the 9 o'clock news that evening, which received 48.3 per cent of the potential audience. He did broadcast on 20 August ('The Few' speech) but oddly the Listening Barometer that day does not record this. Presumably, the figure for his broadcast was subsumed within that for the 9 o'clock news, which was 52.5 per cent.

Date and Time	Description	Audience Share (%)
20/1/40 9.15 p.m.	Talk: 'From the Front Bench': The Rt. Hon. Winston Churchill	34.3
27/1/40 2.35 p.m.	Speech by Mr Winston Churchill from Manchester	35.9
30/3/40 9.20 p.m.	Talk: 'The Progress of the War': The Rt. Hon. Mr Winston Churchill	44.2
19/5/40 9.00 p.m.	News preceded by statement by the Prime Minister	51.0
17/6/40 9.00 p.m.	News preceded by statement by the Prime Minister	52.1
18/6/40 9.00 p.m.	News preceded by speech by Prime Minister	59.8

Date and Time	Description	Audience Share (%)
14/7/40 9.00 p.m.	News preceded by statement by Prime Minister	64.4
11/9/40 6.00 p.m.	Speech by Prime Minister & News	49.5
9.20 p.m.	'Tonight's Talk': Recording of Prime Minister's Speech	18.4
21/10/40 8.30–8.47 p.m.	Broadcast to the people of France by Rt. Hon. Winston Churchill	49.0
23/12/40 9.00 p.m.	Broadcast to Italians by Prime Minister	62.2
9/2/41 9.00 p.m.	Broadcast by the Prime Minister, The Rt. Hon. Winston Churchill	70.0
27/4/41 9.00 p.m.	Speech by the Prime Minister	76.9
22/6/41 9.00 p.m.	Speech by the Prime Minister	57.9
14/7/41 2.20 p.m.	The Prime Minister's Speech to the London County Council	32.5
14/7/41 10.05 p.m.	The Prime Minister's Speech to the London County Council (Recording)	27.3[1]
24/8/41 9.00 p.m.	The Prime Minister	73.5
25/8/41 1.15 p.m.	Prime Minister's Speech (Recording)	16.8
4/9/41 9.15 p.m.	Extracts of Speeches by Prime Minister and Mr Mackenzie King (Recording)	46.9
8/12/41 9.00 p.m.	Speech by Prime Minister	62.9
26/12/41 6.30 p.m.	Speech by Prime Minister to Congress	55.6
30/12/41 7.55 p.m.	Speeches by Mr Mackenzie King and the Prime Minister	57.5
15/2/42 9.00 p.m.	Speech by the Prime Minister	65.4
10/5/42 9.00 p.m.	Speech by the Prime Minister	60.9
21/3/43 9.00 p.m.	Speech by the Prime Minister	73.8
14/5/43 9.00 p.m.	Speech by the Prime Minister	67.8
19/5/43 6.30 p.m.	The Prime Minister Speaks from Congress	53.9
9.00 p.m.	Speech by the Prime Minister (recording)	25.1
31/8/43 9.00 p.m.	Prime Minister's Speech (read by announcer) followed by News	58.5
26/3/44 9.01 p.m.	The Prime Minister	65.5
8/5/45 3.00 p.m.	The Prime Minister	71.5
4/6/45 9.15 p.m.	Election Speech: Prime Minister	48.1
21/6/45 9.15 p.m.	Election Speech: Prime Minister	52.5

[1] This figure included 6.6 per cent who had already heard the speech; the total who heard it on one or both occasions was 53.2 per cent.

Endnotes

INTRODUCTION

1. 'Sir Winston Churchill on "Wonderful Honour"', *The Times*, 1 December 1954; Lord Moran, *Winston Churchill: The Struggle for Survival, 1940–1965*, Constable, London, 1966, p. 616 (entry for 30 November 1954); Winston Spencer Churchill [henceforward WSC], speech of 30 November 1954. Unless otherwise stated, all Churchill's speeches cited are to be found in Robert Rhodes James (ed.), *Winston S. Churchill: His Complete Speeches, 1897–1963*, 8 vols., Chelsea House, New York, 1974.
2. Arthur C. Murray, 'Churchillian Recollections', n.d. (1948?), Elibank Papers, MS. 8818, fo. 13.
3. Speech of 12 November 1941.
4. For brief uses that have previously been made of these files, see David Reynolds, *In Command of History: Churchill Fighting and Writing the Second World War*, Allen Lane, London, 2004, p. 46; Garry Campion, *The Good Fight: Battle of Britain Propaganda and The Few*, Palgrave, Houndmills, Basingstoke, 2009, p. 76, and Allen Packwood, 'Heart versus Head: Churchill Comes to Terms with the Fall of Singapore?' in Brian Farrell (ed.), *Churchill and the Lion City: Shaping Modern Singapore*, National University of Singapore Press, Singapore, 2011, pp. 56–67, at 59.
5. Lord Justice Birkett, 'Churchill the Orator', Richard Dimbleby, 'Churchill the Broadcaster', and Ivor Brown, 'Churchill the Master of Words', in Charles Eade (ed.), *Churchill by His Contemporaries*, Hutchinson, London, 1953, pp. 223–33, 276–84, 132–317; Lord Simon, 'Churchill's Use of English Speech', in James Marchant (ed.), *Winston Spencer Churchill: Servant of Crown and Commonwealth*, Cassell & Co., London, 1954, pp. 29–33; Herbert Leslie Stewart, *Sir Winston Churchill as Writer and Speaker*, Sidgwick and Jackson, London, 1954; Isaiah Berlin, *Mr Churchill in 1940*, John Murray, London, n.d. (1964); Manfred Weidhorn, *Churchill's Rhetoric and Political Discourse*, University Press of America, Lanham, MD, 1987; Frederick Woods, *Artillery of Words: The Writings of Sir Winston Churchill*, Leo Cooper, London, 1992, chapter 5; Robert Rhodes James, 'The Parliamentarian, Orator, Statesman', in Robert Blake and Wm. Roger Louis (eds.), *Churchill*, Oxford University Press, Oxford, 1993, pp. 503–17; Stephen Bungay, 'His Speeches: How Churchill Did It', *Finest Hour*, 112 (Autumn 2001), available online at <http://www.winstonchurchill.org>, consulted 30 January 2007; David Cannadine, *In Churchill's Shadow: Confronting*

the Past in Modern Britain, Penguin, London, 2003 (first published 2002), chapter 4; Jonathan Charteris-Black, *Politicians and Rhetoric: The Persuasive Power of Metaphor*, Palgrave, Basingstoke, 2005, chapter 2; John Lukacs, *Blood, Toil, Tears & Sweat: The Dire Warning*, Basic Books, New York, 2008; Peter Clarke, *Mr Churchill's Profession: Statesman, Orator, Writer*, Bloomsbury, London, 2012. There is also now a considerable literature on Churchill's 1946 'iron curtain' speech, for which a good starting point is John Ramsden, *Man of the Century: Winston Churchill and His Legend Since 1945*, HarperCollins, London, 2002, chapter 4.

6. 'Churchill Speaks', *News from England*, September 1940, Allied airborne leaflets and magazines, Cambridge University Library, OP 110.25.04 (4).

7. 'Listening to Churchill', *Picture Post*, 2 August 1941.

8. Richard Holmes, *The World at War: The Landmark Oral History*, Ebury Press, London, 2007, p. 117.

9. 'Great Britons: Churchill', broadcast on BBC2, 22 November 2002.

10. Sonia Orwell and Ian Angus (eds.), *The Collected Essays, Journalism and Letters of George Orwell*, Vol. II: *My Country Right or Left 1940–1943*, Penguin Harmondsworth, 1970 (first published 1968), p. 86.

11. John Keegan, *Winston Churchill*, Viking Penguin, London, 2002, p. 142.

12. Angus Calder, *The People's War: Britain 1939–1945*, Panther, London, 1971, p. 112.

13. Roy Jenkins, *Churchill*, Macmillan, London, 2001, p. 612.

14. Brian Gardner, *Churchill in His Time: A Study in a Reputation 1939–1945*, Methuen, London, 1968, p. 65.

15. Geoffrey Best, *Churchill: A Study in Greatness*, Penguin Books, London, 2002 (first published 2001), p. 187.

16. Carlo D'Este, *Warlord: A Life of Churchill at War, 1874–1945*, Allen Lane, London, 2009, p. 494.

17. V. G. Trukhanovsky, *Winston Churchill*, Progress Publishers, Moscow, p. 257.

18. John Lukacs, *The Duel: Hitler vs. Churchill 10 May–31 July 1940*, The Bodley Head, London, 1990, p. 148; Clive Ponting, *1940: Myth and Reality*, Hamish Hamilton, London, 1990, p. 2; Clive Ponting, *Churchill*, Sinclair-Stevenson, London, 1994, p. 458; David Reynolds, '1940: The Worst and Finest Hour', in Blake and Louis, *Churchill*, pp. 241–55, at 255; Richard Overy, *The Battle of Britain: The Myth and the Reality*, W. W. Norton & Co., New York, 2001, p. 82.

19. A. J. P. Taylor, 'The War Lords: Churchill', BBC1, broadcast 18 August 1976.

20. Malcolm Smith, *Britain and 1940: History, Myth and Popular Memory*, Routledge, London and New York, 2000, p. 35.

21. Andrew Roberts, *The Storm of War: A New History of the Second World War*, Harper, New York, 2011 (first published 2009), p. 46.

22. Bungay, 'His Speeches'.

23. Norman Rose, *Churchill: An Unruly Life*, Simon and Schuster, London, 1994, p. 269.

24. Robert Mackay, *Half the Battle: Civilian Morale in Britain during the Second World War*, Manchester University Press, Manchester, 2002, pp. 177–8; Michel

Paterson, *Winston Churchill: Personal Accounts of the Great Leader at War*, David and Charles, Newton Abbott, 2005, pp. 255–6.

25. Paul Addison, *Churchill: The Unexpected Hero*, Oxford University Press, Oxford, 2005, p. 169.

26. Landmarks in the literature include: Calder, *The People's War*; Tom Harrisson, *Living through the Blitz*, Collins, London, 1976; Sonya O. Rose, *Which People's War? National Identity and Citizenship in Wartime Britain 1939–1945*, Oxford University Press, Oxford, 2003; and Geoffrey G. Field, *Blood, Sweat and Toil: Remaking the British Working Class, 1939–1945*, Oxford University Press, Oxford, 2011. For a useful survey of the literature, see Mackay, *Half the Battle*, pp. 4–9. Key works on wartime politics include: Paul Addison, *The Road to 1945*, Jonathan Cape, London, 1975; Kevin Jefferys, *The Churchill Coalition and Wartime Politics 1940–1945*, Manchester University Press, Manchester, 1991; and Andrew Thorpe, *Parties at War: Political Organization in Second World War Britain*, Oxford University Press, Oxford, 2009.

27. Anthony King (ed.), *British Political Opinion 1937–2000: The Gallup Polls*, Politico's, London, 2000, p. 184.

28. Mark Roodhouse, '"Fish-and-Chip Intelligence": Henry Durant and the British Institute of Public Opinion, 1936–63', *Twentieth Century British History*, published online 23 May 2012.

29. Mass Observation's surveys covering the years 1940–2 reported somewhat lower levels of satisfaction, with a low point of 66 per cent in March 1942; but there is no reason to think that their methods were more reliable than Gallup's. 'Bulletin No. 1', File Report 1545, December 1942, Mass Observation Archive.

30. Addison, *Churchill*, pp. 170–1.

31. Junius, 'Press Gang', *Tribune*, 30 January 1942.

32. J. G. Ferraby, 'The Limitations of Statistics in the Field of Public Opinion Research', File Report 1666, Mass Observation Archive. This paper was read before the Manchester Statistical Society on 14 April 1943.

33. D. J. Wenden, 'Churchill, Radio and Cinema', in Blake and Louis, *Churchill*, pp. 215–39, at 223.

34. 'The Work of the Home Intelligence Division 1939–1944', INF 1/290, The National Archives [henceforward TNA], quoted in Paul Addison and Jeremy A. Crang (eds.), *Listening to Britain: Home Intelligence Reports on Britain's Finest Hour: May to September 1940*, The Bodley Head, London, 2010, pp. xiii–xiv. There is also a small quantity of relevant material generated by the BBC's Listener Research Department.

35. 'Home Office Review', *Manchester Guardian*, 29 July 1940; Richard North, *The Many Not the Few: The Stolen History of the Battle of Britain*, Continuum, London, 2012, p. 60.

36. Churchill, to his credit, protested at the severity of this sentence: WSC to Herbert Morrison, 19 July 1941, in WSC, *The Second World War*, Vol. II: *The Grand Alliance*, Cassell & Co., London, 1950, p. 720.

37. Anon. diary, 10 May 1942 (5145), Mass Observation Archive. The diarist number, given in brackets, provides the easiest way to locate a given MO diarist in the archive.

38. Mackay, *Half the Battle*, pp. 177–8.

39. Nellie Carver diary, 13 May 1940, Imperial War Museum [henceforward IWM], 379.

40. Mary Cooke (later Potter) diary, 20 May 18940, IWM 17125.

41. Mary Potter, 'My War', unpublished memoir, *c*.2009, IWM 17125.

42. Penny Summerfield, 'Mass-Observation: Social Research or Social Movement?', *Journal of Contemporary History*, Vol. 20, No. 3 (July 1985), pp. 439–52.

43. J. Hinton diary, 13 February 1942 (5335), Mass Observation Archive. Emphasis in original. The number in brackets provides the easiest way to locate a given MO diarist in the archive.

44. Comments reported in Edith Dawson diary, 10 November 1944 (5390), and Edith Oakley diary, 8 November 1944 (5390), Mass Observation Archive.

45. M.A. Pratt diary, 10 May 1942 (5402), Mass Observation Archive.

46. A. White diary, 15 October 1943 (5230), Mass Observation Archive.

47. A. Riley diary, 12 September 1943 (5408), Mass Observation Archive.

48. 'Home Intelligence Weekly Report No. 130', 1 April 1943, INF 1/292, TNA.

49. 'Home Intelligence Weekly Report No. 186', 27 April 1944.

50. M.A. Pratt diary, 9 February 1942 (5402), Mass Observation Archive.

51. Dimbleby, 'Churchill the Broadcaster', p. 281.

52. Dominique Rossignol, *Histoire de la propaganda en France de 1940 à 1944*, Presses Universitaires de France, Paris, 1991, p. 313.

53. This paragraph is indebted to Wenden, 'Churchill, Radio and Cinema', pp. 236–9, and Robert Rhodes James, 'Myths: An Actor Read Churchill's Wartime Speeches over the Wireless', no date, <http://www.winstonchurchill.org/learn/myths/myths/an-actor-read-his-speeches> (consulted 13 July 2012).

54. John Snagge and Michael Barsley, *Those Vintage Years of Radio*, Pitman, London, 1972, p. 36.

55. Charles Catchpole, 'My Finest Hour—by Winston's Stand-in', *Daily Mail*, 1 October 1979.

56. David Irving, *Churchill's War: The Struggle for Power*, Veritas Publishing, Bullsbrook, Australia 1987, p. 313.

57. Warren F. Kimball (ed.), *Churchill & Roosevelt: The Complete Correspondence*, Vol. I: *Alliance Emerging, October 1933–November 1942*, Princeton University Press, Princeton, 1984, p. 42; John Charmley, *Churchill: The End of Glory*, Hodder and Stoughton, London, 1993, p. 411; Ponting, *Churchill*, p. 455.

CHAPTER I

1. Malcolm MacDonald, *Titans & Others*, Collins, London, 1972, pp. 94–5.

2. Roy Foster, *Lord Randolph Churchill: A Political Life*, Clarendon Press, Oxford, 1981, pp. 18–19.

3. Benjamin Disraeli to Queen Victoria, 22 May 1874, William Flavelle Monypenny and George Earle Buckle, *The Life of Benjamin Disraeli, Earl of Beaconsfield*, Vol. II: *1860–1881*, revised edition, John Murray, London, 1929, p. 652.

4. WSC, *My Early Life*, Macmillan, London, 1941 (1930), p. 15. Churchill misdated his memory to 1878; the statute was actually unveiled on 21 February 1880: *Illustrated London News*, 28 February 1880.

5. [No title], *Leeds Mercury*, 24 May 1881.

6. For the culture of the mass meeting in this period, see H. C. G. Matthew, 'Rhetoric and Politics in Britain, 1860–1950', in P. J. Waller (ed.), *Politics and Social Change in Modern Britain*. Brighton, Harvester, 1987, pp. 34–58, and Jon Lawrence, *Electing Our Masters: The Hustings in British Politics from Hogarth to Blair*, Oxford University Press, Oxford, 2009. For a useful comparison of Gladstone and the younger Churchill, see Joseph S. Meisel, 'Words by the Numbers: A Quantitative Analysis and Comparison of the Oratorical Careers of William Ewart Gladstone and Winston Spencer Churchill', *Historical Research*, Vol. 73, No. 182 (October 2000), pp. 262–95.

7. WSC, *Lord Randolph Churchill*, Vol. I, Macmillan, London, 1906, p. 275.

8. WSC, *Lord Randolph Churchill*, Vol. I, p. 277.

9. Quoted in Roland Quinault, 'Churchill, Lord Randolph Henry Spencer (1849–1895)', Oxford Dictionary of National Biography, Oxford University Press, 2004; online edn, September 2010, <http://www.oxforddnb.com/view/article/5404>, accessed 16 August 2012.

10. 'The Political Situation' *The Times*, 21 June 1886.

11. WSC, *My Early Life*, p. 47.

12. Earl of Rosebery, *Lord Randolph Churchill*, Arthur L. Humphreys, London, 1906, p. 72.

13. WSC, *My Early Life*, p. 48.

14. Aylmer Haldane, *A Soldier's Saga*, William Blackwood & Sons, Edinburgh and London, 1948, pp. 119–20.

15. [H. W. Massingham], 'Pictures in Parliament', *Daily News*, 19 February 1901, in Randolph S. Churchill (ed.), *Winston S. Churchill Volume II Companion* [henceforward CV II], Part 1, *1901–1907*, Heinemann, London, 1969, p. 12.

16. 'Parliamentary Sketch', *Yorkshire Post*, 19 February 1901, in CV II, Part 1, p. 16.

17. WSC, *Thoughts and Adventures*, Odhams Press, London, 1947 (first published by Thornton Butterworth, London, 1932), p. 32.

18. See Foster, *Lord Randolph Churchill*, pp. 382–403.

19. Anita Leslie to Randolph S. Churchill, 20 July 1965, quoted in Randolph S. Churchill, *Winston S. Churchill*, Vol. I: *Youth, 1874–1900*, Heinemann, London, 1966, pp. 282–3. For a full account of the two men's relationship, see Michael McMenamin and Curt J. Zoller, *Becoming Winston Churchill: The Untold Story of Young Winston and His American Mentor*, Greenwood World Publishing, Oxford/Westport, CT, 2007.

20. WSC, *My Early Life*, p. 31.

21. For Gibbon, see Roland Quinault, 'Winston Churchill and Gibbon', in R. McKitterick and R. Quinault (eds.), *Edward Gibbon and Empire*, Cambridge University Press, Cambridge, 1997, pp. 317–32.

22. Jeffery Arnett, 'Winston Churchill, the Quintessential Sensation Seeker', *Political Psychology*, Vol. 12, No. 4 (December 1991), pp. 609–21.

23. Martin Gilbert to Randolph S. Churchill, 23 April 1963, Randolph Churchill Papers, RDCH 1/2/30, citing Christabel, Countess of Aberconway. Gilbert quotes the phrase in *Churchill's Political Philosophy*, Oxford University Press, Oxford, 1981, p. 1, but does not give the source.

24. Speech of 26 July 1897.

25. Haldane, *A Soldier's Saga*, p. 120.

26. WSC, 'The Scaffolding of Rhetoric', c.November 1897, Churchill Papers, CHAR 8/13/1–13.

27. WSC, *Savrola: A Tale of the Revolution in Laurania*, Beacon Books, London, 1957 (first published 1899), pp. 65–6. Churchill himself preferred to dictate, often while walking up and down, rather than to make written notes. He had used this technique at Harrow when writing essays for another boy to pass off as his own, in exchange for help with Latin: WSC, *My Early Life*, p. 35.

28. Speech of 17 August 1899.

29. WSC, *My Early Life*, p. 246.

30. *Glasgow Herald*, 19 February 1901, in CV II, Part 1, p. 15.

31. Speech of 13 May 1901.

32. 'Character Sketch: Mr. Winston Churchill MP', *Review of Reviews*, July 1904, pp. 16–24, quotation at 24.

33. John Hulme, 'Winston Churchill, MP: A Study and ...a Story', *Temple Magazine*, 5 (January 1901), pp. 291–6, quotation at 292.

34. Herbert Vivian, 'Studies in Personality IV: Mr. Winston Churchill, MP', *Pall Mall Magazine*, April 1905.

35. Speech of 11 November 1903, quoted in McMenamin and Zoller, *Becoming Winston Churchill*, p. 14.

36. Speech of 29 April 1904.

37. WSC, 'On Making a Maiden Speech in the House', *News of the World*, 25 December 1938, in Michael Wolff (ed.), *The Collected Essays of Sir Winston Churchill*, 4 vols., Library of Imperial History, London, 1976, Vol. II, pp. 421–7, quotations at 422–3.

38. Manfred Weidhorn, *Churchill's Rhetoric and Political Discourse*, University Press of America, Lanham, M D., 1987, chapter 7.

39. These examples and others are enumerated in Ronald Hyam, 'Winston Churchill before 1914', *Historical Journal*, 12 (1969), pp. 164–73, at 173. For the possibility that Churchill may have derived this trope indirectly from the anti-slavery campaigner William Wilberforce, see Richard Toye, *Churchill's Empire: The World that Made Him and the World He Made*, Macmillan, London, 2010, p. 29 and p. 352 n. 135.

40. Hyam, 'Winston Churchill before 1914', p. 172.

41. Speech of 14 March 1914; broadcast of 25 April 1928.

42. Edwin Montagu to H. H. Asquith, 20 January 1909, Edwin Montagu Papers, Box 1 AS1/1/21.

43. Robert Roberts, *A Ragged Schooling*, Flamingo, London, 1984 (first published 1976), p. 52.

44. Colin Cross (ed.), *Life with Lloyd George: The Diary of A. J. Sylvester, 1931–45*, Macmillan, London, 1975, p. 148 (entry for 4 September 1936).

45. See Richard Toye, *Lloyd George and Churchill: Rivals for Greatness*, Macmillan, London, 2007, pp. 71, 75.

46. WSC to Lady Randolph Churchill, 16 May [1898], in Randolph S. Churchill (ed.), *Winston S. Churchill Vol. I Companion, Part II, 1896–1900*, Heinemann, London, 1967, p. 933.

47. Speech of 21 September 1914.

48. David Lloyd George, *Through Terror to Triumph*, Hodder and Stoughton, London, 1915, p. 12.

49. Frank Owen to Thomas Blackburn, 6 August 1952, Thomas Blackburn Papers.

50. 'Anglo-Saxon Unity', *The Times*, 5 July 1918.

51. David Reynolds, *In Command of History: Churchill Fighting and Writing the Second World War*, Allen Lane, London, 2004, p. 105.

52. See for example David Cannadine, *In Churchill's Shadow: Confronting the Past in Modern Britain*, Penguin, London, 2003 (first published 2002), pp. 93–7.

53. Philip E. Tetlock and Anthony Tyler, 'Churchill's Cognitive and Rhetorical Style: The Debates over Nazi Intentions and Self-Government for India', *Political Psychology*, Vol. 17, No. 1 (March 1996), pp. 149–70.

54. WSC to Clementine Churchill, 13 April 1935, in Mary Soames (ed.), *Speaking for Themselves: The Personal Letters of Winston and Clementine Churchill*, Doubleday, London, 1998, p. 399.

55. Harold Nicolson to Ben and Nigel Nicolson, 21 September 1943, in Nigel Nicolson (ed.), *Harold Nicolson: Diaries and Letters, 1939–1945*, Collins, London, 1967, p. 321.

56. Parliamentary Debates, House of Commons, Fifth Series, Vol. 317, 12 November 1936, cols. 1103–4. However, Churchill's broader point was that Baldwin's position had been ambiguous and confusing, because he had also said 'there will be no great armaments'.

57. 'The New Leader and the Old', *The Times*, 1 June 1937.

58. R. A. C. Parker, 'Churchill and Appeasement', Macmillan, London, 2000, pp. 82–3.

59. Philip Williamson, 'Baldwin's Reputation: Politics and History, 1937–1967', *Historical Journal*, Vol. 47, No. 1 (March 2004), pp. 127–68, at 133.

60. WSC, *Lord Randolph Churchill*, Vol. II, Macmillan, London, 1906, p. 247.

61. WSC, 'Parliament is the Stage of Empire Drama', *News of the World*, 1 January 1939, in *Collected Essays of Sir Winston Churchill*, Vol. II, pp. 427–33.

62. Clearly, arguments about foreign policy should not be viewed exclusively in terms of party conflict and competition for office, but these factors were obviously important, as shown in Maurice Cowling, *The Impact of Hitler: British Politics and British Policy*, Cambridge University Press, Cambridge, 1975.

63. Nick Smart (ed.), *The Diaries and Letters of Robert Bernays, 1932–1939*, Edwin Mellen, Lewiston, 1996, p. 63 (entry for 31 March 1933).

64. 'Agenda and Notes on Policy Conference', 21 January 1938, Walter Layton Papers, Box 89/8.

65. Roy Jenkins, *Churchill*, Macmillan, London, 2001, p. 545.

66. Anthony King (ed.), *British Political Opinion 1937–2000: The Gallup Polls*, Politico's, London, 2001, pp. 183–4.

67. N. J. Crowson (ed.), *Fleet Street, Press Barons and Politics: The Journals of Collin Brooks, 1932–1940*, Cambridge University Press for the Royal Historical Society, Cambridge, 1998, p. 253 (entry for 3 September 1939).

68. Speech of 3 September 1939.

69. John Barnes and David Nicholson (eds.), *The Empire at Bay: The Leo Amery Diaries, 1929–1945*, Hutchinson, London, 1988, p. 571 (entry for 3 September 1939).

70. 'Hitler's Speech To-day', *Manchester Guardian*, 6 October 1939.

71. WSC, 'Report of the First Lord of the Admiralty to the War Cabinet No. 1', 17 September 1939, WP (39) 36, CAB 66/1/36, TNA.

72. WSC to Neville Chamberlain, 24 September 1939, in Martin Gilbert (ed.), *The Churchill War Papers*, Vol. I: *At the Admiralty: September 1939–May 1940*, W. W. Norton, New York and London, 1993 [henceforward CWP I], p. 139.

73. Nicolson, *Diaries and Letters, 1939–1945*, p. 31 (entry for 26 September 1939).

74. Speech of 26 September 1939.

75. *Sunday Times*, 13 July 1980, quoted in Paul Addison, *Churchill: The Unexpected Hero*, Oxford University Press, Oxford, 2005, p. 159.

76. WSC to Dudley Pound, 25 April 1940, in CWP I, p. 1134.

77. Stephen Roskill, *Churchill and the Admirals*, Pen & Sword Books Ltd, Barnsley, 2004 (first published 1977), pp. 94–5.

78. Nicolson, *Diaries and Letters, 1939–1945*, p. 31 (entry for 26 September 1939). See also C. W. Moir diary, 27 September 1939 (5156), Mass Observation Archive: 'Main topic of conversation today Churchill's review of the Naval War to date and the contrast it made with Chamberlain's uninspired statement. Heard many people say they thought time would soon come when Chamberlain would go and Churchill replace him'.

79. Geoffrey Shakespeare, *Let Candles Be Brought In*, MacDonald, London, 1949, p. 229.

80. 'Mr. Churchill's Speech Praised in N. America', *Singapore Free Press and Mercantile Advertiser*, 3 October 1939.

81. '"We Are Going On!"', *Evening Post*, 2 October 1939; 'Winston Churchill's Broadcast', *Singapore Free Press and Mercantile Advertiser*, 13 November 1939.

82. 'Nazi Radio Voice Interrupts BBC to Query Churchill', *Vancouver Sun*, 3 October 1939.

83. 'War by Wireless', *Irish Times*, 23 October 1939.

84. Broadcast of 1 October 1939.

85. C. H. Miller diary, 1 October 1939 (5376), Mass Observation Archive.

86. Broadcast of 1 October 1939.

87. Joseph P. Kennedy to Rose Kennedy, 2 October 1939, in Amanda Smith (ed.), *Hostage to Fortune: The Letters of Joseph P. Kennedy*, Viking, New York, 2001, pp. 391–2.

88. Joseph P. Kennedy, 'Memorandum of Conversation with Winston Churchill at Hialeah Race Track on January 31, 1946', in Smith (ed.), *Hostage to Fortune*, pp. 622–3.

89. John Colville, *The Fringes of Power: Downing Street Diaries, 1939–1955*, Hodder and Stoughton, London, 1985, p. 29 (entry for 1 October 1939).

90. 'Review of Broadcasting', *Manchester Guardian*, 4 October 1939.

91. Neville Chamberlain to Hilda Chamberlain, 1 October 1939 and to Ida Chamberlain, 8 October 1939, in Robert Self (ed.), *The Neville Chamberlain Diary Letters*, Ashgate, Aldershot, 2002–5, Vol. IV: *The Downing Street Years, 1934–1940*, pp. 453, 455.

92. C. W. Smallbones diary, 1 October 1939 (5201), Mass Observation Archive.

93. Eleanor Humphries diary, 1 October 1939 (5342), Mass Observation Archive.

94. Broadcast of 1 October 1939.

95. Brenda Cobbett diary, 1 October 1939 (5276), Mass Observation Archive.

96. E. Hill diary, 1 October 1939 (5332), Mass Observation Archive.

97. Elisabeth Crowfoot diary, 1 October 1939 (5292), Mass Observation Archive.

98. R. MacIsaac diary, 1 October 1939 (5138), Mass Observation Archive.

99. Denis Argent diary, 2 October 1939 (5010), Mass Observation Archive.

100. Cowling, *Impact of Hitler*, pp. 368–9. See also Nick Smart, *British Strategy and Politics During the Phony War: Before the Balloon Went up*, Praeger Westport, CT, 2003.

101. 'Hitler's Terms for Peace', *The Times*, 7 October 1939.

102. Cross (ed.), *Life with Lloyd George*, p. 239 (entry for 9 October 1939).

103. Neville Chamberlain to Hilda Chamberlain, 15 October 1939, in Self, *Neville Chamberlain Diary Letters*, Vol. IV, p. 459.

104. W. L. Mackenzie King diary, 11 October 1939, <http://www.collectionscanada.gc.ca>.

105. Parliamentary Debates, House of Commons, Fifth Series, Vol. 352, 12 October 1939, col. 568.

106. Robert Rhodes James (ed.), *'Chips': The Diaries of Sir Henry Channon*, Weidenfeld and Nicolson, London, 1993 (first published 1967), p. 224 (entry for 12 October 1939).

107. Charles Lysaght, *Brendan Bracken*, Allen Lane, London, 1979, p. 166.

108. Neville Chamberlain to Ida Chamberlain, 19 November 1939, in Self, *Neville Chamberlain Diary Letters*, Vol. IV, p. 471.

109. Broadcast of 12 November 1939. For the film, see <http://www.britishpathe.com/record.php?id=24439> (consulted 7 March 2011). It was unusual for Churchill's radio broadcasts to be filmed.

110. Colville, *The Fringes of Power*, pp. 50–1 (entries for 12 and 13 November 1939).

111. Quoted in Self, *Neville Chamberlain Diary Letters*, Vol. IV, p. 471 n. 205.

112. 'Hitler Asks for Loyalty', *The Times*, 31 January 1940.

113. Neville Chamberlain to Ida Chamberlain, 19 November 1939, in Self, *Neville Chamberlain Diary Letters*, Vol. IV, p. 471.

114. P. F. Petherbridge diary, 12 November 1939 (5170), and Denis Argent diary, 12 November 1939 (5010) (citing the reactions of his landlady), Mass Observation Archive.

115. Mary Towler diary, 12 November 1939 (5445), D. I. Masson diary, 12 November 1939 (5145), J. M. MacDougall diary, 12 November 1939 (5363), Mass Observation Archive.

116. Jean Tayler diary, 24 November 1939 (5439), Mass Observation Archive.

117. Arthur Collins diary, 12 November 1939 (5039.1), Mass Observation Archive.

118. 'Brilliant Naval Fighting: Mr. Churchill on Sea Exploits', *The Times*, 19 December 1939.

119. 'Mr. Churchill's Broadcast', *The Manchester Guardian*, 20 December 1939.

120. Mackenzie King diary, 18 December 1939.

121. Speech of 6 December 1939; Reuters report cited in 'New Method of Fighting Submarines', *The Straits Times*, 7 December 1939.

122. WSC to Archibald Carter and others, 19 October 1939, in CWP I, p. 267.

123. Cowling, *Impact of Hitler*, pp. 355–7, 368–9; Smart, *British Strategy*, pp. 74–5.

124. WSC, 'Notes on the General Situation', 25 September 1939, WP (39) 52, CAB 66/2/2, TNA.

125. A table of listening figures is given in the Appendix.

126. Broadcast of 20 January 1940.

127. Ivone Kirkpatrick (for Lord Halifax) to Lancelot Oliphant, 26 January 1940, FO 371/24364, TNA.

128. Quoted in 'Foreign Reaction to Mr. Churchill's Speech', January 1940, FO 371/24364, TNA.

129. 'Music Hall Report', File Report 33, 4 March 1940, Mass Observation Archive.

130. Pravda, quoted in 'Greatest Enemy of Soviet', *Straits Times*, 27 January 1940.

131. Neville Chamberlain to Ida Chamberlain, 27 January 1940, in Self, *Neville Chamberlain Diary Letters*, Vol. IV, p. 492.

132. Parliamentary Debates, House of Commons, 27 February 1940, Vol. 357, col. 1928.

133. David Dilks (ed.), *The Diaries of Sir Alexander Cadogan O.M., 1938–1945*, Cassell & Co., London, 1971, p. 249 (entry for 26 January 1940). For Chamberlain's speech

see 'Rising Might of Britain: Prime Minister's Survey', *The Times*, 1 February 1940, and for evidence that some observers recognized that he was trying to correct Churchill, see 'Our London Correspondence', *Manchester Guardian*, 1 February 1940.

134. Speech of 27 January 1940.

135. 'Mr. Churchill in Manchester', *Manchester Guardian*, 6 January 1940; *London Illustrated News*, 3 February 1940.

136. 'Not an Hour to be Lost', *The Times*, 29 January 1940. The Mosleyites claimed that the hecklers were subjected to violence: 'Churchill Meeting Outrage', *Action*, 8 February 1940.

137. 'A Broadcast Problem for Ministers', *Manchester Guardian*, 6 February 1940.

138. M. M. Corfe diary, 27 January 1940 (5285), Mass Observation Archive.

139. Speech of 27 January 1940.

140. Lord Halifax, 'Publicity in Enemy Countries', WP(R) (40) 105, 29 March 1940, CAB 68/5/55, TNA.

141. François Kersaudy, *Norway 1940*, Arrow Books, London, 1990, pp. 13–36, 44–5.

142. Speech of 30 March 1940.

143. Nance Leacroft to Mass Observation, n.d. but received 8 April 1940 (5356), Mass Observation Archive.

144. J. R. Aldam diary, 27 January 1940 (5006), J. M. MacDougall diary, 29 February 1940 (5363), M. J. Hill diary, 30 March, 1 April and 8 May 1940 (5333), W. C. Eyre Hartley diary, 10 May 1940 (5103), Mass Observation Archive.

145. WM 40 60th Conclusions, Confidential Annex, 3 April 1940, CAB 65/12/15, TNA.

146. Nicolson, *Diaries and Letters, 1939–1945*, p. 70 (entry for 11 April 1940).

147. Colville, *Fringes of Power*, p. 101 (entry for 11 April 1940). In support of Colville's version, it may be noted that Churchill was frequently interrupted by cheers and laughter: 'House of Commons', *The Times*, 12 April 1940.

148. Speech of 11 April 1940.

149. 'Confident of Victory: Mr. Chamberlain Speaks to His Party', *The Times*, 5 April 1940.

150. Quoted in Reynolds, *In Command of History*, p. 126.

151. Parliamentary Debates, House of Commons, Fifth Series, Vol. 360, 7 May 1940, col. 1093.

152. Speech of Alfred Duff Cooper: Parliamentary Debates, House of Commons, Fifth Series, Vol. 360, 7 May 1940, col. 1307. For further examples and discussion, see Kersaudy, *Norway 1940*, pp. 192–3.

153. Parliamentary Debates, House of Commons, Fifth Series, Vol. 360, 8 May 1940, cols. 1278, 1283.

154. Parliamentary Debates, House of Commons, Fifth Series, Vol. 360, 7 May 1940, col. 1150.

155. Percy Harris Diary, 8 May 1940, Percy Harris Papers, HRS/1; Parliamentary Debates, House of Commons, Fifth Series, Vol. 360, 08 May 1940, col. 1266.

156. 'Labour Challenges a Division', *The Times*, 9 May 1940.

157. Barnes and Nicholson, *Empire at Bay*, p. 610 (entry for 8 May 1940).

158. Parliamentary Debates, House of Commons, Fifth Series, Vol. 360, 8 May 1940, col. 1358.

159. 'House of Commons', *The Times*, 9 May 1940.

160. Rhodes James, *'Chips'*, p. 246 (entry for 8 May 1940).

161. Harris Diary, 8 May 1940, Harris Papers, HRS/1.

162. Nicolson, *Diaries and Letters, 1939–1945*, p. 79 (entry for 8 May 1940).

163. Barnes and Nicholson, *Empire at Bay*, p. 610 (entry for 8 May 1940).

164. Parliamentary Debates, House of Commons, Fifth Series, Vol. 360, 8 May 1940, col. 1362; Randolph S. Churchill (ed.), *Into Battle: Speeches by the Right Hon. Winston S. Churchill P.C., M.P.*, Cassell & Co., London, 1941, pp. 198–208. The omissions occur in the *Complete Speeches* too.

165. Nicolson, *Diaries and Letters, 1939–1945*, p. 79 (entry for 8 May 1940); Rhodes James, *'Chips'*, p. 247 (entry for 8 May 1940).

166. See Nick Smart, 'Four Days in May: The Norway Debate and the Downfall of Neville Chamberlain', *Parliamentary History*, Vol. 17, No. 2 (1998), pp. 215–43.

167. '"My Duty Was Plain": Mr. Chamberlain's Broadcast', *The Times*, 11 May 1940.

168. William Armstrong (ed.), *With Malice Toward None: A War Diary by Cecil H. King*, Sidgwick and Jackson, London, 1970, p. 39 (entry for 10 May 1940).

169. Nicolson, *Diaries and Letters, 1939–1945*, p. 84 (entry for 10 May 1940).

170. Parliamentary Debates, House of Commons, Fifth Series, Vol. 360, 13 May 1940, cols. 1501–2. For Garibaldi, see John Lukacs, *Blood, Toil, Tears & Sweat: The Dire Warning*, Basic Books, New York, 2008, p. 47.

171. 'Gallacher Not Told of Debate', *Daily Worker*, 15 May 1940.

172. 'House of Commons', *The Times*, 14 May 1940.

173. Rhodes James, *'Chips'*, p. 252 (entry for 13 May 1940); Lord Davidson to Stanley Baldwin, 14 May 1940, cited in Martin Gilbert, *Winston S. Churchill*, Vol. VI: *Finest Hour, 1939–1941*, Heinemann, London, 1983, p. 332.

174. Andrew Roberts, *Eminent Churchillians*, Weidenfeld and Nicolson, London, 1994, p. 144.

175. 'Rallying Call Given by Churchill; House Votes Confidence', *Saskatoon Star-Phoenix*, 13 May 1940.

176. 'New Government Acclaimed', *Glasgow Herald*, 14 May 1940.

177. Rhodes James, *'Chips'*, p. 252 (entry for 13 May 1940).

CHAPTER 2

1. War Cabinet minutes 14 May 1940, WM (40) 122nd conclusions, TNA CAB/65/7/17.

2. WSC, *The Second World War*, Vol. II: *Their Finest Hour*, Cassell & Co., London, 1949, pp. 38–9, 42.

3. Home Intelligence Report, 18 May 1940, in Paul Addison and Jeremy A. Crang (eds.), *Listening to Britain: Home Intelligence Reports on Britain's Finest Hour: May to September 1940*, The Bodley Head, London, 2010, p. 6.

4. According to one contemporary account, 'The Prime Minister's short and trenchant speech [...] struck the right note with the public because it was the kind of tough talk they wanted to hear after months of woolly optimism'. However, this claim is not replicated in other diary or survey evidence. Mollie Panter-Downes, *London War Notes 1939–1945* (ed. William Shawn), Longman, London, 1972, p. 57 (entry for 19 May 1940).

5. WSC to Brendan Bracken, 4 April 1942, INF1/282, TNA; Ian McLaine, *Ministry of Morale: Home Front Morale and the Ministry of Information in World War II*, George Allen & Unwin, London, 1979, p. 258. Churchill was, however, sometimes shown an extract on 'some controversial topic which is exciting interest': J. H. Peck to C. J. Radcliffe, 30 September 1943, INF 1/285, TNA.

6. Duff Cooper, *Old Men Forget*, Rupert Hart-Davis, London, 1954, p. 280.

7. John Charmley, *Duff Cooper, The Authorised Biography*, Phoenix, London, 1997 (first published 1986), p. 142; '"A Tonic to the Nation"', *The Times*, 22 May 1940.

8. Home Intelligence Reports, 19/20 and 29 May 1940, in Addison and Crang, *Listening to Britain*, pp. 11, 49.

9. Panter-Downes, *London War Notes*, p. 64 (entry for 2 June 1940).

10. WM (40) 138th Conclusions, Minute 1, Confidential Annex, 18th May 1940, CAB 65/13/11, TNA.

11. 'If the battle is to be won, we must provide our men with ever-increasing quantities of the weapons and ammunition they need. We must have, and have quickly, more aeroplanes, more tanks, more guns, more shells. [...] Our task is not merely to win the battle but to win the war'. Neville Chamberlain, 'Notes for Prime Minister's Broadcast', 18 May 1940, Churchill Papers, CHAR 9/176A, 13–14.

12. John Colville, *The Fringes of Power: Downing Street Diaries, 1939–1955*, Hodder and Stoughton, London, 1985, p. 136 (entry for 19 May 1940); '"Tremendous Battle"', *The Times*, 20 May 1940.

13. Broadcast of 19 May 1940.

14. Philip Williamson, 'Christian Conservatives and the Totalitarian Challenge, 1933–40', *English Historical Review*, 115 (2000), pp. 607–42.

15. Andrew Stewart to Lord Hood, 18 May 1940, Churchill Papers, CHAR 9/176A/10.

16. George H. Gallup (ed.), *The Gallup International Opinion Polls: Great Britain 1937–1975*, Vol. I: *1937–1964*, Random House, New York, 1976, pp. 33–4.

17. Home Intelligence Reports, 19/20 and 21 May 1940, in Addison and Crang, *Listening to Britain*, pp. 12, 15.

18. 'Morale Today', 21 May 1940, Mass Observation Archive.

19. Nella Last diary, 19 May 1940 (5353), Mass Observation Archive.

20. Helen D. Millgate (ed.), *Mr. Brown's War: A Diary of the Second World War*, Sutton Publishing, Stroud, 2003 (first published 1998), p. 44 (entry for 19 May 1940).

21. M. M. Paton diary, 22 May 1940 (5394), Mass Observation Archive.

22. Comment of 'G.D.', a solicitor, reported in T. J. Williams diary, 22 May 1940 (5231), Mass Observation Archive.

23. C. Miller diary, 19 and 20 May 1940 (5376), Mass Observation Archive.

24. 'France Told the Facts', *The Times*, 22 May 1940; Home Intelligence Report, 22 May 1940, in Addison and Crang, *Listening to Britain*, pp. 18–20.

25. Statement of 23 May 1940.

26. Speech of 28 May 1940.

27. There are signs that this line was a retrospective 'improvement' by Hugh Dalton—for the purposes of publication—of a slightly less poetic version he recorded at the time. Compare Ben Pimlott (ed.), *The Second World War Diary of Hugh Dalton, 1940–1945*, Jonathan Cape, London, 1986, p. 28 (entry for 28 May 1940) with Hugh Dalton, *The Fateful Years: Memoirs 1931–1945*, Frederick Muller, London, 1957, p. 336.

28. WM 40 (145th Conclusions), Minute 1, Confidential Annex, 18 May 1940, CAB/65/13/24, TNA.

29. WM 40 (145th Conclusions), Minute 1, Confidential Annex, 18 May 1940, CAB/65/13/24, TNA.

30. William Philip Simms, memorandum of 31 May 1940, Churchill Papers, CHAR 9/172/102–3. Emphases in original.

31. Alfred Duff Cooper, undated note and memo, passed on to Churchill with a note from Desmond Morton dated 2 June 1940, Churchill Papers, CHAR 9/171/99–101.

32. Recollections of Sir John Martin, c.1973, <http://www.bbc.co.uk/archive/churchill/11021.shtml> (consulted 5 January 2012).

33. Anthony Eden to WSC, [3?] June 1940, Churchill Papers, CHAR 9/172/104.

34. Frank Wood to E. A. Seal, 3 June 1940, Archibald Sinclair's comments, Churchill Papers, CHAR 9/172/97–8.

35. Dudley Pound, note of 3 June 1940, PREM 3/175/58, cited in Martin Gilbert, *Winston S. Churchill*, Vol. VI: *Finest Hour, 1939–1941*, Heinemann, London, 1983, p. 463.

36. Draft of speech of 4 June 1940, Churchill Papers, CHAR 9/172/23.

37. Alexander Mackintosh, *Echoes of Big Ben: A Journalist's Parliamentary Diary (1881–1940)*, Hutchinson & Co., London, 1945, p. 156.

38. Colville, *Fringes of Power*, p. 148 (entry for 4 June 1940).

39. Mackintosh, *Echoes*, p. 157.

40. Speech of 4 June 1940.

41. 'Lord Rosebery on Questions of Empire', *The Times*, 17 November 1900.

42. Mackenzie King to WSC, 31 May 1940, PREM 4/43B/1, TNA.

43. Mackenzie King diary, 4 June 1940.

44. Lord Lothian to WSC, 26 May 1940, PREM 4/43B/1, TNA.

45. Robert Rhodes James (ed.), *'Chips': The Diaries of Sir Henry Channon*, Weidenfeld and Nicolson, London, 1993 (first published 1967), p. 256 (entry for 4 June 1940).

46. Emanuel Shinwell, 'Winston Churchill on Records', *c.*1964, Michael Wolff Papers, WLFF 2/4.

47. William Armstrong (ed.), *With Malice Toward None: A War Diary by Cecil H. King*, Sidgwick & Jackson, London, 1970, p. 48 (entry for 7 June 1940).

48. Mark Pottle (ed.), *Champion Redoubtable: The Diaries and Letters of Violet Bonham Carter 1914–1945*, Weidenfeld and Nicolson, London, 1998, pp. 224–5 (entry for 11 June 1940).

49. John Barnes and David Nicholson (eds.), *The Empire at Bay: The Leo Amery Diaries, 1929–1945*, Hutchinson, London, 1988, p. 620 (entry for 4 June 1940).

50. German medium-wave broadcast, 'In English for England', 22.15 BST, 5 June 1940, in Daily Digest of Foreign Broadcasts, 6 June 1940, BBC Written Archives.

51. Quoted in WSC, *Their Finest Hour*, p. 355.

52. WSC to Lord Lothian, 9 June 1940, quoted in WSC, *Their Finest Hour*, p. 355.

53. Edward R. Murrow, *This Is London*, Shocken Books, New York, 1985 (first published 1941), p. 125.

54. W. L. Mackenzie King diary, 14 June 1940.

55. For a survey of American and British Press reactions, see 'His Speech Magnificent', *Vancouver Sun*, 5 June 1940.

56. Joseph Cerruti, 'Churchill Calls on America to Help Fight Nazis', *Chicago Daily Tribune*, 5 June 1940; 'Mr. Churchill's Words and Deeds', *Chicago Daily Tribune*, 6 June 1940.

57. 'The "True British Spirit"', *The Times*, Wednesday, 5 June 1940.

58. Alexander Critchley to WSC, 3 June 1940, Churchill Papers CHAR 9/172/87–8.

59. 'Campaign to Prepare Public for Invasion: Memorandum by the Ministry of Information', WP 40 (190), 3 June 1940, CAB 66/8/20, TNA.

60. Doris Melling diary, 4 June 1940, in Sandra Koa Wing (ed.), *Our Longest Days: A People's History of the Second World War*, Profile Books, London, 2008, p. 34.

61. Home Intelligence Report, 5 June 1940, in Addison and Crang, *Listening to Britain*, p. 80. See also 'Morale Today', 5 June 1940, Mass Observation Archive.

62. A. White diary, 4 June 1940 (5230), and also Margery Davis diary, 4 June 1940 (5295), Mass Observation Archive.

63. Vita Sackville-West to Harold Nicolson, 5 June 1940, in Nigel Nicolson (ed.), *Harold Nicolson: Diaries and Letters, 1939–1945*, Collins, London, 1967, p. 93.

64. Nella Last diary, 4 June 1940 (5353), Mass Observation Archive.

65. Evelyn Saunders diary, 5 June 1940 (5420), Mass Observation Archive.

66. 'His Speech Magnificent', *Vancouver Sun*, 5 June 1940.

67. Broadcast of 17 June 1940.

68. Armstrong, *With Malice Toward None*, p. 55 (entry for 20 June 1940).

69. 'Capitulation Talk in Worktown [Bolton]', 19 June 1940, Mass Observation Archive.

70. David Edgerton, *Britain's War Machine: Weapons, Resources and Experts in the Second World War*, Allen Lane, London, 2011, p. 47.

71. Similarly, in his broadcast of 14 July 1940 he said 'We are fighting *by* ourselves alone; but we are not fighting *for* ourselves alone'. And when Hitler invaded Russia Churchill immediately referred to the prior period 'when we had to face the storm alone': broadcast of 22 June 1941. The phrase may have had its first use in a telegram to Roosevelt prior to Dunkirk: 'If necessary, we shall continue the war alone and we are not afraid of that'. WSC to Franklin D. Roosevelt, 15 May 1940, in Warren F. Kimball (ed.), *Churchill & Roosevelt: The Complete Correspondence*, Vol. I: *Alliance Emerging, October 1933–November 1942*, Princeton University Press, Princeton, 1984, p. 37.

72. See Richard Toye, *Churchill's Empire: The World That Made Him and the World He Made*, Macmillan, London, 2010, pp. 204–5.

73. Speech of 18 June 1940.

74. Hansard records 'called'; 'has called' in the broadcast version.

75. Hansard records 'free' rather than 'freed', as in the broadcast.

76. Speech of 18 June 1940, Churchill Papers CHAR 9/172/152.

77. See Marc Wiggam, 'The Blackout in Britain and Germany during the Second World War', Ph.D. thesis, University of Exeter, 2011.

78. See Jonathan Charteris-Black, *Politicians and Rhetoric: The Persuasive Power of Metaphor*, Palgrave, Houndmills, Basingstoke, 2005, pp. 50–3.

79. Pimlott, *Second World War Diary*, p. 42 (entry for 18 June 1940).

80. Paul Einzig, *In the Centre of Things*, Hutchinson, London, 1960, pp. 213–14. The Labour MP Sydney Silverman wrote an article emphasizing the Chamberlainites' failure to cheer Churchill: 'When the House Cheers', *Tribune*, 21 June 1940.

81. War Cabinet minutes, 17 June 1940, WM (40) 170th Conclusions, CAB 65/7/65, TNA.

82. Armstrong, *With Malice Toward None*, p. 55 (entry for 18 June 1940).

83. Nicolson to Sackville-West, 19 June 1940, in Nicolson, *Diaries 1939–45*, p. 97.

84. Home Intelligence Report 19 June 1940, in Addison and Crang, *Listening to Britain*, p. 129.

85. 'Morale', File Report 203, 18 June 1940, Mass Observation Archive.

86. 'Morale', File Report 207, 19 June 1940, Mass Observation Archive.

87. Eleanor Humphries diary, 18 June 1940 (5342), Mass Observation Archive.

88. Margery Davis diary, 18 June 1940 (5295), Mass Observation-Archive.

89. Panter-Downes, *London War Notes*, p. 70 (entry for 22 June 1940).

90. E. Agnes Norman diary, 18 and 19 June 1940 (2450), Mass Observation Archive.

91. John Martin, letter of 21 June 1940, excerpt in John Martin, *Downing Street: The War Years*, Bloomsbury, London, 1991, p. 12.

92. *Daily Mirror*, 19 June 1940.

93. Armstrong, *With Malice Toward None*, p. 55 (entry for 18 June 1940).

94. Home Intelligence Report 20 June 1940, in Addison and Crang, *Listening to Britain*, pp. 134–7. See also Listener Research Section, 'A Listener Research Report: Listeners' Comments on Mr Duff Cooper, Mr J. B. Priestley and Sir Hugh Elles', 2 August 1940, BBC Written Archives.

95. Leo Amery diary, 20 June 1940, Leo Amery Papers, AMEL 7/34; speech of 20 June 1940, in Charles Eade (ed.), *Secret Session Speeches by the Right Hon Winston S. Churchill OM, CH, MP*, Cassell & Co., London, 1946, p. 15.

96. Rhodes James, *'Chips'*, p. 259 (entry for 20 June 1940).

97. Amery diary, 20 June 1940, Amery Papers, AMEL 7/34.

98. Shinwell, 'Winston Churchill on Records', Michael Wolff Papers, WLFF 2/4. On the *Lancastria* incident, see WSC, *Their Finest Hour*, p. 172.

99. Speech of 18 June 1940.

100. Raymond Daniell, 'Churchill in Plea', *New York Times*, 19 June 1940.

101. François Kersaudy, *Churchill and De Gaulle*, Collins, London, 1981, pp. 77–8.

102. 'Weekly Report: Week Ending Friday, 23rd August 1940', File Report 365, Mass Observation Archive.

103. 'Restoration of France', *The Times*, 24 June 1940.

104. 'Extracts from BBC Teleprinter', 23 June 1940, Churchill Papers CHAR 9/172/108.

105. Address of 23 June 1940 in *Le Maréchal Pétain: L'Armistice du 25 Juin 1940: Appels aux Français*, Fédération des Associations Françaises pour le Développement des Relations avec L'Étranger/Comité France-Amérique, Clermont-Ferrand, 1940, p. 11, copy in Philippe Pétain Papers, 2AG/439. This was highly restrained by comparison with German propaganda, which portrayed Churchill's speech as a 'blatant invitation' to the French to betray their own country 'for the sake of the English money-bag'. Deutschlandsender 23 June 1940 (in German for Germany), Daily Digest of Foreign Broadcasts, 24 June 1940, BBC Written Archives.

106. See for example 'Declaration du Maréchal aux Américains', 30 July 1940, Pétain Papers, 2AG/439.

107. Jean-Marie Flonneau, 'L'Évolution de l'opinion publique de 1940 à 1944', in Jean-Pierre Azéma and Francois Bédarida (eds.), *Le Régime de Vichy et les Français*, Fayard, Paris, 1992, pp. 506–22.

108. WSC, *Their Finest Hour*, p. 206.

109. Speech of 4 July 1940.

110. Lord Harmsworth diary, 4 July 1940, Cecil Harmsworth Papers.

111. James Leutze (ed.), *The London Observer: The Journal of General Raymond E. Lee 1940–1941*, Hutchinson, London, 1971, p. 12 (entry for 4 July 1940).

112. 'After His "Oran" Speech: Mr. Churchill Cheered by the House', *Illustrated London News*, 13 July 1940.

113. Rhodes James, *'Chips'*, p. 260 (entry for 4 July 1940).

114. WSC, *Their Finest Hour*, p. 211.
115. Einzig, *In the Centre of Things*, pp. 219–18.
116. 'Weekly Report: Week ending Friday, 23rd August 1940', File Report 365, Mass Observation Archive.
117. The comment of Virginia Woolf's grocer: Anne Olivier Bell (ed.), *The Diary of Virginia Woolf*, Vol. V: *1936–41*, Penguin, London, 1985 (first published 1984), p. 300 (entry for 4 July 1940).
118. Home Intelligence Report, 5 July 1940, in Addison and Crang, *Listening to Britain*, p. 199.
119. J. Howard diary, 5 July 1940 (5111), Mass Observation Archive. Howard was wrong: Churchill often cried. See Martin Francis, 'Tears, Tantrums, and Bared Teeth: The Emotional Economy of Three Conservative Prime Ministers, 1951–1963', *Journal of British Studies*, 41 (2002), pp. 354–87.
120. War Cabinet minutes 11 July 1940, WM (40) 200th Conclusions, CAB/65/8/12, TNA.
121. War Cabinet minutes 14 July 1940, WM (40) 203rd Conclusions, CAB/65/8/15, TNA.
122. Colville, *Fringes of Power*, p. 192 (entry for 12 July 1940).
123. Broadcast of 14 July 1940.
124. 'Weekly Report 20.7.40–27.7.40', File Report 301A, Mass Observation Archive.
125. Broadcast of 14 July 1940.
126. Listener Research Section, 'Listener Research Weekly Report No. 2: Week Ending 27th July 1940', 29 July 1940, BBC Written Archives.
127. Home Intelligence Report, 15 July 1940, in Addison and Crang, *Listening to Britain*, p. 232.
128. Home Intelligence Report, 16 July 1940, in Addison and Crang, *Listening to Britain*, p. 238.
129. L. D. Pexton diary, 19 July 1940, in Ronald Blythe (ed.), *Private Words: Letters and Diaries from the Second World War*, Penguin, London, 1993 (first published 1991), p. 99.
130. Listener Research Section, 'Listener Research Weekly Report No. 2: Week Ending 27th July 1940', 29 July 1940, BBC Written Archives.
131. Rhodes James, *'Chips'*, p. 261 (entry for 18 July 1940).
132. Home Intelligence Report, 20 July 1940, in Addison and Crang, *Listening to Britain*, pp. 248–51.
133. Lord Ismay, *The Memoirs of Lord Ismay*, Heinemann, London, 1960, pp. 179–80. When working on his memoirs, Ismay had trouble working out exactly when this episode occurred. It can be most plausibly dated to 16 August. Lord Ismay to Dermot Boyle, 8 September 1954, and Boyle to Ismay, 3 October 1956, Ismay Papers 1/14/16a–b.
134. Garry Campion, *The Good Fight: Battle of Britain Propaganda and The Few*, Palgrave, Houndmills, Basingstoke, 2009, pp. 33, 76–83.

135. For the issues discussed in this paragraph, see Ben Shephard, *The Long Road Home: The Aftermath of the Second World War*, Alfred A. Knopf, New York, 2011, pp. 33–4.

136. Basil Liddell Hart, 'Talk with the Rt. Hon. H.B. Lees-Smith', 18 July 1940, Liddell Hart Papers, LH 11/1940/73.

137. Anthony Bevir to John Martin, 17 August 1940, Churchill Papers CHAR 9/173B/82, and drafts on the blockade issue, CHAR 9/173B, 177–85.

138. 'Mr. Churchill's Survey', *News Chronicle*, 21 August 1940.

139. Speech of 20 August 1940.

140. Home Intelligence Report, 20 August 1940, in Addison and Crang, *Listening to Britain*, p. 347.

141. Speech of 20 August 1940.

142. Nicolson, *Diaries 1939–45*, p. 109 (entry for 20 August 1940).

143. 'On to the Attack', *Daily Mail*, 21 August 1940.

144. War Cabinet minutes, 19 August 1940, WM (40) 230th Conclusions, CAB 65/8/42, TNA.

145. WSC, *Their Finest Hour*, pp. 361–2.

146. 'US Bases for Defence', *The Times*, 17 August 1940.

147. WSC to Franklin D. Roosevelt, 22 August 1940, in Kimball, *Complete Correspondence*, Vol. I, p. 64.

148. War Cabinet minutes, 21 August 1940, WM (40) 231st Conclusions, CAB 65/8/43, TNA.

149. Speech of 20 August 1940.

150. Colville, *Fringes of Power*, p. 227 (entry for 20 August 1940).

151. *Chicago Daily Tribune*, 21 August 1940.

152. For a survey of the American press, see 'US Optimistic over Britain's Chances', *Singapore Free Press and Mercantile Advertiser*, 22 August 1940.

153. Nicolson, *Diaries 1939–45*, p. 109 (entry for 20 August 1940).

154. Colville, *Fringes of Power*, p. 227 (entry for 20 August 1940).

155. Rhodes James, *'Chips'*, p. 264 (entry for 20 August 1940).

156. Quoted in 'Speech by Confident Man to a Confident Audience', *Straits Times*, 21 August 1940.

157. WSC to Clement Attlee and David Margesson, 12 August 1940, Churchill Papers CHAR 9/173B/225.

158. David Margesson to WSC, 15 August 1940, Churchill papers, CHAR 9/173B/229.

159. Speech of 20 January 1942.

160. Home Intelligence Report, 21 August 1940, in Addison and Crang, *Listening to Britain*, pp. 349–50.

161. Home Intelligence Report, 22 August 1940, in Addison and Crang, *Listening to Britain*, p. 354.

162. Home Intelligence Report, 21 August 1940, in Addison and Crang, *Listening to Britain*, p. 352.

163. O. Smith diary, 21 August 1940 (5427), Mass Observation Archive.

164. Speech of 20 August 1940.

165. A. N. Gerrard diary, 20 and 21 August 1940 (5081), Mass Observation Archive.

166. Armstrong, *With Malice toward None*, p. 66 (entry for 7 August 1940).

167. 'Morale', 20 June 1940, Mass Observation Archive.

168. Chamberlain had reached a high-point of 68 per cent approval in November 1939. Anthony King (ed.), *British Political Opinion 1937–2000: The Gallup Polls*, Politico's, London, 2000, pp. 183–4.

169. Evelyn Waugh to Ann Fleming, 27 January 1965, in Mark Amory (ed.), *The Letters of Evelyn Waugh*, Weidenfeld and Nicolson, London, 1980, p. 630. See also John Howard Wilson, '"Not a Man for Whom I Ever Had Esteem": Evelyn Waugh on Winston Churchill', in Carlos Villar Flor and Robert Murray Davis (eds.), *Waugh without End: New Trends in Evelyn Waugh Studies*, Peter Lang, Berne, 2005, pp. 247–58 at 255.

170. Ludovic Kennedy, 'Introduction', in *War Papers*, Fontana, London, 1989, pp. 5–11, at 6.

171. Lyn Smith, *Young Voices: British Children Remember the Second World War*, Viking, London, 2007, p. 87. Emphases in original.

172. Patricia and Robert Malcolmson (eds.), *Nella Last's Peace: The Post-war Diaries of Housewife, 49*, Profile Books, London, 2008, p. 175 (entry for 14 January 1947).

173. Churchill recorded the speech, and a number of others that had not been broadcast either, in 1949. The recordings were released by Decca in 1964. See the correspondence in the Churchill Papers, CHUR 4/445.

174. Pimlott, *Second World War Diary*, p. 28 (entry for 28 May 1940).

175. Dalton, *Fateful Years*, p. 336.

176. Roy Jenkins, *Churchill*, Macmillan, London, 2000, chapter 32.

177. For examples, see *BBC Handbook 1941*, British Broadcasting Corporation, London, 1941, pp. 17–18. See also Siân Nicholas, *The Echo of War: Home Front Propaganda and the Wartime BBC, 1939–45*, Manchester University Press, Manchester, 1996.

CHAPTER 3

1. Note by WSC, 4 September 1940, Churchill Papers, CHAR 9/174B/119.

2. Robert Rhodes James (ed.), *'Chips': The Diaries of Sir Henry Channon*, Weidenfeld and Nicolson, London, 1993 (first published 1967), p. 265 (entry for 5 September 1940).

3. Home Intelligence Report, 12 September 1940, in Paul Addison and Jeremy A. Crang (eds.), *Listening to Britain: Home Intelligence Reports on Britain's Finest Hour: May to September 1940*, The Bodley Head, London, 2010, p. 398.

4. Draft of speech of 5 September 1940, Churchill Papers, CHAR 9/141B/124.

5. 'An Investor's Note Book: City Confidence Reinforced', *Financial Times*, 7 September 1940.

6. See C. R. Attlee to WSC, 10 September 1940, Churchill Papers, CHAR 9/176A/66.

7. Harold Nicolson to Brendan Bracken, 10 September 1940, Churchill Papers, CHAR 9/176A/47–8. For the impact of bombing on morale, and for the growth of anti-Semitism, see Juliet Gardiner, 'The Blitz Experience in British Society, 1940–1941', in Claudia Baldoli, Richard Overy, and Andrew Knapp (eds.), *Bombing, States and Peoples in Western Europe 1940–1945*, Continuum, London, 2011, pp. 171–83.

8. Naomi Royde Smith, *Outside Information: Being a Diary of Rumours*, London, Macmillan, 1941, pp. 42–3.

9. J. G. Dill to J. H. Peck, 11 September 1940, Churchill Papers, CHAR 9/176A/49.

10. Home Intelligence Report, 13 September 1940, in Addison and Crang, *Listening to Britain*, pp. 418–19.

11. 'Popular Attitudes to War-Time Politics', 20 November 1940, Mass Observation Archive.

12. Quoted in William Armstrong (ed.), *With Malice Toward None: A War Diary by Cecil H. King*, Sidgwick and Jackson, London, 1970, p. 79.

13. See the summary of coverage in Herbert Morrison, 'Subversive Newspaper Propaganda', 8 October 1940, WP (40) 402, CAB 66/12/32, TNA.

14. War Cabinet minutes, 9 October 1940, WM (40) 268th Conclusions, CAB/65/9/30, TNA.

15. Speech of 8 October 1940.

16. Parliamentary Debates, House of Commons, Fifth Series, Vol. 365, 8 October 1940, col. 350.

17. Stuart Ball (ed.), *Parliament and Politics in the Age of Churchill and Attlee: The Headlam Diaries*, Cambridge University Press/Royal Historical Society, London, 1999, p. 222 (entry for 8 October 1940).

18. For an example of the paper's criticism of a Churchill speech, see 'Convention Backing Grows as Churchill Avoids Problems', *Daily Worker*, 20 December 1940.

19. Armstrong, *With Malice toward None*, p. 83 (entry for 12 October 1940).

20. 'Second Weekly Report for Home Intelligence', 11 October 1940, Mass Observation Archive.

21. 'Weekly Report by Home Intelligence, 7th to 14th October 1940', INF 1/292, TNA.

22. Speech of 9 October 1940.

23. See Richard Toye, '"I am a Liberal as much as a Tory": Winston Churchill and the Memory of 1906', *Journal of Liberal History*, 54 (Spring 2007), pp. 38–45.

24. Speech of 12 November 1940.

25. For examples of positive coverage, see 'America and Mr Churchill', *The Times*, 10 October 1940; Dorothy Thompson, 'On the Record', *Milwaukee Sentinel*, 16

October 1940; and Dewitt MacKenzie, 'Churchill's Speech Gives First Sign of Confidence', *Tuscaloosa News*, 22 October 1940.

26. Speech of 9 November 1940.
27. Speech of 5 November 1940.
28. Lord Halifax to WSC, 7 October 1940, Churchill Papers, CHAR 9/174C/308.
29. Speech of 8 October 1940.
30. 'Speech Prominent in Madrid Press', *The Times*, 10 October 1940.
31. Richard Wigg, *Churchill and Spain: The Survival of the Franco Regime, 1940–45*, Routledge, Abingdon, 2005.
32. Speech of 8 October 1940.
33. *Vancouver Sun*, 9 October 1940.
34. John Maffey to Lord Caldecote, 16 July 1940, DO 130/12, TNA.
35. 'Weekly Report by Home Intelligence—No. 6: 4th November to 11th November 1940', INF 1/292, TNA; Elizabeth Cameron [Bowen], 'Notes on Ireland', 21 July 1940, DO 35/1011/3, TNA. See also Edward Corse, 'British Propaganda in Neutral Eire after the Fall of France, 1940', *Contemporary British History*, 22 (2008), pp. 163–80.
36. Speech of 5 November 1940.
37. Joseph Walshe to Eamon De Valera, 13 November 1940, quoted in Brian Girvin, *The Emergency: Neutral Ireland, 1939–45*, Macmillan, London, 2006, p. 171.
38. Andrew Roberts, *Eminent Churchillians*, Phoenix, London, 1995 (first published 1994), pp. 189–90; Richard Toye, *Churchill's Empire: The World That Made Him and the World He Made*, Macmillan, London, 2010, p. 207.
39. For a review of the coverage, see 'Extracts from the British press following Mr Churchill's reference to the Irish Ports on 5 November 1940', National Archives of Ireland, DFA 2002/19/527.
40. Dáil Éireann debates, Vol. 81, 7 November 1940.
41. Elizabeth Cameron [Bowen], 'Notes on Ireland', 9 November 1940, DO 35/1011/3, TNA.
42. 'Dangerous Talk', *Irish Times*, 9 November 1940.
43. Report of 11 November 1940, in Heinz Boberach (ed.), *Meldungen aus dem Reich 1938–1945: Die geheimen Lageberichte des Sicherheitsdienstes der SS*, Vol. V, Pawlak Verlag Herrsching, Berlin, 1984, p. 1749.
44. Corse, 'British Propaganda', p. 168.
45. Broadcast of 30 September 1940.
46. A. B. Watt, 'Parleys with Vichy and Madrid', *Edmonton Journal*, 26 October 1940.
47. David Dilks (ed.), *The Diaries of Sir Alexander Cadogan O.M., 1938–1945*, Cassell, London, 1971, p. 332 (entry for 25 October 1940); Jean Lacouture, *De Gaulle: The Rebel, 1890–1944*, Harvill, London, 1993 (first published in English 1990), pp. 284–5.

48. J. H. Peck to Lord Hood, 19 October 1940, Churchill Papers, CHAR 9/176B/120–1.
49. John Colville, *The Fringes of Power: Downing Street Diaries, 1939–1955*, Hodder and Stoughton, London, 1985, p. 272 (entry for 21 October 1940).
50. In Churchill's English version, the equivalent of the last phrase was 'Hostile ears are listening'. The broadcast did not literally end with this. '"A Day with Churchill" by Michel Saint-Denis', broadcast on the BBC Home Service, 30 November 1959. Transcript in the Michel Saint-Denis Archive, MS Add. 81159.
51. '"A Day with Churchill" by Michel Saint-Denis'.
52. Broadcast of 21 October 1940. Oddly, the version in the *Complete Speeches* refers to Adolphe Thiers in place of Gambetta, to whom Churchill clearly refers in the recording.
53. DeWitt Mackenzie, 'Churchill's Speech Shows First Signs of Confidence', *Tuscaloosa News*, 22 October 1940. Mackenzie was a correspondent for the Associated Press; his columns were widely syndicated.
54. Michael Stenton, *Radio London and Resistance in Occupied Europe: British Political Warfare*, Oxford University Press, Oxford 2000, p. 144. See also Malcolm Anderson, 'The Myth of the "Two Hundred Families"', *Political Studies* 13 (1965), pp. 163–78.
55. 'Propaganda Research Papers 3A Week No. 60: Broadcasts in French during week 21st–27th October', 30 October 1940, Mark Abrams Papers, ABMS 1/2/1.
56. Kathleen Hill to WSC, 20 October 1940, Churchill Papers, CHAR 9/176B/116.
57. Draft of broadcast of 21 October 1940, Churchill Papers, CHAR 9/145/34.
58. '"A Day with Churchill" by Michel Saint-Denis'.
59. 'Propaganda Research Papers 3A Week No. 60: Broadcasts in French during week 21st–27th October', 30 October 1940, Mark Abrams Papers, ABMS 1/2/1.
60. Quoted in Martyn Cornick, '"Fraternity among Listeners". The BBC and French Resistance: Evidence from Refugees', in Hanna Diamond and Simon Kitson (eds.), *Vichy, Resistance, Liberation: New Perspectives on Wartime France*, Berg, Oxford, 2005, pp. 101–13, at 106.
61. Alfred Duff Cooper to WSC, 27 November 1940, Churchill Papers, CHAR 9/176B/130.
62. Examples can be found in the collection of Allied Airborne Leaflets and Magazines produced by the Political Warfare Executive which is to be found in the Cambridge University Library Official Publications Room, OP 110.25.04.
63. Jan Karski, *Story of a Secret State: My Report to the World*, Penguin, London, 2011 (first published 1944), p. 289.
64. 'Slovakian Jews Crowd Streets upon Hearing News of Allied Victories, Nazis Charge', *Jewish Telegraphic Agency*, 26 September 1943.

65. Ben Pimlott (ed.), *The Second World War Diary of Hugh Dalton, 1940–1945*, Jonathan Cape, London, 1986, pp. 127–8 (entry for 20 December 1940).

66. Speech of 19 December 1940.

67. Malcolm Muggeridge (ed.), *Ciano's Diary 1939–1943*, Heinemann, London, 1947, p. 320 (entry for 20 December 1940).

68. War Cabinet minutes, WM (40) 309th Conclusions, 23 December 1940, CAB/65/10/29, TNA.

69. Dilks, *Cadogan Diary*, p. 343 (entry for 23 December 1940).

70. Alexander Cadogan to private secretary, 10 Downing Street, 23 December 1940, Churchill Papers, CHAR 9/176B/209. The suggestions in this note were Halifax's.

71. A later reference to 'nineteenth-century Liberalism' was included in the speech as broadcast.

72. Halifax to WSC, 20 December 1940, covering speech draft, Churchill Papers, CHAR 9/176B/210–15.

73. Broadcast of 23 December 1940.

74. Cadogan to private secretary, 10 Downing Street, 23 December 1940, Churchill Papers, CHAR 9/176B/209.

75. Broadcast of 23 December 1940.

76. Broadcast of 23 December 1940.

77. Nigel Nicolson (ed.), *Harold Nicolson: Diaries and Letters, 1939–1945*, Collins, London, 1967, p. 131 (entry for 23 December 1940).

78. Broadcast of 23 December 1940.

79. See Oliver Harvey diary, 26 December 1940, Oliver Harvey Papers, MS Add. 56386.

80. 'A Broadcast to Italy', *The Times*, 24 December 1940.

81. 'Appeal to Italians', *Glasgow Herald*, 24 December 1940.

82. 'Huge American Audience', *The Times*, 24 December 1940; 'Appeal to Reason', *Sydney Morning Herald*, 25 December 1940.

83. 'Churchill: Cajoler', *St Petersburg Times*, 29 December 1940.

84. 'England to Italy', New York Times, 25 December 1940.

85. J. W. T. Mason, 'Today's War Moves', *Pittsburgh Press*, 24 December 1940.

86. E. A. Seal to WSC, 21 December 1940, Churchill Papers, CHAR 9/176B/208.

87. Lord Hood to John Colville, 26 December 1940, CHAR 9/176B/197.

88. 'Churchill Speech Printed in Italy in Abridged Form', *Milwaukee Journal*, 26 December 1940.

89. 'Il Duce Answers Churchill's Plea', *Lawrence Daily Journal-World*, 24 December 1940.

90. 'Propaganda Research Papers 3A Week No. 51-2/40: Broadcasts in French for the French Listener during the two weeks 16th–29th December 1940', 3 January 1941, Abrams Papers, ABMS 1/2/1.

91. 'Fascist Anger with Mr Churchill', *The Times*, 27 December 1940.

92. 'Fourth Weekly Report for Home Intelligence', 24 October 1940, Mass Observation Archive.

93. 'Report on the War in December Diaries', February 1941, Mass Observation Archive.

94. J. Lippold diary, 23 December 1940 (5132), Mass Observation Archive. See also Vere Hodgson, *Few Eggs and No Oranges: A Diary*, Dennis Dobson, London, 1976, p. 93 (entry for 23 December 1940), and Helen D. Millgate (ed.), *Mr Brown's War: A Diary of the Second World War*, Sutton Publishing, Stroud, 2003 (first published 1998), p. 81 (entry for 23 December 1940).

95. C. H. Miller diary, entry covering 21–5 December 1940 (5367), Mass Observation Archive.

96. E. Oakley diary, 23 and 24 December 1940 (5390), Mass Observation Archive.

97. J. H. Millington, letter to Mass Observation, 28 December 1940 (5135), Mass Observation Archive.

98. WSC, *The Second World War*, Vol. II: *Their Finest Hour*, Cassell & Co., London, 1949, pp. 550–1.

99. E. A. Seal to WSC, 16 January 1941, PREM 4/70/2, TNA.

100. Report of 6 March 1941, in Boberach, *Meldungen aus dem Reich*, Vol. V, p. 2093.

101. Desmond Flower to Kathleen Hill, 21 May 1940, Churchill Papers, CHAR 8/803/173.

102. Brendan Bracken to Kathleen Hill, 15 July 1940, Churchill Papers, CHAR 8/803/166.

103. G. P. Putnam's to WSC, 4 September 1940, Churchill Papers, CHAR 8/803/165.

104. Frederick Woods, *Artillery of Words: The Writings of Sir Winston Churchill*, Leo Cooper, London, 1992, p. 72.

105. Bracken to Hill, 15 July 1940, Churchill Papers, CHAR 8/803/166.

106. Hill to Bracken, 12 February 1941, Churchill Papers CHAR 8/803/109.

107. Charles Eade (ed.), *The Unrelenting Struggle: War Speeches by the Right Hon. Winston S. Churchill*, Cassell & Co., London, 1942.

108. WSC, *Into Battle*, Cassell & Co., London, 1941, p. viii; WSC, *Blood, Sweat, and Tears*, Putnam's, New York, 1941, p. x.

109. The post-1941 volumes were edited by Charles Eade, editor of *The Sunday Dispatch*, Randolph having joined the army.

110. The post-war volume of *Secret Session Speeches* (1946) sold nearly 60,000 copies. For sales figures and details of translations, see Woods, *Artillery of Words*, pp. 72–3.

111. At least in the case of *Into Battle*: see Kathleen Hill to WSC, 16 February 1941, Churchill Papers, CHAR 8/803/106.

112. See, for example, 'Expressions of Opinion in the Swedish Press Regarding Churchill's Speeches', Churchill Papers, CHAR 8/803/291–322.

113. See the correspondence in the Emil Oprecht Papers, MS Oprecht 11.30, 13.3, and 14.12.
114. A. S. Hodge to F. D. W. Brown, 20 May 1942, Churchill Papers, CHAR 8/803/210–11. Churchill sent a letter of thanks to Oprecht for his efforts; WSC to Emil Oprecht, 25 May 1942, Oprecht Papers, MS Oprecht 3.25.
115. For Churchill's fears that criticisms of the production effort would 'do us very great harm in America', see Charles Eade diary, 24 July 1941, Charles Eade Papers, EADE 2/1.
116. Colville, *Fringes of Power*, p. 333 (entry for 11 January 1941).
117. Speech of 17 January 1941; 'Invasion Harder Now: We Stand Four-Square', *News Chronicle*, 18 January 1941.
118. Speech of 22 January 1941; Ball, *Parliament and Politics*, p. 238 (entry for 22 January 1941).
119. Colville, *Fringes of Power*, p. 355 (entry for 9 February 1941).
120. David Stafford, *Churchill and Secret Service*, Abacus, London, 2000 (first published 1997), pp. 232–3.
121. 'Nazis Say US Being Deceived by Churchill', *Kentucky New Era*, 10 February 1941; 'Germans Say Churchill Speech Pessimistic', *Lewiston Morning Tribune*, 11 February 1941; 'Propaganda Research Papers 3A Week No. 7/41: Broadcasts in French for the French Listener for the week 10th–16th February', 19 February 1941, Abrams Papers, ABMS 1/2/1; 'War Cabinet: Report on Foreign Broadcasts 01.00 Monday, 10th February, to 01.00 Tuesday 11th February 1941', Churchill Papers CHAR 9/181A/88; Fred Taylor (ed.), *The Goebbels Diaries 1939–1941*, Sphere Books, London, 1983 (first published 1982), p. 229 (entry for 11 February 1941).
122. Broadcast of 9 February 1941.
123. Broadcast of 9 February 1941.
124. James Leutze (ed.), *The London Observer: The Journal of General Raymond E. Lee 1940–1941*, Hutchinson, London, 1971, p. 258 (entry for 27 April 1941).
125. See James Lansdale Hodson, *And Yet I Like America*, Victor Gollancz, London, 1945 (entry for 7 June 1944).
126. Eade diary, 6 March 1941, Eade Papers, EADE 2/1. The visitor in question was J. B. Conant, President of Harvard University.
127. 'Churchill Talk Was Aimed at Senate—Clark', *Chicago Daily Tribune*, 11 February 1941.
128. *Milwaukee Journal*, 10 February 1941; *Los Angeles Times*, 10 February 1941.
129. 'Mr Churchill's Speech', *The Times*, 11 February 1941.
130. 'Senator Wheeler Has Another Idea', *Windsor Daily Star*, 10 February 1941.
131. 'Mr Churchill and His Cause', *Chicago Daily Tribune*, 11 February 1941.
132. 'The War in MO Diaries: February 12–28th '41', 3 March 1941, Mass Observation Archive.
133. M. Davis diary, 9 February 1941 (5295), Mass Observation Archive.
134. Hodgson, *Few Eggs*, p. 115 (entry for 11 February 1941).

135. Pamela Slater diary, 9 February 1941 (5425), Mass Observation Archive.

136. M. J. Hill diary, 9 February 1941 (5333), Mass Observation Archive.

137. Tom Harrisson, 'Morale in 1941', File Report 568, Mass Observation Archive. This is dated '4.2.41', which is clearly an error (likely for 14 February), as the report discusses Churchill's speech in the second week of February. Harrisson's covering letter, to Mary Adams of MoI, is dated 15 February. Emphasis in original.

138. 'Weekly Report by Home Intelligence—No. 19: 5th to 12th February 1941', INF 1/292, TNA.

139. A. W. Martin and Patsy Hardy (eds.), *Dark and Hurrying Days: Menzies' 1941 Diary*, National Library of Australia, Canberra, 1993, p. 50 (entry for 9 February 1941).

140. Rhodes James, *'Chips'*, p. 299 (entry for 9 April 1941).

141. Ball, *Parliament and Politics*, pp. 247–8 (entry 10 April 1941).

142. 'Note on Morale', File Report 677, 14 April 1941, Mass Observation Archive.

143. Speech of 9 April 1941; Larry Rue, 'Churchill Talk Seen as Appeal for US Convoys', *Chicago Daily Tribune*, 10 April 1941.

144. W. I. Mallet to John Colville, 25 April 1941, Churchill Papers, CHAR 9/181B/133.

145. 'Notes by Mr Harriman', n.d. but c.25–7 April 1941, Churchill Papers, CHAR 9/181B/209–11.

146. Broadcast of 27 April 1941.

147. Associated Press, 'Churchill Speech Arouses Interest', *Lawrence Journal-World*, 28 April 1941.

148. Mollie Panter-Downes, *London War Notes 1939–1945* (ed. William Shawn), Longman, London, 1972, p. 146 (entry for 4 May 1941).

149. E. A. Stebbing diary, 27 April 1941 (5205), Mass Observation Archive.

150. 'Note on Churchill's Speech', File report 676, 28 April 1941, Mass Observation Archive. Emphasis in original.

151. Nigel West (ed.), *The Guy Liddell Diaries*, Vol. I: *1939–1942: MI5's Director of Counter-Espionage in World War II*, Routledge, London, 2005, p. 145 (entry for 6 May 1941).

152. Martin and Hardy, *Dark and Hurrying Days*, p. 119 (entry for 26 April 1941).

153. Parliamentary Debates, House of Commons, 5th Series, Vol. 371, 7 May 1941, col. 880.

154. Rhodes James, *'Chips'*, p. 303 (entry for 7 May 1941).

155. Speech of 7 May 1941.

156. Pimlott, *Second World War Diary*, p. 199 (entry for 7 May 1941).

157. Earl Winterton diary, 7 May 1941, in Earl Winterton, *Orders of the Day*, Cassell & Co., London, 1953, p. 271.

158. Ball, *Parliament and Politics*, p. 251 (entry for 7 May 1941).

159. Speech of 7 May 1941.

160. John Martin, note of 19 May 1941, Churchill Papers, CHAR 9/178B/112.

161. The uncorrected version of Churchill's speech was accidentally put out over the news-ticker. By comparing this text with the speech as given, we can deduce that Winant's suggestions resulted in the passage on American help. Theodore C. Achilles to John Martin, 9 May 1941, Churchill Papers, CHAR 9/178B/113—14.

162. Speech of 7 May 1941.

163. Taylor, *Goebbels Diaries*, p. 355 (entry for 9 May 1941).

164. P.J. Grigg to F.A. Grigg, 9 May 1941, P.J. Grigg Papers, PJGG 9/6/13.

165. James Landale Hodson, *Before Daybreak*, Victor Gollancz, London, 1941, p. 55 (entry for 8 May 1941).

166. Earl Winterton diary, 27 May 1941, Earl Winterton Papers, 46.

167. 'Impressions of Parliament', *Punch*, 18 June 1941.

168. Winterton, *Orders*, p. 271.

169. Pimlott, *Second World War Diary*, p. 222 (entry for 10 June 1941).

170. Speech of 10 June 1941.

171. E.A. Stebbing diary, 11 June 1941 (5205), Mass Observation Archive. Emphasis in original.

172. Draft of speech of 10 June 1941, Churchill Papers, CHAR 9/178B/180.

173. Churchill Papers, CHAR 9/178C/312. It is not clear who the author of this note was.

174. See 'Crete Atrocities Alleged', *Sydney Morning Herald*, 7 June 1941.

175. 'Second Weekly Report (New Series)', 16 June 1941, Mass Observation Archive; Armstrong, *With Malice toward None*, p. 134 (entry for 15 July 1941).

176. R. J. Minney, *The Private Papers of Hore-Belisha*, Collins, London, 1960, pp. 294—5.

177. Draft of speech of 10 June 1941, Churchill Papers, CHAR 9/178B/169.

178. Speech of 10 June 1941.

179. 'Second Weekly Report (New Series)', File Report 738, File Report 738, 16 June 1941, Mass Observation Archive.

CHAPTER 4

1. It was said that Churchill had told journalists, 'You've no need to worry. Hitler will be fighting Russia before the end of the month'. ('Second Weekly Report (New Series)', File Report 738, 16 June 1941, Mass Observation Archive.) He had indeed spoken to a group of editors, and had told them that 'Germany is now concentrating very large forces on the Russian borders', but had suggested that Stalin might make concessions rather than fight. W. P. Crozier, *Off the Record: Political Interviews 1933—1943* (ed. A. J. P. Taylor), Hutchinson, London, 1973, pp. 226—7 (entry for June 1941).

2. John Colville, *The Fringes of Power: Downing Street Diaries, 1939—1955*, Hodder and Stoughton, London, 1985, p. 404 (entry for 21 June 1941). In a later recollection Colville added the words 'in the House of Commons': untitled chapter

by John Colville in John Wheeler-Bennett (ed.), *Action This Day: Working with Churchill*, Macmillan, London, 1968, pp. 47–138, at 89.

3. Clare Sheridan to WSC, 22 June 1941, Churchill Papers, CHAR 9/182B/142.
4. Alison Selford interview, 2005, IWM oral history 28637.
5. 'Nazi-Red Menace Gives Britain Biggest Break of War', *Pittsburgh Press*, 23 June 1941.
6. H. Knatchbull-Hugessen to Foreign Office, 22 and 23 June 1941, FO 954/28, TNA.
7. Lord Beaverbrook and David Farrer, 'The Second Front', in A. J. P. Taylor, *Beaverbrook*, Hamish Hamilton, London, 1972, p. 475. According to Taylor, this document was written 'shortly after the end of the war'.
8. Colville in Wheeler-Bennett (ed.), *Action This Day*, p. 89; Colville, *Fringes of Power*, p. 405 (entry for 22 June 1941).
9. David Dilks (ed.), *The Diaries of Sir Alexander Cadogan O.M., 1938–1945*, Cassell & Co., London, 1971, p. 389 (entry for 22 June 1941).
10. Colville, *Fringes of Power*, pp. 405–6 (entry for 22 June 1941).
11. 'Sir Stafford Cripps' notes', n.d. but 22 June 1941, Churchill Papers, CHAR 9/151/130–7.
12. Colville, *Fringes of Power*, p. 405 (entry for 22 June 1941).
13. Broadcast of 22 June 1941.
14. Frank R. Kent, 'The Great Game of Politics', *Toledo Blade*, 24 June 1941; 'UK Policy Given', *Montreal Gazette*, 23 June 1941.
15. Broadcast of 22 June 1941.
16. Broadcast of 22 June 1941.
17. J. M. Martin to Viscount Hood, 15 July 1941, PREM 4/70/2, TNA.
18. Broadcast of 22 June 1941.
19. Broadcast of 22 June 1941.
20. Broadcast of 22 June 1941.
21. Gabriel Gorodetsky (ed.), *Stafford Cripps in Moscow 1940–1942: Diaries and Papers*, Vallentine Mitchell, Edgware, 2007, p. 114.
22. David Carlton, *Churchill and the Soviet Union*, Manchester University Press, Manchester, 2000, pp. 88–9.
23. Broadcast of 22 June 1941.
24. Norman and Jeanne Mackenzie (eds.), *The Diary of Beatrice Webb*, Vol. IV: *1924–1943: 'The Wheel of Life'*, Virago, London, 1985, pp. 470–1 (entry for 23 June 1941).
25. George Orwell, *Diaries* (ed. Peter Davison), Harvill Secker, London, 2009, p. 315 (entry for 23 June 1941).
26. 'Germany vs. Russia, a Dream Come True', *Tuscaloosa News*, 23 June 1941.
27. 'But—Says Boake Carter', *Palm Beach Post*, 27 June 1941.
28. The words were those of Assistant Secretary of State Sumner Welles: 'US and Russian Conflict', *The Times*, 24 June 1941.
29. 'Moscow Reports "Bulk of Nazis Hurled Back"', *Vancouver Sun*, 23 June 1941.

30. 'Prime Minister's Broadcast', *The Times*, 24 June 1941.
31. Geoffrey Hosking, 'The Second World War and Russian National Conscious-ness', *Past & Present* 175 (2002), pp. 162–87.
32. 'Stalin's Call to Arms', *The Times*, 4 July 1941.
33. Robert Rhodes James, *Victor Cazalet: A Portrait*, Hamish Hamilton, London, 1976, pp. 261–3.
34. John Colville to WSC, 22 August 1941, Churchill Papers, CHAR 9/182B/250–2.
35. Broadcast of 24 August 1941.
36. Nicholas Tamkin, *Britain, Turkey and the Soviet Union, 1940–45: Strategy, Diplomacy and Intelligence in the Eastern Mediterranean*, Palgrave, Basingstoke, 2009, p. 30.
37. War Cabinet minutes, 30 June 1941, WM (41) 64th Conclusions, CAB/65/18/43, TNA.
38. Tamkin, *Britain, Turkey and the Soviet Union*, p. 108.
39. H. Knatchbull-Hugessen to Foreign Office, 2 July 1941, FO 954/28, TNA.
40. Tamkin, *Britain, Turkey and the Soviet Union*, chapter 5.
41. Fred Taylor (ed.), *The Goebbels Diaries 1939–1941*, Sphere Books, London, 1983 (first published 1982), p. 427 (entry for 24 June 1941).
42. 'Churchill Sprach', *Kladderadatsch*, 13 July 1941.
43. Winston Churchill, *Mein Bundesgenosse*, Nibelungen-Verlag, Berlin, 1942, p. 102; Broadcast of 20 January 1940.
44. Martin Gilbert, *Finest Hour: Winston Churchill 1939–1941*, Heinemann, London, 1983, p. 1137; Carlton, *Churchill and the Soviet Union*, p. 87.
45. Malcolm Muggeridge (ed.), *Ciano's Diary 1939–1943*, Heinemann, London, 1947, p. 363 (entry for 23 June 1941).
46. 'Third Weekly Report (New Series)', File Report 753, 23 June 1941, Mass Observation Archive.
47. 'Home Intelligence Weekly Report No. 38', 18–25 June 1941, INF 1/292, TNA.
48. 'Home Intelligence Weekly Report No. 39', 25 June–2 July 1941, INF 1/292, TNA.
49. 'Third Weekly Report (New Series)', File Report 753, 23 June 1941, Mass Observation Archive.
50. M. A. Pratt diary, 22 June 1941 (5402), Mass Observation Archive.
51. James Leutze (ed.), *The London Observer: The Journal of General Raymond E. Lee 1940–1941*, Hutchinson, London, 1971, p. 444 (entry for 5 November 1941).
52. War Cabinet minutes, WM (41) 62nd Conclusions, 23 June 1941, CAB 65/18/41, TNA.
53. Andrew Thorpe, *Parties at War: Political Organization in Second World War Britain*, Oxford University Press, Oxford, 2009, p. 39.
54. 'Today in Britain', *Vancouver Sun*, 30 June 1941. Gallacher's quotation of Churchill's speech of 14 April 1937 was basically accurate.

55. Internal CPGB documents quoted in Herbert Morrison, 'Communist Party Policy', WP (41) 169, 18 July 1941, CAB 66/17/42, TNA.

56. Paul Addison, *The Road to 1945*, Jonathan Cape, London, 1975, pp. 134–41.

57. War Cabinet minutes, WM (41) 62nd Conclusions, 23 June 1941, CAB 65/18/41, TNA.

58. WSC, *The Second World War*, Vol. II: *The Grand Alliance*, Cassell & Co., London, 1950, p. 133; 'Home Intelligence Weekly Report No. 38', 18–25 June 1941, INF 1/292, TNA.

59. John Martin to WSC, 8 July 1941, Churchill Papers, CHAR 9/182B/152–3.

60. R. W. Fenn diary, 14 July 1941 (5065), Mass Observation Archive.

61. Minutes of National Council, 19/20 July 1941, Peace Pledge Union Archive, London; Minutes of Executive Committee, 17 July 1941, National Peace Council Papers, NPC 2/6, London School of Economics. I am grateful to Richard Overy for these references.

62. Mark Connelly, 'The British Debate', in Igor Primoratz (ed.), *Terror from the Sky: The Bombing of German Cities in World War II*, Berghahn Books, Oxford, 2010, pp. 181–202.

63. 'Production Again', *Manchester Guardian*, 22 July 1941.

64. David Edgerton, *Britain's War Machine: Weapons, Resources and Experts in the Second World War*, Allen Lane, London, 2011, chapter 5; Richard Overy, *Why the Allies Won*, Jonathan Cape, London, 1995, pp. 198–9.

65. Edward Bridges, 'Speech on Production: Covering Note', n.d. but July 1941, PREM 4/85/1, TNA.

66. See H. Henderson Stewart to WSC, 22 July 1941, and Stewart's accompanying report, PREM 4/85/1, TNA.

67. Colville, *Fringes of Power*, p. 421 (entry for 28 July 1941).

68. Speech of 29 July 1941. The Supply Departments were: the Controller's Department of the Admiralty; the Ministry of Supply; and the Ministry of Aircraft Production.

69. Speech of 29 July 1941.

70. 'Page 70', 29 July 1941, PREM 4/85/1, TNA.

71. Speech of 29 July 1941.

72. 'Home Intelligence Weekly Report No. 44', 31 July–6 August 1941, INF 1/292, TNA.

73. Robert Rhodes James (ed.), *'Chips': The Diaries of Sir Henry Channon*, Weidenfeld and Nicolson, London, 1993 (first published 1967), p. 310 (entry for 29 July 1941). See also Stuart Ball (ed.), *Parliament and Politics in the Age of Churchill and Attlee: The Headlam Diaries*, Cambridge University Press/Royal Historical Society, London, 1999, p. 266 (entry for 29 July 1941).

74. Cazalet's diary entry for 29 July 1941, quoted in Rhodes James, *Victor Cazalet*, p. 263. See also John Harvey (ed.), *The War Diaries of Oliver Harvey 1941–1945*, Collins, London, 1978, p. 26 (entry for 3 August 1941), and William Armstrong

(ed.), *With Malice Toward None: A War Diary by Cecil H. King*, Sidgwick and Jackson, London, 1970, p. 137 (entry for 30 July 1941).

75. 'Impressions of Parliament', *Punch*, 6 August 1941.

76. Elizabeth Nel, *Mr Churchill's Secretary*, Hodder and Stoughton, London, 1958, pp. 29, 36—8.

77. Speech of 29 July 1941.

78. Jon Meacham, *Franklin and Winston: A Portrait of a Friendship*, Granta Books, London, 2005 (first published 2004), pp. 104—5.

79. Reprinted in 'Declaration by United Nations', Cmd. 6388, London, 1942.

80. Sonya O. Rose, *Which People's War? National Identity and Citizenship in Wartime Britain 1939—1945*, Oxford University Press, Oxford, 2003, pp. 62—3. In his speech of 9 September 1941, however, Churchill claimed that 'a Joint Declaration by Great Britain and the United States is a process of a totally different nature' from a statement of peace or war aims.

81. 'Home Intelligence Weekly Report No. 46', 13—20 August 1941, INF 1/292, TNA; 'Mr Attlee's Broadcast', *The Times*, 15 August 1941.

82. 'Eleventh Weekly Report (New Series)', File Report 832, 18 August 1941, Mass Observation Archive.

83. 'Home Intelligence Weekly Report No. 48', 27 August—3 September 1941, INF 1/292, TNA. For the speech's reception, see also 'Thirteenth Weekly Report (New Series)', File Report 855, 1 September 1941, Mass Observation Archive.

84. Andrew Schvil diary, 24 August 1941 (5192), Mass Observation Archive.

85. Anonymous diary, 24 August 1941 (5290), Mass Observation Archive.

86. 'What of Russia?', *Daily Mirror*, 25 August 1941.

87. Harvey, *War Diaries*, p. 36 (entry for 25 August 1941). Emphasis in original. This remark seems to have reflected Eden's concerns. See T. L. Rowan to WSC, 24 August 1941, Churchill Papers CHAR 9/182B/281.

88. Gorodetsky, *Stafford Cripps in Moscow*, p. 146 (entry for 25 August 1941).

89. 'Home Intelligence Weekly Report No. 48', 20—27 August 1941, INF 1/292, TNA.

90. *Daily Herald*, 25 August 1941.

91. Broadcast of 24 August 1941; 'Churchill Sees Britain and America as "Armed Police" to Enforce World Peace', *Painsville Telegraph*, 25 August 1941. The fact of the negotiations had not previously been publicly known.

92. 'Japanese Claim Churchill Lies of Peace Moves', *Palm Beach Post*, 26 August 1941.

93. 'Says Japan to Carry on Task', *Windsor Daily Star*, 26 August 1941.

94. 'Churchill's Slap at Japan Hailed by Administration', *Pittsburgh Press*, 25 August 1941.

95. 'Mr Churchill Tells Us', *Chicago Daily Tribune*, 26 August 1941.

96. Broadcast of 24 August 1941.

97. Chaim Weizmann to Lord Moyne, 26 August 1941 (copy), Churchill Papers, CHAR 9/182B/239. See also Harvey, *War Diaries*, p. 37 (entry for 28 August 1941).

98. Nicholas Terry, 'Conflicting Signals: British Intelligence on the "Final Solution" through Radio Intercepts and other Sources, 1941–1942', *Yad Vashem Studies* 32 (2004), pp. 351–96.

99. Speech of 10 November 1941.

100. Report of 28 August 1941, in Heinz Boberach (ed.), *Meldungen aus dem Reich 1938–1945: Die geheimen Lageberichte des Sicherheitsdienstes der SS*, Vol. VIII, Pawlak Verlag Herrsching, Berlin, 1984, p. 2698.

101. 'Churchill's broadcast', *Indian Express*, 26 August 1941.

102. M. A. Pratt diary, 24 August 1941 (5402), Mass Observation Archive.

103. War Cabinet minutes, WM (41) 89th, 4 September 1941, CAB 65/19/25, TNA.

104. J. G. Winant to Cordell Hull, 4 November 1941, *Foreign Relations of the United States: Diplomatic Papers 1941*, Vol. III: *The British Commonwealth / The Near East and Africa*, United States Government Printing Office, Washington, DC, pp. 181–4.

105. Speech of 9 September 1941.

106. Wm. Roger Louis, *Imperialism at Bay: The United States and the Decolonization of the British Empire, 1941–1945*, Oxford University Press, Oxford, 1977, p. 132, quoting a minute by Macmillan of 1 September 1942.

107. Pamela Slater diary, 9 September 1941 (5425), Mass Observation Archive.

108. M. S. Venkataramani and B. K. Shrivastava, *Roosevelt, Gandhi, Churchill: America and the Last Phase of India's Freedom Struggle*, Sangam Books, London, 1997 (first published 1983), p. 23.

109. Nigel Nicolson (ed.), *Harold Nicolson: Diaries and Letters, 1939–1945*, Collins, London 1967, p. 185 (entry for 9 September 1941).

110. Speech of 9 September 1941.

111. Nicolson, *Diaries 1939–1945*, p. 185 (entry for 9 September 1941).

112. Ball (ed.), *Parliament and Politics*, p. 274 (entry for 30 September 1941).

113. D. Argent diary, 17 October 1941 (5010), Mass Observation Archive.

114. 'First Weekly Digest (Third Series)', File Report 899, 6 October 1941, Mass Observation Archive.

115. 'Hitler and Russia', *The Times*, 4 October 1941.

116. Speech of 12 November 1941.

117. Kevin Jefferys (ed.), *Labour and the Wartime Coalition: From the Diary of James Chuter Ede 1941–1945*, The Historians' Press, London, 1987, p. 23 (entry for 12 November 1941).

118. Speech of 29 October 1941. Emphasis in original. Churchill had made a previous wartime visit to the school, on 18 December 1940.

119. Harvey, *War Diaries*, p. 60 (entry for 4 November 1941); Dilks, *Cadogan Diaries*, pp. 410–11 (entry for 5 November 1941).

120. FDR to WSC, 7 November 1941, in Warren F. Kimball (ed.), *Churchill & Roosevelt: The Complete Correspondence I: Alliance Emerging October 1933–November 1942*, Princeton University Press, Princeton, 1984, p. 267.

121. Speech of 10 November 1941; and the draft of the same speech in the Churchill Papers, CHAR 9/152B/166. Churchill also deleted a sentence suggesting that Hirohito's life might be at risk if he opposed war: 'But in a country where statesmen are assassinated by young army officers if they are thought to be lacking in aggressive spirit, no one can tell what folly may be committed'.

122. L. N. Adamson diary, 10 November 1941 (5004), Mass Observation Archive.

123. 'Home Intelligence Report No. 59', 19 November 1941, INF 1/292, TNA.

124. 'Final Warning', *Singapore Free Press*, 11 November 1941.

125. 'Tokyo's Answer to Churchill', *Sydney Morning Herald*, 12 November 1941.

126. 'Japanese Silent about Churchill Warning on War', *Spartanburg Herald*, 12 November 1941.

127. L. N. Adamson diary, 10 November 1941 (5004), Mass Observation Archive.

128. WSC, *Grand Alliance*, p. 540.

129. War Cabinet minutes, 8 December 1941, WM (41) 125th Conclusions, CAB/65/20/18, TNA.

130. J. H. Peck, 'Timing of British Declaration of War on Japan', 8 December 1941, Churchill Papers, CHAR 9/149B/121.

131. Speech of 8 December 1941.

132. Andrew Schvil diary, 8 December 1941 (5192), Mass Observation Archive.

133. Phyllis Lewis diary, 8 December 1941 (5360), Mass Observation Archive.

134. C. R. Woodward diary, 8 December 1941 (5235), Mass Observation Archive.

135. Robert J. Nichols diary, 8 December 1941 (5163), Mass Observation Archive.

136. 'Report by Parliamentary Private Secretary', 12 December 1941, with WSC's marginal comments, George Harvie-Watt Papers, HARV 1.

137. 'Mr Churchill's White House Audience of 30,000', *Manchester Guardian*, 27 December 1941.

138. Recollections of Garrison Norton, quoted in Martin Gilbert, *Road to Victory: Winston S. Churchill 1941–1945*, Heinemann, London, 1986, p. 29.

139. Lord Moran, *Churchill at War 1940–45*, Robinson, London, 2002, p. 15 (entry for 26 December 1941).

140. WSC, *Grand Alliance*, p. 595.

141. WSC, *Grand Alliance*, p. 595.

142. Speech of 26 December 1941.

143. Moran, *Churchill at War*, p. 15 (entry for 26 December 1941).

144. Speech of 26 December 1941.

145. Moran, *Churchill at War*, p. 16 (entry for 26 December 1941).

146. David E. Lilienthal, *The Journals of David E. Lilienthal*, Vol. I: *The TVA Years 1939–1945*, Harper and Row, New York, 1964, p. 419 (entry for 26 December 1941).

147. *Washington Post*, 27 December 1941, quoted in Meacham, *Franklin and Winston*, p. 154.

148. Weekly Political Summary, 30 December 1941, in H. G. Nicholas (ed.), *Washington Despatches 1941–1945: Weekly Political Reports from the British Embassy*, University of Chicago Press, Chicago, 1981, p. 9.

149. WSC, *Grand Alliance*, p. 596.

150. 'Home Intelligence Weekly Report No. 65', 31 December 1941, INF 1/292, TNA.

151. Edith Dawson diary, 26 December 1941 (5296), Mass Observation Archive.

152. R. M. Dhonau diary, 27 December 1941 (5301), Mass Observation Archive.

153. M. A. Pratt diary, 26 December 1941 (5402), Mass Observation Archive.

154. Moran, *Churchill at War*, pp. 17–20 (entries for 27–9 December 1941).

155. Mackenzie King diary, 30 December 1941.

156. Speech of 30 December 1941.

157. Draft of speech of 30 December 1941, Churchill Papers, CHAR 9/153/94.

158. Speech of 30 December 1941.

159. Moran, *Churchill at War*, p. 20 (entry for 31 December 1941).

160. Elisabeth Barker, *Churchill and Eden at War*, Macmillan, London, 1978, pp. 50–1.

161. Speech of 30 December 1941.

162. Royal Institute for International Affairs, *Review of the Foreign Press*, Series A, No. 118, 5 January 1942.

163. Charles De Gaulle to WSC, 31 December 1941, PREM 3/120/10A, TNA.

164. François Kersaudy, *Churchill and De Gaulle*, Collins, London, 1981, p. 175.

165. 'Home Intelligence Weekly Report No. 65', 31 December 1941, INF 1/292, TNA.

166. J. Frewin diary, 30 December 1941 (5072), Mass Observation Archive.

167. R. M. Dhonau diary, 30 December 1941 (5402), Mass Observation Archive.

168. L. N. Adamson diary, 30 December 1941 (5004), Mass Observation Archive.

169. C. R. Woodward diary, 30 December 1941 (5235), Mass Observation Archive.

170. This was a comment that came specifically from the Southern Region, but it was echoed by four other regional reports and by information from postal censorship. 'Home Intelligence Report No. 66', 7 January 1942, INF 1/292, TNA.

CHAPTER 5

1. F. B. Chubb diary, 26 December 1941 (5039.5), Mass Observation Archive. It was not literally true that Britain had no planes in Malaya; Churchill had spoken of a shortage, not a complete absence.

2. Press conference at Government House, Ottawa, 31 December 1941, in David Dilks (ed.), *The Great Dominion: Winston Churchill in Canada, 1900–1954*, Thomas Allen, Toronto, 2005, p. 221.

3. Winston S. Churchill, *The Second World War*, Vol. IV: *The Hinge of Fate*, Cassell & Co., London, 1951, p. 81.

4. See, in particular, Raymond Callahan, 'Churchill and Singapore', in Brian Farrell and Sandy Hunter (eds.), *Sixty Years On: The Fall of Singapore Revisited*, Eastern Universities Press, Singapore, 2002, pp. 156–72; Christopher Bell, 'The "Singapore Strategy" and the Deterrence of Japan: Winston Churchill, the

Admiralty, and the Dispatch of Force Z', *English Historical Review*, 116 (2001), pp. 604–34; Christopher Bell, 'Winston Churchill, Pacific Security, and the Limits of British Power, 1921–41', in John H. Maurer (ed.), *Churchill and Strategic Dilemmas before the World Wars*, Frank Cass, London, 2003, pp. 51–87; and David Reynolds, *In Command of History: Churchill Fighting and Writing the Second World War*, Allen Lane, London, 2004, pp. 294–8.

5. 'The Manoeuvres at Singapore', *The Times*, 5 February 1937; David Reynolds, *In Command of History*, p. 115; Richard Toye, 'An Imperial Defeat? The Presentation and Reception of the Fall of Singapore', in Brian Farrell (ed.), *Churchill and the Lion City: Shaping Modern Singapore*, National University of Singapore Press, Singapore, 2011, pp. 108–22.

6. Hamilton quoted in Herbert Russell, '"Vulnerability" Again', *United Services Review*, 23 December 1937, copy in Ian Hamilton Papers 17/88; 'Greater East Asia', *The Times*, 1 April 1941.

7. For a contemporary assessment of the political and press stereotypes surrounding Japan, see 'The Campaign in the Far East', File Report 1090, 12 February 1942, Mass Observation Archive.

8. The segment, entitled 'News from Singapore', was released on 15 January 1942. It is available at <http://www.britishpathe.com>.

9. Lord Moran, *Winston Churchill: The Struggle for Survival 1940–1965*, Sphere Books, London, 1968 (first published 1966), p. 43.

10. Speech of 27 January 1942.

11. Nigel Nicolson (ed.), *Harold Nicolson: Diaries and Letters, 1939–1945*, Collins, London 1967, p. 207 (entry for 27 January 1942).

12. Stuart Ball (ed.), *Parliament and Politics in the Age of Churchill and Attlee: The Headlam Diaries*, Cambridge University Press/Royal Historical Society, London, 1999, p. 290 (entry for 27 January 1942).

13. Speech of 29 January 1942.

14. WSC, *Hinge of Fate*, p. 62.

15. Lord Harmsworth diary, 29 January 1942, Cecil Harmsworth Papers.

16. D. Hurley diary, 29 January 1942 (5116), Mass Observation Archive.

17. M. Collins diary, 27 January 1942 (5282), M. J. Hill diary, 27 January 1942 (5333), Mass Observation Archive.

18. 'Home Intelligence Weekly Report No. 69', 28 January 1942, INF 1/292, TNA.

19. 'Home Intelligence Weekly Report No. 70', 4 February 1942, INF 1/292, TNA.

20. Cripps broadcast of 8 February 1942, quoted in Peter Clarke, *The Cripps Version: The Life of Sir Stafford Cripps*, Allen Lane, London, 2002, pp. 264–5.

21. C. R. Woodward diary, 8 February 1942 (5235), Mass Observation Archive.

22. R. W. Fenn diary, 9 February 1942 (5065), Mass Observation Archive.

23. Mark Pottle (ed.), *Champion Redoubtable: The Diaries and Letters of Violet Bonham Carter, 1914–1945*, Weidenfeld and Nicolson, London, 1998, p. 235 (entry for 11 February 1942).

24. F. E. Smith diary, 8 February 1942 (5203), Mass Observation Archive.

25. 'Summary Report on Prestige of Government Leaders', 16 April 1942, Mass Observation Archive.

26. Mollie Panter-Downes, *London War Notes 1939–1945* (ed. William Shawn), Longman, London, 1972, p. 205 (entry for 14 February 1942).

27. Helen D. Millgate (ed.), *Mr. Brown's War: A Diary of the Second World War*, Sutton Publishing, Stroud, 2003 (first published 1998), p. 149 (entry for 15 February 1942).

28. Broadcast of 15 February 1942.

29. John Barnes and David Nicholson (eds.), *The Empire at Bay: The Leo Amery Diaries, 1929–1945* Hutchinson, London, 1988, p. 774 (entry for 16 February 1942).

30. Barnes and Nicholson, *Empire at Bay*, p. 773 (entry for 15 February 1942).

31. Nicolson, *Diaries 1939–45*, pp. 211–12 (entries for 15 and 16 February 1942).

32. William Barkley, 'They'll Blame Churchill for the Weather Next', *Daily Express*, 17 February 1942.

33. Quoted in 'Churchill Assures British Allies are Capable of Squaring All Accounts', *Evening Independent* (St Petersburg, Florida), 16 February 1942.

34. Millgate, *Mr. Brown's War*, p. 149 (entry for 15 February 1942).

35. Dorothy Medd diary, 15 February 1942 (5372), M. Collins diary 16 February 1942 (5282), Andrew Schvil diary, 15 February 1942 (5192), Mass Observation Archive.

36. R. W. Fenn diary, 16 February 1942 (5065), A. White diary, 16 February 1942 (5230), Mass Observation Archive.

37. Judy Roberts diary, 15 February 1942 (5410), Mass Observation Archive.

38. Robert Rhodes James (ed.), *'Chips': The Diaries of Sir Henry Channon*, Weidenfeld and Nicolson, London, 1993 (first published 1967), p. 321 (entry for 13 February 1942); George Orwell, 'The British Crisis: London Letter to *Partisan Review*', 8 May 1942, in Sonia Orwell and Ian Angus (eds.), *The Collected Essays, Journalism and Letters of George Orwell*, Vol. II: *My Country Right or Left, 1940–1943*, Penguin, Harmondsworth, 1970 (first published 1968), pp. 246–7.

39. Denis Argent diary, 15 February 1942 (5010), Mass Observation Archive. In the same entry, Argent commented, 'To call Churchill "the greatest regenerator of our history" is to ignore everything that's being said in every gathering of soldiers about "that bastard Churchill"'.

40. Pam Ashford diary, 16 February 1942, in Simon Garfield (ed.), *Private Battles: How the War Almost Defeated Us*, Ebury Press, London, 2007 (first published 2006), p. 214.

41. 'Home Intelligence Weekly Report No. 72', 18 February 1942, INF 1/292, TNA.

42. BBC Listener Survey Department, 'A Listener Report: The Prime Minister's Broadcast before the 9.00 p.m. News on Sunday, 15th February 1942', LR/713, 3 March 1942, BBC Written Archives.

43. This report suggested that, by contrast, there had been only 2 per cent unfavourable comments on Churchill's previous two broadcasts from America. 'Opinion on the Cabinet Changes', File Report 1111, 24 February 1942, Mass Observation Archive.

44. Interestingly, Goebbels, who had spent much of 1941 predicting the collapse of the British Empire, published an article in November of that year suggesting that this was unlikely to take place imminently. Ernest K. Bramsted, *Goebbels and National Socialist Propaganda 1925–1945*, The Cresset Press, London, 1965, p. 423.

45. 'Workers' Challenge', 'In English for England', 16 February 1942, quoted in Daily Digest of Foreign Broadcasts, 16–17 February 1942, BBC Written Archives.

46. Talk by William Joyce, 16 February 1942, quoted in Daily Digest of Foreign Broadcasts, 16–17 February 1942, BBC Written Archives.

47. 'Home Intelligence Weekly Report No. 65', 31 December 1941, INF 1/292, TNA.

48. Report of 19 February 1942, in Heinz Boberach (ed.), *Meldungen aus dem Reich 1938–1945: Die geheimen Lageberichte des Sicherheitsdienstes der SS 1938–1945*, Vol. IX, Pawlak Verlag Herrsching, Berlin, 1984, pp. 3338–9.

49. Report of 29 January 1942, in *Meldungen aus dem Reich 1938–1945*, Vol. IX, pp. 3221–2.

50. Voice of Free Arabs, 16 February 1942, quoted in Daily Digest of Foreign Broadcasts, 16–17 February 1942, BBC Written Archives.

51. 'In Afrikaans for South Africa', 16 February 1942, and 'In Hindustani for India', 16 February 1942, both quoted in Daily Digest of Foreign Broadcasts, 16–17 February 1942, BBC Written Archives.

52. 'Monthly Intelligence Summary no. 7', 6 July 1942, quoted in Philip Woods, 'From Shaw to Shantaram: The Film Advisory Board and the Making of British Propaganda Films in India, 1940–1943', *Historical Journal of Film, Radio and Television*, Vol. 21 (2001), 293–308, at 299.

53. Mackenzie King diary, 15 February 1942.

54. Weekly Political Summary, 19 February 1942, in H. G. Nicholas (ed.), *Washington Despatches 1941–1945: Weekly Reports from the British Embassy*, University of Chicago Press, Chicago, 1981, p. 19.

55. Julian Huxley, 'What Churchill's Visit Has Meant to the US', *Picture Post*, 10 January 1942.

56. Walter Lippmann, 'The Post-Singapore War in the East', *Montreal Gazette*, 21 February 1942.

57. Lord Halifax to Anthony Eden, 24 February 1942, FO 954/29B, TNA. Emphasis in original.

58. Rhodes James, *'Chips'*, p. 322 (entry for 17 February 1942).

59. Speech of 17 February 1942.

60. Rhodes James, *'Chips'*, p. 322 (entry for 17 February 1942).

61. Nicolson, *Diaries 1939–45*, p. 212 (entry for 17 February 1942).

62. 'Home Intelligence Division Weekly Report No. 73', 25 February 1942, INF 1/292, TNA.

63. Barnes and Nicholson, *Empire at Bay*, p. 775 (entry for 17 February 1942).

64. Kevin Jefferys (ed.), *Labour and the Wartime Coalition: From the Diary of James Chuter Ede 1941–1945*, p. 51 (entry for 18 February 1942).

65. 'Home Intelligence Division Weekly Report No. 73', 25 February 1942, INF 1/292, TNA.

66. Speech of 24 February 1942.

67. Barnes and Nicolson, *Empire at Bay*, p. 787 (entry for 11 March 1942).

68. Jeffreys, *Labour and the Wartime Coalition*, p. 62 (entry for 11 March 1942).

69. Speech of 11 March 1941.

70. Rhodes James, *'Chips'*, p. 324 (entry for 11 March 1942).

71. Barnes and Nicolson, *Empire at Bay*, p. 787 (entry for 11 March 1942).

72. Draft for speech of 24 February 1942, Churchill Papers, CHAR 9/183C/245. For this episode, see Allen Packwood, 'Heart versus Head: Churchill Comes to Terms with the Fall of Singapore?' in Farrell, *Churchill and the Lion City*, pp. 56–67, at 59.

73. P. J. Grigg to WSC, n.d. but February 1942, Churchill Papers, CHAR 9/183C/237–8.

74. Speech of 24 February 1942.

75. 'Summary Report on Prestige of Government Leaders', File Report 1207, 16 April 1942, Mass Observation Archive.

76. Speech of 23 April 1942.

77. See 'Singapore Inquiry Needed "to Clear the Air"', *Sydney Morning Herald*, 28 January 1946; 'Defence of Singapore's Vanquished', *The Straits Times*, 31 July 1947; and the correspondence in PREM 8/316, TNA.

78. Speech of 23 April 1942.

79. Callahan, 'Churchill and Singapore', p. 160.

80. Speech of 23 April 1942.

81. Ball, *Parliament and Politics*, pp. 308–9 (entry for 23 April 1942).

82. Rhodes James, *'Chips'*, p. 327 (entry for 23 April 1942).

83. Nicolson, *Diaries 1939–45*, pp. 223–4 (entry for 23 April 1942).

84. Jefferys, *Labour and the Wartime Coalition*, p. 70 (entry for 23 April 1942).

85. Speech of 23 April 1942.

86. Ben Pimlott (ed.), *The Second World War Diary of Hugh Dalton, 1940–1945*, Jonathan Cape, London, 1986, p. 416 (entry for 23 April 1942).

87. Jefferys, *Labour and the Wartime Coalition*, p. 70 (entry for 23 April 1942).

88. Pimlott, *Second World War Diary*, p. 416 (entry for 23 April 1942).

89. George Harvie-Watt, 'Report by the Principal Private Secretary', 1 May 1942, Harvie-Watt Papers, HARV 2/1.

90. John Harvey (ed.), *The War Diaries of Oliver Harvey 1941–1945*, Collins, London, 1978, p. 121 (entry for 5 May 1942).

91. Broadcast of 10 May 1942.
92. Leonard Adamson diary, 11 May 1942 (5004), Mass Observation Archive. Emphasis in original.
93. Edith Dawson diary, 11 May 1942 (5296), Mass Observation Archive.
94. Cecil Miles diary, 3 May 1942 (5150), Mass Observation Archive.
95. 'Home Intelligence Division Weekly Report No. 85', 20 May 1942, INF 1/292, TNA.
96. O. Sutherst diary, 10 May 1942 (5433), Mass Observation Archive. Although dated 10 May, this entry was written up the following day.
97. Christopher Gould to Vera Denise Russell, 11 May 1942, IWM 12542.
98. Denis Argent diary, 10 May 1942 (5010), Mass Observation Archive.
99. M. A. Pratt diary, 10 May 1942 (5402), Mass Observation Archive.
100. E. A. Stebbing diary, 12 May 1942 (5205), Mass Observation Archive.
101. Anne Chisholm and Michael Davie, *Beaverbrook: A Life*, Pimlico, London, 1993 (first published 1992), p. 431.
102. Broadcast of 10 May 1942.
103. 'Home Intelligence Division Weekly Report No. 85', 20 May 1942, INF 1/292, TNA.
104. Anthony Beevor, *The Second World War*, Little, Brown and Company, New York, 2012, p. 332.
105. Broadcast of 10 May 1942.
106. War Cabinet Conclusions, Confidential Annex, WM (43) 58th, 7 May 1942, CAB/65/30/9, TNA.
107. B. S. Inglis diary, 11 May 1942 (5118), Mass Observation Archive.
108. 'Home Intelligence Division Weekly Report No. 85', 20 May 1942, INF 1/292, TNA.
109. Report of 18 May 1942, in Heinz Boberach (ed.), *Meldungen aus dem Reich 1938–1945: Die geheimen Lageberichte des Sicherheitsdienstes der SS 1938–1945*, Vol. X, Pawlak Verlag Herrsching, Berlin, 1984, p. 3746.
110. John Ellis van Courtland Moon, 'Chemical Weapons and Deterrence: The World War II Experience', *International Security*, Vol. 8, No. 4 (Spring 1984), pp. 3–35.
111. Alex Danchev and Daniel Todman (eds.), *War Diaries 1939–1945: Field Marshall Lord Alanbrooke*, Phoenix, London, 2002 (first published 2001), p. 269.
112. WSC, *Hinge of Fate*, p. 346.
113. WSC, *Hinge of Fate*, p. 352; Nicolson, *Diaries 1939–45*, p. 231 (entry for 1 July 1942).
114. WSC, *Hinge of Fate*, p. 353.
115. Duff Hart-Davis (ed.), *King's Counsellor: Abdication and War. The Diaries of Sir Alan Lascelles*, Phoenix, London, 2007 (first published 2006), p. 36 (entry for 1 July 1942).
116. Rhodes James, *'Chips'*, p. 334 (entry for 1 July 1942).
117. Parliamentary Debates, House of Commons, Fifth Series, Vol. 381, 1 July 1942, col. 245.

118. Parliamentary Debates, House of Commons, Fifth Series, Vol. 381, 2 July 1942, col. 528.

119. Speech of George Garro-Jones, Parliamentary Debates, House of Commons, Fifth Series, Vol. 381, col. 562.

120. Ball, *Parliament and Politics*, p. 323 (entry for July 1942).

121. Vere Hodgson, *Few Eggs and No Oranges*, Dennis Dobson, London, 1976, p. 245 (entry for 5 July 1942).

122. Speech of 2 July 1942.

123. FDR to WSC, 2 July 1942, in Warren F. Kimball (ed.), *Churchill & Roosevelt: The Complete Correspondence*, Vol. I: *Alliance Emerging, October 1933–November 1942*, Princeton University Press, Princeton, 1984, p. 517.

124. Lionel Randle diary, 2 July 1942 (5176), Mass Observation Archive.

125. A. White diary, 2 July 1942 (5230), Mass Observation Archive.

126. C.W. Gardner diary, 2 July 1942 (5076), Mass Observation Archive.

127. 'Home Intelligence Division Weekly Report No. 92', 9 July 1942, INF 1/292, TNA.

128. Report of 8 July 1942, in Boberach, *Meldungen aus dem Reich 1938–1945*, Vol. X, p. 3911.

129. David Carlton, *Churchill and the Soviet Union*, Manchester University Press, Manchester, 2000, pp. 101–2.

130. Speech of 8 September 1942.

131. Speech of 8 September 1942.

132. Ashley Jackson, *The British Empire and the Second World War*, Hambledon Continuum, London, 2006, p. 66.

133. Charles Peake to Dorothy Halifax, 21 September 1942 Halifax Papers, Borthwick Institute of Historical Research, A2.280.32.

134. War Cabinet minutes: Confidential Record, WM (42) 122nd Conclusions, 9 September 1942, CAB/65/27/38, TNA.

135. Cabinet Secretary's notebook: WM (42) 122nd Meeting, 9 September 1942, CAB 195/1, TNA.

136. 'Home Intelligence Division Weekly Report No. 102', 17 September 1942, INF 1/292, TNA.

137. A. R. Mudaliar to G. Laithwaite, 21 September 1942, in Nicholas Mansergh (ed.), *The Transfer of Power 1942–7*, Vol. III: *Reassertion of Authority, Gandhi's Fast and the Succession to the Viceroyalty 21 September 1942–12 June 1943*, HMSO, London, 1971, p. 3.

138. Barnes and Nicholson, *Empire at Bay*, p. 832 (entry for 9 September 1942).

139. Barnes and Nicholson, *Empire at Bay*, p. 832 (entry for 10 September 1942).

140. Robert Pearce (ed.), *Patrick Gordon Walker: Political Diaries 1932–1971*, The Historians' Press, London, 1991, p. 113 (entry for 1 October 1942).

141. Speech of 10 September 1942.

142. The Indian press reaction is summarized in 'A Chorus of Criticism', *The Times*, 14 September 1942.

143. 'Reports of a Press Conference held by Mr Jinnah', 13 September 1942, in Nicholas Mansergh (ed.), *The Transfer of Power 1942–7*, Vol. II: *'Quit India' 30 April–21 September 1942*, HMSO, London, 1971, p. 958.

144. India League, *The Prime Minister on India: An Examination of Mr. Churchill's Statement on India in the House of Commons on the 10th September 1942*, India League, London, 1942, p. 17, in Fabian Colonial Bureau Papers, Box 1/5, MSS Brit. Emp. S365.

145. Lord Halifax to Anthony Eden, 14 September 1942, Halifax Papers, Churchill College, HLFX 2. Emphasis in original.

146. 'Home Intelligence Division Weekly Report No. 102', 17 September 1942, INF 1/292, TNA.

147. Diary of Corporal Terry (first name unknown), 12 September 1942 (5210), Mass Observation Archive.

148. A. L. Baker diary, 10 September 1942 (5016), Mass Observation Archive.

149. Speech of 12 October 1942.

150. 'Home Intelligence Division Weekly Report No. 107', 22 October 1942, INF 1/292, TNA.

151. Speech of 31 October 1942. The speech was published in 1943.

152. 'Home Intelligence Division Weekly Report No. 107', 22 October 1942, INF 1/292, TNA.

153. Speech of 10 November 1942.

154. Speech of 10 November 1942.

155. Dominique Rossignol, *Histoire de la propaganda en France de 1940 à 1944: L'Utopie Pétain*, Presses Universitaires de France, Paris, 1991, pp. 311–13.

156. Wm. Roger Louis, *Imperialism at Bay: The United States and the Decolonization of the British Empire, 1941–1945*, Oxford University Press, Oxford, 1977, p. 8.

157. 'Commonwealth of the World', *The Times*, 28 October 1942.

158. Brendan Bracken, 'Mr. Wendell Willkie's Broadcast', WP (42) 501, 2 November 1942, CAB 66/30/31, TNA.

159. Mackenzie King diary, 5 December 1942.

160. '"Old Imperialistic Order"', *The Times*, 18 November 1942.

161. Weekly Political Summary, 8 December 1942, in Nicholas, *Washington Despatches*, p. 122. Not all American commentators took Willkie's side, though. See Richard Toye, *Churchill's Empire: The World that Made Him and the World He Made*, Macmillan, London, 2010, p. 231.

162. '"Great Design" in Africa', *The Times*, 11 November 1942.

163. 'Home Intelligence Division Weekly Report No. 111', 19 November 1942, INF 1/292, TNA.

164. A. Schofield diary, 11 November 1942 (5423), Mass Observation Archive.

165. 'Morale in November 1942', 1 December 1942, Mass Observation Archive.

166. R. W. Fenn diary, 14 November 1942 (5065), Mass Observation Archive.

167. It is unclear whether this comment referred to Churchill's Mansion House speech (or a repeat of it) or to a news report of his war review in the Commons the next day. M. A. Pratt diary, 11 November 1942 (5402), Mass Observation Archive.

CHAPTER 6

1. François Kersaudy, *Churchill and De Gaulle*, Collins, London, 1981, p. 222.
2. 'Home Intelligence Weekly Report No. 113', 3 December 1942, INF 1/292, TNA.
3. Kersaudy, *Churchill and De Gaulle*, pp. 223–4.
4. WSC to Franklin D. Roosevelt, 17 November 1942, in Warren F. Kimball (ed.), *Churchill and Roosevelt: The Complete Correspondence*, Vol. II: *Alliance Forged, November 1942–February 1944*, Princeton University Press, Princeton, 1984, p. 7.
5. 'Statement on the Temporary Political Arrangements in North and West Africa', 17 November 1942, in Samuel Rosenman (ed.), *The Public Papers and Addresses of Franklin D. Roosevelt, 1942 Volume: Humanity on the Defensive*, Harper, New York, 1950, pp. 479–80; Kersaudy, *Churchill and De Gaulle*, p. 225.
6. Elisabeth Barker, *Churchill and Eden At War*, Macmillan, London, 1978, pp. 65–6.
7. John Harvey (ed.), *The War Diaries of Oliver Harvey 1941–1945*, Collins, London, 1978, pp. 192–3 (entries for 25 and 28 November 1942).
8. 'Churchill's Speech Today May Shed Light on France', *St. Petersburg Times*, 29 November 1942.
9. Broadcast of 29 November 1942.
10. M. C. Towler diary, 29 November 1942 (5445), Mass Observation Archive.
11. Margaret Congdon diary, 29 November 1942 (5283), Mass Observation Archive.
12. J. Hinton diary, 29 November 1942 (5335), Mass Observation Archive.
13. Broadcast of 29 November 1942.
14. 'Home Intelligence Weekly Report No. 113', 3 December 1942, INF 1/292, TNA.
15. Nella Last diary, 29 November 1942 (5353), Mass Observation Archive.
16. Broadcast of 29 November 1942.
17. 'Churchill's Report', *Pittsburgh Press*, 30 November 1942.
18. Broadcast of 29 November 1942.
19. 'RAF Follows up Churchill Words with Italy Raid', *Berkeley Daily Gazette*, 30 November 1942.
20. Malcolm Muggeridge (ed.), *Ciano's Diary 1939–1943*, Heinemann, London, 1947, p. 530 (entry for 1 December 1942).
21. 'Mussolini Makes Reply to Churchill's Speech', *Tuscaloosa News*, 2 December 1942.
22. Muggeridge, *Ciano's Diary*, pp. 530–1 (entry for 2 December 1942).
23. 'Home Intelligence Weekly Report No. 114', 10 December 1942, INF 1/292, TNA.
24. Winston S. Churchill, *The Second World War*, Vol. IV: *The Hinge of Fate*, Cassell & Co., London, 1951, p. 573.
25. Nigel Nicolson (ed.), *Harold Nicolson: Diaries and Letters, 1939–1945*, Collins, London 1967, p. 266 (entry for 10 December 1942).

26. Notes for speech of 10 December 1942, Churchill Papers CHAR 9/187B/157, 190–6.

27. There were also other minor deletions and alterations made in order to avoid giving offence to the Americans. Edward Bridges to WSC, 1 January 1946, Churchill Papers, CHUR 4/5B, fos. 241–3; Charles Eade (ed.), *Secret Session Speeches by the Right Hon Winston S. Churchill OM, CH, MP*, Cassell & Co., London, 1946, pp. 76–96.

28. Typescript of the *Secret Session Speeches*, Charles Eade Papers, 3/1.

29. The passage was at last published in Kersaudy, *Churchill and De Gaulle*, pp. 227–8. Kersaudy did not, however, note the 'red rag' remark.

30. Robert Rhodes James (ed.), *'Chips': The Diaries of Sir Henry Channon*, Weidenfeld and Nicolson, London, 1993 (first published 1967), p. 346 (entry for 10 December 1942).

31. Kevin Jefferys (ed.), *Labour and the Wartime Coalition: From the Diary of James Chuter Ede 1941–1945*, The Historians' Press, London, 1987, p. 114 (entry for 10 December 1942).

32. WSC, *Hinge of Fate*, p. 576.

33. Herbert Morrison, 'Civil Administration and Security in French North and West Africa', 18 December 1942, WP (42) 594, CAB 66/32/24, TNA.

34. David Stafford, *Churchill and Secret Service*, Abacus, London, 2000 (first published 1997), pp. 290–4.

35. For the complexities surrounding this statement, see Tuvia Ben-Moshe, 'Explaining an Historical Puzzle: Freudian Errors and the Origin of the Declaration on the Policy of "Unconditional Surrender" in the Second World War', *Political Psychology*, Vol. 14, No. 4 (December, 1993), pp. 697–709.

36. 'Mass Observation Bulletin', February 1943, Mass Observation Archive.

37. Speech of 3 February 1943. Churchill made a further speech, to the New Zealand Division, the following day.

38. F. J. Reber diary, 9 February 1943 (5177), Mass Observation Archive.

39. Speech of 11 February 1943.

40. Foreign Broadcast Information Service, 'Daily Report: Foreign Radio Broadcasts', 13 February 1943, FBIS-FRB-43-038.

41. 'Home Intelligence Weekly Report No. 124', 18 February 1943, INF 1/292, TNA.

42. Speech of 11 February 1943.

43. 'Home Intelligence Weekly Report No. 124', 18 February 1943, INF 1/292, TNA.

44. Broadcast of 21 March 1943.

45. Foreign Broadcast Information Service, 'Daily Report: Foreign Radio Broadcasts', 27 March 1943, FBIS-FRB-43-074.

46. 'Churchill's Speech Interests Russians', *New York Times*, 24 March 1943.

47. 'Churchill Speech Praised by Hoover', *Lewiston Daily Sun*, 23 March 1943; 'Hailed by United Nations', *Glasgow Herald*, 23 March 1943.

48. Weekly Report, 28 March 1943, in H. G. Nicholas (ed.), *Washington Despatches 1941–1945:Weekly Reports from the British Embassy*, University of Chicago Press, Chicago, 1981, pp. 170–1.

49. Broadcast of 21 March 1943.

50. Weekly Report, 28 March 1943, in Nicholas, *Washington Despatches*, p. 171. See also 'The Post-War World', *The Times*, 23 March 1943.

51. John Carter Vincent to Cordell Hull, 8 April 1943, *Foreign Relations of the United States: Diplomatic Papers: 1943: China*, US Government Printing Office, Washington DC, 1957, p. 47.

52. 'Mme. Chiang Disappointed by Churchill Post-War Program Revealed Sunday', *St. Petersburg Times*, 23 March 1943.

53. Office of the Military Attaché in Chungking to the Director of Military Intelligence, War Office, 8 April 1943, WO 208/421, TNA.

54. 'Mr. Eden Outlines the Aims for Peace', *The Times*, 27 March 1943.

55. Weekly Political Summary, 3 April 1943, in Nicholas, *Washington Despatches*, p. 171; Chiang Kai-shek to T.V. Soong, 22 May 1943, in Wu Jingping and Tai-chun Kuo (eds.), *Select Telegrams between Chiang Kai-shek and T.V. Soong*, Fudan University Press, Shanghai, 2012, p. 512; WSC, *Hinge of Fate*, pp. 712–13.

56. 'Churchill Talks of Extended War', *Free-Lance Star*, 22 March 1943.

57. Broadcast of 21 March 1943.

58. A. White diary, 21 March 1943 (5230), Mass Observation Archive.

59. Jon Meacham, *Franklin and Winston: Portrait of a Friendship*, Granta Books, London, 2004, p. 218.

60. Broadcast of 14 May 1943. The speech seems to have been devised as a means to boost flagging Home Guard morale. See Thomas Moore to G. S. Harvie-Watt, 29 January 1943, Churchill Papers, CHAR 9/194A/34–5.

61. R. H. Allott diary, 14 May 1943 (5001), Mass Observation Archive.

62. 'Home Intelligence Weekly Report No. 137', 20 May 1943, INF 1/292, TNA.

63. W. L. Mackenzie King diary, 19 May 1943.

64. Speech of 19 May 1943.

65. Michael Wright to T. L. Rowan, 18 May 1943, and Lord Halifax to WSC, 15 May 1943, Churchill Papers, CHAR 9/194A/123, 126–7.

66. 'Demands Rise for Offensive against Japan', *Pittsburgh Press*, 18 May 1943; 'Churchill Speech Smooths Controversy over Strategy', *Edmonton Journal*, 20 May 1943.

67. Mackenzie King diary, 19 May 1943.

68. Speech of 19 May 1943; 'Attack Japan Now, Congressmen Urge', *Pittsburgh Press*, 20 May 1943.

69. Arthur Krock, 'In the Nation: The House of Commons Technique in Congress', *New York Times*, 20 May 1943.

70. *Yomiori-Fochi*, quoted in Foreign Broadcast Information Service, 'Daily Report: Foreign Radio Broadcasts', 21 May 1943, FBIS-FRB-43-121.

71. Cabinet Secretary's notebook, WM (43), 81st Meeting, 5 June 1943, CAB 195/2, TNA.
72. Drew Pearson, 'Washington Merry-Go-Round', *Lodi News-Sentinel*, 25 May 1943.
73. Felix Frankfurter to Lord Halifax, 19 May 1943, Churchill Papers, CAR 9/194A/176.
74. 'Washington Reassured by Churchill Address', *Edmonton Journal*, 20 May 1943.
75. 'Roosevelt's Pledge to China', *Sydney Morning Herald*, 22 May 1943.
76. Nicholas, *Washington Despatches*, pp. 192–3; WSC, *Hinge of Fate*, p. 714.
77. Speech of 19 May 1943.
78. 'Churchill Helps Lay Foundation of FDR's Fourth Term Campaign', *St. Petersburg Times*, 26 May 1944.
79. John Morton Blum (ed.), *The Price of Vision: The Diary of Henry A. Wallace*, Boston, Houghton Mifflin Company, 1973, p. 207 (entry for 22 May 1944).
80. Speech of 19 May 1943.
81. 'Fighting French Upset', *Milwaukee Journal*, 20 May 1943.
82. See David Dilks (ed.), *The Diaries of Sir Alexander Cadogan O.M., 1938–1945*, Cassell & Co., London, 1971, p. 532 (entry for 21 May 1943).
83. 'Home Intelligence Weekly Report No. 138', 27 May 1943, INF 1/292, TNA.
84. J. R. Reber diary, 20 May 1943 (5177), Mass Observation Archive.
85. N. E. Underwood diary, 20 May 1943 (5447), Mass Observation Archive.
86. M. R. J. Wilmett diary, 19 May 1943 (5460), Mass Observation Archive.
87. Lionel Randle diary, 20 May 1943 (5176), Mass Observation Archive.
88. Alex Danchev and Daniel Todman (eds.), *War Diaries 1939–1945: Field Marshal Lord Alanbrooke*, Weidenfeld and Nicolson, London, 2001, p. 410 (entry for 24 May 1943).
89. Speech of 8 June 1943.
90. Kersaudy, *Churchill and De Gaulle*, p. 286.
91. Nicolson, *Diaries 1939–45*, p. 299 (entry for 8 June 1943); 'Home Intelligence Weekly Report No. 141', 17 June 1943, INF 1/292, TNA.
92. Speech of 30 June 1943.
93. 'Home Intelligence Weekly Report No. 144', 8 July 1943, INF 1/292, TNA.
94. Dilks, *Cadogan Diaries*, p. 546 (entry for 26 July 1943).
95. 'Home Intelligence Weekly Report No. 148', 5 August 1943, INF 1/292, TNA.
96. Speech of 27 July 1943.
97. Nicolson, *Diaries 1939–45*, p. 309 (entry for 27 July 1943).
98. Rhodes James, '*Chips*', p. 373 (entry for 27 July 1943).
99. John Barnes and David Nicholson (eds.), *The Empire at Bay: The Leo Amery Diaries, 1929–1945*, Hutchinson, London, 1988, p. 901 (entry for 27 July 1943).
100. 'Churchill on Mussolini: Then and Now', *Tribune*, 30 July 1943.

101. David Lawrence, 'Today in Washington', *New London Evening Day*, 28 July 1943; Walter Lippmann, 'The King and Badoglio', *Montreal Gazette*, 29 July 1943; 'OWI Broadcast under Criticism from Roosevelt', *Ottawa Daily Citizen*, 28 July 1943; 'Is Italy Asking for Armistice Terms?', *Indian Express*, 29 July 1943.

102. 'Troops Called Out to Check Unrest in Milan', *Glasgow Herald*, 29 July 1943.

103. A. B. Holness diary, 11 August 1943 (5338), Mass Observation Archive. See also William Armstrong (ed.), *With Malice Toward None: A War Diary by Cecil H. King*, Sidgwick and Jackson, London, 1970, p. 229 (entry for 23 August 1943).

104. G. F. Glover diary, 31 August 1943 (5318), Mass Observation Archive.

105. H. B. Monck diary, 31 August 1943 (5157), Mass Observation Archive.

106. Lionel Randle diary, 31 August 1943 (5176), Mass Observation Archive.

107. G. South diary, 1 September 1943 (5429), Mass Observation Archive.

108. 'Home Intelligence Weekly Report No. 153', 9 September 1943, INF 1/292, TNA.

109. L. N. Adamson diary, 1 September 1943 (5004), Mass Observation Archive.

110. Broadcast of 31 August 1943.

111. 'Home Intelligence Weekly Report No. 153', 9 September 1943, INF 1/292, TNA.

112. 'The Premier's Broadcast', *Manchester Guardian*, 2 September 1943; John Martin to George Steward, 5 September 1943, Churchill Papers, CHAR 9/195/98; W. P. Crozier, *Off the Record: Political Interviews 1933–1943* (ed. A. J. P. Taylor), Hutchinson, London, 1973, p. 379 (entry for 22 October 1943).

113. Weekly Political Summary, 12 September 1943, in Nicholas, *Washington Despatches*, p. 240.

114. 'Churchill Clarified Matters', *Lewiston Evening Journal*, 1 September 1943.

115. 'See Tri-Power War Parley as Certainty', *Schenectady Gazette*, 1 September 1943.

116. Foreign Broadcast Information Service, 'Daily Report: Foreign Radio Broadcasts', 9 September 1943, FBIS-FRB-43-209.

117. Speech of 6 September 1943.

118. Weekly Political Summary, 12 September 1943, in Nicholas, *Washington Despatches*, p. 244.

119. 'Prime Minister's Speech at Harvard', WP (43) 398, 20 September 1943, CAB 66/40/48, TNA, quoting *New York Times*, 7 September 1943, *St Louis Post-Dispatch*, 7 September, *Chicago Daily Tribune*, 8 September 1943, *Wheeling Intelligencer*, 8 September 1943, and *Baltimore Sun*, 7 September 1943.

120. Lord Moran, *Churchill at War 1940–45*, Robinson, London, 2002, p. 142 (entry for 7 September 1943).

121. Stuart Ball (ed.), *Parliament and Politics in the Age of Churchill and Attlee: The Headlam Diaries*, Cambridge University Press/Royal Historical Society, London, 1999, p. 383 (entry for 21 September 1943).

122. Harold Nicolson to Ben and Nigel Nicolson, 21 September 1943, in Nicolson, *War Diaries 1939–45*, pp. 320–1.

123. Speech of 21 September 1943.

124. Parliamentary Debates, House of Commons, Fifth Series, Vol. 392, 22 September 1943, cols. 304–14.

125. J. Greenwood diary, 22 September 1943 (5088), Mass Observation Archive.

126. A. White diary, 27 September 1943 (5230), Mass Observation Archive.

127. N. E. Underwood diary, 22 September 1943 (5447), Mass Observation Archive.

128. 'Home Intelligence Weekly Report No. 156', 30 September 1943, INF 1/292, TNA.

129. Geoffrey G. Field, *Blood, Sweat and Toil: Remaking the British Working Class, 1939–1945*, Oxford University Press, Oxford, 2011, pp. 116–17.

130. Viscount Cranborne to WSC, n.d. (October 1943), Churchill Papers, CHAR 9/192C/320.

131. Speech of 13 October 1943.

132. Jack Wilkes, 'Lords and Commons', *Tribune*, 15 October 1943.

133. 'Coal Nationalisation Issue Deferred', *Glasgow Herald*, 14 October 1943.

134. G. F. Glover diary, 14 October 1943 (5318), N. E. Underwood diary, 13 October 1943 (5447), Mass Observation Archive.

135. 'Coal Comfort', *The Economist*, 16 October 1943.

136. Nicolson to Ben and Nigel Nicolson, 21 September 1943, in Nicolson, *War Diaries 1939–45*, p. 320.

137. He did make an uncontentious speech on 28 October proposing a Select Committee to consider the rebuilding of the House of Commons.

138. Speech of 9 November 1943.

139. 'Home Intelligence Weekly Report No. 163', 18 November 1943, INF 1/292, TNA.

140. E. A. Stebbing diary, 9 November 1943 (5205), Mass Observation Archive.

CHAPTER 7

1. 'Baroness Asquith of Yarnbury [Violet Bonham Carter] in Conversation with Kenneth Harris', *The Listener*, 17 August 1967.

2. David Dilks (ed.), *The Diaries of Sir Alexander Cadogan O.M., 1938–1945*, Cassell & Co., London, 1971, p. 597 (entry for 18 January 1944).

3. 'Brighton and a Letter', *The Times*, 1 February 1944. See also 'Mr. Churchill to Brighton', *The Times*, 2 February 1944, and G. S. Harvie-Watt, *Most of My Life*, Springwood Books, Windlesham, 1980, pp. 141–2.

4. 'Home Intelligence Weekly Report', 10 February 1944, INF 1/292, TNA.

5. Margaret Kornitzer diary, 11 February 1944 (5349), Mass Observation Archive.

6. Edith Dawson diary, 7 February 1944 (5296), Mass Observation Archive. Emphasis in original.

7. A. W. Martin and Patsy Hardy (eds.), *Dark and Hurrying Days: Menzies' 1941 Diary*, National Library of Australia, Canberra, 1993, p. 112 (entry for 14 April 1941).

8. Corporal Terry diary, 2 February 1944 (5210), Mass Observation Archive.

9. Nigel Nicolson (ed.), *Harold Nicolson: Diaries and Letters, 1939–1945*, Collins, London 1967, p. 347 (entry 7 February 1944).

10. Ben Pimlott (ed.), *The Second World War Diary of Hugh Dalton, 1940–1945*, Jonathan Cape, London, 1986, p. 709 (entry for 22 February 1944).

11. John Harvey (ed.), *The War Diaries of Oliver Harvey 1941–1945*, Collins, London, 1978, pp. 330, 332–3 (entries for 8 and 21 February 1944).

12. Speech of 22 February 1944.

13. Kevin Jefferys (ed.), *Labour and the Wartime Coalition: From the Diary of James Chuter Ede 1941–1945*, p. 172 (entry for 22 February 1944).

14. Speech of 22 February 1944.

15. 'Britain "Facing Two Ways"', *Sydney Morning Herald*, 25 February 1944.

16. Harvey, *Diaries 1941–1945*, pp. 333 (entry for 25 February 1944).

17. Foreign Office to Moscow, 25 February 1944, FO 954/20A, TNA.

18. Decrypted telegram from the Turkish ambassador in Moscow to the Turkish Ministry of Foreign Affairs, 29 February 1944, HW 1/2573, TNA.

19. Foreign Broadcast Information Service, 'Daily Report: Foreign Radio Broadcasts', 28 February 1944, FBIS-FRB-44-051.

20. Foreign Broadcast Information Service, 'Daily Report: Foreign Radio Broadcasts', 23 February 1944, FBIS-FRB-44-047.

21. 'Home Intelligence Weekly Report No. 178', 2 March 1944, INF 1/292, TNA.

22. Weekly Political Summary, 27 February 1944, in H. G. Nicholas (ed.), *Washington Despatches 1941–1945: Weekly Reports from the British Embassy*, University of Chicago Press, Chicago, 1981, p. 321.

23. Speech of 22 February 1944.

24. War Cabinet minutes, Confidential Annex, WM (44) 23rd, 21 February 1944, CAB 65/45/15, TNA.

25. Elisabeth Barker, *Churchill and Eden At War*, Macmillan, London, 1978, pp. 162–77.

26. 'Sforza Criticizes Churchill's Speech', *New York Times*, 26 February 1944.

27. 'Churchill Abandons Us: Italian Liberal', *Palm Beach Post*, 28 February 1944; 'Italian Strike Protest', *Sydney Morning Herald*, 1 March 1944.

28. Lord Stansgate diary, 24 February 1944, Stansgate Papers, ST/254/7.

29. 'The Principle of Legitimacy', *New Statesman & Nation*, 26 February 1944.

30. For which, see David Cannadine, *In Churchill's Shadow: Confronting the Past in Modern Britain*, Allen Lane, London, 2002, chapter 3.

31. Anthony Eden to WSC, 19 February 1944, Churchill Papers, CHAR 9/197C/264.

32. Pimlott, *Second World War Diary*, p. 709 (entry for 22 February 1944).

33. Speech of 22 February 1944.

34. 'Home Intelligence Weekly Report No. 178', 2 March 1944, INF 1/292, TNA.

35. John Colville, *The Fringes of Power: Downing Street Diaries, 1939–1955*, Hodder and Stoughton, London, 1985, p. 475 (entry for 22 February 1944).

36. Harvie-Watt, *Most of My Life*, p. 145. This was on 2 March 1944.

37. John Martin to WSC, 1 March 1944, Churchill Papers, CHAR 9/204A/12.

38. Cabinet minutes, 21 March 1944, WM (44) 37th, CAB 65/41/37, TNA.

39. Broadcast of 26 March 1944.

40. M. C. Towler diary, 26 March 1944 (5445), Mass Observation Archive.

41. 'Home Intelligence Weekly Report No. 183', 6 April 1944, INF 1/292, TNA.

42. Speech of 21 April 1944.

43. Cordell Hull to J. G. Winant, 4 May 1944, *Foreign Relations of the United States: Diplomatic Papers 1944*, Vol. II: *General: Economic and Social Matters*, United States Government Printing Office, Washington, DC, 1967, p. 40; Lord Halifax to Anthony Eden, 6 May 1944, FO 954/30B, TNA.

44. Richard Wigg, *Churchill and Spain: The Survival of the Franco Regime, 1940–45*, Routledge, Abingdon, 2005, chapter 6.

45. Dean Acheson, *Present at the Creation: My Years in the State Department*, W. W. Norton, New York, 1969, p. 61.

46. Pimlott, *Second World War Diary*, p. 749 (entry for 24 May 1944).

47. Dilks, *Cadogan Diaries*, p. 630 (entry for 24 May 1944).

48. John Barnes and David Nicholson (eds.), *The Empire at Bay: The Leo Amery Diaries, 1929–1945*, Hutchinson, London, 1988, p. 985 (entry for 24 May 1944).

49. The passages in question were present in Churchill's speech notes; there is no question of him having improvised them off the cuff. See Churchill Papers, CHAR 9/163B/192–200.

50. Speech of 24 May 1944.

51. Harold Nicolson to Ben and Nigel Nicolson, 24 May 1944, in Nicolson, *Diaries 1939–45*, pp. 372–3.

52. Pimlott, *Second World War Diary*, p. 748 (entry for 24 May 1944).

53. *ABC*, 26 May 1944, quoted in Enrique Moriadellos, *Franco frente a Churchill: España y Gran Bretaña en la Segunda Guerra Mundial (1939–1945)*, Ediciones Península, Barcelona, 2005, p. 363.

54. Foreign Broadcast Information Service, 'Daily Report: Foreign Radio Broadcasts', 27 May 1944, FBIS-FRB-44-128.

55. 'Spain: Reactions to Mr. Churchill's Speech of the 24th May', 9 June 1944, HW 1/2930, TNA.

56. Decrypted telegram from the Turkish chargé d'affaires in Madrid to the Turkish Foreign Ministry, 31 May 1944, HW 1/2930, TNA.

57. Decrypted telegram from the Japanese ambassador to the Japanese Minister of Foreign Affairs, 29 May 1944, HW 1/2883, TNA.

58. 'Reactions on Spain', *The Economist*, 3 June 1944.

59. *Daily Times* (Beaver and Rochester), 24 May 1944; *News and Courier* (Charleston SC), 25 May 1944. But see also 'Churchill Praise of Franco Stirs Rift', *Christian Science Monitor*, 25 May 1944.

60. Nicholas, *Washington Despatches*, p. 363.

61. Speech of 24 May 1944. This was in part a way of rationalizing the alliance with the Soviet Union. Churchill claimed that the Russian state had undergone 'a remarkable broadening of its views. The religious side of Russian life has had a wonderful rebirth'. He also noted the abolition of the Comintern.

62. Nicholas, *Washington Despatches*, p. 363.

63. Press Conference of 30 May 1944, in Samuel Rosenman (ed.), *The Public Papers and Addresses of Franklin D. Roosevelt, 1944–45 Volume: Victory and the Threshold of Peace*, Harper, New York, 1950, p. 143; 'Roosevelt Criticizes Spain, Taking Issue with Churchill', *New York Times*, 31 May 1944; C. R. Blackburn, 'Diplomats Deny any Split between Churchill and Roosevelt on Spain', *Ottawa Citizen*, 2 June 1944.

64. 'FDR Must Keep Health Gains', *Tuscaloosa News*, 30 May 1944.

65. WSC to FDR, 4 June 1944, in Warren Kimball (ed.), *Churchill & Roosevelt: The Complete Correspondence*, Vol. III: *Alliance Declining, February 1944—April 1945*, Princeton University Press, Princeton, 1984, pp. 162–3.

66. 'Home Intelligence Weekly Report No. 191', 2 June 1944, INF 1/292, TNA.

67. J. Greenwood diary, 24 May 1944 (5088), Mass Observation Archive.

68. Edith Dawson diary, May 1944 (5296), Mass Observation Archive.

69. E. A. Stebbing diary, 26 May 1944 (5205), Mass Observation Archive.

70. Kathleen Hill to John Martin, 27 May 1944, PREM 4/70/2, TNA.

71. 'Good Europeans?', *The Economist*, 27 May 1944.

72. Eden to WSC, 1 August 1944, Churchill Papers, CHAR 9/200A/72–5.

73. Mark Pottle (ed.), *Champion Redoubtable: The Diaries and Letters of Violet Bonham Carter*, Weidenfeld and Nicolson, London, 1998, p. 318 (entry for 1 November 1944).

74. *Daily Herald*, 18 June 1945.

75. Harvie-Watt, *Most of My Life*, p. 156.

76. Nicolson, *Diaries 1939–45*, p. 375 (entry for 6 June 1944); Speech of 6 June 1944.

77. Angus Calder, *The People's War: Britain 1939–1945*, Panther, London, 1971, p. 645; Speech of 22 February 1944. For the state of British knowledge about the German V-weapon programme, see James Goodchild's forthcoming University of Exeter Ph.D. thesis.

78. 'Home Intelligence Weekly Report No. 196', 6 July 1944, INF 1/292, TNA. In his Mexico Embassy speech on 15 June Churchill said that 'the months of this summer may, by the victories of this Allied campaign, bring full success to the cause of freedom'.

79. Harvie-Watt, *Most of My Life*, p. 162

80. Speech of 6 July 1944.

81. Nicolson, *Diaries 1939–45*, p. 387 (entry for 6 July 1944).

82. Jefferys, *Labour and the Wartime Coalition*, p. 185 (entry for 6 July 1944).

83. A. B. Holness diary, 6 July 1944 (5338), Mass Observation Archive.

84. J. Greenwood diary, 7 July 1944 (5088), Mass Observation Archive.

85. Nellie Carver diary, 6 July 1944, IWM.379.

86. 'Morale in July 1944', 1 August 1944, Mass Observation Archive.

87. 'Home Intelligence Weekly Report No. 197', 13 July 1944, INF 1/292, TNA.

88. 'Home Intelligence Weekly Report No. 198', 20 July 1944, INF 1/292, TNA.

89. Herbert Morrison to WSC, 11 July 1944, PREM 4/70/2, TNA.

90. W. M. Challis diary, 13 July 1944 (5271), Mass Observation Archive.

91. Walter Citrine, 'Interview with the Prime Minister re. Flying Bombs, 28th July 1944', 1 August 1944, Walter Citrine Papers, 10/6.

92. Speech of 2 August 1944.

93. 'Home Intelligence Weekly Report No. 201', 11 August 1944, INF 1/292, TNA.

94. Lionel Randle diary, week of 31 July–7 August 1944 (5176), Mass Observation Archive.

95. Peter Clarke, *The Last Thousand Days of the British Empire*, Allen Lane, London, 2007, pp. 65–6.

96. Lord Ismay, *The Memoirs of Lord Ismay*, Heinemann, London, 1960, p. 375.

97. Speech of 16 September 1944.

98. Brian Bond (ed.), *Chief of Staff: The Diaries of Lieutenant General Sir Henry Pownall*, Vol. II: *1940–1944*, Leo Cooper, London, 1974, p. 190 (entry for 10 October 1944).

99. 'Home Intelligence Weekly Report No. 208', 28 September 1944, INF 1/292, TNA.

100. He took Eden's advice to omit from this speech a comment about his 'close association' with Roosevelt, on the grounds that 'Dewey and the Republicans might seize upon it and pretend that it was intended to assist the President in the election campaign'. Draft of speech of 16 September 1944, and undated note conveying Eden's advice, Churchill Papers, CHAR 9/201A/40–1.

101. Nicolson, *Diaries 1939–45*, p. 402 (28 September 1944). Churchill's precise words were, '"Not in vain" may be the pride of those who have survived and the epitaph of those who fell'.

102. 'Home Intelligence Weekly Report No. 209', 5 October 1944, INF 1/292, TNA.

103. Speech of 28 September 1944.

104. William R. Langdon to Cordell Hull, 13 October 1944, *Foreign Relations of the United States: Diplomatic Papers 1944*, Vol. VI: *China*, United States Government Printing Office, Washington, DC, 1967, p. 172.

105. Colville, *The Fringes of Power*, p. 522 (entry for 5 October 1944).

106. 'Mr. Churchill Eulogizes Old Friend', *Palestine Post*, 8 November 1944.

107. Parliamentary Debates, House of Commons, 5th Series, Vol. 404, 17 November 1944, col. 2242.

108. E. A. Stebbing diary, 9 11 1944 (5205), M. J. Brierley diary, 9 November 1944 (5261), K. Hey diary, 10 November 1944 (5331), Mass Observation Archive.

109. Views reported in K. Hey diary, 10 November 1944 (5331), Mass Observation Archive.

110. M. J. Brierley diary, 9 November 1944 (5261), Mass Observation Archive.

111. See the famous passage in WSC, *The Second World War*, Vol. VI: *Triumph and Tragedy*, Cassell & Co., London, 1954, p. 198. For an understanding of the context, see Albert Resis, 'The Churchill-Stalin Secret "Percentages" Agreement on the Balkans, Moscow, October 1944', *American Historical Review*, Vol. 83, No. 2 (April 1978), pp. 368–87.

112. The National Popular Liberation Army (ELAS) was the military wing of the National Liberation Front (EAM). The National Democratic Greek League was known as EDES. This paragraph draws on Andrew Thorpe, '"In a Rather Emotional State"? The Labour Party and British Intervention in Greece, 1944–5', *English Historical Review*, Vol. 493 (2006), pp. 1075–105, and A. J. Foster, 'The Politicians, Public Opinion and the Press: The Storm over British Military Intervention in Greece in December 1944', *Journal of Contemporary History*, Vol. 19 (1984), pp. 453–94.

113. WSC to Roland Scobie, 5 December 1944, in WSC, *Triumph and Tragedy*, p. 252.

114. Stettinius's comments were linked to ongoing Anglo-American tensions about the Italian government and the position of Count Sforza. See 'US Government and Count Sforza', *The Times*, 6 December 1944, and 'Stettinius Urges Full Freedom', *Evening Independent*, 7 December 1944.

115. Colville, *Fringes of Power*, p. 533 (entry for 5 December 1944).

116. M. A. Pratt diary, 7 December 1944 (5402), Mass Observation Archive.

117. Anon. diary, 10 December 1944 (5068), Mass Observation Archive.

118. Parliamentary Debates, House of Commons, Fifth Series, Vol. 406, 8 December 1944, col. 908.

119. War Cabinet minutes, 7 December 1944, WM (44) 162nd Conclusions, Confidential Annex, CAB 65/48/14.

120. Speech of 8 December 1944.

121. '"Allies at Ringside"', *Daily Mirror*, 9 December 1944.

122. Colville, *Fringes of Power*, p. 534 (entry for 8 December 1944).

123. Harold Nicolson to Nigel and Ben Nicolson, 8 December 1944, in Nicolson, *Diaries 1939–45*, p. 416.

124. Jefferys, *Labour and the Wartime Coalition*, p. 199 (entry for 8 December 1944). Andrew Thorpe suggests that Churchill's provocativeness may have had a political purpose: 'It [...] seems likely that he was deliberately truculent with his Labour critics in order to push them into more extreme positions, to compromise them—or rather to allow them to compromise themselves—by taking up positions that were so pro-ELAS that they would embarrass the party once the dust had settled in Athens'. '"In a Rather Emotional State"?', pp. 1088–9.

125. Barnes and Nicholson, *The Empire at Bay*, p. 1022 (entry for 8 December 1944).
126. Jefferys, *Labour and the Wartime Coalition*, p. 200 (entry for 8 December 1944).
127. A Gallup poll in January 1945 found that 43 per cent approved of Churchill's handling of the Greek problem and that 38 per cent disapproved, but we do not have equivalent figures for the previous month. George H. Gallup (ed.), *The Gallup International Opinion Polls: Great Britain 1937–1975*, Vol. I: *1937–1964*, Random House, New York, 1976, pp. 104–5.
128. 'Home Intelligence Weekly Report No. 219', 14 December 1944, INF 1/292, TNA.
129. 'Greece', December 1944, File Report 2190, Mass Observation Archive.
130. WSC, 'Greece: Note by the Prime Minister', WP (44) 766, 31 December 1944 (enclosing a censorship summary for the week ending 16 December), CAB 66/60/16, TNA.
131. WSC to Harry Hopkins, 9 December 1944, Churchill Papers, CHAR 9/203B/258.
132. Weekly Political Summaries, 10 and 17 December 1944, in Nicholas, *Washington Despatches*, pp. 473, 476.
133. Speech of 15 December 1944.
134. Colville, *Fringes of Power*, p. 535 (entry for 14 December 1944).
135. Foreign Broadcast Information Service, 'Daily Report: Foreign Radio Broadcasts', 19 December 1944, FBIS-FRB-44-304.
136. Herbert L. Matthews, 'Balts in Rome See Countries Doomed', *New York Times*, 17 December 1944.
137. 'City's Polish Leaders Flay Churchill Stand', *Milwaukee Sentinel*, 18 December 1944.
138. Nicholas, *Washington Despatches*, p. 476.
139. Decrypted German Foreign Ministry press circular, 18 December 1944, HW 1/3388, TNA.
140. James W. Blackwell, 'The Polish Home Army and the Struggle for the Lublin Region', University of Glasgow PhD thesis, 2010, p. 164.
141. Colville, *Fringes of Power*, p. 536 (entry for 19 December 1944).
142. Comment of a 55-year-old man reported in 'Greece', File Report 2190, December 1944, Mass Observation Archive.
143. Foster, 'Politicians, Public Opinion and the Press', p. 486.
144. Comment of a 35-year-old woman reported in 'Greece', File Report 2190, December 1944, Mass Observation Archive.
145. Robert Rhodes James (ed.), *'Chips': The Diaries of Sir Henry Channon*, Weidenfeld and Nicolson, London, 1993 (first published 1967), p. 385 (entry for 15 January 1945).
146. Speech of 18 January 1945. It had been Lord Cherwell's idea to refer to EAM/ELAS as 'Trotskyists', as 'this would distinguish them from the orthodox Russian communists and put many of their supporters here in a hole'. Cherwell to WSC, 11 January 1945, Churchill Papers, CHAR 9/205D/462.

147. Speech of 18 January 1945.

148. Jefferys, *Labour and the Wartime Coalition*, p. 204 (entry for 18 January 1945).

149. Colville, *Fringes of Power*, p. 553 (entry for 18 January 1945).

150. Parliamentary Debates, House of Commons, Fifth Series, Vol. 407, 18 January 1945, col. 479.

151. Gallup, *Gallup International Opinion Polls*, p. 103.

152. Nicholas, *Washington Despatches*, p. 505.

153. Speech of 14 February 1945.

154. Nicolson, *Diaries 1939–45*, p. 437 (entry for 27 February 1945).

155. This paragraph and the following one draw on David Reynolds, *In Command of History: Churchill Fighting and Writing the Second World War*, Allen Lane, London, 2004, p. 469.

156. Pimlott, *Second World War Diary*, p. 836 (entry for 23 February 1945).

157. Draft of speech of 27 February 1945, Churchill Papers, CHAR 9/206A/126.

158. Nicolson, *Diaries 1939–45*, p. 437 (entry for 27 February 1945).

159. Jefferys, *Labour and the Wartime Coalition*, p. 204 (entry for 27 February 1945, but misdated 26 February).

160. Speech of 27 February 1945.

161. WSC, *Triumph and Tragedy*, p. 351.

162. WSC to Clement Attlee and James Stuart, 14 February 1945, Churchill Papers, CHAR 9/206B/207.

163. Colville, *Fringes of Power*, p. 565 (entry for 27 February 1945). Colville did not listen to the speech but as noted above he had read it in draft.

164. Nicolson, *Diaries 1939–45*, p. 436 (entry for 27 February 1945).

165. Parliamentary Debates, House of Commons, Fifth Series, Vol. 408, 28 February 1945, col. 1422.

166. For a detailed breakdown, see 'Votes of Credit for War Expenditure: Committee', 19 January 1945, Churchill Papers, CHAR 9/206B/209.

167. Stuart Ball (ed.), *Parliament and Politics in the Age of Churchill and Attlee: The Headlam Diaries*, Cambridge University Press/Royal Historical Society, London, 1999, p. 448 (entry for 28 February 1945).

168. 'Home Intelligence Weekly Report No. 219', 14 December 1944, INF 1/292, TNA.

169. Ronnie Scott (ed.), *The Real 'Dad's Army': The War Diaries of Col. Rodney Foster*, Viking, London, 2011, p. 324 (entry for 27 February 1945).

170. Weekly Political Summary 3 March 1945, in Nicholas, *Washington Despatches*, 521.

171. Speech of 15 March 1945.

172. Speech of 28 March 1945.

173. Clementine Churchill to WSC, 30 March 1945, in Mary Soames (ed.), *Speaking for Themselves: The Personal Letters of Winston and Clementine Churchill*, Doubleday, London, 1998, p. 520.

174. Colville, *Fringes of Power*, p. 222 (entry for 28 March 1945).

175. 'Death of Roosevelt', 13 April 1945, Mass Observation Archive.

176. Elizabeth Nel, *Mr. Churchill's Secretary*, Hodder and Stoughton, London, 1958, p. 173.

177. Speech of 17 April 1945.

178. Broadcast of 8 May 1945.

179. Lord Moran, *Churchill At War 1940–45*, Constable and Robinson, London, 2002, p. 305 (entry for 8 May 1945).

180. A. Riley diary, 8 May 1945 (5408), Mass Observation Archive.

181. Vere Hodgson, *Few Eggs and No Oranges: A Diary*, Dennis Dobson, London, 1976, p. 473 (entry for 8 May 1945).

182. Mary E. Lelean diary, 9 May 1945 (5358), Mass Observation Archive. Emphasis in original.

183. Broadcast of 13 May 1945.

184. The episode is discussed in detail in John Ramsden, *Man of the Century: Winston Churchill and His Legend Since 1945*, HarperCollins, London, 2002, pp. 250–4. For the longer-term context, see Richard Toye, '"Phrases Make History Here": Churchill, Ireland and the Rhetoric of Empire', *Journal of Imperial and Commonwealth History*, Vol. 38 (2010), pp. 549–70.

185. Eamon De Valera, broadcast of 16 May 1945, in Richard Aldous (ed.), *Great Irish Speeches*, Quercus, London, 2007, pp. 82–7.

186. Ramsden, *Man of the Century*, p. 254.

187. John Maffey to Eric Machtig, 21 May 1945, DO 35/1229, TNA. I am grateful to Martin Thomas for supplying me with a copy of this document.

CHAPTER 8

1. Broadcast of 4 June 1945.

2. Charles Eade diary, 31 August 1945, Charles Eade Papers. There was a slightly different emphasis in his remarks to the editor of *The Times* at around the same time: 'He offered no explanation [for his defeat] himself except to say ironically that it might have been different "If I had done my broadcasts differently and if we had had a little more of your support"'. Donald McLachlan, *In the Chair: Barrington-Ward of The Times, 1927–1948*, Weidenfeld and Nicolson, London, 1971, p. 209.

3. See, for example, Kenneth Harris, *Attlee*, Weidenfeld and Nicolson, London, 1995 (first published 1982), pp. 255–6; and Peter Hennessy, *Never Again: Britain, 1945–1951*, Vintage, London, 1993, pp. 82–3.

4. 'Churchill's Crazy Broadcast', *Daily Herald*, 5 June 1945.

5. Anthony Beevor, *The Second World War*, Little, Brown, New York, 2012, p. 763.

6. J. R. Aldam diary, 27 January 1940 (5006), Mass Observation Archive.

7. W. C. Eyre Hartley diary, 10 May 1940 (5103), Mass Observation Archive.

8. Margaret Kornitzer diary, 15 May 1940 (5349), Mass Observation Archive.

9. *MO: Mass Observation's Bulletin*, 16 August 1943, Mass Observation Archive.

10. Speech of 22 January 1941.

11. 'Political Unity after the War', *The Times*, 23 January 1941.

12. Andrew Thorpe, *Parties at War: Political Organization in Second World War Britain*, Oxford University Press, Oxford, 2009, p. 20.

13. Douglas Hacking to WSC, 26 March 1941, Churchill Papers, CHAR 9/181A/111–17.

14. 'Home Intelligence Division Weekly Report No. 78', 1 April 1942, INF 1/292, TNA.

15. R. W. Fenn diary, 4 April 1942 (5065), Mass Observation Archive.

16. Speech of 26 March 1942.

17. G. S. Harvie-Watt, *Most of My Life*, Springwood Books, Windlesham, 1980, p. 117.

18. Richard Toye, *Lloyd George and Churchill: Rivals for Greatness*, Macmillan, London, 2007.

19. Martin Daunton, *Just Taxes: The Politics of Taxation in Britain, 1914–1979*, Cambridge University Press, Cambridge, 2002, p. 135.

20. Richard Toye, '"I am a Liberal as much as a Tory": Winston Churchill and the Memory of 1906', *Journal of Liberal History*, Vol. 54 (2007), pp. 38–45. See also Malcolm Baines, 'The Liberal Party and the 1945 General Election', *Contemporary Record*, Vol. 9, No. 1 (Summer 1995), pp. 48–61.

21. E. H. H. Green, *Ideologies of Conservatism*, Oxford University Press, Oxford, 2002, p. 253.

22. Michael David Kandiah, 'The Conservative Party and the 1945 General Election', *Contemporary Record*, Vol. 9, No. 1 (Summer 1995), pp. 22–47.

23. Richard Acland, the leader of the radical left-wing Common Wealth party, observed, 'Winston would never have made that speech if CW candidates had all lost their deposits'. Acland to Tom Wintringham, 9 April 1943, quoted in Geoffrey G. Field, *Blood, Sweat and Toil: Remaking the British Working Class, 1939–1945*, Oxford University Press, Oxford, 2011, p. 332 n. 99.

24. Elizabeth Nel, *Mr Churchill's Secretary*, Hodder and Stoughton, London, 1958, p. 97.

25. Lord Keynes to WSC, 17 March 1943, T172/2001, TNA.

26. Draft (dated 3 March 1943) of broadcast of 21 March 1943, Churchill Papers, CHAR 9/193A/85–116.

27. Cabinet Secretary's notebook, WM (43) 43rd Meeting, 19 March 1943, CAB 195/2, TNA.

28. Ben Pimlott (ed.), *The Second World War Diary of Hugh Dalton, 1940–1945*, Jonathan Cape, London, 1986, p. 569 (entry for 22 March 1943).

29. Kevin Jefferys (ed.), *Labour and the Wartime Coalition: From the Diary of James Chuter Ede 1941–1945*, The Historians' Press, London, 1987, p. 130 (entry for 24 March 1943).

30. 'Great Reception for Premier's Speech', *Glasgow Herald*, 23 March 1943.

31. Broadcast of 21 March 1943; Jefferys, *Labour and the Wartime Coalition*, p. 129 (entry for 21 March 1943).

32. Kevin Jefferys, *The Churchill Coalition and Wartime Politics 1940–1945*, Manchester University Press, Manchester, 1991, p. 122.

33. W. P. Crozier, *Off the Record: Political Interviews 1933–1943* (ed. A. J. P. Taylor), Hutchinson, London, 1973, pp. 226–7 (ed. A. J. P. Taylor), Hutchinson, London, 1973, p. 345 (entry for 26 March 1943).

34. Broadcast of 21 March 1943.

35. Stuart Ball (ed.), *Parliament and Politics in the Age of Churchill and Attlee: The Headlam Diaries, 1935–1951*, Cambridge University Press for the Royal Historical Society, Cambridge, 1999, pp. 361–2 (entry for 21 March 1943).

36. John Barnes and David Nicholson (eds.), *The Empire at Bay: The Leo Amery Diaries, 1929–1945*, Hutchinson, London, 1988, p. 878 (entry for 21 March 1943).

37. Jefferys, *Labour and the Wartime Coalition*, pp. 129–30 (entries for 21 and 24 March 1943).

38. Pimlott, *Second World War Diary*, p. 569 (entry for 24 March 1943).

39. William Stewart, 'Churchill Speech Charged with Planning "Khaki Election"', *Vancouver Sun*, 23 March 1943.

40. James Lansdale Hodson, *Home Front*, Victor Gollancz, London, p. 310 (entry for 23 March 1943).

41. Paul Addison, *The Road to 1945*, Jonathan Cape, London, 1975, p. 227.

42. W. P. Crozier, *Off the Record: Political Interviews 1933–1943* (ed. A. J. P. Taylor), Hutchinson, London, 1973, p. 345 (entry for 26 March 1943).

43. A point noted briefly in Addison, *The Road to 1945*, p. 228.

44. N. E. Underwood diary, 22 March 1943 (5447), Mass Observation Archive.

45. M. J. Brierley diary, 21 March 1943 (5261), Mass Observation Archive.

46. L. N. Adamson diary, 22 March 1943 (5004), Mass Observation Archive.

47. E. A. Stebbing diary, 21 and 24 March 1943 (5205), Mass Observation Archive.

48. J. Hinton diary, 21 March 1943 (5335), Mass Observation Archive. Emphasis in original.

49. 'Home Intelligence Weekly Report No. 129', 25 March 1943, INF 1/292, TNA.

50. 'Summary of Morale in March 1943', 1 April 1943, Mass Observation Archive.

51. Listener Research Bulletin, LR 1643, 3 April 1943, BBC Written Archives.

52. Anthony King (ed.), *British Political Opinion 1937–2000: The Gallup Polls*, Politico's, London, 2001, p. 2.

53. 'Mr Churchill's Plan Cheers City', *Financial Times*, 23 March 1943.

54. Broadcast 26 March 1944.

55. 'Home Intelligence Weekly Report No. 182', 30 March 1944, INF 1/292, TNA.

56. Listener Research Bulletin, LR 2525, 11 April 1944, BBC Written Archives.

57. 'Home Intelligence Weekly Report No. 183', 6 April 1944, INF 1/292, TNA.

58. Speech of 15 March 1945.

59. Edith Dawson diary, 16 March 1945 (5296), Mass Observation Archive.

60. Speech of 15 March 1945.

61. Winston Churchill to Lord Croft, 17 March 1945, Croft Papers, CRFT 1/8.

62. 'Major Lloyd-George's Future', *The Times*, 20 March 1945.

63. Churchill to Ralph Assheton, 11 June 1945, Churchill papers, CAC, CHAR 2/554/14.

64. There were also smaller subheadings: 'Prime Minister's Broadcast Attack on Socialism' and 'Policy Abhorrent to British Ideas of Freedom.' *The Times*, 5 June 1945.

65. Quoted in Paul Addison and Jeremy A. Crang (eds.), *Listening to Britain: Home Intelligence Reports on Britain's Finest Hour: May to September 1940*, The Bodley Head, London, 2010, p. xv.

66. Parliamentary Debates, House of Commons, 5th Series, Vol. 406, 20 December 1944, col. 1862. For further examples, see Richard Toye, 'Winston Churchill's "Crazy Broadcast": Party, Nation, and the 1945 Gestapo Speech', *Journal of British Studies*, Vol. 49, No. 3 (July 2010), pp. 655–80, at 661.

67. See, for example, C. R. Attlee, *The Labour Party in Perspective*, Victor Gollancz, London, 1937, p. 60.

68. 'Celticus' (Aneurin Bevan), *Why Not Trust the Tories?*, Victor Gollancz, London, p. 84. See also 'Gracchus' (Tom Wintringham), *Your MP*, Victor Gollancz, London, 1944, p. 81.

69. 'July Election Nearer', *The Times*, 22 May 1945.

70. Duff Hart-Davis (ed.), *King's Counsellor: Abdication and War: The Diaries of Sir Alan Lascelles*, Weidenfeld and Nicolson, London, 2006, p. 327.

71. *Speaker's Handbook 1945*, The Labour Party, London, 1945, p. 179. See also Scott Kelly, '"The Ghost of Neville Chamberlain": *Guilty Men* and the 1945 Election', *Conservative History Journal*, Vol. 5 (Autumn 2005), pp. 18–24.

72. This paragraph draws on Joanne Reilly, *Belsen: The Liberation of a Concentration Camp*, Routledge, London, 1998, esp. chapter 2.

73. F. A. Hayek to Paul Addison, 13 April 1980, quoted in Paul Addison, *Churchill on the Home Front 1900–1955*, Jonathan Cape, London, 1992, p. 383.

74. Hayek to 'The Principal Private Secretary to the Prime Minister', 15 March 1944, Churchill Papers, CHAR 2/253, fo. 17.

75. Waldron Smithers to Churchill, 9 October 1944, Churchill Papers, CHAR 2/497, fo. 31.

76. Richard Cockett, *Thinking the Unthinkable: Think-Tanks and the Economic Counter-Revolution, 1931–1983*, Fontana Press, London, 1995 (first published 1994), pp. 92–3.

77. Speech of 14 February 1920.

78. Ben Jackson, 'At the Origins of Neo-Liberalism: The Free Economy and the Strong State, 1930–1947', *Historical Journal*, Vol. 53 (2010), pp. 129–51. For

Hayek's belief in a 'minimum income' see *The Road to Serfdom*, Routledge and Kegan Paul, London, 1962 (first published 1944), p. 89.

79. *New Horizon*, April 1945, quoted in David Dutton, *Liberals in Schism: A History of the National Liberal Party*, I. B. Tauris, London, 2008, p. 142. Similar arguments, directed at Labour's nationalization plans, were made by some grassroots Conservatives: Thorpe, *Parties at War*, p. 176.

80. John Colville, *The Fringes of Power: Downing Street Diaries 1939–1955*, Hodder and Stoughton, London, 1985, p. 606; Hart-Davis, *King's Counsellor*, p. 331.

81. Mary Soames, *Clementine Churchill*, Penguin, Harmondsworth, 1981 (first published 1979), p. 545.

82. Cockett, *Thinking the Unthinkable*, p. 94.

83. Winston Churchill to Harry S. Truman, 12 May 1945, in United States Department of State, *Foreign Relations of the United States: Diplomatic Papers: The Conference of Berlin (The Potsdam Conference), 1945*, Vol. I, United States Government Printing Office, Washington DC, 1960, pp. 8–9.

84. Richard Overy, *The Morbid Age: Britain between the Wars*, Allen Lane, London, 2009, pp. 282–3; Ann Deighton, *The Impossible Peace: Britain, the Division of Germany and the Origins of the Cold War*, Clarendon Press, Oxford, 1993, p. 221.

85. Asa Briggs, *The History of Broadcasting in the United Kingdom*, Vol. IV: *Sound and Vision*, Oxford University Press, Oxford, 1979, p. 627 n. 4.

86. Colville, *Fringes of Power*, p. 606.

87. In fact, Churchill did not oppose the nationalization of the Bank when the new government legislated for this in 1946: Hugh Dalton, *High Tide and After: Memoirs, 1945–1960*, Frederick Muller, London, 1962, p. 45.

88. See Philip Williamson, *Stanley Baldwin: Conservative Leadership and National Values*, Cambridge University Press, Cambridge, 1999.

89. Jon Lawrence, *Speaking for the People: Party, Language and Popular Politics in England, 1867–1914*, Cambridge University Press, Cambridge, 1998, esp. pp. 106–7.

90. Speech of 14 April 1905.

91. 'Was Worth 50 Seats to Labour', *Daily Herald*, 6 June 1945.

92. Robert Rhodes James (ed.), *'Chips': The Diaries of Sir Henry Channon*, Weidenfeld and Nicolson, London, 1993 (first published 1967), p. 408 (entry for 5 June 1945).

93. Ball, *Parliament and Politics*, p. 462.

94. 'Tory Doubts on Premier's Broadcast', *Manchester Guardian*, 6 June 1945.

95. 'Churchill's Crazy Broadcast', *Daily Herald*, 5 June 1945.

96. 'Churchill Claims He is Leading National Govt.', *Daily Mirror*, 5 June 1945.

97. 'Labour Case for Socialism', *The Times*, 6 June 1945.

98. Published on 31 July 1945 in *The Evening Standard*, the cartoon was called 'The Two Churchills'. It showed one Churchill, 'The leader of humanity', sitting on a pedestal, commiserating with the other one, 'The Party Leader' down below.

'Cheer up!' he tells him. 'They will forget *you* but they will remember *me* always'.

99. Mary Soames, *Clementine Churchill*, p. 545.

100. *Daily Herald*, 6 June 1945.

101. This theme was taken up in the Labour-supporting press. See, for example, Maurice Kitching, 'New Zealand is Insulted', *Reynolds News*, 10 June 1945, and F. A. Cooper, 'Where Labour Has Ruled for 27 Years and They've Never Seen a Gestapo Man', *Reynolds News*, 24 June 1945. Cooper was writing about Queensland, of which he was Premier.

102. 'Labour Case for Socialism', *The Times*, 6 June 1945.

103. For Morrison, see 'The Road to Serfdom', *Daily Express*, 6 June 1945, and for the broader Labour reaction to the book, see Richard Toye, *The Labour Party and the Planned Economy 1931–1951*, Royal Historical Society, London, 2003, pp. 136–8.

104. Cockett, *Thinking the Unthinkable*, p. 5.

105. Speech of 4 June 1945.

106. 'Prof. Von Hayek', *Daily Telegraph & Morning Post*, 6 June 1945.

107. 'The Road to Serfdom', *Daily Express*, 6 June 1945.

108. Mark Pottle (ed.), *Champion Redoubtable: The Diaries and Letters of Violet Bonham Carter 1914–1945*, Weidenfeld and Nicolson, Lodon, 1998, pp. 350–1 (entries for 4 and 6 June 1945).

109. John Barnes and David Nicholson (eds.), *The Empire at Bay: The Leo Amery Diaries, 1929–1945*, Hutchinson, London, 1988, p. 1046 (entries for 4 and 5 June 1945). The text in fact gives 'rodomontage', a clear error.

110. Barnes and Nicholson, *Empire at Bay*, p. 1046.

111. Margaret Thatcher, *The Path to Power*, HarperCollins, London, 1995, p. 45.

112. Quoted in Austin Mitchell, *Election '45: Reflections on the Revolution in Britain*, Fabian Society/Bellew Publishing, London, 1995, p. 69.

113. 'He's the Silliest Candidate of the Election', *Daily Mirror*, 28 June 1945.

114. R. B. McCallum and Alison Readman, *The British General Election of 1945*, Geoffrey Cumberlege/Oxford University Press, London, 1947, p. 148.

115. See Morrison's comments in 'Churchill's Crazy Broadcast', *Daily Herald*, 5 June 1945.

116. Steven Fielding, 'What Did "The People" Want? The Meaning of the 1945 General Election', *Historical Journal*, Vol. 35 (1992), pp. 623–39, at 631.

117. The Nuffield survey did concede that 'the opposition papers had almost a monopoly of abuse' but the target of this remark was the press, not politicians: McCallum and Readman, *British General Election*, p. 190.

118. Emrys Hughes, '"Gestapo Will Get You"', *Forward*, 9 June 1945.

119. Michael Foot, 'Why this "National" label is a shameful fraud', *Daily Herald*, 19 June 1945.

120. See 'Rejoinders to Premier's Broadcast', *Manchester Guardian*, 6 June 1945, and '"Tory Gestapo Put Gag on Leading Scientists"', *Reynolds News*, 17 June 1945.

For examples relating to Tory MPs' alleged Fascist sympathies see Kelly, '"The Ghost of Neville Chamberlain"', p. 21.

121. 'Cripps Answers Churchill', *Forward*, 16 June 1945.
122. 'Tories and Mr Churchill', *Manchester Guardian*, 12 June 1945.
123. 'Axis Aid by Tories', *Sunday Pictorial*, 17 June 1945.
124. 'Liberals are Rallying in the West', *News Chronicle*, 9 June 1945. For Morrison's comments, see 'Churchill's Crazy Broadcast', *Daily Herald*, 5 June 1945.
125. 'Report on the General Election, June–July 1945', File Report 2270A, October 1945, Mass Observation Archive.
126. A. White diary, 4 June 1945 (5230), Mass Observation Archive.
127. J. Greenwood diary, 5 June 1945 (5088), Mass Observation Archive.
128. M. Clayton diary, 5 June 1945 (5275), Mass Observation Archive.
129. A. B. Holness diary, 4 June 1945 (5338), Mass Observation Archive.
130. Edith Oakley diary, 5 June 1945 (5390), Mass Observation Archive.
131. J. Lippold diary, 4 and 5 June 1945 (5312), Mass Observation Archive.
132. Addison, *The Road to 1945*, p. 266; Fielding, 'What Did "The People" Want?', p. 632.
133. Harold Macmillan to WSC, 8 June 1945, Churchill Papers, CHAR 2/556/23–4.
134. Draft of broadcast of 13 June 1945, Churchill Papers, CHAR 9/208B/106.
135. Broadcast of 13 June 1945.
136. 'Mr Churchill in the North', *The Times*, 27 June 1945.
137. Broadcast of 21 June 1945.
138. Broadcast of 30 June 1945.
139. 'Report on the General Election, June–July 1945', File Report 2270A, October 1945, Mass Observation Archive.
140. Vita Sackville-West to Harold Nicolson, 22 June 1945, in Nigel Nicolson (ed.), *Harold Nicolson: Diaries and Letters 1939–1945*, Collins, London, 1967, p. 472.
141. 'Election Observations, June–July 1945', File Report 2267, Mass Observation Archive.
142. 'Crowds Cheer and Jeer', *Manchester Guardian*, 5 July 1945.
143. Lord Moran, *Churchill at War*, Robinson, London, 2002, p. 310 (entry for 22 June 1945).
144. R. F. Harrod, *The Prof: A Personal Memoir of Lord Cherwell*, Macmillan, London, 1959, p. 255.
145. 'Opening Salvo', *News Chronicle*, 5 June 1945.
146. The Liberals put up only 306 candidates (there were 640 constituencies). A Gallup poll conducted after the campaign closed found that 'about 23 per cent. of the total electorate would have voted for the Liberal Party, given the opportunity': '58 Per Cent. Opposed Election', *News Chronicle*, 26 July 1945.
147. A point made effectively in 'The Unfinished Task', *The Spectator*, 8 June 1945.
148. Soames, *Clementine Churchill*, p. 544.

CONCLUSION

1. This was the implication of the section on Churchill in 'Bulletin No. 1', File Report 1545, December 1942, Mass Observation Archive.

2. 'Bulletin No. 1', File Report 1545, December 1942, Mass Observation Archive.

3. Paul Addison, *Churchill: The Unexpected Hero*, Oxford University Press, Oxford, 2005, p. 169.

4. Comments of George. W. Bush, 16 July 2001, quoted in Richard Toye, 'The Churchill Syndrome: Reputational Entrepreneurship and the Rhetoric of Foreign Policy since 1945, *British Journal of Politics & International Relations*, Vol. 10 (2008), pp. 364–78, at 364.

5. For a parallel case, see Catriona Pennell, *A Kingdom United: Popular Responses to the Outbreak of the First World War in Britain and Ireland*, Oxford University Press, Oxford, 2012.

6. However, his various attempts to silence the press, and to quash criticism by demanding votes of confidence, are potentially open to criticism. See Brian Gardner, *Churchill in his Time: A Study in a Reputation 1939–1945*, Methuen & Co., London, 1968, p. xv.

7. Lord Moran, *Winston Churchill: The Struggle for Survival, 1940–1965*, Constable, London, 1966, p. 292 (entry for 2 September 1945).

8. Speech of 30 November 1954.

9. E. Bliss (ed.), *In Search of Light: The Broadcasts of Edward R. Murrow* (London, 1968), p. 237, quoted in David Cannadine, *In Churchill's Shadow: Confronting the Past in Modern Britain*, Penguin, London, 2003 (first published 2002), p. 107.

10. Clement Attlee, 'The Man I Knew', *Observer*, 31 January 1965, in Frank Field (ed.), *Attlee's Great Contemporaries: The Politics of Character*, Continuum, London, 2009, p. 157.

List of Archival Collections

CAMBRIDGE

Churchill Archives Centre
Mark Abrams Papers
Leo Amery Papers
Randolph Churchill Papers
Winston Churchill Papers
Charles Eade Papers
Lord Halifax Papers
George Harvie-Watt Papers
Michael Wolff Papers
Trinity College
Walter Layton Papers
Edwin Montagu Papers

CAVERSHAM

BBC Written Archives Centre

EXETER

University of Exeter Special Collections
Thomas Blackburn Papers
Cecil Harmsworth Papers

LONDON

Imperial War Museum
The National Archives
British Library
Oliver Harvey Papers
Michel Saint-Denis Archive
British Library of Political and Economic Science
Walter Citrine Papers

Liddell Hart Centre for Military Archives, King's College
Ian Hamilton Papers
Hastings Ismay Papers
Basil Liddell Hart Papers
Parliamentary Archives
Percy Harris Papers
Stansgate Papers

OXFORD

Bodleian Library
Earl Winterton Papers
Rhodes House
Fabian Colonial Bureau Papers

YORK

Borthwick Institute of Historical Research
Lord Halifax Papers

DUBLIN

National Archives of Ireland

PARIS

French National Archives
Philippe Pétain Papers

ZÜRICH

Zentralbibliothek
Emil Oprecht Papers

LIST OF ELECTRONIC DATABASES AND INTERNET RESOURCES

Foreign Broadcast Information Service (USA)
Jewish Telegraphic Agency, <http://www.archive.jta.org/>
W. L. Mackenzie King diary, 11 Oct. 1939, <http://www.collectionscanada.gc.ca>.
Mass Observation Archive

Picture Acknowledgements

Index